PETRARCH AND HIS WORLD

la mia angosciosa e desperata vita
—Rime *CXLIX*

drawings by Alison Mason Kingsbury

PETRARCH
AND HIS WORLD

MORRIS BISHOP

Indiana University Press · Bloomington · 1963

PREFACE

THE FIRST TWELVE CHAPTERS OF THIS BOOK served as the substance of the Patten Foundation Lectures at Indiana University in the spring of 1962. To the officials of that university, to the late Mr. Will Patten, the generous donor of the Foundation, and to the faithful auditors I am much indebted.

Most of the work of preparation was done in the Cornell University Library's superb Fiske Petrarch Collection. My gratitude to the first collector, Willard Fiske, and to the magnanimous custodians of the Collection is profound.

The book is intended for those who may have some interest in Petrarch, but little, presumably, in the quarrels of critics and interpreters. Therefore, although many of my outright statements are in fact disputable, I have generally accepted what seemed to me the best conclusions, and have gone on.

Translations from Petrarch's works, both prose and verse, are my own, unless otherwise indicated.

M. B.

THE PATTEN FOUNDATION

Mr. Will Patten of Indianapolis (A.B., Indiana University, 1893) made, in 1931, a gift for the establishment of the Patten Foundation at his Alma Mater. Under the terms of this gift, which became available upon the death of Mr. Patten (May 3, 1936), there is to be chosen each year a Visiting Professor who is to be in residence several weeks during the year. The purpose of this prescription is to provide an opportunity for members and friends of the University to enjoy the privilege and advantage of personal acquaintance with the Visiting Professor. The Visiting Professor for the Patten Foundation in 1962 was

MORRIS BISHOP

CONTENTS

ILLUSTRATIONS

PETRARCH AND HIS WORLD

1304

AREZZO

I: BOYHOOD

> *When I think upon the affairs and fortunes*
> *of men, their uncertain and sudden chances*
> *and changes, truly I find nothing almost more*
> *frail, nothing more unquiet, than man's life.*
>
> —De remediis, *Preface*

"I WAS BORN IN AREZZO. IN A BACK STREET, Garden Lane, was the seed cast, and there sprang that arid flower, that insipid fruit that was I," said Petrarch, with a belittlement in which he expected no one to concur. The house of his birth in that small Tuscan city has somehow got lost, but the Casa del Petrarca, wearing its plaque like a medal, will do as well as another.

It was the twentieth of July, 1304. By a happy symbolism he entered this world as day was dawning. His birth was difficult; the doctor and the midwife despaired of saving mother and child. "Thus even before birth I began to know danger, and I crossed the threshold of life under the loom of death."

He was born in exile from noble Florence, and all his life he was an exile. Though he was to see his city only twice, and briefly, he called himself a Florentine, and signed his name proudly Franciscus Petracchi de Florentia. In those days a man's city, not his country, was his spiritual home; from her he received his legal identity and social pride, and to her he gave his passionate love, or, if he felt himself unkindly used, his hatred.

His father, Ser Petracco, or Petraccolo, dell' Ancisa, had been an honorable citizen of Florence. (Once and for all, Italian proper names of that century accepted no convenient rule. Some men paraded a family name; thus Dante Alighieri. More used a patronymic—the father's name as a Latin genitive or, in Italian, preceded by *di;* thus Franciscus Petracchi or Francesco di Petracco. And displaced men appended the name of their home town, with *di* or *da* or an adjectival ending, and such a name was likely to become permanent. Thus Petracco dell' Ancisa, or Leonardo da Vinci, or Giulio Romano. Our Francesco in manhood found, no doubt, the diminutive Petracco a little inelegant. He latinized it to Petrarca or Petrarcha, which we have anglicized to Petrarch. The Ser which preceded many names was no more than Signore; it was a title prized by notaries and such, though it carried no more honorability than Esquire today.)

Petrarch's family came from Ancisa, or Incisa, a small town in Florentine territory, fifteen miles southeast of the city. They were small landholders, by no means noble. His great-grandfather, Garzo, he remembers as virtuous and shrewd. The townsmen consulted him on business matters, contracts, marriages, and public affairs. Though no man of letters, he was sought out by scholars for his sound judgments. He died in the room he was born in, at 104, and, like Plato, on his birthday.

The family removed to Florence in the mid-thirteenth century, but kept their country home. The great-grandfather, Garzo, the grandfather, Ser Parenzo, and the father, Ser Petracco, were notaries. A notary was then, as in Latin countries today, a diploma'd expert in business and administrative law, something like an English solicitor. He drew contracts and statutes, handled estates, couched governmental records and edicts in legal form, organized local elections. He accompanied the mayor and judges, often illiterate, when they administered justice, and whispered constantly in their ears. His was a respectable and respected profession, demanding probity and caution, and hostile always to the wild imagination.

Petrarch's father, Ser Petracco or Petraccolo, must have been born about 1266. Early writers describe him as worthy, active, prudent, and eloquent. But even in a notary passion may lurk. Ser Petracco, at fifty, discerned in a mirror his first white hairs, and made such an uproar that he roused the whole neighborhood.

Florence was solidly Guelf, or pro-Papal, but the Guelfs were divided into two parties, the conservative bourgeois Whites and the radical Blacks, a union of the populace and the proscribed nobility. At the century's end the Whites were in power, and evidently Ser Petracco was numbered among them. He held some comfortable appointments, though his son alleges that he verged

on poverty. For two months, from December 15, 1300 to the following February, he was Notary to Florence's governing board, the
College of Priors. This is interesting, for during the same months
Dante was one of the Priors. Dante and the Petracchi were close
friends, bound by common literary tastes.

At about this time, with Fortune smiling, Petracco married
Eletta, said to be of the famous Canigiani family (although Petrarch, who could be snobbish enough at moments, never makes
such a claim). The rising notary, in his mid-thirties, could dream
of a happy and honorable public and private life.

But Fortune frowned. The Blacks gained control of Florence in
the winter of 1301-1302. Dante and 600 prominent Whites were
banished from the city, with the assurance that they would be
burned alive if they should ever reappear. However, Ser Petracco,
who had kept his skirts carefully clean, continued to serve the
Black government until, on October 20, 1302, he was charged with
forging an instrument injurious to a powerful Black. Surely the
charge was baseless, a device for ousting a servant inherited from
the Opposition. He was condemned to pay a fine of a thousand lire
within ten days or have a hand chopped off. He avoided both alternatives by fleeing, with his young wife. He thus ensured the confiscation of his property in Florence.

He went to Arezzo, fifty miles away, and found refuge in a nest
of Florentine exiles. His character and judgment must have been
commended among them, for he was chosen secretary to a peace
mission of banished Whites to Florence, in April 1304. There was
much embracing and emotion in the square of Santa Maria Novella, under a pouring rain. But the negotiations ended in a fight,
and Petracco fled, with the other negotiators, on June 9. The exiles
then had recourse to arms. In mid-July they marched on Florence,
and on the very day of Petrarch's birth they stormed their native
city, but vainly. It is not clear if Ser Petracco was among the attackers. Probably, from marital affection or notarial prudence, he
remained in Arezzo.

Now began his wandering years, surely hard ones, for a notary's
success depends on his record and records, his business repute, his
knowledge of local men, property, ordinances. We do not know
where or how he made a living.

In February 1305, when the boy Francesco—called "Checco" in

the home—was seven months old, Florence granted permission to Signora Petracco and her child to reside in her father-in-law's ancestral home in Incisa. According to a dear family story, the baby was transported from Arezzo to Incisa in a sort of sling depending from a stout stick borne over a mounted servant's shoulder. In fording the flooded Arno the horse slipped and fell; the servant nearly lost his life in saving that of the child. And thus the intellectual history of western Europe owes its debt to a nameless courageous servant.

Incisa is a pretty riverside town, bounded by vineyarded hills. Here the boy learned to speak the pure Tuscan idiom. This is important; the cradle is the poet's first school. One is reminded of George Santayana's plaint, in the introduction to his book of poems in English: "I never drank in in childhood the homely cadences and ditties which in pure spontaneous poetry set the essential key."

The proscribed father returned on furtive visits, resulting in the birth of a second son, who died, and of a third, Gherardo, born in 1307.

The ruling Blacks of Florence offered Ser Petracco an opportunity to return. He had after all served in turn the Whites, the Blacks, and the Whites; he might readily again change color. A decree of February 1309 proposed to absolve him of all guilt against the Republic, but required him first to set foot in the city prison, then to issue forth and walk bareheaded and penitent to the Baptistery, where he would make a suitable offering and receive absolution. But this humiliation he refused, perhaps suspecting that only the first step of the ceremony would be carried out. Thus, when in 1311 an amnesty was declared by the Florentine Blacks, Ser Petracco—and Dante Alighieri and others—were specifically excepted from pardon.

Surrendering all hope of return to the homeland, Ser Petracco removed his family, in the summer of 1311, to Pisa, the ancient rival and enemy of Florence. Revisiting the city after 650 years, he would find it familiar, for the cathedral, the baptistery, the leaning tower, the Campo Santo, already stood. Pisa was filled with Guelf exiles, from Florence and elsewhere. Exiles, émigrés, are sadly known to us now; we are aware of their courage, their willingness to turn to any trade, and the perpetual ache of their uprooting.

How Ser Petracco lived, how he fed his family, we do not know.

In March and April 1312 the Emperor-elect, Henry VII, made a long visit to Pisa, on his way to be crowned in Rome. This was probably the occasion when, as Petrarch remembers, he saw Dante, whose old friendship with the Petracchi was tightened by shared misfortunes. Dante was now a wanderer, importuning Henry VII with his political dreams, which included the capture of Florence for the benefit of the émigrés. But Henry showed no disposition to besiege that stout city.

A new hope glimmered for Ser Petracco. The Pope, Clement V, a Frenchman and a tool of the French King Philip the Fair, had been elected in 1305. He was "the shameless harlot" for whom Dante reserved, while he was still alive, a special pit among the simonists in hell. Pope Clement refused to take his high seat in Rome, where indeed he might not have been safe. He could not forget the slap administered to the face of his predecessor, Boniface VIII, by Sciarra Colonna, the most resounding slap in history. Clement preferred to take the Papal Court with him in a long tour of France. In 1309 he chose as the seat of his papacy the small city of Avignon, in what is now southern France, but was then an outlying possession of the French king of Naples, Charles II of Anjou. King Charles lived far away, and was willing to let the Pope rule supreme in his city. Avignon had other advantages. It stood at the crossing of main highways, at about the center of Catholic Christendom. It adjoined the Comtat Venaissin, papal territory. And unlike bloody Rome, it was at peace.

By 1312 Avignon was a boom town, just the place for an unemployed notary with a few influential friends. Apparently Ser Petracco went there alone, to make a trial of new fortunes. He found plenty of work to do. On October 26, 1312 he was appointed proctor, or solicitor, for some members of the great Florentine banking house of Frescobaldi, imprisoned on the complaint of the Treasurer of King Edward II of England. (We do not know the charge against them; perhaps usury, or reluctance in advancing money to King Edward, a bad risk.)

The news Ser Petracco sent to Pisa was encouraging, and, probably in the winter of 1312-13, his wife and two sons set forth to join him. Francesco was eight, old enough to observe and remember. They rode along the famous ancient coast road, sadly dilapi-

dated since Roman times. Forty years later Petrarch recalled the
journey, in a letter to the Doge and Council of Genoa:

> I was just a boy, and I remember only confusedly what I saw, like
> something dreamed. But I still keep vividly in memory the enchant-
> ment of your Riviera, so beautiful that it seemed rather celestial than
> of this earth, or like the homes of the blest in the Elysian Fields, con-
> ceived in poets' fancy, among gracious hills, with delicious pathways
> opening to the bosoms of green valleys. Stupendous to the gaze tow-
> ered on high the mass of superb palaces, and at the foot of the cliffs
> stood your citizens' marble pleasure-mansions, truly regal, such as the
> noblest city might envy; while art, overmastering nature, clothed the
> sterile summits of your mountains with cedar, vines, and olives. One
> looked in amazement at those alluring caves among the rocks, where
> hid great gold-pillared rooms, echoing with the sound of breaking
> waves and dripping with moisture. At sight of them the gaping sailor
> dropped his oars in wonder.

At Genoa the party found a ship bound for Marseilles. The sea
journey was grievous. Petrarch was always prone to seasickness,
and nowhere can one be more seasick than in a small craft on the
Mediterranean. The ship was driven ashore near Marseilles in a
winter storm; "It was a miracle that I was not thrust beyond the
pale of life." He learned to fear and hate the sea, and afterward
chose, whenever possible, the jogging path along the shore.

Whether on the journey or a little later, the Petracchi met the
Sette family, emigrants from the Genoa region. A son, Guido Sette,
small, intelligent, and delicate in appearance, was almost exactly
Francesco's age. The two families and the boys became close
friends, and the friendship lasted their lives long.

From Marseilles the party traveled overland, seventy miles
through a pleasant, rich country, to Avignon. Their first impression was a shock. Until the coming of the Pope and his Court
Avignon had been a quiet little riverside city of 5,000 or 6,000 inhabitants. The arrival of the Papal Court affected it as would the
establishment of the United Nations in a rural American county
seat. Cardinals' trains were billeted in the homes of the local
nobility and gentry, petitioners and office-seekers camped in the
streets, on the walls, in cemeteries. Indeed, the cemeteries were the
only open spaces in the city, and were used for business meetings.
These must have been unusually horrid, for we are told that

burials, in the universal crowding, were so shallow that pigs were forever rooting up the deceased.

For a vigorous notary eager to begin a new career Avignon obviously offered a splendid opportunity. The town was filled with activity, with newcomers, with money. Every papal expropriation of private homes, every building or street-widening project, with upset of ancient rights, every scheme of ruthless progress, every dispute among greedy, swarming, uncomfortable men, brought business to notaries. The town had struck oil; holy oil, in this case.

But the city was no place for a mother and two small sons. They apparently remained there briefly, while the boys attended some sort of school. Then a home was discovered for Signora Petracco, and for Signora Sette and her family, in the town of Carpentras, fifteen miles east of Avignon. Thus they could escape the city's hurly-burly, while receiving occasional visits from the fortune-seeking husbands.

Carpentras was the capital of the Comtat Venaissin, a private domain of the papacy. The town lies in a rich, well-watered plain, vine and olive country. Ten miles to the east rise the first Alpine foothills, with Mont Ventoux standing a mile high above the plain. The town boasts a fine triumphal arch, inspiring young imaginations with a sense of ancient Rome's continuing presence. It boasts also the possession of the Holy Bit, made for Emperor Constantine's horse, and incorporating one of the nails from the True Cross. In Petrarch's time the town had a considerable Jewry, thriving under the benevolent eye of the Avignon Popes.

The émigrés found in Carpentras—or perhaps they brought with them—an admirable schoolmaster, Convenevole da Prato. He too was an émigré. He had been a scholarly notary in Prato, near Florence. In late middle age he had fled from the troubles to welcoming Pisa. Like so many unfortunates, he turned to teaching, and he could well have given there the boy Francesco his first Latin lessons. He was a simple, warm-hearted, enthusiastic little man (*homunculus simplicissimus*). He was forever full of mighty literary projects. "After finding a magnificent title," remembers Petrarch affectionately, "and writing a fine preface—which, coming first in a book, should be the last thing one writes—he would turn his inconstant, fantastic wits to another project." He was always borrowing books. Years later he borrowed Petrarch's unique copy of Cicero's *De gloria,* and pressed by extreme need he pawned it. Petrarch hunted the book desperately, and vainly; and the learned world has ever since been hunting as vainly the lost work of Cicero. But even this crime against scholarship could not quell Petrarch's affection for the kindly schoolmaster.

We read much of the barbarous cruelties of medieval schools, of the whipping of boys even to death. We may be sure that the rod was little used in Convenevole's school. How fortunate was Petrarch to be led to learning by this sweet old man and excellent scholar! He loved his pupils, and Petrarch most of all. Some twenty years later Cardinal Giovanni Colonna, who was very fond of Convenevole, said to him with a smile: "Magister, among all those fine pupils you are so proud of, is there a little place for our Francesco?" The master's eyes filled with tears, and at first he could not speak. Then, says Petrarch, "he swore by God that he had never loved any so well as the poor little fellow that was I."

(Beware of large generalizations about the medieval, or any, mind, about medieval, or temporal, or national character. Beware of turning schoolmasters, notaries, poets, into types. There are always the kind and the cruel, the wise and the stupid, the proud and the humble. There is no common character of the schoolmaster; there are only men and women who teach school.)

We have no specific record of Petrarch's early studies. He had certainly learned his letters young. There is an old story, told by fourteenth-century Filippo Villani, that Francesco, when a small child, would ask what his father was writing, and if he received a facetious or irritated answer he was broken-hearted; he tried secretly to reproduce script, and learned by his own effort to read and write. The story does not sound unlikely. The father, a man of culture, recognized the boy's intelligence and promise. On a trip to Paris Ser Petracco bought a fine manuscript of the compilations of Isidore of Seville, and brought it back as a present for his schoolboy son.

In Convenevole's school Petrarch presumably studied the usual subjects—primarily Latin grammar, with a little elementary logic, rhetoric, and arithmetic. He learned Latin as no one can learn it today. It was a living language to him, in the ordinary commerce of the school as it was in the streets of cosmopolitan Avignon. All (but one) of his voluminous extant letters are in Latin, and even

his marginal comments in his books. He thought in Latin as readily as in Italian. At the same time he kept up his Italian in the
home, with his mother and with Italian émigrés. Inevitably also he
learned the Provençal of the countryside and of the servants. He
apologized, years later, for not knowing French, but surely he was
unduly modest, for he read French easily, and, linguist as he was,
he must have readily converted his Provençal into French in his
travels in France.

In school he discovered Cicero, *"Cicero meus,"* and fell in love
with his rolling periods. He called Cicero his father, Virgil his
brother. He says:

> From my early youth, when the other boys were studying only in
> Prosper and in Aesop, I gave myself wholly to Cicero, whether through
> natural sympathy or at the suggestion of my father, who always held
> that author in highest veneration and who would himself have at-
> tained some high reputation if domestic cares had not occupied his
> noble intelligence, and if exile with a numerous family had not con-
> strained him to turn his powers to other ends. At that age I was in-
> capable of understanding what I read, but I took so much delight in
> the harmonious disposition of the words that any other book I read
> or heard read seemed to me to give off a graceless, discordant sound. I
> must admit that this was not a very juvenile judgment, if one may
> call judgment what was not based on reason. But certainly it is re-
> markable that while I didn't understand anything, I already felt ex-
> actly what I feel today, when after all I do understand something,
> little though it be. That love for Cicero increased day by day, and my
> father, amazed, encouraged my immature propensity through pater-
> nal affection. And I, dodging no labor that might aid my purpose,
> breaking the rind began to savor the taste of the fruit, and couldn't
> be restrained from my study.

He confesses thus his early susceptibility to the sound of words.
This is a poet's quality. Next, he began to find his way through
beautiful words to beautiful thought, to break the rind and savor
the taste of the fruit. He remembers that while his companions
were concentrating on forms and rules of language, "I was noting
down the substance of the thought—the pettiness of this life, its
brevity, haste, tumbling course, its hidden cheats, time's irrecover-
ability, the flower of life soon wasted, the fugitive beauty of a
blooming face, the flight of youth, the trickeries of age, the wrin-
kles, illnesses, sadness and pain, and the implacable cruelty of

indomitable death." Already he was oppressed by the sense of time
and its hurry toward the end.

He developed his memory, later phenomenal; he was said to
have 20,000 Latin verses by heart. He brought to his reading his
own vivid imagination. He felt the old Roman world to be present, his own. His schooling determined his whole life, says a critic;
he never swerved from the principles and courses then learned.
"Latin culture was his life; for his predecessors it was something
outside. In Petrarch antiquity creates a new conception of existence." This new conception was later to be termed Humanism.

His moral as well as his mental education was tended by his
master and parents. "What fear of God I possessed in those days!"
he exclaims. "What religious emotion! What love of uprightness!
And how I pondered on death!" This faith too he never disavowed
or questioned.

He profited physically by his country boyhood. He calls himself not robust, but very dextrous and agile. He became an indomitable walker, even a mountain-climber, and a vigorous gardener.
He was not one of the unhappy little destined clerics one still sees
in Italy, cassocked and confined in decorum at the age of ten.

It was a blessed stage in sunny Carpentras. Fifty years later,
writing to his old schoolmate, Guido Sette, Petrarch remembers
there only joy, security, peace at home, liberty in public, and
country silence round about.

One fine day Ser Petracco and Guido Sette's uncle, visiting their
families in Carpentras, proposed a country jaunt to the famous
Fontaine de Vaucluse, a dozen miles away, to see the mysterious
swirling pool, where long-hidden underground waters of the river
Sorgue furiously emerge under high overhanging limestone cliffs.
Petrarch wrote his friend, many years later:

> When the matter was broached, our boyish eagerness to go along was
> excited. And since it appeared that we could not safely be trusted to
> ride alone, a servant was assigned to each of us, to bestride the horses
> behind us and hold us in the saddle. How we had to plead with
> mother—my own natural mother, and yours too by her love, and the
> best of all mothers I have ever seen! At length she yielded, though
> full of fears and good advice. So we set forth, with your uncle, the
> remembrance of whom is still a pleasure to me. When we got to the
> Fountain (I remember it as if it were today), I was so struck by the

strange character of the place that I said, in such childish words as I could find: "Here is a place that is just right for me, where I would rather live than in the greatest of cities!"

The elders were likewise charmed. Apparently Guido's uncle bought a country property near by, for Petrarch recalled to Guido: "I will remind you of our trips and our stays in your house near the fountain of the Sorgue, sometimes talking all day long from morning to evening, forgetting even to eat, and sometimes staying up all night with our books, and seeing the dawn come up without feeling any slightest need of repose and sleep. There is no distance of place or time that can cancel such things from my mind."

Thus he learned young to recognize and to love natural beauty. He was always a countryman, pining in the great cities. He responded sensuously to the sights and sounds of the countryside; he knew the awe and terror of mountains. The purling of brooks tinkles forever in his writings. Of course there were others who felt such noble emotions, but lacking letters they made no report to posterity. If Petrarch did not exactly discover the love of wild nature, he established it as a literary convention for all later times.

It was a happy boyhood, and one that prepared him, with no one's intention or awareness, for his destiny. Already young Petrarch was assembling the equipment of a poet.

II: COLLEGE DAYS

> *Rule a child till he is fourteen; then advise*
> *him, don't force him. Let God and nature*
> *guide him. In my case, the struggle against*
> *nature was vain.*
>
> —Rerum memorandarum *III, 99*

SER PETRACCO WAS PROPERLY AMBITIOUS, eager that his promising sons should rise in the world, outdo himself. Since a lawyer outranked a notary, in prestige and opportunity, he was determined that the boys should be Doctors of Civil Law.

Much of Christendom was ruled by canon law, administered mostly by clerics under the eye of the Church. But the Roman civil law, with its ancient Code of Justinian, had never disappeared in Italy and southern France. From the eleventh century onward, with the founding of the University of Bologna, civil law gained importance, prospering at the expense of canon law. Civil law opened a career to bright young men who had no taste for holy orders. Its Doctors were much in demand, serving as judges, magistrates, ambassadors, and counselors to princes. It was well adapted to the needs of the rising commercial cities, in Italy and elsewhere. Canon law, for instance, condemned out of hand usury, or lending money at interest; civil law was much more accommodating to bankers and businessmen. At the beginning of the fourteenth century King Philip the Fair of France, in a dispute with Pope Boniface, rested his demands on civil law. Thus, says the historian Milman, "the hierarchy found, almost suddenly . . . a grave intellectual aristocracy, equal to themselves in profound erudition, resting on ancient written authority, . . . of which they were perfect masters, opposing to the canons of the Church canons at least of greater antiquity."

Ser Petracco determined his sons' lives with no thought that

they might object. He was doing them, in fact, the utmost paternal
favor. The training of a civil lawyer was very long and expensive,
requiring at least eight years in residence at a law school. One
concludes that Ser Petracco was prospering, though he may have
had to scrape and sacrifice. He could have sent his Checco to the
well reputed Law School of the University of Avignon, but no, he
must have the more famous school at Montpellier.

Ser Petracco informed his elder son that he was to be a lawyer,
and that he would enter the University of Montpellier in the
autumn of 1316. The announcement probably did not disturb the
boy. At twelve one accepts parental decisions readily enough, without realizing their import. Francesco could have known only that
a lawyer's calling was high and noble, and that, in his beautiful
gown, he received universal obeisance. For him the important
thing was that his chum Guido Sette would matriculate with him
at Montpellier.

Some writers have called Ser Petracco a tyrant for cribbing
Francesco's poetic spirit in legal bonds. But there was no such
thing as a gainful literary career in those days; and plenty of loving fathers of all times have distrusted a boy's tendency to dreami-
ness, judging that a good sound legal training will persuade him
to keep his feet on the ground. Johann Kaspar von Goethe put his
son Wolfgang to the law, and nobody called him a tyrant.

Thus in the early autumn of 1316 Francesco, Guido, and perhaps one of the parents made the eighty-five-mile journey from
Carpentras to Montpellier, over the hot ancient roads, through
cities, like Nîmes, still redolent of Rome. Montpellier was a typical
medieval city. However picturesque it might appear to our eyes,
with its crowded Gothic buildings, its damp narrow dark arcades,
its winding alleys jammed with workers' stands, it seemed normal
enough to the travelers. Most of the city was ruled by the King of
Majorca, though a corner belonged to the King of France. The
Spanish connection brought in many Spaniards and even Moors,
and the Jewish population was large. The swarming students
added to the city's cosmopolitan character. Petrarch remembers
chiefly the throng of students and teachers, the rich merchants,
and tranquillity and peace.

The Law School occupied a large ogival building, which has
long since disappeared. There Francesco and Guido attended lec-

tures, often uncomprehending, often bored. They began with pre-
law work: Grammar, Dialectic, and Rhetoric, remnants of the
Three Arts of the ancient Trivium. Grammar meant drill in reading and writing Latin, not so much the high Latin of ancient
Rome as that of medieval legal authorities. Dialectic, or Logic,
dealt with the rules and methods of argument, in the service of
legal needs. Rhetoric, or the art of persuasion, had less to do with
literary excellence than with the composition of convincing pleas
before judges and juries.

For Petrarch, grammar, dialectic, and rhetoric may have had
their compensations, but the actual study of the law can have offered few. The professor expounded the text of the Roman codes,
and then embarked on the commentaries, distinctions, glosses,
and glosses on glosses that had congregated about every article. A
celebrated case was put by the famous Raymond Lull. An ass
grazing by a river enters an empty boat, chews the mooring rope,
is carried away, sinks with the boat, and is drowned. Who is
responsible for the damages? Answer: the ass's owner bears four-
fifths, the boat's owner one-fifth. For the ass has caused four torts,
elementative, vegetative, sensitive, and imaginative, whereas the
boat's owner has caused only an elementative tort.

The students were officially held to good behavior. They were
bound to attend many church services, and they were forbidden
to dress sumptuously, to gamble, dance, or attend the carnival.
Nevertheless student hot blood would burst forth. In 1319 there
was a real riot, stemming from the students' effort to import their
own wine in defiance of the town's protective system.

Petrarch probably held aloof from such affrays. He was a quiet,
studious youth, but studious rather of ancient poets than of legal
manuals. His father, on a visit to Montpellier, had therefore to
administer a dramatic reproof. Says Petrarch:

> Since he wanted above all things to open for me a road to wealth, I
> had to apply myself to civil law, and to learn what the law decrees
> about commodate and mutual loans, about wills and codicils, about
> rural and urban property, and I had to put aside the works of Cicero,
> which contain the laws most salutary for life. In my law studies I spent,
> or rather entirely wasted, seven years. And, to amuse you or stir your
> pity, I'll tell you what once happened. With uncanny foresight, I kept
> in a hiding place all the books I had been able to collect of Cicero and

of certain poets. Well, I heard Father condemn such books as impediments to that study which was supposed to be the source of fat earnings; and with these eyes I saw Father pull them out of their secret place and throw them in the fire with an air of scorn, as if they were heretical writings. Anguished by this spectacle, as if I were myself cast on the fire, I burst out in cries of woe. Thereat Father, as I well remember, was moved by my grief. He pulled out of the fire two volumes already scorched, and smiling at my tears he held out to me with one hand Virgil and with the other Cicero's *Rhetoric,* and said: "Here; take this one as an occasional recreation for your mind and the other to comfort and aid you in your law studies." In gratitude I dried my tears.

It seems strange that Ser Petracco, a scholar himself and a booklover, with a special cult for Cicero, should toss books, scarce and costly, on the flames. A really prudent notary would have merely confiscated the books and sold them. Nevertheless the story has the ring of truth. Ser Petracco was not invariably a prudent notary. Passion is stronger than prudence; and passion could not resist the symbol of a consuming fire.

In Montpellier the boy certainly made, or continued, his acquaintance with the Provençal poetry of the Troubadours. Their bloom had already passed, but their songs of love and springtime were still sung in the streets by jongleurs, who would intersperse their melodies with acrobatics and conjuring tricks. Petrarch knew the Provençal poets well; he mentions fifteen of them in his *Triumph of Love,* and his own poetic doctrine was deeply influenced by them. In these years he must also have learned to play the lute, to which he sang his own songs in later years.

During his stay in Montpellier, most likely in 1318 or 1319, his mother died. He loved this "best of all mothers" dearly; her death brought him his first experience of overwhelming, irremediable grief. His grief demanded expression, and, being what he was, he found the expression in a poetic tribute. He wrote his first extant poem, thirty-eight Latin hexameters for the thirty-eight years of his mother's life.

> Receive, O Mother most holy, these funeral measures.
> Incline to my song, if virtue by heaven rewarded
> may fitly accept a terrestrial filial tribute.
> What pledge may a sorrowing son depose on the altar

of thee in the spirit Elect, as in name and in person?
Only the vow to preserve in perpetual presence
thy virtue, humble and humbling, thy saintly devotion,
and thy soul's majesty, cloaked in the modest demeanor
in thy far girlhood first learned, and in beauty preservèd,
luminous still and serene, till the final leave-taking. . . .
Hope now and fortune abandon the sorrowful dwelling,
with the kind mother departing, the balm of our spirits;
and under the burdening stone I too lie buried.

His grief was genuine, his love for his mother deep. But if we
contemplate coldly his pain, we observe that he has already found
a means of solace, in the transmutation of pain into beautiful, well
ordered poetic statement. All his great poetry was to spring from
pain. He uses somewhere the phrase *quaedam dolendi voluptas,* a
certain pleasure in grieving. This pleasure in grieving he learned,
perversely, to seek.

And the cold observer will note the lines reading: "I should like
to utter these few words testifying to my grieving heart, and more
shall I say otherwhere; thy glory, dear Mother, shall ring to all
time through my lips." Already he had in mind a poetic career;
and already he was possessed by the dream of worldly fame.

In 1320 Ser Petracco summoned his sixteen-year-old son back
from Montpellier and informed him that he would continue his
law studies in Bologna, in company with his brother Gherardo,
aged thirteen. We do not know what prompted the change of plan,
but plenty of plausible reasons present themselves. The University of Bologna had the most famous school of civil law, and Ser
Petracco may have been dissatisfied with Montpellier or with his
son's progress. Or, like other expatriates, he may simply have
wanted his sons to have experience of Italian life and language.
At any rate, his decision to send the two boys so far away indicates
that his finances were in good order.

In time for the autumn term, Francesco, Gherardo, and the inseparable Guido Sette went off to college. Their journey must have
been delightful, along the narrow coast-road—too narrow even for
loaded pack-mules to pass—looping around innumerable headlands above the blue Mediterranean, then up and over the Apenines and down into the Lombard plain. The constant fear of
brigands would hardly have diminished their delight.

Italy was a revelation. The boys gaped at the magnificence of the cities, with their broad paved streets, high palaces, churches, and monumental tombs. In the suburbs of such cities as Genoa they passed sumptuous villas, with gardens, fountains, and grottoes. When, then or later, they were invited into noble houses, they saw luxury unknown in France, with large high-windowed rooms hung with embroidered silk or gilded leather, amply furnished, and decorated with paintings, majolicas, bronzes, and ivories.

Bologna was the finest city Francesco had ever seen. "Nothing fairer or freer could be found in the whole world," he recalls. Bologna was in transformation from medieval huddle to the spacious city we know today, with widening of the streets, the creation of open piazzas, the construction of the Palazzo del Comune and the Palazzo del Podestà and the churches of San Domenico, San Giacomo, and San Francesco. Its 180 towers, topped by the Torre Asinelli, over 300 feet high, made the city seem from afar to be invaded by giants stepping over the ruinous walls. A leaning tower rivaled that of Pisa. To be sure, outward magnificence masked the usual accepted drawbacks of urban life. A story is told of a poor scholar, begging through the city, mostly in vain, for his education, and often falling into "that Bologna mud that smells like corpses."

The city was called Fat Bologna, *pinguis Bononia*. Its citizens loved to give banquets. Its rich farming country supplied good living, and the sausage that has gained a worldwide fame, matched only by those of Frankfurt and Vienna. Petrarch's taste for salty meats, which he confesses in old age, was surely whipped by Bologna's salamis and sausages.

It was a luxurious, easygoing, amorous town. Gambling was rife. Bolognese women were famous for their beauty and their rich adornments. They wore crowns with pearls, or garlands threaded with gold and silver, and veils of lace. Bare necks contrasted with gowns of peacock-colored or crimson silk, woven with flowers or pictured images, with open sleeves hanging halfway to the ground. These were often tossed over the shoulder to display a bare arm. The women bore much ornament, belts with gold or gems, gold bracelets, gilded buttons and pins, begemmed purses. They were said to be free in their behavior. Even the convents were pervaded by the license borne on the soft air. These were oc-

casionally invaded by student bands, as today are women's dormi-
tories in the springtime. In 1332 four convents were ordered destroyed as a punishment for bad behavior of the inmates. In the
streets courtesans from all Italy and from foreign lands plied their
smiling trade. They wore long trains to distinguish them from
honest women, to indicate both their shame and their accessibility.

Presumably in wanton Bologna Petrarch made his acquaintance
with profane love, both with the heavenly goddess and with
Venus Libentina. He was a sensual man, unable, as he confesses,
to conceive of abstinence from amorous commerce. He was likewise one of the world's great celebrants of chaste fidelity to the
ideal woman. This is no paradox; the art of love comprises many
minor arts.

More reluctantly, he followed his courses in the University.

Bologna boasts that its University, dating from the eleventh
century, is the oldest in Europe. Its specialties were, and are, Law
and Medicine. Its constitution was unique in its time, and unique
it still remains. It was a *universitas,* a society, or aggregate, of
students. (*Studium generale* are the words translated by our modern "university.") The University possessed no buildings or other
properties. Classes were held in hired halls, public buildings, or
open porches, and general meetings in churches and monasteries.
The students elected their own Council and two Rectors from
their own number, and the Council chose the professors, paid
them, supervised them rigorously, and discharged them if they did
not behave. (The only modern parallel of which I am aware is the
Art Students' League in New York.) The Council likewise defended the students against grasping landlords and booksellers,
and against any usurpation of their rights by the city authorities.
The Council would yield to the city government in the case of
certain civil crimes, but its statutes provided that no student might
be tortured except with the sanction of a Rector and in his presence. To maintain student rights the Council had a powerful
weapon—the threat of emigration. Three times in the thirteenth
century the University flitted off to rival cities.

The treatment of the professors represents a student's dream of
bliss. I do not know why I should not copy E. H. R. Tatham's excellent summary, which is itself a summary of the excellent Hast-
ings Rashdall.

If a Professor wanted a single day off, he had to ask first his own students, and then the Rectors and Council. He might not create holi-
days, for which there was a fine of forty *solidi*, and his pupils were
bound to inform against him on pain of perjury. If he failed to secure
an audience of five for an "ordinary" or three for an "extraordinary"
lecture, he was treated as absent and fined accordingly. (Sometimes a
Professor had to bribe students to attend his lectures, or he made an
arrangement by which they attended in turn.) If he left the town he
had to deposit a security for his return. Punctuality was rigidly enforced. The Professor must begin when the bell of St. Peter's rang for
mass, under a penalty of twenty *solidi* for each offence, though he
may begin earlier; he must not go on one minute after the bell for
tierce, and if the students remained they were fined ten *solidi*. He
was fined if he skipped a chapter or decretal, and he might not postpone any difficulty to the end of the lecture, lest that be made an
excuse for evasion. At Bologna it was a sign of dissent or ironic applause to "bang books" at the lecturer.

The law texts were divided into sections known as *puncta*, and he
must reach each *punctum* by a certain date. [Hence our word *punctuality*.] At the beginning of the academic year he had to deposit ten
Bologna lire with a banker, from which his fines were deducted by the
Rectors. There was a committee of students called *Denunciatores
Doctorum*, appointed, according to the statutes, for the Doctors' spiritual good. The law books were divided among the Professors, so that
all subjects might be lectured on within two, or at most four, years.
In Petrarch's time many of the Professors were salaried; but there
were probably also fees for each course, which were collected by dele-
gated students.

The professors were few in number, and their classes generally
crowded. The effort of the students to hear and understand the
lecturer's Latin, to write notes on the knee with goose-quill and
inkhorn in the numbing cold of a Bologna winter, is surely a tribute to the boys' desire for a legal education. Surely also those who,
like our hero, had little of such desire found reasons aplenty for
absence. The statutes punished only the Faculty, not the students,
for non-attendance. Though Petrarch must have heard read and
expounded the essential Digests, Decretals, and Codes, only once
in all his work (in *Familiares* IX 5) does he mention any of them
or recall phrases or anecdotes from them. He may have profited,
however, from the *Dictamen*, or Art of Composition. This was
Bologna's specialty. It consisted in the writing of private letters,

official briefs and bulls, and legal documents. It partook of both grammar and law, and if taught by a competent instructor may well have developed Petrarch's feeling for Latin prose style.

Misplaced though he was, he honored his Alma Mater. He praised the good order and vigilance of the student government and the majesty of the professors. "Our stay there was a gift of heaven," he reminds his brother, "though we often had to complain of our friends' greed." This means no doubt that the two boys were better supplied with funds than their companions.

He wore the prescribed costume, a tunic with a hood, and a black cloak or gown, opening in the front, secured with a brooch or clasp. He was forbidden to carry arms (although a student who had reason to fear assassination could get a special license to bear weapons). He lived probably with Gherardo and Guido in a house rented by a student group, an embryo fraternity, with their own furniture, dining arrangements, and servants. He wrote, in his reminiscent letter to Guido Sette:

> It is both pleasant and painful to recall in these hard days the memory of happier ones. There cling in my memory, and surely in yours, indelible vestiges of that time when I was one of the student band. I had become an ardent youth, more daring than I had been or than I should have been. I ran with the group; on holidays we would roam far afield, so far that often the light abandoned us in the countryside, and we would return in the dark night. The gates stood wide open; or if by chance they were shut, the walls did not baffle us. Only a weak palisade, half in ruins, surrounded that intrepid city. What need was there of walls or bulwarks in time of peace? There were plenty of ways of getting in, and one could choose the easiest; there was nothing difficult or suspicious about it.

He remembered happily the singing and dancing in the streets. He watched the ceremony of the Presentation of the Snow. At the first snowfall the Councilors of each Student Nation, attended by their beadles, formally presented a snowball in a basin to the Gonfaloniere (or High Bannerman), the Ancients of the City, the Archbishop, the Rector of the College of Spain, the Papal Legate and vice-Legate, and received presents from each. There were other functions, uniting parade and combat, such as the Italians still love—jousts and pallio races. And the egg game. Before the assembled professors, clergy, nobility, and populace, students wear-

BOLONIA

ing leather helmets with tiny eye-holes and bearing ten-foot poles issued forth from a painted castle in the piazza. Opposing them appeared another student band carrying baskets of eggs. The eggs flew, and the spattered knights hit blindly with their poles at the attackers, to the spectators' joy.

Other diversions illustrate the brutality of medieval humor. There was the *festa della porchetta*. A boiled pig was thrown from the balcony of the Palazzo Comunale to the mob below, and when the daring charged for the prize they were sprinkled with the boiling water in which the pig had been cooked. And there was the horrible cat game. A man bare to the waist, with his head shaved, entered a cage with a cat. Forbidden the use of his hands, he was supposed to kill the cat with his teeth. But some students were revolted by this ugly spectacle, and saluted the Knight of the Cat with stones and melon rinds.

The students provided on occasion their own tumults. Petrarch was inevitably involved in the great student uprising of 1321. It came about thus: a student of canon law, with sixteen armed companions, abducted a notary's daughter, who was also a niece of the famous Giovanni d'Andrea, Professor of Canon Law. The father, with a band of citizens, stormed the seducer's lodging-house, defended by the embattled students. The culprit was taken. The Mayor condemned him to decapitation, and on the following day his head was publicly removed. But the students, already legal sophisters, and a good many of the professors protested the violation of student privileges, for the unruly young man had been denied the right to appeal for a trial by the Rector of his Student Council. Obtaining no satisfaction from the municipality, the students abandoned Bologna in a body and retreated to Imola, twenty miles away, taking with them their professors and leaving behind their debts and unfulfilled contracts. A year of parleys ensued, with the Pope intervening on the side of the students. Finally it was agreed that the Mayor should "receive discipline" in public, and the students should erect an expiatory chapel.

Thus for a year and a half, from March 1321 to October 1322, the University was practically suspended. Petrarch seized the opportunity to make a trip to Venice with his "preceptor," and no doubt with Gherardo and Guido. The party certainly passed through Rimini, and probably through Padua and Ferrara, cities later dear to him. Perhaps also Ravenna, where Dante died on September 13 or 14, 1321; but Petrarch did not see the dying poet, or he would somewhere have told us. His only recorded impression of Venice was one of prosperity and joy. We do not know where he spent the rest of the immense vacation.

Francesco resumed then his studies at Bologna in October 1322. Our next date is December 29, 1324, when he borrowed from a Bologna money-lender 200 lire, a considerable sum. Francesco was in Avignon in February 1325, according to a note in his copy of Augustine's *De civitate Dei,* bought in that month. We do not find him again in Bologna until October 1325, for the opening of the next college year.

Why the sudden need of money? And why the trip to Avignon, interrupting his studies? It is tempting to suppose that it was to attend, or to oppose, the remarriage of his father.

It used to be assumed that Ser Petracco and his wife Eletta died at about the same time in April 1326, since Petrarch says: "I gave up my studies when the care of my parents deserted me." But in the course of the last century certain awkward documents have turned up in Florentine records, which point to the existence of a second wife and also of an illegitimate daughter. The matter is very complicated, and its resolution is perhaps impossible, since the pieces never seem quite to fit. What seems to me the best solution is the following:

Some time before 1308 Ser Petracco begat a daughter, Selvaggia, a by-blow of his wandering years. On April 12, 1324 she married, in Florence, Giovanni de Summofonte, and her father provided a dowry, wretchedly small, of thirty-five florins. Petrarch never mentions her, understandably, though some early writers tell an absurd tale about a presumably legitimate sister.

Ser Petracco's wife, Eletta, died at an unspecified date. Petrarch says he lost her "in his first adolescence," and "at the Pythagorean fork," or parting of the ways, when a boy chooses the upward or the downward path in life. But how did he conceive of the *prima adolescentia?* And of the Pythagorean fork? He uses the latter phrase with reference to his own son at the age of eleven or twelve. But his mother's death occurred when he was old enough to write a Latin elegy for her; say fifteen or sixteen, or about 1319.

A few years later, and very likely in 1325, Ser Petracco married

Niccolosa di Vannis Sigoli. The Sigoli were Florentine Whites, and they could have been living in exile in Avignon. Niccolosa could conceivably have been the mother of Selvaggia, born out of wedlock.

Ser Petracco died in the spring of 1326. Five years later his widow put in a claim for some Florentine property of Petracco's, which had apparently escaped confiscation. She evidently moved to Florence. She is mentioned in a document of May 20, 1363 as living.

Petrarch, usually very profuse about his family affairs, never mentions her. His failure to do so proves nothing one way or the other. But the assumption of her existence gives a new and better meaning to some of his puzzling statements, e.g.: "In a single day Fate laid me, my hopes and wealth, low, and my family and house." (If this be taken to refer to the banishment from Florence, he was not yet born and could have had no hopes; if to the death of his father, with no stepmother existing, he would at least have had some hopes and wealth.) Again: "Though I experienced much harsh and unworthy treatment from my early youth, and—what increases the injury—from those from whom I had no reason to deserve such treatment, to whom did I ever return evil for evil?" And a new significance is given to a confidence to Gherardo:

> This curse [of faithless guardianship] followed us from childhood on. Whether it was fate or our simplicity, when adolescents and alone in the world, we were seen to be unsuspecting and made to be fooled. The old proverb runs: "Opportunity makes the thief." To put it in a nutshell, brother, this curse brought us from riches to poverty. Or rather—and here we may recognize God's hand—it turned us from our harried life to peace, and lifted our burdens. We soon saw what happened to those who loaded themselves with our spoils. The spoils were struck from their hands, and we saw the spoilers come down to a sad death, or lingering in extreme poverty and a miserable old age.

At any rate, Francesco and Gherardo were back in the University of Bologna for the scholastic year beginning in October 1325. And on April 26, 1326, three weeks after the opening of the spring term, the brothers suddenly left the University to return to Avignon. Almost certainly the reason was the news of their father's death or of his hopeless illness. Thus they did not take their final examinations or receive the doctorate, with its license to practice.

They had spent a good part of six years at Bologna, and were ready to leave. (Petrarch confuses us by saying that he spent three years there; he probably meant that, counting out the two long absences, he had fulfilled a three-year course.)

Years later Professor Giovanni d'Andrea of Bologna accused Petrarch of being a deserter, for abandoning the law when he was beginning to master it. He replied: "Nothing is well done that is done contrary to nature. She made me a lover of solitude, not of the law courts. Be assured of this: either I have never done anything worth while, which is quite possible, or, if I have, these were my luckiest, if not my wisest acts—to go to Bologna and to leave it."

The law was to him simply uncongenial. He grieved that he had lost in its study many precious years, of which man has so few. "I couldn't reconcile myself to making a merchandise of my mind," he says. When a young friend asked his advice about undertaking the study of civil law, he replied that laws are good, necessary, and useful in the world, but that those who apply the laws may be either bad or good, and the pity is that more are attracted to the law schools by greed than by the love of justice.

> They don't understand or they distort the laws described by our fathers with so much profundity and keenness; they dishonor justice, served in the past with so much zeal. What a venal trade they have made! Their tongues, hands, intelligence, soul, glory, fame, time, faith, friendships—all are for sale—and for just what they are worth! And what a contrast of times and customs! Our fathers armed justice with sacred laws; these prostitute it, stripped and defenseless; those held truth precious, these fraud; those gave the people secure, impregnable judgments; these feed their quarrels with tricks and sophistries; and the very abuses they are supposed to destroy with their legal arms they try to render immortal.

Though Petrarch profited little or not at all from his law studies, his years in Bologna were of great service to his developing mind. He admired and respected certain of his professors. Filippo Formaglini, who was perhaps his tutor, endorsed his note for 200 lire. (What professor today would give such student aid? However —a troubling thought—a number of the Faculty were involved in money-lending to students through go-betweens.) Formaglini's beautiful wife Novella was the daughter of the famous Professor Giovanni d'Andrea. We should perhaps scout the ancient story that on occasion she lectured in her father's stead, from behind a curtain to avoid upsetting the class by her beauty. Hers was a learned family; her mother advised the Professor on his courses, and her sister was one of the rare contemporaries who knew Greek. Acquaintance with such a family must have been truly educational. Petrarch probably knew also Cino da Pistoia, a professor with a wide knowledge of the Latin classics and a poet. Some of his songs of love and nature are to be found in every anthology of Italian poetry. At his death in 1337 Petrarch wrote for him an obituary sonnet.

Important also to Petrarch were his college companions. The friends one makes at twenty are likely to remain friends forever. There was Tommaso Caloiro, with whom he corresponded as long as Tommaso lived; and Luca Cristiani and Mainardo Accursio, to whom he proposed, in 1349, a common residence dedicated to good fellowship and the Muses; and Giovanni da Rimini, to whom he wrote, after twenty years, asking news. And of course Guido Sette, who stayed on in Bologna to take his degree. Guido returned to Avignon, became an important legal counselor to the Papal Court, and ended as Archbishop of Genoa. His lifelong intimacy with Petrarch never faltered.

Petrarch's chief profit from his stay in Bologna was literary. Bologna stood on the edge of Tuscany, and had close relations with Florence. Many Florentines attended the University, and Tuscan was the common tongue of the Italian students. Petrarch stabilized and corrected his knowledge of the language in which he was to write his great poetry.

At the same time he did not lose touch with the Provençal poetic tradition. Provençal had a good deal of currency among the literary-minded. Some Italian *trovatori,* including Dante's, and Browning's, Sordello, wrote by preference in Provençal. And in the streets one could often hear wandering jongleurs from Provence, attracted by the Provençal and French students in the University.

Bologna was a kind mother to poets. There Guido Guinizelli had lived in the latter part of the preceding century, and had there originated the *dolce stil nuovo,* the sweet new style, which Dante adapted and made immortal in his *Vita Nuova.* Briefly, the sweet new style demands elevation, nobility, both in style and in substance. In its theory (Platonic), the will directs the lover's intellect

toward the true object of its desire, which is beauty, not any material object; in the adoration of beauty resides the lover's happiness.
The sweet new style idealizes love and the beloved. Love rises from
its sensual origins to a realm of purity, where it blends with the
divine. The beloved becomes God's emissary on earth; her purpose
is to guide the poet, to redeem him from earthly evil, to purify
him in beauty. Thus the beloved takes on some of the attributes
of divinity, and the poet, by way of earthly love, attains to love
divine. And thus human feelings claim the dignity of permanent
moral values.

> Since the intellectual faculty was considered to be the distinguishing
> characteristic of the human being, to love humanly was to love intel-
> lectually. The highest quality of the beautiful woman would thus be
> her transparency, the quality which permitted the lover to glimpse
> the soul, the ideal, through the fleshly envelope; and the function of
> the beauty of woman would be to set man on the upward path, mak-
> ing manifest to him in the first place through his senses that beauty
> which his intellect could afterward follow upward to its source in the
> absolute.

The poetic sense was abroad in Bologna during Petrarch's stay.
(Notaries were especially fecund; perhaps they were bored with
their wills and contracts.) Students, imitating their elders, tried
their hands at poems of adoration, divinity-merging, and despair.
Thus Petrarch, at the all-important age of twenty, found precious
encouragement and rivalry in the group. Thus he wrote, and
destroyed, and wrote again, and by trial and error struggled to find
a form of expression which should be true, and beautiful, and his
own.

III: AVIGNON, 1326

That western Babylon, worst of cities, very like to hell.

—Fam. *XI 6*

THE WESTERN WORLD IN 1326 WAS IN ITS USUAL parlous condition. The long struggle for dominance between papacy and Empire had weakened both parties. The papacy had won, in a way, by establishing its claim to temporal power and possessions. The Pope, a ruler among other rulers, at the same time maintained his anointed superiority to them, and his right to settle their disputes on temporal matters. He was both judge and interested party. However, he could enforce his judgments only with spiritual weapons, excommunications and interdictions, which the mighty had learned to take lightly. To punish a prince materially he had to borrow the armed forces of other princes, members of the European concert; and these other princes would lend their soldiery only for a price, or for their own advantage. The papal overlordship was somewhat in the position of the United Nations today.

The papacy's attainment of temporal power was in some ways disadvantageous to it. In the common mind the papacy became a state among states, the Pope an earthly prince, fighting his rivals with the purposes and methods of power politics. As the Pope gained land and wealth he lost spiritual authority and the reverence of his charges. In the early years of the century Clement V, under pressure from Philip the Fair of France, tortured the Knights Templar and burned fifty-four of them, until he collected enough evidence from their screams to abolish the order and confiscate its immense properties, largely for the benefit of King Philip. Catholic laymen generally condemned the papal action, and still do. (The Grand Master of the Templars, Jacques de Molay, who called the Pope an unjust judge as he burned, has become the patron of a lay order with three million members in the United States alone.)

The current Pope, chosen in 1316, was John XXII, formerly Cardinal Jacques d'Euse, Bishop of Avignon. He came from Cahors, in Aquitaine, which was subject to England but French in sympathy. He was very thin and short, strikingly ill-favored, pale, and weak of voice. He was compared to Zaccheus, little of stature, who climbed up a tree his Lord to see. He was simple, modest, abstinent, industrious and energetic, and a considerable scholar in theology and canon law. He was in terror of magicians, who evoked evil spirits, especially Diana, against him. The Bishop of Cahors, in fact, stuck pins in a wax image of his person; the Pope protected himself by obtaining at great cost a serpent's horn. He was charged with nepotism, with appointing a swarm of needy relatives to lucrative posts. One of his first acts was to create fifteen new cardinals, eight of them from his natal diocese of Cahors, and only one of them Italian. His excellent financial management was frequently termed avarice. According to Giovanni Villani, whose brother helped make the inventory, the papal hoard included 18 million florins in specie and 7 million more in plate and jewels. (A gold florin was the price of a sheep.) If the figure is correct, as it most likely is not, the treasure weighed ninety-six tons.

He was not a miser; he was saving largely in view of a crusade against the infidels, which never came to pass. He had a certain taste for display and luxury. His pillows were edged with ermine; the liveries of his servants cost over 8,000 florins a year. John XXII was, however, austere in comparison with his predecessor, Clement V, and his successor, Benedict XII.

The Emperor was Louis of Bavaria, chosen by the German Electors in 1326. Promptly excommunicated by the Pope, he responded by declaring the Pope deposed for heresy and by creating an Antipope. Though he succeded in getting himself crowned Emperor in Rome by his Antipope, he was driven out of Italy in shameful flight. This was the end of Dante's and the Ghibellines' dream of an Emperor who should unite Italy in peace and prosperity.

As papacy and Empire weakened, Europe's kingdoms became

stronger. The fragmenting tendency of feudalism was checked by vigorous rulers and by a growing sense of nationalism. France, England, Aragon, Castile, Naples gained in might and turned their arms against one another. The days of the Crusades, when Europe could unite in common purpose against the paynim, were over. The only crusade that John XXII could contrive was one against his personal enemies, the Visconti of Milan.

His reign was shaken by a case that distressed the devout. A radical and powerful party in the Franciscan order tried to take seriously the rule of absolute poverty enjoined by Christ, the Apostles, and St. Francis. The Pope condemned these "Observants," or "Spirituals," for heresy. (For if their principle were accepted, where would be the papal claims to temporal possessions?) The Observants did not submit, but called the Pope a heretic, the Church no true Church. As Franciscan Little Brothers roasted for quoting Christ's words, spectators muttered angrily.

Heresy was rife, as every reader of Dante knows. Simple illuminates preached bizarre evangelical doctrines to simple enthusiasts. The failure of the Crusades left a residue of doubt and cynicism among the common people. Even in the mid-thirteenth century a monkish chronicler notes: "When the Friars Minor and Preachers begged alms in France in Christ's name, men gnashed their teeth on them; then, before their very faces, they would call some other poor man and give him money and say: 'Take that in Mahomet's name, for he is stronger than Christ.' "

Faith was of course still general and active, but it was affected by a decline in public and private morals, by the cynical power politics of rulers, by the cupidity and pride of the Church's masters, and by the misconduct of many in the lower ranks of the clergy. Although saints, such as Catherine of Siena, led their saintly lives, although some orders, as the Carthusians, demanded the utmost in devotion and austerity, although the Franciscan Spirituals and numberless obscure parish priests were holy men, sacrificing themselves in quiet labors, the morality of churchmen was comparatively low. The Church offered a career, opening the way to possibly immense rewards, for poor, ambitious, intelligent men; indeed, it was the only profitable career accessible to the lowborn. Today a young man or woman takes the vows in relative maturity, with a well-tested vocation, without thought of worldly success. "One who doubts his ability to live chaste would not choose the Church, any more than a timid man would choose an army career." But in those days many a youth took orders with no expectation of living chaste. Boccaccio's pictures of lewd clerics were of course exaggerated, satirical, unjust, but they contained enough truth to be acceptable to contemporary readers.

In the organized Church a priest was regarded as an indispensable official intermediary between man and God. His chief duty was to perform the sacraments necessary in the present life and for the soul's salvation. Vices did not disqualify him or invalidate the sacraments; he was not absolutely obliged to set an example of edifying conduct. Many of the high clergy, and even Popes, had their mistresses, and lowly priests their lemans. After all, the requirement of clerical celibacy was still only recent.

The prestige of the Church had suffered from the removal of the papal seat from Rome to Avignon in 1309. The name of Rome, that sonorous monosyllable, was a powerful magic throughout Christendom, as it still is. (Imagine transferring the Vatican to perhaps Indianapolis!) It is true that Rome was hardly more than a heap of ruins, inhabited by some 20,000 Romans with a villainous reputation, ruled by a few great families in high fortresses, at perpetual war with one another. Even the Pope was not safe in Peter's seat. In 1303 Boniface VIII had been taken prisoner by the Colonna, sword in hand. But however justly the Popes feared domination in Rome by nobles leading savage mobs, they shocked Italy by their removal to Avignon, where they fell under French domination. Just how far papal policy was subject to French policy is disputed by French and Italian historians, and it is noteworthy that Petrarch, who accuses the Papal Court of every crime, never says that it serves French ambitions. Nevertheless its sympathies were pro-French and anti-Italian. During most of the fourteenth century the Popes were French, and appointed French and Gascon cardinals in sufficient numbers to outvote the Italians.

The life of the Court was marked by display and conspicuous consumption, for *magnificentia* was regarded as an obligation of a ruler. An eyewitness describes a great party given by two cardinals to Pope Clement V in 1308. A cardinal attended by twenty chaplains met the master, and ushered him into a hall hung with splendid tapestries. Four knights and sixty-two squires waited on the diners, and were rewarded by the Pope with rich presents. There were nine courses, each consisting of three elaborate *pièces montées*; for instance, a pastry castle containing a roasted stag, roebucks, and hares. After the fourth course a cardinal presented to the Pope a white charger worth 400 florins and two rings, one with an enormous sapphire, the other with a no less enormous topaz. Each of the sixteen cardinals present received a ring, as did twenty other distinguished guests, and each of the twenty-four guards had his present. After the fifth course appeared a fountain spurting five kinds of wine. The margins of the fountain were garnished with peacocks, pheasants, partridges, and cranes. The interval between the seventh and eighth courses was occupied by a tourney in the dining hall. After the ninth course, a concert. Then dessert: two edible trees, one silver-colored, bearing gilded apples, pears, peaches, figs, and grapes, the other green, blooming with multicolored candied fruits. After dessert, the chef and thirty of his assistants performed a dance. The Pope then retired to his apartment, and had wine and spices brought.

We have also a description of Benedict XII setting forth on a journey, around 1340. First came a white horse, led by grooms; then a chaplain and squires carrying the papal pallium, or white wool yoke, and three red hats on poles; then two pontifical barbers, with red cases containing the Pope's vestments and tiara; then a subdeacon with a cross, followed by a mule with the Corpus Christi; then the Pope himself on a white horse, under a dais held aloft by six nobles, and followed by a squire with his mounting stool; then his train of chamberlains, stewards, prelates, and abbots: and finally his almoner, tossing coins to the crowd.

The Pope naturally lived well. His fruits, vegetables, oil, and fowls were the choicest of the Avignon region, which is still a gastronomic holy land. Sheep and cattle for his table were driven down from Alpine pastures. He was well supplied with game, including deer. His sea fish came from Marseilles; fresh-water fish were brought in tanks down the Rhone and were kept in a *piscarium*. He dazzled his visitors with forks, still hardly known. He had gold forks for roast meat and figs, and crystal ones for strawberries.

The cardinals lived close to their master, except when they were sent out on embassies and missions. They numbered about twenty-four in these years, a fourth of them Italian, the rest French or Gascons (from English Aquitaine), with an occasional Englishman or Spaniard. Each had his palace, in Avignon or nearby Villeneuve, where some may still be admired. The cardinals rivaled the Pope in magnificence, spending their revenues lavishly for jewels, plate, enameled plaques for their gloves, brocades, ermine and marten furs, rare weaves from Syria, lace for their shoes and stockings, cups engraved with serpent tongues to detect poison, even golden bits for their horses. Each cardinal had his court of prelates and laymen, theologians and lawyers, notaries and physicians, and the indeterminate hangers-on, the free-loaders who always gather where money is nobly spent.

The business of the Curia, or Papal Court, was enormous. Many hundred clerics and laymen of all ranks were employed to run the Church's affairs, doctrinal, administrative, legal, and financial, even to coin its money in the papal mint. Most of them spent their days writing, writing forever. Think of the copies necessary of a bull, encyclical, or pastoral letter, to be broadcast to every diocese! Think of the bookkeeping in a worldwide collection bureau! Incoming correspondence had to be summarized for the attention of department chiefs; every outgoing document had to be copied for the files. As there was no means of duplication, each copy of an official document had to be closely checked for accuracy. If a scribe made a mistake he had to do his job over, without pay. Since there were no newspapers, a résumé of reports brought in by couriers was handwritten daily for the top executives. The secretarial staff was ill paid, but it was accused of utilizing its many opportunities for petty graft.

The working conditions and living conditions were intolerable, even for those undemanding times. John XXII, promoted from the bishopric of Avignon, continued to live in his palace, beside the cathedral, where now rises the northwest wing of the Palace of the Popes. He built some hasty additions, entirely insufficient, and found in the city whatever quarters he could for his workers. He must have provided some sort of canteen, for work began with daylight, and the chief of the day's two meals came at nine or ten in the morning. (The mainstay, in the Italian tradition, was a minestra, with a little meat, sometimes with cheese, almonds, cinnamon, or cloves. Lasagne, ravioli, and rice dishes were popular, as well as fish on fast days. We find rather surprising references to salted whale meat. Sugar and honey were rare and costly. Everything was highly spiced; imported pepper was used even by peasants. And of course garlic and onions were consumed in great quantity. A Byzantine author said in 1202 that all Byzantines were undone by the breath of the conquering French crusaders.)

The scribes at work suffered from crowding and cold. The rooms were heatless, though a writer could warm his numb hands with a *chauffe-mains*, a container with hot coals. The worst drawback to efficiency was lack of light. Glass windows were rare, except in churches, and at best they were hardly transparent, bossed with lumps like bottle-bottoms. Most panes were of parchment or oiled cloth. The high winds of Avignon forbade the opening of a window, to disturb the ranged papers. On dark days one could use a tallow candle, which smelt foul, and required constant trimming of the wick. Candles of beeswax were too expensive for use, except in church ceremonies. Small brass lamps with oil, like those of the Romans, existed, but they were probably too feeble for office use. Good eyesight was essential for scribes; we should be tolerant of their errors. To be sure, spectacles were coming in, for those with well-lined purses. The first reference to them, it is said, appeared in 1299.

The employees of the Papal Court lived where they could in the bulging city. If one looks at a plan of Avignon one perceives, well within the present walls (which were not begun till 1349), a sort of inner sac, marked by a series of streets somewhat wider than the average—the Rue Grande de Fusterie, the Rue Joseph Vernet, the Rue des Lices, the Rue Philonarde. These trace the line of the earlier ramparts. Within this sac lived somehow the papal employees, the old Avignonnais, and the numberless representatives of the service industries: notaries, physicians, merchants, musicians, goldsmiths, restaurateurs, servants, hostlers, and those who used to be called so nicely night-soil men. When dark put an end to the long day's writing the scribes rose stiff from their hard stools and descended through unlighted streets to the city. There was no place to go except the taverns, nothing to do, except to drink, to dice, to wench. (One could not even *danser en rond* on the bridge of St. Bénézet, for it is only four meters wide, and the traffic on it was heavy. But probably the original phrasing of the song was

"Sous le pont d'Avignon.") The authorities were tolerant of moral lapses. It was noted that there were eleven bawdy-houses in the city, to only two in Rome. In 1311 a bishop asked for a decree forbidding prostitutes to live too close to churches, the Papal Palace, and cardinals' houses, and requiring them to pay fees to the Pope's Marshal.

"Dismal Avignon on its horrid rock," as Petrarch calls it, was an uncomfortable city, unplanned, insanitary, its dust and filth blown by the everlasting mistral. But its inhabitants claimed that the high wind blew away diseases; hence the saying: *Avenio, cum vento fastidiosa, sine vento venenosa*; Avignon, unpleasant with a wind, poisonous without it. The city's bad smell, *odor terribilis,* was famous. But Petrarch admits to an old friend that it didn't smell so bad when they were young together. He describes with loathing the noisy crowds, speaking every barbarous tongue, asking their way in bewilderment, begging for food. The streets, he says, resound with the clang of blacksmiths' hammers; a butcher slaughters a steer in front of his shop; a passing cart splashes all indiscriminately with mud. Again, Petrarch calls his city

> the most dismal, crowded, and turbulent in existence, a sink overflowing with all the gathered filth of the world. What words can express how one is nauseated by the rank-smelling alleys, the obscene pigs and snarling dogs, and the rumble of wheels, shaking the walls, and the carts blocking the twisting streets! So many races of men, such horrible beggars, such arrogance of the rich! In short, so many discordant human beings of diverse customs, such a clamor of mingling voices, and such a throng of jostling bodies!

Socially, Avignon resembled a small New England city with a giant army camp on its outskirts. While the merchants rejoiced, the gentry, often evicted from their homes, huddled in cramped quarters and regarded the newcomers with hostility and disdain. In general they kept themselves to themselves, though of course a cardinal or an archbishop might have his entrée in an old noble household, as, in the New England town, a major general may be asked to tea.

The new settlers tended to group themselves according to nationality, although well-established men of affairs, like Ser Petracco, gradually formed their own groups of congenial, cultured friends, of whatever racial origin. Italians monopolized the luxury trades and the higher levels of banking. The lower levels, or usury, were in the hands of Jews. The Italians had their own consuls, confraternities, and festivals; they numbered at one time 600 families. Most of them were Tuscan; among them Petrarch could keep fresh his Tuscan speech. True gravity, the morality of life, he says, are proper to the Italians, whereas the French are keen, facetious, light in speech and in bodily movement, jokers, gay singers, hard drinkers, mighty eaters.

Men wore breeches and doublet, and over them a gown, with a hood tossed back except in bad weather. The correct length of the gown varied from year to year, causing much dispute among fashionable young men. The short French gown to half-calf was favored; extremists wore them so short as barely to cover the buttocks. These scant costumes were regarded as scandalous. Petrarch mocked fashion's decrees, "gowns now hiding the feet, now revealing our shameful parts, sleeves that now sweep the ground, now pinion the elbow, belts that now confine the breast, now hang down below the belly." A worker or a gentleman riding on a journey put on a girdled knee-length blouse, such as the hunters wear in the famous wall-paintings of the Palace of the Popes, or the characters in Giotto's frescoes in Padua. Gloves were rare and expensive. The linen shirt first became general in the fourteenth century. The shirts turned to rags, the rags to paper; paper made printing possible, and printing made our world. Underclothing was of linen; cotton was an imported rarity. The commoners' underclothing, if any, was of rags, often of hempen cloth. Imagine hempen shorts! The commoner wore sabots or coarse leather boots, the gentlemen soft, tight heelless shoes or slippers. Every man carried a knife or poniard slung across his stomach; this was by turns a tool, a table utensil, and a weapon.

Women in the home wore a loose house dress of wool, linen, or hemp, more rarely cotton, or they donned one of their men's old gowns. Their public and party dresses were often magnificent, brightly colored, adorned with furs and gems. At this time they were very low cut; preachers called them "windows of hell." Women had no hats, but wore a bandeau, a silk veil, or a crown of flowers. The hair hung loose until marriage, and then was divided in two tresses raised in a large chignon.

As for manners and morals, one may venture generalizations

only insecurely. The old established families, the conscientious clerics, the godfearing artisans, certainly led exemplary lives. But bad examples, especially of violence, were set them by the great. Treason and perfidy, which so horrified Dante, were rife. The fear of poison was universal among Italy's tyrants; an invitation to dinner aroused the utmost forebodings. The tradition of medieval justice persisted, that disputes should be settled by personal combat, and that God would ensure the victory of the just man. Knifeplay was common, even among clerics. On the other hand, the rise of the mercantile ideal in Italy tended to substitute the bourgeois code of law, order, and security for the knightly ideal of honor at the sword's point.

Women were in general religious, moral, high-minded. Boccaccio's wanton wives existed, no doubt, not only as an escapist's dream. But Boccaccio also wrote a book about women of noble character, *De claris mulieribus* (which has had no popular success), and even in his *Decameron* there is no hint of misbehavior among the gentle youths and maidens who lived unchaperoned in their Settignano villa. The Italians, with their strong sense of family obligation, required impeccable behavior of their women, and were likely to punish any infraction with death. There is no good reason to suppose that moral looseness was commoner in the early fourteenth century than in other centuries.

Intellectually, Avignon was by no means a barren land. It had its own little University. The tradition of the Provençal poets was still treasured; poetic improvisers were welcomed in the houses of the great. The establishment of the Papal Court brought to it scholars, musicians, learned lawyers, many of them devotees of classical literature, many of them adepts of poetry and the arts. These rudimentary humanists formed a caste, a club, in which Petrarch could feel at home.

Such was the city to which Francesco and Gherardo returned in 1326. It must have seemed very crude and mean after the splendors of Bologna. It was a frontier city, where various traditions met and warred—French and Italian, lay and papal, chivalrous and businesslike, pious and self-seeking, *naïf* and sophisticated—medieval, in short, with strong hints of the modern.

IV: YOUNG MAN ABOUT TOWN

> *I have wasted years; but I never lost a day*
> *without realizing it, so that in the snares of*
> *business or in pleasure's heat I would still*
> *say: "Alas, this day is reft from me, never to*
> *return!"*
>
> —Fam. *XVI* 11

"I CAN'T BOAST OF REMARKABLE GOOD LOOKS," wrote Patrarch to posterity, with a little smirk, "but in my greener years I was thought pleasant enough. I had a high complexion, with skin between white and brown, sparkling eyes, and for a long time very acute vision, which failed me when I was over sixty, so that, reluctantly, I had to have recourse to glasses." In another letter he admits that he thought himself handsome; to him might have been addressed Virgil's warning: "Fair youth, trust not too much to your fresh bloom."

Boccaccio fills out the picture by describing Petrarch as somewhat above middle height, with a round handsome face, neither light nor dark, but of an intermediate complexion, fitting for a man of worth. He had a grave movement of the eyes, and a cheerful, penetrating gaze. He was mild of manner, restrained of gesture, with a ready, infectious laugh, but never the loud foolish outburst. His voice was powerful and well modulated. He was normal in his gait, placid and humorous in converse. Remember also that he was quick and active of body, though not exceptionally strong. His hair was reddish-blond, but to his grief it began to turn gray before he was twenty-five. He consoled himself with the recollection that Virgil and Numa Pompilius were similarly afflicted. In Petrarch's *Secretum,* his St. Augustine accuses him of too much satisfaction with his appearance, and he protests only weakly. Unfortunately our only authentic portrait of him is a mere sketch, in profile, of a full-fleshed man in later years, three-fourths swaddled in a monastic cowl.

He was equipped to make a good impression, and his charm of person was enhanced by charm of personality. An acquaintance asserts that Petrarch held auditors breathless, for fear he would stop talking. Boccaccio says that he could hold the simple without their wearying, but rather to their delight:

> They are so ensnared that they would grant to be true the story that Naricius's ships were wrecked by the sirens' songs, for they are similarly spellbound by the charm of his talk. And others aver that the very bees that bedewed the lips of the child Plato, and of Ambrosius too, with honey of Cyrrhan thyme, did the same for him. His affability is so exceptional that, whereas many illustrious men are disappointing in the encounter, he surpasses all expectations.

His material situation in these years is far from clear. His statements have already been quoted about Fate laying low his hopes and wealth, about subjection to harsh and unworthy treatment, about the misdeeds of guardians, whom God properly punished. Add to these a sentence in a letter to Gherardo: "What shall I say of the tempests in the courts, and the lawsuits, which are enough to make not only the tribunals but the whole world odious to me?" Add a reminiscence that his father possessed a splendid manuscript of Cicero, and that the executors of his estate, intent on despoiling his patrimony, which they thought very rich, handed the manuscript over to Francesco, not out of good will, but because they did not recognize its value. These texts would fit with the supposition that a stepmother existed, on bad terms with the two boys; that Ser Petracco's will favored her at the expense of his sons; that the sons contested the will, and that at length it was upheld in the courts; that the young men lived well, though briefly, on their great expectations; and that, though they must have received some legacy, they were before long reduced to seeking employment or patronage.

For a time at least they lived the carefree life of young men about town. In his letter to Gherardo, who had become a Carthusian monk in the sternest of monasteries, Francesco recalls those happy days.

> You remember, my dear fellow, what our situation was then, and how some hard-won pleasure was mixed with our bitterness. . . . You remember how strong and how foolish was our desire for fine clothes—

AVINIONE

which I admit I still feel, though every day less. You remember the endless boredom and bother of putting them on and putting them off, morning and evening. And how we feared that a hair would be displaced, and a breeze would upset the proper structure of our coiffure! And how we had to dodge the animals coming every which way in the streets, so that our perfumed, spotless gowns wouldn't get a splash of mud or have their folds disarranged by jostling! How vain are men's cares, especially young men's! Why all this anxiety in our minds? Simply to please the eyes of others. Well, whose eyes? Those of a lot of people who found no favor in our own. Seneca, in a letter to Lucilius, says: "Who ever put on a purple gown, except to show it to somebody?" It's idiocy to regulate our lives not according to intelligent reason but to suit popular fads, and to call in as judges of our lives those whose own lives we despise. No one chooses for a captain someone with a sword wound on his back, nor for pilot someone famous for his shipwrecks. We choose those whom we admire, and we trust our business to those who have brilliantly handled their own. And so to follow the fashions of the idiot mob, whose manners we laugh at and whose lives and opinions we despise, is to be more idiotic than the mob. . . .

A commoner's costume is more useful, adaptable, and practical than that of a king. But we thought quite differently in those days. We thought it worth any trouble to be looked at, and as Persius says, to have people point at us and say: "There he goes!" . . .

What shoes we wore! They were supposed to protect our feet, of which they were in fact the fierce and unrelenting enemies. They would have crippled me completely, if, warned by extreme necessity, I hadn't preferred to shock other people rather than to squeeze my bones and nerves out of shape. And what of our curling-irons and our artful locks, which cost us labor and pain and robbed us of sleep? What pirate could have tortured us more cruelly than we did ourselves! How often in the morning we saw in the mirror red wounds on our foreheads, so that when we wanted to show off our beautiful hair we had to hide our faces! . . .

Just think how late we watched and how hard we worked so that our folly should be widely known and so that we might become the town's talk! How we would distort our pronunciation and upset the normal word order! In short, what didn't we do so that our affectations, which we should properly have rooted out, or at least hidden out of shame, should be applauded and admired? . . . Remember those swarms of visitors and their struggles to salute us, and how we sweated and labored to appear here and there in public, immaculate and magnificent! . . .

And O dear Jesus, how eagerly we sought out a love not merely
mortal but mortiferous, whose deceptive sweetness, mixed with pain,
Thou didst permit us to taste, lest in ignorance we should think it
something very fine! . . . What sighs, what laments, what tears we
cast to the winds! And how, like madmen resisting their physician, we
thrust aside Thy hand, which sought to apply Thy sovereign balm to
our wounds! Now, Gherardo, tell me, you who have changed from
God's enemy to his friend, from his adversary to his citizen, what
resemblance is there between our silly songs, full of false and indecent
praise of loose women and shamefully revealing our lusts, and those
sacred songs and midnight psalms, with which now you sleeplessly
resist the assaults of the old enemy!

These memories of his own and Gherardo's popularity and
wanton courses could well have upset the penitent monk and
have forced him to some disciplinary flagellation.

Although we may recognize in Petrarch's recollections a touch
of literary exaggeration and more than a touch of complacency, we
can take them as clear evidence of his social success in Avignon.
Why not, indeed? He was twenty-two, handsome of person, well-
bred, compelling in his speech and thought, careless of his money.
He was just back from college, full of collegiate jokes and songs,
with anecdotes of the older Italian world to impress the rather
colonial society of Avignon. He was also a poet, singing his own
songs to favored ears with lute accompaniment. In proper circumstances he revealed his extraordinary knowledge of Roman
history and of ancient literature. Of course he was popular, and of
course he enjoyed his popularity.

He found conquests easy in the Avignon half-world, among the
light women who gather where sturdy lonesome males abound. He
makes no secret of his freedoms. He confesses that, while inwardly
abhorring fleshly sins, he was carried away by the fire of youth and
by his ardent temperament, that his body warred bitterly against
him, that he was one of a youthful pleasure-seeking band, though
not the worst among them. He also tells us that he was shyer than
a stag; but shyness would not be inconsistent with membership in
a youthful pleasure-seeking band.

He may have undertaken amorous enterprises on a higher social
level. In his *Triumph of Love* Cupid says to him: "I've been expecting you for a long time, since from your early years you gave

such presage of your character." Petrarch replies: "True enough; but love's distresses frightened me so that I abandoned the adventure. Nevertheless my breast is still marked, my clothing torn." We have a hint of masculine rivalries, a duel. He reminds his brother, in the letter quoted above: "Some fought with the tongue, some with treacheries, some with the sword. I speak briefly to one who knows what I am talking about." However, these references are too vague for us to build on.

Genuine love, turning to adoration, he surely did not know until he met Laura. He probably played the conventional game permitted by the Provençal tradition of the Courts of Love, revived in the Avignon region in the early fourteenth century. The troubadour picked a respectable noble married lady and to her addressed his songs of adoring despair, extolling her beauties and blaming her chaste rigor. The lady listened with satisfaction, and permitted at most a kiss of the beloved hand. The husband listened with equal satisfaction, and perhaps gave the troubadour a present; as today fine ladies have their artistic protégés who write heart-smitten poems, which the husband keeps in pocket and proudly shows to his friends. No one's reputation suffered; quite the contrary. The poems were copied, passed about, and admired. With luck one might eventually hear them sung in the streets by a jongleur.

None of Petrarch's juvenilia persist, for in later years, with regard for his reputation, he destroyed them. Vain though it is to judge poems that do not exist, we may at least assume that they were written in the Provençal tradition, and perhaps in that language. He would later show his debt to Provençal, in his prizing of form and technique, in the use of Provençal verse forms, in his liking for obscurity, double meanings, and the elaborate "conceit," or far-fetched analogy. But Petrarch brought with him from Bologna a deep admiration for the Italian "sweet new style," with its typical forms, the sonnet, the canzone, the madrigal, and with its elevation of the beloved from the sensual to the spiritual world. He was influenced also by admiration for Dante, who had succeeded in writing the greatest of serious poems in the vulgar tongue.

"In my youth," he wrote to Boccaccio, "I had conceived a grandiose work in Italian, and had already assembled the stone, lime, and wood for the foundations. But I reflected that our times would not appreciate it." Of his project we know no more than this, but we may be sure that it thrilled the ladies of the Avignon salons.

Not all of Petrarch's time was given to poetry and social success. He was already a humanist scholar in embryo, a passionate lover of ancient wisdom and beauty. To extend his knowledge he needed elder scholars to give him guidance, encouragement, and inspiration. These he found in the persons of Raimondo Soranzo and of Giovanni of Florence.

Soranzo was a venerable man, a lawyer, who pled in suits before the papal Curia. In at least one case he boldly denounced the papal policy, and thus lost all chance of favor and advancement. He was a book-collector, specializing in Livy and Roman history. Petrarch helped him in his researches and freely borrowed his books. Soranzo gave him fatherly advice and affection and no doubt useful introductions and possibly even money for his secretarial services.

To Giovanni of Florence Petrarch pays a loving tribute.

When I was a youth there was a certain old man from Florence, with venerable gray hair and notable austerity of character. He was also a more than ordinary literary scholar, although he was one of the Pope's writers, whom we know to be rather laborious than intelligent. He had done his work with industry and fidelity for more than fifty years. His age, integrity, and chiefly his sweet, gentle, eloquent conversation gave him an air of benevolent authority. His name was Ioannes, and his only other name was that of Florence, his home town; and I think that was the first cause of our common affection, for I don't think there was anything else in me to attract him. . . .

This great man came to admire, love, and encourage my small talent. May Christ reward him, for I owe him much, and he did not live to a time when I could prove my indebtedness to him. He never saw me without prodding me sharply and stirring my young mind, with fatherly kindness, to virtue and knowledge, and especially to the love of God. . . .

Well, once when I had a good deal on my mind I went to see him, and found him alone and buried as usual in his studies. The dear man was delighted to see me. "Why do you look so much more worried than usual?" he said. "Am I mistaken, or has something happened?"

Said I: "You aren't mistaken, though what has happened is not new. I am tortured by an old trouble. You know how hard I've worked, and you know my ambitions. You know how I have been struggling to rise above the common run of people. . . . I haven't lacked earnest purpose and hard work, and I must have some talent, to judge from your own testimony, if for no other reason. You have loudly praised my exceptional abilities in the presence of many, and they were convinced, knowing that you always tell the truth. You have often warned me in your gentle voice that I should exercise my mind in higher studies, and not by my laziness allow so great a gift of God and nature to lie useless. Under such urging I worked all the harder, and nothing seemed difficult to me. I pressed on, and passed all my hours in the study of letters, and tried not to waste any in idleness. Not content with conventional teachings, I kept trying for something new, flattering myself that I was not laboring in vain, but that I promise something important and praiseworthy for the future. But now, in the very midst of my eager study, when I thought I was gradually getting close to some achievement, I feel that I have sunk to the bottom, and all the springs of my intelligence seem to have dried up. I don't know why this sudden plague has struck me. What used to seem easy now seems impossible, and where I used to run at full speed now I pick my way step by step, with such hesitation that I can hardly move. I am dull instead of bright, poor rather than rich, timid instead of courageous; I was a master, and now I'm a learner. I'm nearly desperate, and I come to you because you have brought me to this situation. I confess I know nothing at all; and I want you to tell me whether I should give up what I've begun, or try some new course in life—or what?"

I said all this and a lot besides, crying and shouting like a child. He didn't stand it long, but said: "My son, don't waste time in complaining that might better be spent in thanking God. You are better off than you think, for when you thought you knew so much you didn't know anything, and when you realized your ignorance you took a giant step forward. Now at last, when you think you know nothing, you are beginning to know something. For hidden places are now revealed, whose existence you couldn't even perceive as long as you thought so magnificently of yourself. A mountain-climber begins to see things that he couldn't imagine from below. A man who wades into the sea realizes its depth, and knows he's going to need a boat to venture farther. So, since you say I'm responsible for your present situation, I not merely urge you, I command you to continue what you've begun. God will be with you, have no doubt."

When I had heard these words, like an oracle from heaven, I went away cheered and full of hope.

The wise old man was diagnosing a disease common in the intellectual world, and particularly in graduate schools. It might be called graduate colic, or intellectualepsy. It is the dryness, or *siccitas,* of the mystics. The learning faculty seems dead; intellectual curiosity vanishes; the ends and aims of study are regarded as worthless. The victim longs to abandon learning in favor of life, which, though imperfectly defined, seems like something very bold, free, and gay. The only cure for this disease is time.

How Petrarch lived during these years is far from clear. It is supposed that he obtained some employment at the Papal Court, or that he supported himself and Gherardo by teaching. However, he never mentions such occupations, and I find it hard to picture him copying or editing among the lowly scribes he despised, or drumming Latin grammar into boys' brains. He may have found a patron free with money, but he gives us no hint of one until he entered the Colonna household in 1330. The fashionable life he describes could not possibly have been led on the returns from some modest labors. I think it most likely that his father's legacy and the negotiable expectations it aroused supported him during at least the five years between 1326 and 1330, and that he kept going for a time on grants and loans. He speaks of his "gay, free youth," when, with his companions in poverty, he scorned the might of money.

At any rate, he became a cleric, in order to qualify for a job at Court, and eventually for a benefice, which would give him the revenues of an ecclesiastical living. He was tonsured; a round patch of hair was clipped from the skull's crown, thus ruining his stylish coiffure. Authorities dispute whether or not he took the four minor orders of acolyte, exorcist, reader, and doorkeeper. With all allowance for the laxity of the fourteenth-century Church, I find it hard to believe that he could have held his important benefices, as chaplain, canon, and archdeacon, without the minor orders. These, to be sure, imposed few obligations, except celibacy, and even celibacy was often avoided by a dispensation. However, a loose-living young man could find the vow of celibacy rather a convenience than a drawback.

If one condemns Petrarch for taking orders without a vocation, one should remember that he had no reasonable alternative. There was no career for an intellectual outside the Church, except law, the notariate, and the merchant world, for all of which he was entirely unfitted. Even the professional army did not exist.

We see, then, Petrarch in his mid-twenties as something of a celebrity in Avignon society, charming all by his personality and by his reputation as a poet. We see him also as a serious scholar, frequenting learned elders, delighting in the study of the ancient classics, writing Latin with unusual elegance. We see him finally as a very troubled young man, proudly conscious of his superiority, but seeing no use for his abilities, no clear path through life, except by way of the Church, whose obligations he detested. He passed through many moments of despair, wondering if there was any future for him in the world. And his apprehensions were increased by his responsibility for Gherardo, who was no scholar, who was then something of a libertine, and who was always in need of money.

In his state of depression, self-questioning, self-condemnation, and misgivings about his future life, he made matters far worse. He fell in love.

V: LAURA

*Go to, hope a God's name, since there is
nothing more pleasant unto thee than to be
deceived.*

      —De remediis (Phisicke against Fortune),
       I 109

THE DEAREST OF PETRARCH'S BOOKS WAS HIS
Virgil (which is now in the Ambrosian Library in Milan).
On its flyleaves he wrote family records and noted the
deaths of friends, as others do in their Bibles. Here he preserves
for his secret meditation the greatest experience in his life, the
love of Laura and her death, as Pascal kept the Memorial of his
mystical illumination always sewn in the lining of his coat. Here
is Petrarch's Memorial:

> Laura, illustrious for her own virtues and long celebrated in my
> poems, first appeared to my eyes in my early manhood, in the Church
> of St. Clare in Avignon, in the 1327th year of Our Lord, on the sixth
> of April, at the early morning service. And in the same city, in the
> same month of April, on the same sixth day, at the same first hour in
> the year 1348, her light was subtracted from that of the world, when I,
> by chance, was in Verona, ignorant, alas, of my fate. The sad news
> reached me in Parma, in a letter from my friend Ludovicus, on the
> 19th of May, in the morning. That very chaste and lovely body was
> laid to rest in the church of the Franciscan Brothers on the very day
> of her death, at evening. But her soul has, I am persuaded, returned
> to the heaven whence it came, as Seneca says of Scipio Africanus. As
> a memorial, afflicting yet mixed with a certain bitter sweetness, I have
> decided to make this record in this place of all places, which often
> falls under my eyes, that I may reflect that there can be no more
> pleasure for me in this life, and that, now that the chief bond is
> broken, I may be warned by frequently looking at these words and by
> the thought of the flying years that it is time to flee from Babylon.
> This, by God's grace, will be easy for me, when I think courageously

and manfully of the past's vain concerns and empty hopes and unexpected outcomes.

How typically Petrarchan this is, with its genuine emotion, its intrusion of author's complacency ("long celebrated in my poems"), its touch of pedantry ("as Seneca says of Scipio"), its quick transition from tears for Laura to self-analysis ("affliction mixed with bitter sweetness"), its sense of God's favor in providing a miraculous coincidence between the hour of his meeting Laura and that of her death!

Who was Laura?

There were two Lauras: the heroine of Petrarch's poetic romance, and the Laura of fact. Petrarch's Laura is described in his own statements, mostly in his Italian poems. The Laura of fact is preserved in an ancient Avignon tradition, reinforced by scholarly researches during the last two centuries.

Petrarch's heroine was of an ancient, rich, noble or semi-noble family. She was born in a small town, at the foot of hills, not far from Avignon and Vaucluse. She lived in Avignon; "I loathe seeing my lovely treasure in that muck." She was younger that he, but married; for his tête-à-têtes would have been hardly conceivable with a noble maiden. Since he fell in love at twenty-two, she was at least sixteen, at most twenty-one; she was born between 1306 and 1311. Someone was jealous; presumably her husband. She had a number of children. In Petrarch's private *Secretum*, his St. Augustine sneers: "That magnificent body, now worn out with illnesses and frequent childbirths, has lost much of its pristine vigor."

She was beautiful, of course. Augustine makes his charge admit that her beauty had first allured him. However, the descriptions of her beauty are never very detailed and specific, in the manner of modern realism. (After all, we are told few exact details of Beatrice and her physique, or of the beloved in the Song of Songs, or even of the Dark Lady of the Sonnets.) Laura's hair was gold, her complexion snowy, though flushing on occasion. Her eyelashes were ebony, her eyes black. (Could it be that she dyed her hair?) Her mouth was angelic, full of pearls and roses. She sang sweetly, in a thrilling voice. She was fond of finery, twined pearls and gems in her hair, and wore silk gloves, then rare and costly. She was captivated by her own beauty; Petrarch regarded her mirror as his

chief rival, and warned her of the fate of Narcissus. She could be
gay enough with her women companions, but she was often silent,
and Petrarch loved her smiling muteness, encouraging him to
talk. He does not conceive that perhaps she had nothing to say.
She did not care for poetry, even for Petrarch's. This seemed to
him astounding, since poetry is the greatest force in the world. She
did not prize or even notice Love's irresistible power. She was prudent, modest, indomitably chaste. She permitted no compromising visits; all her encounters with Petrarch seem to take place outdoors. As to her death and hasty burial in the Franciscan church,
there are suggestions of the Great Plague; "a sudden tempest from
the east" submerged her (*Rime* CCCXXIII). Again, in Eclogue X,
"a pest-bearing chariot, a wet south wind invaded us and laid low
my joy, the Laurel, among the prostrate trees."

This is nearly all we know of Petrarch's Laura. I picture her
as Flora in Botticelli's Primavera, golden-haired, flower-crowned,
barefoot on a flowery sward, pure, unfleshly, unearthly, and probably illiterate.

And who was the Laura of fact?

An ancient Avignon tradition alleged that she was a girl named
Lauretta, of the house of de Sade (or de Sauze, or di Salso). She
was said to be about eighteen when Petrarch fell in love with her
in 1327. In 1520 an Italian biographer, Alessandro Vellutello, visited Avignon and talked with an old gentleman, Gabriel de Sade,
who reported the family tradition. A number of variant stories
were, to be sure, current in the city. In the mid-eighteenth century
a scholarly abbé, J. F. X. de Sade, uncle of the unholy Marquis,
undertook a serious investigation, especially in the family ar-
chives. He found a Laura or Lauretta de Noves, daughter of Audibert and Ermessenda de Noves, who married Hugues de Sade.
Audibert de Noves was a chevalier, of an eminent Provençal family, lords of the village of Noves, ten miles southeast of Avignon.
The de Sades were of the same class of wealthy gentry. They were
owners of prosperous weaving mills in Avignon. Their arms were
carved on the bridge of Avignon in 1177. The contract of marriage
is dated January 16, 1325; normally the wedding would follow immediately on the signature of the contract. The document stipu-
lates a handsome dowry: 6,000 livres tournois with a round O
(whatever those are), two costumes, one green, one scarlet, with

squirrel-fur tassels, a silver crown, a bed and equipment. Since this Laura could hardly have been less than fifteen at marriage, she was born in 1310 or earlier.

Hugues de Sade was philoprogenitive. Laura bore eleven children. The eldest, Augière, went somehow astray after her marriage, and was confined in a convent by papal order when she was only twenty-one; her father left her an insulting five sous in his will. No doubt she caused her mother much grief.

In the spring of 1348 the Great Plague came to Avignon, causing such ravages as we can hardly conceive. It is said that half the population of the city died. On April 3, 1348, at the height of the plague, Laura de Sade made her will. It states that she is "of sound mind, but weak in body." She asks to be buried in the Franciscan church, in which the de Sade family had built chapels. She then disappears from the family records. Her husband remarried in the following November.

The family records no longer exist. Most of them perished in an attack on the family château during the Revolution. However, the Abbé de Sade had the genuineness of Laura's will attested by two notaries and seven persons of high standing. There is no reason to doubt the Abbé's good faith or to suspect his competence. His book, in three great volumes, is a monument of Petrarchan scholarship, indeed of historical-critical literary scholarship; his scrupulousness can be checked in his transcription of many medieval documents which are still extant.

Now put together Petrarch's Laura and Laura de Sade and see how they fit. The name of Laura; the suitable age; the gentle birth; the origin in a village near Avignon; the wealth; the illnesses and frequent childbirths; the burial in the Franciscan church—at all these points the two Lauras coincide. As for the death of the two, the coincidence is almost as compelling. Petrarch's Laura died in the morning of April 6, 1348, and was buried in the evening. The haste strongly suggests that she died of the plague, and the presumption is borne out by other statements of the poet. Laura de Sade was sick, and made her will, on April 3, 1348. She was certainly dead very soon after. The plague commonly killed in three days.

The identification seems to me certain. The chances that there were in the small city of Avignon two rich, well-born young ladies

named Laura, of the right age, married, with many children, who
died on or about April 6, 1348 and were buried in the Franciscan
church, are infinitesimal. Add to this the ancient tradition that
Petrarch's Laura was a member of the de Sade family, and the case
would appear closed.

Not all the critics agree, however. Many have alleged, and some
still do, that there was no real Laura; she was merely an ideal in
the poet's mind, or she was an abstraction for poetry or philosophy. Her origin, they say, was verbal—the name Laura, lending
itself to triple puns, *il lauro*, the laurel-tree, *l'aura*, the breeze,
l'auro, gold. Many have been revolted by the thought of Laura's
marriage and motherhood, and have insisted, with the slenderest
of proof, that she was a wild woodland virgin, roaming the hills
around Vaucluse.

The identification of the two Lauras as one entails, it is true,
certain awkwardnesses. One of them is the astounding coincidence
that Laura died twenty-one years, to the very hour, from the moment that Petrarch first caught sight of her.

The date and hour when Petrarch first saw Laura in church and
was unholily transfixed by Cupid's arrow in the very midst of
Mass were recorded and stated long before Laura's death. Number
III of the *Rime* fixes the moment on Good Friday. Number XXX
states: "If I mistake not in my count, seven years ago today I began
to go sighing." LXII records that eleven years have passed, and
that on this day Christ was crucified. Petrarch poetically records
the eleventh year of his subjection, and the fourteenth, and the
sixteenth, and the seventeenth. In CCXI he states specifically: "In
the year 1327, exactly at the hour of prime on the sixth of April,
I entered the labyrinth." He repeats the statement in his *Triumph
of Death*.

The trouble is that the sixth of April, 1327, was not Good Friday but Monday in Holy Week. Petrarch's assimilation of the two
dates is an error, deliberate or unconscious. We can take our
choice; Petrarch fell in love on Monday, April 6, or on Good Friday, April 10. Various reconciliations have been offered; one that
has found wide favor is that the theologians of the time speculated
much on the actual date of Christ's death, and concluded, on the
basis of Biblical texts and astronomical calculations, that the Cru-

cifixion took place on April 6, A. D. 30; hence Petrarch was smitten on Monday, but called it Good Friday.

This does not seem to me very satisfactory. I would rather say that the assimilation of Good Friday to the sixth of April represents the victory of subconscious desire over conscious memory. Secretly, Petrarch compared his own tragedy to that of Christ. He may also have remembered that Dante's Divine Comedy begins on Good Friday. The day was charged with inspiration; on Good Friday 1338 he conceived the idea of his epic poem, *Africa*. His first dated recall of his enamorment was in 1334, seven years after the fact. In seven years his memory had had plenty of time to adapt itself to the demands of poetic pertinence.

But what of the amazing coincidence that his Laura died twenty-one years to the hour from the moment he first saw her in the church of St. Clare? Can we believe this? The answer depends on one's capacity for belief. It could have happened, of course. Laura de Sade was sick, probably of the plague, on April 3, 1348, and the plague works quickly. If one objects to coincidence on the ground of mathematical probability, one may suppose that Petrarch's close friend Ludovicus, whom he called Socrates, writing to inform him of Laura's death, and well aware of the fatal date of the enamorment at prime on April 6, put her death at the same hour, perhaps as a mere supposition, and that Petrarch transformed the supposition into a fact. Many other miracles have had such an origin.

Other questions arise about the identification of Petrarch's Laura with Laura de Sade. How did the poet and his beloved communicate? Probably in Provençal. The old Avignon gentry were sufficient to themselves, and we have no indication that Laura knew any language but her own. However, the Italians swarming about the Papal Court made Italian current on the streets of Avignon, and Laura may have picked up some knowledge of it, enough to read and applaud, if not quite appreciate, the poems addressed to her. She must have found some of Petrarch's elaborate conceits difficult. Perhaps her indifference to Petrarch's poetic pleas was due in part to her failure to understand them.

Another recurring question is: how well known was Petrarch's adoration of Laura? If his love, proclaimed in hundreds of poems, was common knowledge, why is there any question about her identity? The answer is that his love of Laura de Sade was indeed well known in Avignon, and that the memory of it was still preserved two hundred years later. But local gossip did not last in the era of oral communication as it does in the era of syndicated tittle-tattle, and the actual Laura faded, and her image was replaced by the ideal figure of Petrarch's poems.

Many writers maintain that the poet sedulously kept the secret of his love from all but the beloved. No one who has lived in a small city can believe this. If a beautiful young married woman of the aristocracy is constantly attended by a sighing poet, himself a striking figure, with a lute, people are going to talk. Petrarch did not really try very hard to keep the secret. He had the great Simone Martini paint her portrait for him. His friend Sennuccio del Bene knew her well, and so did Ludovicus, who sent news of her death. His love-poems were widely diffused; he sent them to friends on request, and there is an old story that, reciting his love-poems, he held spellbound his dinner companions. They must have inquired, and learned, the name of the original. He and Laura visited an elderly friend in his garden, who gave them each a rose, exclaiming: "The sun never saw such a pair of lovers!" Someone told Laura that Petrarch really loved another, to whom his poems were actually addressed, and Laura was only the cover. She was furious.

On the other hand, his close, dear friend, Giacomo di Colonna, wrote him in 1336, long after the enamorment, a *iocosa epistola,* applauding him for presenting himself to the world as brilliant, wise, and sober. And your famous devotion to Laura? "I don't believe there is any Laura. You made her up." Petrarch was stung, though recognizing the writer's facetious purpose:

> You say that I have invented the beautiful name of Laura to have something to talk about and to get everyone talking about me, and that there's no Laura in my life except the poetic Laurel, to which obviously I aspire through long and persistent toil. And you say of the living and breathing "laurel," whose beauty, I claimed, had enthralled me, that the whole business is made up, the sighs pretended, the poems fictitious. Well, I wish that your joke were true, that it were all pretense and not passion! But believe me, no one can keep up a pretense for long without great effort; to labor without advantage to appear

mad is the height of madness. Further, though in health we can simu-
late illness in our actions, we can't counterfeit actual pallor. And you
know well both my pallor and my pains, so that I am afraid you are
making fun of my disease, with the Socratic humor that is called irony.

This passage has been frequently adduced by critics who maintain that Laura was a mere poetic allegory, or that Petrarch con-
cealed her identity from even his best friend. But Petrarch makes
more than clear that Bishop Giacomo was ironic. The essence of
irony is that one assumes to be true what writer and reader know
to be not true, or vice versa.

(Anyway, it is dangerous to present particular phrasings of these
early letters as conclusive evidence. Petrarch did not set about collecting his *epistolarium* until 1350; we never know if the early
letters are taken from filed copies or from first drafts, or if they
are total reconstructions.)

And what of the husband, Hugues de Sade? He cannot have
taken the poet very seriously, as a menace to his happiness, or he
would have prevented any meeting between his wife and her
adorer. After all, the tonsured clerk, the penniless son of a notary,
with no standing in the world, could not have been a serious rival.
His meetings with Laura were casual encounters, usually in company. Hugues de Sade knew well the Provençal tradition of the
infatuate poetic suppliant. If the poet wanted to sigh at dawn beneath his wife's window, there was no great harm done. Nevertheless, at times he thought the wooer went a bit too far; he confined
Laura to the house. One day Petrarch met a group of young ladies,
who were all well informed of his passion (*Rime* CCXXII):

> "My strolling ladies, gossiping busily,
> pensive, yet gay; for lack of her, alone;
> your sweet companion, whether is she flown?
> Where is my life? Where is the death of me?"
> "We're gay, because she's quick in memory,
> pensive, because her absence we bemoan.
> A jealous heart has marked her for his own,
> forbidding to the world felicity."
>
> "Who can hold lovers in such harsh oppression?"
> "Why, the soul's free; but body still must hearken,
> as women know, to wrath that domineers.
> But often the face transcribes the heart's confession,

and we have seen her stately beauty darken,
and her eyes liquid with a dew of tears."

Is it, really, of any importance whether Laura was a real person, any particular real person whom we may still faintly revivify, or merely a creation of Petrarch's poetic imagination? Many say that the poetic creation is all that matters, and that the effort to find a long-dead human being behind it is a meaningless waste of time. Nevertheless, readers always want to know how much is true in any fiction, as writers are usually reluctant to tell; and I think the readers are right. Most of us are concerned about life as well as art. We want to know what the life was that the poet has transformed, though into something better than life. However we may admire an abstraction, we want it to be an abstraction of something, hence of reality. Our first question at sight of an abstract painting is: "But what is it *of?*" If we admire a poem, we are usually not content to read it merely as a poem. Our curiosity urges us to discover the poet, and the reality of his emotion, and the material of his inspiration.

Thus we have a right to seek the real Laura who is responsible for the existence of one of the world's great collections of poems. We should be pleased, I think, to find her in the exemplary Avignon housewife, chaste and gay, doing her marital and maternal duty, and on the whole rather bored with the poet who was to make her name a familiar symbol for at least two-thirds of a millennium.

VI: LOVE—APPASSIONATO

And I am one of those who joy in weeping.
                                                        —Rime *XXXVII*

ETRARCH'S *RIME,* OR *CANZONIERE,* AS WE NOW
call his collection of poems in Italian, is an autobiograph-
ical novel in verse, telling the story of a man's love-life. It
begins with passionate profane love, seeking its fleshly end. This
love, mingling hope and despair, is frustrated by the lady's chastity
and is gradually purified by her virtue. The profane love is transformed to the love of the ideal, to the love of God. The climax is
the death of Laura. Then memory turns backward, to retrace the
story with a new understanding, a new resignation to God's will.
The experience closes with a great hymn of thankfulness to the
Virgin.

Petrarch worked on his book intermittently almost to the day
of his death, revising phrases, patching and transposing, altering
the poems' order. He divided the book into two parts, corresponding to the life and death of Laura. (But the division is not fast;
two and a half years after the calamity he wrote a poem complaining of Laura's rigor, and put it among those celebrating Laura living.) He never quite finished his task. Late in life he inserted at
the end of each part a group of poems previously excluded, which
are out of place chronologically and rather miscellaneous in content. Many others recall and express a state of mind anterior to
the moment of composition. And it is almost certain that a few
were addressed to other women than Laura, and that the poet, unwilling to discard them, fitted them awkwardly into his scheme.
He included in his book poems that are moral, political, or mere
letters to friends, entirely unrelated to his love. These digressions

serve, at least, to give a factual background to the novel's theme,
and make it a book of life as well as a book of love.

The book in its final form consists of 366 poems, the leap-year
number. Is this a mere coincidence? Most commentators think so,
but it seems to me that Petrarch, with his sense of the mystic sig-
nificances of numbers, knew what he was about in addressing 365
poems to human beings and a final one to the Virgin.

The arrangement is based upon three principles, determined
(by Ernest H. Wilkins) to be a generally but not strictly chronological order; variety in content; and variety in form. The canzoni
are so placed as to break up long sequences of sonnets; the political
poems interrupt long sequences of love poems. "This mingling of
forms is a major innovation on the part of Petrarch."

His book begins with an address to his readers, a preface, obviously written late in his life:

> You who give ear to sorrow, as you scan
> these rhymes, and hearken to the sighs that fed
> my heart, since first in youth it was misled—
> was it myself? Was it another man?—
> oh, recollect that passion has no plan.
> So, for the various styles here gatherèd,
> give me no pardon; pity give instead.
> Vain hope, vain grief, speak only as they can.
>
> Now well I know that long to the world my name
> was mockery, a public fable merely,
> and suddenly shame is in my heart supreme.
> And all the fruit of all my love is shame;
> shame, and repentance, and the knowing clearly
> that all our joy is only a brief dream.

Are we to believe this introductory disavowal of the whole
work? Are we to accept that shame was supreme in his heart? Certainly not. This is false modesty; indeed, perhaps all modesty is
false modesty. Petrarch had created in his middle years a new public image of himself, that of the learned, pious sage, and it pleased
him to refer to his famous poems as mere trifles, *nugellae*, in the
vulgar tongue. But his diffusion of the book, its "publication" as
manuscripts could then be published, his continuing revision of it,
are reason enough to reject his disclaimers. He always loved his
own young poetry, as he did his young self.

In the second sonnet, the proper beginning, he tells how Amor picked up his bow again and struck him a mortal blow. Much has been made of the "again" (*riprese*) to prove that Petrarch had been in love before. Probably he had; but the syllable *ri* is useful in filling out the line. In the third sonnet he gives us the time of the disaster—Good Friday. "My woes began at the moment of the world's pain." In the fourth the beloved is introduced; she was born in a *picciol borgo,* a small town. In the fifth we are told her name, by the author's device of setting significant syllables close together: LAUdando . . . REal . . . TAci . . . LAUdare . . . REve-rire. (Though the heroine is commonly named Laura, she was probably called, in life, Laureta, or Laurette.) In the sixth he tells us of his ardor and of Laura's virtuous rejection of it.

Thus we have had the exposition of the novel: the setting, the place, the time, the characters, the statement of the theme; and also the tone and form—realism elevated to poetry by the strict music of the sonnet.

He proceeds with the endless story of baffled love. But as the sonnet form is beginning to thump in the sensitive ear, he breaks the succession with a ballata (XI) . Laura has taken offense at his impetuosity:

> Madonna, never does your veil discover
> your face, in any fashion,
> since you surprised my too-unwary passion
> unriddling the dear secret of a lover.
>
> Once I was strong and kept my hunger hidden
> in a mind dead to all except desire,
> and your kind eyes brought ease to my despair.
> But Love betrayed me; and I watched retire
> your tender smile. I saw your beauty chidden
> and a veil bound about your yellow hair.
> What I most loved, I see not anywhere;
> the prudent veil is drawn
> in every weather; and my life is gone
> because the light of your eyes is clouded over.

In XV he is going on a journey, perhaps to Lombez in 1330. He keeps turning back, heavy-footed, grieving, and wonders how his body can live so far from its soul. Love answers that it is the priv-ilege of lovers to be freed from all their human qualities. In fact

he had a delightful summer vacation in Lombez, with three dear
and jolly friends. In XVII and XVIII he is so moved at the thought
of parting from Laura that he prefers not to see her. In XIX it is
the opposite; he seeks the pain of parting.

XXII is a sestina, a Provençal form consisting of six six-line
stanzas and an envoy of three lines. It is built on only six rhyme-
words, which must be repeated in varying order in each stanza,
and the first line of each stanza must end with the same word as
the last line of the preceding stanza. The six rhyme-words recur at
the mid-point and at the end of the lines of the three-line envoy.
The aesthetic pleasure of the reader is derived from the variation
within a strict pattern, from the insistent repetition of the rhyme-
words, which must be so set that they seem inevitable, with no
straining of the thought. Here are two stanzas (not consecutive)
and the envoy from this sestina:

> When the night drives away the shining day,
> when evening makes the antipodean dawn,
> musing, I gaze upon the cruel stars
> which have created me from sentient earth;
> and then I curse the day I saw the sun,
> for I am changed to a wild man of the wood. . . .
>
> Would I were with her from the last of the sun,
> when there's no light except the indifferent stars,
> through a long night! O never come the dawn!
> O never let her root in the green wood,
> eluding my arms, as happened on the day
> Apollo hunted Daphne down to earth!
>
> But I'll be under earth in the dry wood
> or ever the tiny stars have followed day,
> or ever comes the sun to such sweet dawn!

XXIII is the first of the canzoni. A canzone is an originally Provençal form, adopted and developed by Petrarch's Italian predecessors. It is a long poem; XXIII consists of eight twenty-line stanzas and a nine-line envoy. The metrical scheme is elaborate, with
an intricate pattern of long and short lines and of rhymes. Italian
critics generally prize the canzone as the supreme Italian verse-
form, and Petrarch's canzoni as supreme above all canzoni.

This canzone XXIII is a summary of his love story.

In my first youth I was free, scorned by Amor. Now I have become
a byword for hopeless love. Many years passed since Love's first assault;
I had grown a crust on my heart. Love summoned the aid of Laura,
and turned me from a living man into a green laurel-tree, anchored in
earth. Or, to alter the figure, she opened my breast, took out my heart
with her hand, and bade me be silent. Then she turned me into stone,
again into a fountain. I wept my boldness for years. I resumed my
form, and one day I saw her bathing naked in a pool; and I was
changed, like Actaeon, to a stag. But I must love her still, for she has
banished all other pleasure from my heart.

Critics have labored long upon these allegories. And as critics
are as prurient as anyone else, they have been fascinated by the
passage about Laura naked in the pool. It runs:

> Once in the greenwood hunting, all alone,
> I came upon my wild one, fierce and fair,
> in a pool bathing, bare,
> while the hot sun incontinently shone.
> And since no other sight could so delight me,
> I greedily stared, and she was anger-shamed;
> and in my eyes—a vengeful reprimand—
> she spattered water with the heel of her hand.

The critics recall that medieval ladies certainly bathed, and that
we find no record of medieval bathing-suits. Boccaccio has a number of bathing scenes. In the *Decameron* a group of ladies immerse
themselves, naked, with a servant guarding access to the pool.
However, in Petrarch's context of classical mythological meta-
morphoses, the episode proves nothing about Laura de Sade's
debonair personal habits.

Petrarch now falls into a long-lasting state of baffled love,
pleading, reproaching, sighing, and writing poems. Intense emotion, heightened sensibility, systematic thwarting, make the natural soil of poetry.

Laura fell ill, and the poet was torn with apprehension and
thoughts of death, as in XXXIII:

> It was the hour when Venus sent her ray
> from orient skies; and still to northward burned
> the gentle star that heavenly Juno spurned.
> It was the hour when, in the chilly gray,
> the barefoot hags arose, their fires to lay,

and drowsy spinning-wheels reluctant turned.
It was the hour when dreaming lovers learned
that fancied joy dies with the truthful day.

And in that hour my hope was but a wraith,
or but a stub of candle, guttering green;
when lo! in vision did I see her rise—
although how changed from that which she had been!—
I heard her say: "How little is your faith!
You'll look again upon these living eyes!"

He sought solitude, but not so much for escape as for the pleasure of meditation on his misery (**XXXV**) :

Pensive I stray, in desert pathways turning
my heavy solitary steps and slow,
yet quick to flee, if the sand's records show
man vagrant near to eager eyes' discerning.
There is no veil so thick to hide my yearning,
no eye so dull it would not straightway know
that I am he whose joy is spent to woe,
so does my outward write my inward burning.

Therefore I think each wood and ragged spot
and field and river knows how I am tried.
All the wild knows what only one knows not.
I cannot find such barren ways and grim
that Love comes not forever at my side,
talking with me, and I do talk with him.

In this poem one will have noticed the animation of wild nature by the poet's spirit, an identification of his emotion with the earth's life. This is not new, of course; the Greeks had done it first. But Petrarch established, for all his successors, the doctrine of nature's emotional sympathy with the lover. The doctrine was to become the "pathetic fallacy" of the Romantics, and it has by no means disappeared today.

His thoughts ran much on death, on suicide (**XXXVI**) :

If I believed that death could make an end
to love's long torture that has laid me low,
my hand would long ere this have dealt the blow
to summon up oblivion, my friend.
But since I fear that I would but descend

from tears to tears, from woe to a worse woe,
on the gulf's edge, with half a step to go,
irresolute, above the black I bend.

Oh, it were time the pitiless bow were drawn,
the cord pulled taut, aim taken carefully,
time that the shaft into my heart were gone!
Thus I pray Love, and that deaf deity,
Death, whose pale colors I have now put on.
Why is she silent? She has forgotten me.

XXXVII is a canzone, probably written in Italy. Petrarch is far
away; only the hope of seeing Laura again keeps him alive. He
states a frequently-recurring thought: "How strange a quality of
the human mind, that one often loves whatever novelty may start
a storm of sighs! And I am one of those who joy in weeping. It
even seems that I seek out means to fill my eyes with tears and my
heart with pain." This phenomenon might have occurred to a
reader before it did to the author.

XL is out of place in the amorous litany. The poet writes to a
friend in Rome, asking the loan of a volume of St. Augustine. "If
love or death don't interfere with the new tapestry I am weaving,
and if I can free myself from the clinging bird-lime while I am
putting some great truths together, perhaps I shall write a work
midway between the ancient and the modern styles, so that, I dare
say, you will hear of it even in Rome." To what work he refers is
not clear; it is at least clear that his thoughts were running on a
literary project to be new and sensational in form. It is clear also
that since he could refer to his love as "clinging bird-lime" he
used a different vocabulary with his men friends and with Laura.
There is no question of insincerity; in addressing Laura he used
one set of emotional impulses and utterances and with his men
friends another. The hero of the *Canzoniere* is one Petrarch; there
were others.

He breaks the series of sonnets and canzoni with a madrigal, a
sweet country idyll (LII) :

Diana, naked in the chilly pool,
brought no more rapture to the greedy eyes
of him who watched her splashing in the cool
than did my glimpse of a maiden unaware,

washing a veil, the gossamer garment of
her lovely and unruly golden hair.
Wherefore, although the sky burn hot above,
I shake and shiver in a storm of love.

The lover struggled against his affliction. For a moment he
thought he had gained a cure, but he relapsed. Laura promised
him a rendezvous, and stood him up. The poet voiced his dolorous
reproach (LVI) :

It is the hour—unless my agony
have shook my wits, my reckoning belying—
it is the hour in pity promised me;
but as I speak, the promised hour is flying.
What shadow chilled the seedling, ripe to free
its essence into sunny fructifying?
'Twixt hand and grain what wall rose suddenly?
Within the cotes what hungry beast came prying?

I do not know; but this I realize:
that by Love's trickery I have been led.
Love! How he dangled joy before my eyes,
masking the pain he destined for my prize!
What were those wise old words that once I read?
"Call no man happy till the day he dies!"

The endless courtship follows its doomed course. Laura was
kind for a moment (LXI) ; the poet blesses the day, love, and his
subjection, in a burst of joy. He reveals in passing that he has
made her famous: "Blessed be all the writings in which I have
brought her fame." She bows to him in the street, and he is ravished with delight (LXIII) . LXVII seems to be a kind of joke. He
sees a laurel, tries to reach it, falls in a hidden stream. "At least,
instead of having my eyes, as usual, raining tears, I got my feet wet
for a change." But it is really a joke, or a solemn super-conceit?
Love reveals to him, on his way to Rome in 1337, that one cannot resist or hide from one's fate—to love (LXIX). He sets down
three long canzoni on Laura's eyes (LXXI to LXXIII) . He admits
therein that Laura has transformed his life, made it holy and
happy, instead of noxious and burdensome, but that reason has
ceased to control his actions. He admits further that writing his
poems pricks and inflames him (a typical confession of a real liter-

ary man) . He begins to hope for freedom, but fears that the only
freedom for him is death (LXXVI) :

> Love with his promises cajoling me,
> to his old prison led me; clapped the door
> upon me; and the keys he handed o'er
> to my relentless foe, his votary.
> Alas, bemused and blind, I could not see
> until too late their guileful secret war.
> And it is only now I come once more,
> struggling and halting, to my liberty.
>
> And though there be an end of durance now,
> under familiar chains I still must bend.
> I've writ my heart upon my eyes and brow,
> and you will read it, you will comprehend.
> And seeing my prison pallor, you will vow:
> "You've but a little walk to death, my friend."

For all his protests of purification and spiritualization, he reveals the sensual basis of his love in LXXVIII: "How lucky were
you, Pygmalion, to possess a thousand times what I ask for only
once!"

Such is the story he records in, roughly, the first eighty poems
of the *Canzoniere*. The first stage of his love, that of passionate desire, came to an end at the latest in 1336, although many poems
written later recall and express the earlier mood. In that year he
sought and found many distractions, including mountain-climb-
ing and travel. In his letter on the ascent of Mont Ventoux, in
April 1336, nine years after his meeting with Laura, he calls his
love evil and perverse, and treats it as a calamity. By the end of the
year he set off for Rome, returning to Avignon only in August
1337. Immediately after his arrival he bought a small country
house in Vaucluse, and lived there out of Laura's reach. In 1337
he became the father of an illegitimate child.

The love of men for women springs from concupiscence, although, like the strutting courtship of birds, it may assume many
forms imposed by biological inheritance and social tradition.

Petrarch, immersed in the classics, was much influenced by the
ancient concept of love. The Romans distinguished between *amor*
and *libido,* but their *amor* was markedly libidinous. The gods,

headed by Jupiter, spent most of their time pursuing and fecun-
dating the goddesses and the daughters of men. Yet the ancients
were aware of love spiritualized by longing, of the mortal pains of
unrequited love. They could applaud lifelong fidelity, as that of
Philemon and Baucis; they could tell idylls of constancy, as that
of Daphnis and Chloe.

The monks of the Middle Ages, poor tortured celibates, developed their own theory. Women, headed by Eve, were put on earth
to tempt good men to their damnation. They were little better
than demons, and carnal love was itself demonic. The one defense
of the sexual business, says Pascal, is that it is the only known
method of producing saints. A woman's body, in the clerical view,
was a thing of horror, a *saccum stercoris*. Petrarch was inevitably
troubled by these teachings. His St. Augustine, in the *Secretum*,
urges him to escape Laura's thrall by meditating on the filthiness
of the feminine body.

In revulsion against these inhuman valuations appeared, in the
twelfth century, the concept of Courtly Love. According to this
doctrine, human passion is an ennobling force, and the beloved
woman is the incarnation of unattainable beauty. Medieval idealism, represented by the Church's thought, art, and architecture,
by feudalism and chivalry, by devotion to the Virgin Mary, found
a corresponding expression in social life and literature. A modern
critic, Mario Casella, says that the ideal conception of love derives
from Platonic-Augustinian thought, and that it is fundamental
in the doctrinal systemization of Thomism; it is an aspect of the
theory of knowledge. Love is a force, developing and perfecting
the individual in his yearning for beauty:

> . . . it became the dominating motive of a life stylized according to
> forms of courtesy. . . . The feeling of life as beautiful culminated in
> eternal spiritual youth. The lord of Courtesy was love, but a love
> which is inward superbundance, elective spontaneity, the constant
> vocation and clothing of the soul. Above all it is gentility or nobility
> of feeling—scorn for all forms of violence, respect for human indi-
> viduality, secure control and composure of the passions, aspiration
> toward an ideal of life in which, by the light of knowledge, the virtues
> of action may be completed and harmonized.

The theory, says Casella, remains constant from the time of its
first formulation to that of Petrarch. "Love is the desire of beauty,

our essential delight; it is the contemplation of the intelligence through the senses, and its intuition through the movements of the heart. Ideal beauty arises beyond sensible pleasure; its recognition is the culminating moment of an intellective process through which the subject, within that beauty, recognizes itself in the intentions of its own profundities."

The troubadours were the chief celebrants of Courtly Love. Petrarch inherited from them not only the general idea, but many developments of thought and language. Such are his conceits on battles, imprisonments, chains, on the escape of his heart from his breast, on the potency of his lady's eyes, on purification by fire, on the melting ice of emotion, on passion which files, gnaws, makes sick, and cures.

It is interesting to compare the precepts in the manual of Courtly Love written by Andreas Capellanus at the end of the twelfth century with Petrarch's behavior. Andreas demands that the lover conceal his passion from the world. If he meets his beloved in public, he must not try to communicate with her by signs, but should treat her almost like a stranger. Beware of communication, anyway; too much conversation decreases love. "Everybody knows that love can have no place between husband and wife." Among the rules of love are these: every lover regularly turns pale in the presence of the adored one; when a lover suddenly catches sight of his beloved his heart palpitates; and he whom love torments eats and sleeps very little.

Courtly Love journeyed to Italy, and was developed by the stilnovisti and Dante. The inamorata became a divinity descended to earth; to her the poets addressed their prayers, as to any saint. She became a religious and a metaphysical symbol.

Petrarch accepted, then, the tradition of Courtly Love, but with a difference. He abandoned the philosophic content of the stilnovisti. His Laura has commonly no allegorical meaning. Dante's Beatrice represented divine revelation; Laura represents only herself. She is a real woman, whose faults of character are clearly stated. Most of the poems are essentially realistic. They take their rise from actual incidents, which provoke the poet's emotions and reflections. They present the idealization of the real, or the realization of the ideal.

Petrarch loves Laura humanly before he loves her angelically.

His love takes its rise from sensual desire: *il caldo desio . . . m'infi-amma*. And Laura's steady resistance to his desire produced po-etry, as the resistance in an electric filament produces light.

And Laura? Some modern writers and readers are still indig-nant at her obduracy. (Macaulay called her "a heartless co-quette.") Why did not that unimportant little Avignon house-wife bring some solace to the great poet?

Well, in the first place, she couldn't. Adultery with security in a small city is always difficult, if not impossible. Petrarch was liv-ing in the palace of the Cardinal Colonna, no place for an assigna-tion. A rendezvous in the ill-famed quarters of some go-between was hardly thinkable, the dangers of recognition forbidding. If lovers sought the Avignon countryside, they would have had to walk or ride horseback for miles to some secluded grove, and then miles back, and the chances of being observed would have been high. At most of Petrarch's meetings with Laura other women were evidently present. His rare happy private interviews were probably arranged by the discreet withdrawal of Laura's waiting-women. But how could she count on their discretion? Her hus-band, we remember, was jealous, and the noble code required that an unfaithful wife be immediately poniarded.

One may rejoin that Boccaccio's *Decameron* gives evidence that adultery was nevertheless extremely common. In rebuttal, I note that Boccaccio's tales are largely fantasies, and that his incessant theme is the procuring of ingenious devices by which lovers may meet. His gallants are forever waiting for the merchant husband to leave town, and they are adept at wall-climbing. Boccaccio makes clear that wives and their maids were closely watched, and

In the second place, Laura didn't want to. She was a respectable that the penalty for discovery was dire.

matron, pregnant or nursing most of the time. She took her fam-ily obligations, her marriage vows, and her maternal duties seri-ously. She was pleased to have the adulation of the poet, within the limits permitted by society. But when he suggested *that,* she recoiled. More of *that?* She had far too much of it already. To leave her husband for a penniless cleric? Impossible! To enter on the perilous path of adultery? What on earth for? The only reason the poet could suggest was pity for his sufferings. But pity was hardly a sufficient motive for getting into so much trouble. His groans and sighs for pity evoked only Laura's anger or her Mona Lisa smile.

Any competent rake could have pointed out to Petrarch his error. To compass a woman's downfall one must capture her heart. One must undo her, paralyze her resistance by her admiration for the lover's strength, courage, beauty, power. Pity is no good. Ask for pity, and that is all you'll get. One must actually—even though temporarily—love her. One must be fascinated by all of her, by her beauty, her character, her adornments, her friends, her small accomplishments, her silly mannerisms, her dull anecdotes. One must forever breathe, with conviction, You, You, You, not Me, Me, Me.

But Petrarch was fascinated only by himself. Most of his love-poems are not so much celebrations of his beloved's merits as they are analyses of his own feelings in certain situations, usually the sequel of a rebuff. Even his three canzoni on his lady's eyes barely mention her eyes; they deal almost entirely with his own sufferings. We prize them as masterpieces of self-analysis; but self-analysis is not a means of amorous conquest. For his purposes, he was analyzing the wrong self.

Laura, then, didn't want to, and she couldn't. And I suspect that Petrarch didn't really much want to either. He had no more desire to ruin his career by a public scandal than did Laura. He enjoyed the study of his woe, as he confesses. He certainly enjoyed the thought that he was creating a new series of love-poems, to match and outdo those of his predecessors, including Dante, and he enjoyed his reputation as one of the foremost younger poets of his time. Long hopeless fidelity was the mark of the character he presented to the public. Long hopeless fidelity is the poet's best line. One may amuse oneself by imagining that one day Laura might have decided to "yield." How Petrarch would have fled! She would have ruined his whole book.

VII: SEEING THE WORLD

> *Such was my youthful ardor and eagerness*
> *to see new things that I would have gone to*
> *far China, to the Indies, to the ultimate land*
> *of Taprobane.*
>
> —Sen. IX 2

THUS PETRARCH, IN HIS MID-TWENTIES, LIVED
in Avignon, giving his time to love, to poetry, and to the
study of the great ancient classics. He was welcome in the
old noble houses of the city, though not as an eligible young man.
He frequented also, with an eye to advantage, the palaces of the
Papal Court. Of these his favorite resort was the home of Cardinal
Giovanni Colonna. Petrarch's long intimacy with the Colonna, one
of the great families of the Western world, began.

The Colonna appeared in Rome in the ninth century, took root
firmly just to the north of Trajan's Forum, and there, in their
enormous Palazzo Colonna, they still are. By the end of the thirteenth century they dominated the city from the Porta del Popolo
to the Quirinal, with their various strongholds, including the converted mausoleum of Augustus. Outside the walls they had their
suburban castles, at Palestrina and elsewhere.

In the wane of the thirteenth century the master of the mightiest branch of the Colonna was Stefano. His power terrified Pope
Boniface VIII, who favored the Colonna's old enemies, the Orsini,
and their new enemies, the Caetani, of whom the leader was the
Pope's nephew. In 1297 Stefano Colonna declared the Pope an
illegitimate ruler, and robbed a papal convoy on the Appian Way
of 200,000 gold florins. Boniface proclaimed a crusade against the
Colonna, razed their Palestrina castle, and forced them into exile.
But in the famous Anagni outrage of 1304 Sciarra Colonna, Stefano's brother, had the satisfaction of sacking the Pope's palace
and smiting the elderly Pope with his steel gauntlet. Boniface died

of shock and shame, the quarrel was compounded, and Stefano was admitted again to Rome, under proper guarantees, while the following Popes abandoned the Holy City in favor of unholy but peaceful France.

Stefano Colonna married Gaucerande de l'Isle-Jourdain, whose great properties lay just southwest of Toulouse. The marriage was celebrated by proxy, but not by proxy Gaucerande gave Stefano seven stalwart sons and six daughters. Of these the two that most concern us are Giovanni and Giacomo.

Giovanni entered the Church, and rose speedily to become a cardinal in December 1327. He then established himself in Avignon, with suitable magnificence, in fifteen adjoining houses on the site of the present Palais Municipal. The old owners were summarily ousted by the papal billeters. Cardinal Giovanni had all the Colonna ability, with the gracious charm of his French mother. His house was a rendezvous of eminent visitors, and Petrarch, the interesting young poet-scholar, soon had his entrée there. In 1328 or 1329 a clerical Colonna, Landolfo, canon of Chartres, stopped in Avignon, and lent Petrarch his copy of the precious Chartres Livy. Petrarch copied and collated it, finding many valuable variants. His book passed in the fifteenth century into the hands of the famous Lorenzo Valla. Only recently Giorgio Billanovich recognized it in the British Museum, with Petrarch's and Valla's notes.

Giacomo Colonna was Stefano's youngest son. He studied law in Bologna in Petrarch's time, but did not make the young poet's acquaintance. Giacomo returned to Rome with his degree, took the tonsure, and, though no priest, was immediately appointed chaplain to the Pope, with fat benefices besides.

He was more Colonna than clerk. In the early months of 1328 the Emperor, Louis of Bavaria, came to Rome and had himself crowned by representatives of the Roman people, in despite of Pope John XXII. He then announced the Pope to be a usurper, a heretic, and Antichrist. The Pope replied with a bull of anathema and excommunication, declaring the Emperor's coronation void. But a bull does not become effective until it is published, and for a time no prudent Roman would undertake the publication. Then Giacomo, with four masked companions, took his stand before the door of San Marcello (on the present Corso). He read to a

thousand gaping Romans the bull of excommunication, and tacked
it to the church door. The five mounted their horses, charged
through the mob, and rode unmolested through the city's gate and
on to safety. Giacomo then announced his readiness to defend the
bull with the sword.

Such gallantry deserved and received papal gratitude. Pope
John issued a brief, promoting Giacomo to a bishopric, but requiring that he take the subdiaconate within a year as a step to full
priesthood. Petrarch says that the elevation was made without
Giacomo's knowledge or desire, that there was no ambition in his
sweet character.

The bishopric was that of Lombez, a small town about thirty-
five miles southwest of Toulouse. It was the poorest and most in-
significant of episcopates, but it stood only a few miles from Giacomo's mother's estate of l'Isle-Jourdain, and the castles round
about were populated by his relatives.

The young Bishop scrupulously fulfilled the ecclesiastical re-
quirements laid upon him. He came to Avignon probably in the
autumn of 1329, and lodged with his brother while he prepared
for his episcopal duties. A bit of a poet himself, he sought out
Petrarch, who was captured forthwith by the Bishop's character
and quality of mind and spirit. In a moment Giacomo Colonna
became Petrarch's best friend, and so he remained until his untimely death. Petrarch never loved any man as he loved Giacomo.
He said: "With a hint in his calm face he could have drawn me to
go beyond the Indies." It used to be thought, in the world's innocence, that the utter, pure devotion of two high-minded young
men was one of love's most beautiful manifestations, and so, if we
will, we may still regard it.

In the last months of his life Petrarch described Giacomo Colonna as

> that incomparable man, the remembrance of whom is both sweet and
> bitter to me. The world was not worthy of him. Christ wanted him
> for his own, robbed us of him, and took him back to heaven. . . . As
> he used to tell me, he had often seen me in Bologna, when I was just
> out of boyhood, and he had been attracted by me without knowing
> who I was or where I came from, only recognizing from my gown that
> I was a fellow student. . . . [When he came to Avignon he saw me
> again.] Having obtained exact information about me, he had me sum-

moned. Nothing was more sweet and delightful than his presence, and
no man on earth was more serious, eager, wise, virtuous, more modest
in prosperity, more stout and constant in adversity. I don't speak from
others' report, but from the testimony of my own eyes. None could
match him in eloquence: he held men's hearts in his hand. Whether he
was addressing his clergy or the people, he would sway the minds of
his hearers to his purpose. In his letters and in informal speech he was
so frank that you would look into his heart and need no commentary,
so clearly did his words express his thoughts. His affection for his
flock was unexampled, his liberality toward his friends tireless, his pity
for the poor inexhaustible, his affability constant toward all. Horace
would have called him the perfect gentleman *ad unguem*, to his finger-
tips. Such was his majesty of countenance and bearing that, seeing him
in a crowd, you would have singled him out as a prince.

When this man had seen me only twice he so won me with his
brilliant talk that he occupied the chief place in my spirit, which he
has never quitted, nor can he ever do so. He was then about to leave
for his bishopric in Gascony, and unaware, I think, of his spell over
me, he begged what he could have commanded, that I accompany him
on his journey. . . . O hurrying time, O fleeting life! Forty-four years
have passed since that summer; it was the happiest summer of my life.

The young Bishop invited Petrarch to be his guest on the trip
to Lombez, with all expenses paid, naturally. He invited also two
other young men, to make a cheery foursome in the reputedly dismal bishopric.

The first was a Belgian musician, from a small village near
Liége. His name was Lodewyck Heyliger, latinized as Ludovicus
Sanctus, but Petrarch promptly rechristened him Socrates, because
of his knowledge and wisdom. Seeking his fortune in Avignon, he
became the music master of Cardinal Colonna's private chapel.
He was exactly of Petrarch's age. He possessed a singularly
winning character, and unalterable good humor. He was always
ready with his lute to sing songs gay or sober. Certainly he provided settings for Petrarch's poems, and gave the poet the tech-
nical advice of the musician. It was he who informed Petrarch of
Laura's death. When he died, Petrarch called him "the companion and consolation of my life."

The second friend was Lello di Stefano dei Tosetti, a Roman
gentleman in the service of the Colonna family. He is said to have
been one of Giacomo's four masked attendants in the hazardous

publication of the papal bull. Petrarch, with his amiable pedantry, changed his name to Laelius, after the lieutenant and faithful friend of Scipio Africanus.

Petrarch's friendship with Socrates and Laelius never faltered. To them he wrote innumerable letters; with them he had nothing to hide, no pretense to support. Several times he proposed that they should find a common house and live together in scholarly concord. Nevertheless, he did not regard them as he did Giacomo Colonna. With them he was the dominant friend, expecting kindly services. But to Giacomo he was subject. Giacomo was unique in his life.

In April 1330 the four friends, with their train of ecclesiastics and servants, set forth on the 200-mile journey to Lombez. As far as Montpellier the Roman road was familiar to Petrarch. He had sight, beyond, of the old cities of Béziers, Narbonne, and Carcassonne. In Toulouse there was a necessary pause for the new Bishop to do homage to his Archbishop and Metropolitan. One is tempted to suppose that the party attended the poetic contest for the Golden Violet, held annually on the first of May, which was declared a public holiday in honor of poetry.

At Toulouse the party left the highway and turned southwest to Lombez. Petrarch found the small town dirty and ill built, the country arid, the climate harsh, the inhabitants boorish. The region was afflicted by terrible thunderstorms, firing peasants' houses and filling Petrarch with a peculiar fear. The diocese was a new creation; the Bishop was inadequately lodged in a Benedictine abbey. His cathedral was the abbey church. The best that a modern *Atlas pittoresque de la France* can say of it is: "c'est un édifice en briques digne d'attirer un moment l'attention." The sole glory of the monastery, the body of St. Majan, had been stolen by rival monks to make a pilgrimage center. (The money value of relics led to many an abuse. St. Thomas Aquinas, on a journey, fell ill and died at the monastery of Fossanuova. The monks immediately decapitated him and boiled the body for its precious bones. Petrarch himself tells of St. Romualdus of Ravenna, who escaped from France by feigning madness, since the people proposed to kill him in order to make sure of his relics.)

The barren surroundings of Lombez did not damp the spirits of the four friends. Though they must have visited the castles of

Giacomo's maternal relatives, they found most of their happiness in each other and in long discussions of poetry, music, classic wisdom, and religion. (Giacomo proclaimed Jerome the greatest of the Church fathers, while Petrarch upheld Augustine.) There were times for mirth and frolic. Giacomo rallied Petrarch on his prematurely gray hair; and I suspect that all of them rallied him about Laura de Sade. It is incredible that four bosom friends, hearty young men in their twenties, should have failed, whether clerks or no, to speak of love.

What of Laura, anyway? How does the poet's despair, his haggard woe, fit with this happiest of summers? It is simple enough. The poet's agony is perfectly genuine, but it is not continuous. There is time enough in life, even in its crises, for many moods. The poet Lamartine, while summoning death to bind him to his dying Elvire, was at the same time eagerly hunting a post in a *sous-préfecture*. And Petrarch, in his entranced summer with his three boon friends, was taking a vacation from agony.

The summer of 1330 ended. Petrarch, Socrates, and Laelius returned to Avignon; the Bishop may have accompanied them. Personally or by letter, Giacomo recommended to his brother, Cardinal Giovanni Colonna, that Petrarch be taken into the Cardinal's official household.

Thus Petrarch found a patron. On patronage, ecclesiastical, political, and personal, he was to live for the rest of his life. We are supercilious about patronage today, unreasonably so, for patronage is widespread under other names. The son-in-law vice-president of a family business, the college roommate in a high appointive government post, lives on patronage. He may, of course, be supremely competent. And in justice to Petrarch we must remember that no author could live on the product of his work, until the coming of printing and protected copyrights.

Petrarch's status in Cardinal Colonna's establishment is not clear. He was officially called *capellanus continuus commensalis,* or regular table-companion chaplain, but of course he could administer no sacred rites. His Ciceronian Latin style would qualify him as a superior sort of secretary. His training in the civil law would make him useful in business pertaining to abbey lands, ecclesiastical fiefs, disputes with communes and with noble houses. As a presentable poet and scholar, he could be produced to impress distinguished guests. He was for a time tutor to the Cardinal's nephew, Agapito Colonna. Perhaps in this task he gained his life-long dislike of formal teaching.

Clearly he repaid the Cardinal for his support. Clearly also his master's rule was light, permitting the poet time to write, the scholar time to study. "Serving him was better than living inde-pendent," confesses Petrarch, "for without him I could never have enjoyed a really free and tranquil life." In service, obviously, one may be free and tranquil, and in independence a slave.

The Cardinal's regard for him was made evident in an incident that Petrarch recalled with complacency. A quarrel broke out in the high-mettled household, and swords were drawn. The Card-inal intervened and assembled his staff. He bade them all, includ-ing one of his brothers, a churchman, swear on the Gospels to tell the truth. Petrarch held out his hand to swear; the Cardinal re-moved the book, saying: "From you your word is enough."

Though Petrarch's situation would seem to many poets ideal, he was restless and unhappy. His love affair remained in its state of painful arrest. He was worried about his brother Gherardo, who was weak and capricious, always in need of money, and without any gainful position or any prospects in the world. Chiefly Pe-trarch was distressed by his failure to compass his literary ambi-tions. True, his love-poems were widely copied and sung. But we have seen that he assembled materials for a grandiose work in Italian, which came to nothing, and that he planned a mighty work of scholarship, which ever eluded him. He wrote a Latin comedy called *Philologia philostrati,* in imitation of Terence. Pre-sumably he destroyed it later. Contemporaries asserted that it was better than Terence, but this is probably an obituary exaggera-tion. He tried, with more success, a new line—political poetry. He wrote, probably in 1331, a long Latin epistle on the state of Italy and the Empire. He recalls Italy's past glories, and blames her present discord and servitude on foreign barbarians. The old val-orous spirit of Italy must be roused! Romans may again cross in triumph the Rhine, the Seine, the Garonne! Italy, unite, and prove your strength! This in substance is the message that the poet will proclaim throughout his life.

At the same time he was performing valuable services to liter-ary scholarship, both in collecting and in editing great works of the Romans. He asked the many foreign visitors to the Cardinal's palace to hunt Cicero manuscripts for him, and kept on reminding the visitors of their promises. "No one can doubt that the loss of the sweet solace of literary manuscripts is more damnable than commerce with demons," he once wrote. He sent appeals and money (whose money?) to France, Germany, Spain, and Greece. And in his quiet study he worked out a system of critical editing which he taught to others, and thus the "literary codex" assumed its standard form. (In contrast to the close-packed monastic manuscript, the "literary codex" is a big book with ample margins for notes, with the text collated, revised, and corrected.) The supreme example is his Livy, now in the British Museum. It is called the first scholarly edition. Petrarch assembled the best available manuscripts, transcribed part of them himself and had the rest done by copyists, blending the best readings, with emendations, variants, and notes. Traditionally, the copying of sacred texts was regarded as meritorious; "every word of the Lord that is copied deals Satan a wound," said Cassiodorus. Petrarch saw equal merit in the copying of the Latin classics. But he recognized that editing is much more the scholar's duty than copying. (The lesson has not yet been universally learned.) Petrarch's model of procedure was exciting to scholars of his time, and of ours. Billanovich calls Petrarch "a Master, without a chair, in a European Academy of affectionate friends."

In spite of all, he was ill at ease, itching for change. He could never stay long in one place, doing the same thing over. "Incola ceu nusquam, sic sum peregrinus ubique," he says; I am at home nowhere, a stranger and wanderer everywhere.

In the spring of 1333 he had an opportunity to allay his restlessness by making a tour to Paris, the Low Countries, and the Rhine. Why, and how? Cardinal Colonna must have paid the fairly high expenses, and he must have expected some return. Probably Petrarch carried dispatches from the Cardinal, and acted as a minor ambassadorial agent in his political and business affairs. Perhaps he collected feudal and ecclesiastical dues from his patron's far-flung holdings. However, Petrarch tells his St. Augustine, in the *Secretum*, that the real purpose of his journey was to shake off his obsession with Laura. And in the *Epistle to Posterity* he admits: "Although I pretended other purposes to get the ap-

proval of my superiors for the journey, the real reason was my
eager desire to see new things."

Surely the reallest reason was his eager desire to see new things.
Young men have always felt this desire, which no doubt serves
some biological purpose, but before Petrarch's time they never, or
at least very seldom, thought of expressing it in durable words.
Petrarch has been called the first tourist, the first to travel for
pleasure alone, and indeed it is hard to think of a predecessor, for
even Herodotus wandered with a book in mind. Petrarch always
loved change and movement. He says he would have gone to the
Holy Land, were it not for fear of seasickness. He wrote a small
guidebook for visitors to Egypt, though he had never got beyond
Naples. Even in old age he loved to travel on a map, with the aid
of books and imagination. One of his distinctions in the history of
modern thought is his formulation of the eager desire to see new
things as a motive of human behavior.

He discovered, for the coming world, the profitable delights of
travel. He said: "It's a peasant virtue to stay on one's own land and
to know the qualities of one's soil and the habits of cattle, and to
draw profit from one's water, trees, and seeds, and to watch the
changes of weather, and to be learned about rakes and grub-hoes
and plows. But it's the quality of a noble and aspiring mind to see
many lands and the customs of many peoples, and to observe and
remember them."

He was aware, as were few in his century, of natural beauty and
the world's wonder. In his *De remediis utriusque fortunae* (I
quote the fine sixteenth-century translation by Thomas Twyne,
Phisicke against Fortune) he gives good reasons for banishing
melancholy:

> So many shows and kinds of things, which by strange and marvellous
> means do serve to your delight; moreover, so great virtue in roots, so
> many juices of herbs, such pleasant variety of so many sorts of flowers,
> so great concord of smells and colors and tastes, and sounds rising of
> contraries, so many living creatures in the air, upon the land, and in
> the sea, serving only to your use and created only to do man pleasure.
> ... Add hereunto, moreover, the prospect of the hills, the openness of
> the valleys, the shadowy woods, the cold Alps, the warm shores. Add
> also so many wholesome streams of water, so many sulfurous and
> smoking lakes, so many clear and cool fountains, so many seas within

PARIGI

and round about the earth. . . . Add lastly some lakes, as big and broad almost as the sea, and ponds lying in bottoms, and rivers falling down headlong from the tops of hills, with their brinks full of flowers and pleasant herbs, and, as Virgil saith, "the bedchambers of the shores, and meadows green with running streams." What shall I need to speak of the foaming rocks that lie upon the sounding shore, and the moist dens, and the fields yellow with corn, and the budding vineyards, and the commodities of cities, and the quiet of the country, and the liberty of wilderness? And also the most glorious and bright spectacle of all, which is the circumference of the starry firmament, that continually turneth about with incomprehensible swiftness, wherein are fastened the fixed stars!

(One is reminded of St. Francis's *Song of the Creatures.* But whereas the saint saw the world's wonders and delights uniting in a choir of praise, Petrarch lauds them for their beauty alone.)

Thus equipped with eager curiosity, Petrarch set out in the spring of 1333, with some unnamed companions, on the great ancient highway to Paris. The road's surface, if not its firm foundation, had suffered much since Roman times. Landed gentry and abbots kept up the local roads, for their own interest, but few were concerned with the trunk highways. Clerical orders helped somewhat, rebuilding bridges and repairing breaks as a pious work, to be paid in the next life. But the roadsides were overcome with trees and bushes, and great pools lurked in the midway, through which men and animals splashed together.

The traffic was heavy. Much of it was local, but much was national and international commerce. Wool traveled from England to Florence by pack-mule, and returned as fine robes and gowns. A vast quantity of Oriental goods, cotton, silk, spices, was transported by road to the north. The wine business alone was enormous. Northern France, England, and the Low Countries had developed discriminating palates, and demanded the products of their favorite southern vineyards. Sheep and cattle, walking to market, competed with horsemen and footmen. There was probably more commercial traffic even than today, for about seventy pack-animals and a score of muleteers and guards would be required to convey the contents of a ten-ton truck. Think of the business originating in Avignon, the outflow of briefs, encyclicals, admonitions, agents, and new appointees with their trains, vessels, and vestments, and the inflow of information, claims and claimants, protests and protestors, money and treasure!

Little traffic went on wheels, only ox-drawn carts carrying produce to a nearby town. The gentry and the well-to-do rode, caring for their own steeds or hiring fresh horses at relay-stations along the way. King's couriers and other hurried messengers went at a gallop, short-cutting across fields with impunity. A courier brought news of Pope John XXII's election from Lyons to York, over 800 miles with the Channel to cross, in ten days. Most of the wayfarers went afoot, scuffing through horse- and mule-droppings, slipping in mud, bespattered by the mounted gentry.

Everyone was on the roads: monks and nuns, on their proper business; mendicant friars, who had no business but begging; disreputable hedge-priests and gyrovagues; ribald students, visiting various universities for good educational reasons or none; wandering preachers and pardoners; pilgrims returning from St. James of Compostela, with the scallop-shell, the *coquille Saint-Jacques*, on cap and gown and on bread-bag, to keep off thieves; papal postmen, *cursores*; minstrels, gleemen, tumblers, quacks and drugsellers; pedlars, tinkers, seasonal workmen, and peasants out of bond; discharged soldiers, outlaws, beggars, and thieves. By night the gentlemen would seek out a castle near the road, where hospitality was a noble obligation. The middle class stopped in inns, notorious for their crowding, discomfort, and vermin. The poor were received in the guest-houses of monasteries; and the poorest, the outlaws and outcasts, slept under the stars or the rain. It took a gay heart and a stout stomach to be a tourist in those days. But Petrarch says that in youth he always reached his journey's end too soon, whereas in old age he was glad to arrive.

Thus he came to Paris, which he thought overrated, in comparison with Italian cities. He later wrote to a French friend: "Permit me to say, you are over-obsessed with your Paris Petit Pont and its high arches. The murmur of the Seine flowing under tickles your ears too much, and too much French dust has settled on your shoes." He was chiefly impressed by the Rue du Fouarre, Straw Street, so called because young Ph.D.'s, or the equivalent, there upheld their theses, and the street was spread with straw to diminish the rival din.

Leaving Paris probably in May 1333, Petrarch and his party

went north to Ghent in Flanders. He alleged later that he had seen the Rhine at the point where it divides in two, so apparently he visited Arnhem or Nijmegen in southern Holland. The party then turned south. Their course took them near Beeringen, the native village of his friend Socrates; one is tempted to suppose that Socrates was a fellow traveler. Hearing that Liège was rich in old books, Petrarch made his companions halt there while he searched. He found indeed two speeches of Cicero that were new to him (one of them the famous *Pro Archia*) and these he copied, though the only ink he could find was yellow as saffron. From Liège the travelers turned east to Aachen, or Aix-la-Chapelle, where Charlemagne lies buried. In Petrarch's report to Cardinal Colonna he tells a long story about Charlemagne. The Emperor, it appears, was infatuated with a girl, who died. He had her body embalmed and embraced it in mad transports. (Love is a filthy, unjust servitude!) A bishop found a magic ring under the corpse's tongue. He removed it, and the Emperor then loved him. The bishop threw the ring in a marsh, which became Charlemagne's favorite haunt. The Emperor built a church on the marsh and remained there the rest of his life.

On June 22 Petrarch continued his journey eastward to Cologne. He remarked the beautiful cathedral under construction. (He was usually oblivious to architecture. On only one other occasion, I think, did he call a building beautiful; he admired the golden glitter of St. Mark's in Venice.) He was chiefly impressed by a St. John's Eve ceremony beside the Rhine. A great band of lovely women assembled by the bank, turned up their sleeves, and bathed their white arms in the stream. It was believed that the sins and misfortunes of the year would thus be washed away—to infect the shores of England, says Petrarch with a smile.

On June 29, he left his companions, to return to Avignon alone. He was in a hurry, for he had word that Bishop Giacomo Colonna, summoned to Rome, proposed to take him as a traveling companion. Rome was of all places in the world the one that Petrarch most longed to see.

His course took him through the forest of the Ardennes, then more far-spreading than it is today. He entered the dark woods with foreboding. Off the great highways the woodland roads were unmarked and bewildering; one easily went astray. (Hence all the

old stories of lost wanderers finding rescue in a lorn woodcutter's
hut or an enchanted castle.) The Ardennes forest has always been
a bloody land, to our own time. In 1333 some little war was in
progress, as menacing to a traveler as a great war, for the looting
of passers-by was the soldiers' privilege.

At least, on his solitary journey, he could think of Laura, and
he could fit rhymes together. He liked to compose verses on horseback, to the jog of hooves, inditing them later at an inn table. He
wrote (CLXXVI) :

> In the inhospitable woodland reaches
> where men-at-arms all vigilantly ride,
> I go secure, with hardihood for guide.
> Love's sun alone brightens the forest-breaches!
> And I go singing—so little prudence teaches!—
> singing of her, and how she doth abide
> in the very eyes of me! And by her side
> are maids and ladies—why, they're firs and beeches!
>
> I think I hear her, hearing the rustling air,
> the boughs, the leaves, the voice of birds complain,
> and muttering waters through the forest flee.
> I think I've never been so happy where
> the shadowy silent wildwood horrors reign—
> save that my sun looks all too pale on me!

In Lyons he had bad news. The quarrel between the Colonna
and the Orsini in Rome had broken out, with assaults on castles,
with the seizure of Tiber bridges, which each party held as private
property, exacting profitable tolls. Pope John XXII, who favored
the Colonna faction, sent Giacomo Colonna urgently to Rome to
compose the quarrel. The Bishop had already left Avignon, taking
Laelius with him as companion. Petrarch was bitterly disappointed. He had to content himself with writing a sonnet to the
Bishop, urging him to attack the she-bear and her cubs, the Orsini,
in their lair and destroy them. Petrarch descended the Rhine comfortably by boat, and resumed his old position in the Cardinal's
household.

Well, he had had a fine trip. He had somewhat satisfied his
eager desire to see new things. And he had stimulated his passion
for book-hunting. When, on his course, he saw some old monastery in the distance, he would turn aside and inquire if the library

contained some manuscripts of ancient texts. He had the conscious purpose of preserving the treasures of antiquity for posterity.

He was not, of course, the first in the field. At the end of the thirteenth century two early Paduan humanists, Lovato and Mussato, rescued many priceless manuscripts from nearby monasteries. There were others. Shortly after Petrarch's return to Avignon (probably), he met Richard de Bury, England's Keeper of the Privy Seal, author of *Philobiblon,* or *The Love of Books.* Sir Richard was a great collector. He bequeathed five wagon-loads of books to what is now Trinity College, Oxford, with the stipulation that they should be made accessible to poor students. With him Petrarch engaged in a long discussion about the location of the island of Thule.

Petrarch's passion for books was not selfish. He was well aware of the irreparable losses of the world's stock of knowledge due to the neglect and ignorance of its keepers. He was aware also that he lived at a crucial moment of history. He assailed those who allowed ancient books to be lost by intolerable negligence, by the infamy of their own sterility. "Pliny's *History of the Roman Wars* disappeared in our own times. Our descendants will have no knowledge of the past. I am as if on the frontiers of two peoples, looking forward and backward." He spoke with uncanny perception.

VIII: THE ASCENT OF MONT VENTOUX

Now it's my whole desire and all my pleasure
up to the highest mountain-ridge to climb.

—Rime *CXXIX*

POPE JOHN XXII DIED ON DECEMBER 4, 1334, aged ninety. The conclave met immediately. The six Italian cardinals, led by Giovanni Colonna, fought to elect a Pope who would pledge himself to return the papacy to Rome. The French and Gascon cardinals fought as determinedly for one who would remain in Avignon. A deadlock was broken by the choice of Cardinal Fournier, who, though a Gascon, was uncommitted. He was taken by surprise. "My Lords, you have elected an ass!" he exclaimed. He was crowned as Benedict XII on January 8, 1335. Then, on his papal white palfrey, he was conducted by the red-robed cardinals on black steeds to the old Bishop's Palace occupied by Pope John.

Benedict was tall and fat, high-colored, loud-voiced, in contrast to John, short and lean, pinched and pinching. He was a mighty eater and drinker. Perhaps he is best remembered today for two words: *Bibamus papaliter,* let's drink papally. Lowborn, Benedict had entered the Cistercian order, had distinguished himself as a theologian, and had risen, amid general respect, to the cardinalate. He was acclaimed for the monkish virtue of humility, which is perhaps not a prime papal virtue. He said his morning mass in his white Cistercian habit; then putting off his cowl he would kiss it, and say: "Farewell, monk!" And donning his pontificals: "Welcome, Lord Pope!"

One of the new Pope's first acts was to appoint Petrarch to a canonry in the cathedral of Lombez, on the recommendation of Cardinal Colonna. A canon is a cathedral officer, charged with such tasks as the regulation of services and ceremonies. His duties are likely to be light, his revenues ample. A titular canon would commonly entrust his duties to a working priest of the cathedral for a small fee and keep most of the revenues for himself. The system may seem to us abusive, but it was so well established that no one, least of all Petrarch, discerned in it any moral flaw, any more than a modern stockholder questions his right to dividends derived from others' labor.

Here intervenes a troublesome, though not very important, problem. Petrarch thrice refers to a stay by the Britannic Ocean, or the English Channel, where he heard "no murmur of a Latin tongue." This journey is hard to fit into the known chronology of his life. There was time for it in the spring or summer of 1335. He could have gone to Lombez to take possession of his canonry, and then turned north to Brittany, where he would have heard in the streets no murmur of a Latin tongue. But why should he go to Brittany? Perhaps on some business for Cardinal Colonna, who held a benefice in Bayeux, which is close to Brittany.

Petrarch otherwise served the Cardinal's interests and his own convictions by writing a poetic appeal in Latin to the new Pope to return to Rome. The appeal is put in the mouth of Rome herself, who is represented as a distraught matron deserted by her spouse, the Pope. The figure is unfortunately complicated by the matron's simultaneous appeal to a second unfaithful spouse, the Emperor. The poem did not move the papal spouse to embrace his tearful, though bigamous, bride. His agents reported that Rome was in bloody turmoil, with the Colonna and their enemies fighting for control of the Tiber bridges. Rome was no place for a Pope.

In the autumn of this year 1335 Petrarch found himself further involved in public affairs. The rising tyrant of Verona, Mastino della Scala, was expanding his tyranny by seizing various north Italian cities, including Parma. The ousted tyrant of Parma appealed to the Pope, on the ground that he had honestly bought the city. Mastino sent to Avignon as his representatives his uncle, Azzo da Correggio, with two lawyers, Guglielmo da Pastrengo and another. These envoys engaged Petrarch as their spokesman, because of his personal relations, his knowledge of the ins and outs of the Papal Court, and his training in legal procedure. Petrarch insists that he accepted the case only out of friendship for the envoys, and that he conducted it on a high level, without aspersion of persons or imputation of base motives. He must have been at least competent, for the Pope decided in favor of his clients.

Azzo da Correggio and Guglielmo da Pastrengo became Petrarch's lifelong friends. Azzo, handsome of person, physically mighty (he was nicknamed "Bronze-Foot"), was possessed of a keen wit and a remarkable memory. He displayed all the courtly gentility that was later to be the mark of the Renaissance man. He was trained to the Church, until better opportunities opened for him in the tyrant trade, and he had the cultured manners of a prelate. Guglielmo da Pastrengo was lawyer, poet, and scholar, and a gallant with the ladies. He had even some knowledge of Greek. He later wrote an alphabetic dictionary of all authors, sacred and profane, of every age and country. This is said to be the first biographical dictionary. The two represent the types to whom Petrarch naturally clove. Azzo, like Bishop Giacomo Colonna, was the handsome patrician with a tincture of letters, the man of power and action, a confident master of his world. He was the man whose gifts of place and person Petrarch could never match, the man he would have liked to be. Guglielmo was the learned scholar, a little dry perhaps, honoring and admiring Petrarch, willing to put himself forever second, to repay his superior's kindness with devotion. He was one of Petrarch's lesser selves, a flattering reflection.

Meanwhile Petrarch's reputation as a poet was growing and spreading. Young Boccaccio, in Naples, discovered his work, and listened with rapture to the new voice. At Petrarch's death in 1374 Boccaccio wrote: "I was totally his, for forty years or more."

Adulation, however agreeable, did not bring the poet happiness. He was troubled and ill at ease. With his high view of the poet's mission he found his domestic position in the Cardinal's household a little demeaning. His scholarly purposes remained unfulfilled. His love for Laura brought him endless exasperation.

In this pass Augustine's *Confessions* came to him as a consolation and a revelation. His own copy led its peculiar life. It was a present from his one-time confessor, Dionigi da Borgo San Sepolcro, an Augustinian monk and Doctor of Theology. Father Dionigi recognized in his charge's spirit a state similar to that of St. Augustine in youth. He gave Petrarch a pocket copy of the *Confessions*, which the poet had not read. The book was Petrarch's cherished companion for forty years. It journeyed with him to a mountain top, and once, in its owner's pocket, it was near drowning with him in the sea.

Previously he had prized only classic literature, and had regarded works of Christian piety with contempt. He remembers: "With my overwhelming love for profane letters I thought, in my youthful arrogance, sacred literature crude, rough, and inelegant, and I despised it. But the reading of this book produced in me a tremendous change." The fact is, he found himself in Augustine, as have so many other troubled souls. The saint's frank account of his youthful sins and errors, of his struggles for self-understanding and self-mastery, fitted Avignon as well as Carthage. Petrarch felt that he was living again the first part of the *Confessions*. The second part, the complete conversion, the sainthood, lay still in the future's murk.

Petrarch's melancholy state may be explained by the brutal solutions of everyday bourgeois common sense. He was a vigorous, sensual, and very emotional man, now past thirty. He was vowed to clerical rectitude, for which he had no vocation. Nature summoned him to take a mate, to beget children and guard their growth, to perform gladly, for their sakes, the humdrum tasks of shelter-building and food-getting, at the cost of bidding farewell to poetry. But for social and economic reasons he was defying the physiological imperative, as Remy de Gourmont used to call it. His furtive visits to the lights-of-love of Avignon brought him no solace; they merely exchanged lust for disgust. Yet he could not conquer his lusts.

In his fits of depression he would often stare out his window at the heights of Mont Ventoux, snow-topped or shimmering in summer heat, thirty miles away to the northeast. The mountain became an obsessive symbol. As a boy in Carpentras he had dwelt at its foot. The idea of climbing out of the ugly world to its pure summit possessed him.

One evening in the spring of 1336 his purpose was precipitated by classical authority. He happened to read in Livy that King Philip of Macedon climbed Mount Hemus (the present Mount Balkan in Bulgaria) to find out whether one could see from its summit both the Black Sea and the Adriatic. Here was his justification. "What is not blamed in the case of an aged king should be excusable, it seemed to me, for a young man in private life."

The decision was far more original than it would appear today.

There is no clear record that anyone ever climbed a mountain for
pleasure or mere curiosity from the time of King Philip of Macedon to that of Petrarch. True, there is the case of King Peter of
Aragon in the thirteenth century, who is said to have climbed
Mount Canigou in the Pyrenees only to see what was on the summit. There he found a lake with monstrous hovering dragon,
darkening the face of heaven with his breath. I think we may rule
this out. We may rule out also the Alpine hermits, who sought
their high retreats only to escape the world; and even Empedocles,
who climbed Mount Etna in order to throw himself in the crater.
Of course there were hunters, pursuing game to the upper fast-
nesses, and shepherds seeking stray sheep or goats. However,
except for a nameless shepherd who will soon appear, Petrarch
remains the first recorded Alpinist, the first to climb a mountain
because it is there.

> Thinking about a companion [he wrote to his former confessor,
> Dionigi da Borgo San Sepolcro], I found hardly any of my friends
> entirely suitable, remarkable to state; for even among one's intimates
> a perfect concord of purpose and character is very rare. One was too
> phlegmatic, another too eager; one too slow, another too quick; one
> too gloomy, one too gay; one to dull, one more prudent than I should
> like. I was frightened by the muteness of one, the talkativeness of
> another, by the overweight of one, by another's leanness and weakness.
> The cold incuriosity of one, the officiousness of another discouraged
> me. Those are defects which are tolerable enough at home, but they
> are much too serious on a journey. . . . Finally I looked for aid to my
> own family. I turned to my younger brother, Gherardo. He was de-
> lighted by the idea.

Probably by design, for Petrarch had a great sense of anniver-
saries, he planned the ascent for April 26, 1336, exactly ten years
from the day he and Gherardo had left Bologna. The date was
well chosen. The snows were gone, the great heats had not yet
come, and there was a full moon.

On the 24th the brothers, with two stout servants, rode to
Malaucène, a small village at the foot of the mountain. At this
season the surrounding meadows are bright with narcissus. The
party rested for a day and reconnoitered their route.

Mount Ventoux, *Mons Ventosus,* Windy Mountain, rises only
1,912 metres, 6,273 feet, above sea level, and Malaucène is already

MONTE
VENTOSO

at an altitude of 226 metres. The ascent would hardly even be called mountaineering today. However, the upper levels are barren and craggy, with a high ridge falling away in cliffs; and in Petrarch's time it was trackless. A hard day's work lay before the brothers and the forgotten servants.

They left before dawn, and climbed (probably) a steep path to a Benedictine priory, of which the ruins still remain. From then on they had to find their own way.

> Among the mountain's ridges we met an old shepherd, who tried to discourage us from the ascent with much talk, saying that fifty years before, with an ardent youthful purpose like ours, he had climbed to the very summit, and that he had got nothing from it but toil and repentance, and torn clothes and scratches from the rocks and briars. Never, he said, had he heard that anyone else either before or after had ventured to do the same.

The old shepherd had visited the Delectable Mountain and had seen no beauty, no symbol. Bunyan might have called him Mr. Twarn't-Much.

> His shouted discouragements merely increased our eagerness, as young men's minds are naturally hostile to good advice. So the old man, recognizing that his efforts were useless, went with us a little way among the rocks and pointed out to us a steep course, crying many counsels and warnings to our retreating backs. We had left with him our extra clothing and other baggage, and kept only what was necessary for the climb. And so we mounted eagerly upward.

The course was plain enough. The mountain rises eastward in a steep, fairly continuous ridge to the summit. The north side of the ridge is precipitous; the south side is buttressed by a series of ribs, between which lie folds, hollows, or what are called in north England combes or coombs. Down these combes the melting snows course, to make valleys below. Now barren, the slopes were then forested with beeches and firs. But the wind-beaten crests were probably open, a stony mass interspersed with bloodthirsty upland scrub and brush. Today a motor road follows, more or less, the route taken by Francesco and Gherardo.

> But, as often happens, fatigue soon followed our strenuous effort. We sat down on a rock, and then went on more slowly, I especially keeping a more modest pace. My brother chose the shortest and steep-

est way, directly up the ridge. Softer than he, I kept turning along the
slopes, and when he called to me and pointed to the shorter way, I kept
answering that I would find an easier approach on another side, and I
didn't mind a longer course which would not be so steep. But this was
merely an excuse for laziness. While the others kept to the high ridge I
wandered in the combes without finding any gentler upward path, and
I just lengthened my journey and increased my useless labor. After this
vain, perplexing wandering I decided to climb straight up. Exhausted
and anxious, I found my brother seated, refreshed by his long wait for
me. But hardly had we left that ridge than what do I do but forget my
previous digression and again tend to take a downward course! And
again, rounding the combes and looking for an easy way, I landed in
much difficulty. Thus I kept putting off the trouble of climbing; but
man's wit can't alter the nature of things, and there is no way for any-
body to reach the heights by going down.

In short, to my brother's great amusement and to my fury, the same
thing happened to me three or four times within a few hours. Being so
befooled, I sat down in a combe. My thought quickly turned from the
material to the spiritual, and I said to myself, in approximately these
words: "What you have experienced so often today in the ascent of
this mountain certainly happens to you and to many who are striving
for the blessed life. But the spiritual straying is not so easily to be
perceived, for the movements of the body are in the open, while those
of the soul are hidden and invisible. The life that we call blessed is
situated on a high place; and narrow, we are told, is the way that leads
to it; and many hills stand in the way, and we must advance from
virtue to virtue up shining steps. The summit is the ultimate goal, the
terminus of the road on which we journey. . . .

"What," I said to myself, "holds you back? Surely nothing but the
level road that seems at first sight easier, amid base earthly pleasures.
But after much wandering you will either have to climb upward
eventually with your long-borne burden to the heights of the blessed
life, or lie sluggishly in the valley of your sins. And if—I shudder at the
thought!—the darkness and the shadows of death find you there, you
will spend an eternal night in perpetual torture."

These thoughts, remarkably enough, spurred my mind and body to
accomplish what remained to be done. God grant that my soul may
follow the road for which I long day and night, as today I journeyed
with my corporeal feet, conquering all difficulties! . . .

One hill dominates all the others; it is called by the mountaineers
Filiolus, or Little Son; why, I don't know, unless by antiphrasis, for it
seems the father of all the mountains round about. There is a small
level space at the top. There, exhausted, we came to rest.

On the small level space stands today a bleak observatory. The name Filiole is now given to an icy spring and a tiny rivulet near by.

Every climber knows the inward uplift that comes with the conquering of his peak. The mood has certainly its source in the organism. The thinness of the upper air, breathed in gulps after long labor, brings a dizzy exaltation to the brain. One feels a light-headed visionary excitement. One looks, godlike and alone, down on the immense world out of which one has climbed, and up to the nearness of heaven.

> At first, affected by the rare quality of the air and by the wide-spreading view, I stand as if stunned. I look about. Clouds lie far below. The tales of Athos and Olympus seem less incredible, when what I had read of them comes true on this less famous mountain. I look toward Italy, whither most my soul inclines. The noble snow-topped Alps seem close by, far away though they are. I admit that I sighed for the Italian skies, evident more to my thought than to my eyes, and unspeakable longing invaded me to see again my friend [Giacomo Colonna] and my native land, although I reproached myself for this somewhat unmanly weakness. . . .
>
> Then a new thought came to me, rather of time than space. I said to myself: "Today ten years have passed since you finished your youthful studies and left Bologna. Oh immortal God! Oh immutable Wisdom! What changes in your character have these years seen!" I suppress much, for I have not yet reached a safe harbor, from which to look back on the storms of the past. The time will perhaps come when I shall review all my past deeds in their order, prefacing them with the words of your St. Augustine: "I wish to recall the filth of my past and the carnal corruptions of my soul, not that I love them, but that I may love thee, O my God!" Indeed, an obscure and toilsome course lies before me. What I used to love, I love no longer. No, I am lying. I love it still, but more moderately. No, again I have lied. I love, but with more shame, more sadness; and now at last I have told the truth. This is the fact: I love, but I love what I long not to love, what I should like to hate. I love nonetheless, but unwillingly, under compulsion, with sadness and mourning. I feel in myself, wretchedly, the sense of Ovid's famous line: "I shall hate if I can; otherwise I shall love in my own despite."

This is one of the rare passages in which Petrarch refers in his letters to the love of Laura. He reveals more than he would ever utter in his poems of longing and fidelity, intended for her eyes and ours. He tells his confessor, and he tells us, how under the devotion lay rebellion, weariness of love, and even hate.

> "Less than three years have passed since that perverse and guilty desire that totally possessed me and that reigned without opposition in my heart's chambers began to find a champion struggling against it. Between the two impulses a gruelling battle has long been fought in my mind by the two men within me, and the outcome is still uncertain."

Thus Petrarch dates his revulsion against earthly love, his yearning for the spiritual life, from his escape from Avignon in 1333. He continues:

> Thus my thoughts ran back over the previous ten years. Then I transported my distresses to the future, and I asked myself: "If you should by chance prolong this transitory life for ten years more, and continue approaching virtue, cultivating your new dispositions, breaking down your old obstinacy, could you not then, with luck, encounter death at forty and calmly renounce that residuum of life that dwindles into old age?" Such thoughts as these, Father, ran through my mind. I was happy at my progress, I wept for my imperfections, and I wept for the common inconstancy of human actions; and I forgot what the place was, why I had come there, and how I must have looked to the others.
>
> Then dismissing my troubles to some more suitable occasion, I looked about me and saw what I had come to see. It was already time to think of starting back, for the sun was descending and the great shadow of the mountain was extending below. Roused and warned, I look back to the west. The Pyrenean range, boundary of France and Spain, was not visible, not because of any intervening obstacle, but because of the weakness of human vision.

The Pyrenees, 20 miles away, are in fact visible from Mont Ventoux on a clear morning. The afternoon haze prevented Petrarch from seeing them.

> On the other hand I could see clearly the Cévennes to the right, and to the left the sea beyond Marseilles and Aigues-Mortes. The Rhone itself lay under our eyes.
>
> While I was admiring all these features, now recognizing some earthly object, now uplifting my soul, like my body, it occurred to me to look at the *Confessions* of Augustine, the gift of your love. (I keep it always with me, for the sake of the author and of the donor. It's of pocket size, but it contains infinite sweetness.) I open it, to read what-

ever may start forth; what but pious and devout words could start
forth? Now by chance it opened to the tenth book. My brother stood
intently by, waiting to hear what Augustine would say through my
lips. I call God to witness, and my brother too, that the first words on
which my eyes fell were these: "Men go to admire the high mountains
and the great flood of the seas and the wide-rolling rivers and the ring
of Ocean and the movements of the stars; and they abandon themselves."

I was stunned, I admit. Asking my brother, who was eager to hear
more, not to bother me, I shut the book. I was angry with myself for
admiring the things of this world, when I should have learned long
since from the pagan philosophers themselves that nothing is admirable except the soul, beside which nothing is great.

Then, sated with sight of the mountain, I turned my inward eye
upon myself, and from that time no one heard me utter a word until
we got to the bottom. That quotation had given me enough food for
thought, and I couldn't imagine that it had emerged by chance. I was
sure that what I had read had been written for me and for no one
else. . . .

I thought in silence of the vanity of men's purposes. Neglecting the
nobler part of themselves, they disperse themselves in a multitude of
trifles and waste themselves in vain shows, and look abroad for what
they could find within. I wondered also at the nobility of our human
spirit—unless, degenerate, it has wandered from its primitive origins
and has turned to shame what God gave it for honor. How often, on
the descent, I turned around and looked back at the mountain peak!
It seemed hardly more than a cubit high, in comparison with the
height of human thought, unless this is plunged in the filth of earth!
. . . How eagerly we should strive to tread beneath our feet, not the
world's heights, but the appetites that spring from earthy impulses!

Note, in this fine passage, that in his self-accusations to his confessor Petrarch can acclaim the nobility of the human spirit. Even
while announcing his submission to the divine he can celebrate the
nobilitas animi nostri. This is why Petrarch is a precursor of the
Renaissance and of modern times.

Amid these surging emotions, with no consciousness of the rough
and stony way, I came back in deep night to the little country inn from
which I had set forth before daybreak. The full moon gave us welcome
assistance as we descended. Then, while the servants were busy getting
a meal, I retired to a private room to write all this to you hastily and
extemporaneously. I was afraid that if I should put it off and go to

another place my mood might change and I would lose my eagerness to write you.

This last bit is a little too much. We can hardly credit that after some eighteen hours of strenuous ascent and descent Petrarch could have written an enormous Latin letter of about 6,000 words, including a number of exact quotations from the poets. We may reasonably suppose that while waiting for dinner he jotted down notes for the letter, and later elaborated it in literary form.

At any rate, it is a remarkable letter. It probes with acuity his troubled spiritual state. It also expresses for the first time that mountain-awe which has become a commonplace of human feeling, as of literature. This is one of the new pleasures, like speed, that civilization has discovered. Many a modern reader has been exasperated that Petrarch's appreciation of nature, of a View, turned so quickly to religious introspection, that instead of nature jottings he gives us an allegory of the Blessed Life. Critics have deplored that on the edge of romantic pantheistic identication with nature he stopped short to open his Augustine. Wordsworth would have melted into deity—

> Rapt into still communion, that transcends
> The imperfect offices of prayer and praise.

And Byron:

> I become
> Portion of that around me; and to me
> High mountains are a feeling.

Petrarch could not so far overpass his time. His uplifted spirit could find terms of statement only in religious exaltation. In the world below he had been passing through a critical stage, trying to shake off his obsession with Laura, trying to fight the demon of carnality. He had found moving sympathy and help in the confessions of a kindred soul. In the rarefaction of the upper air his heightened sensibility stirred him to egotistic examination of his own state. In a devout mind such thought can only be religious. Most religion is egotistic.

IX: ROME, 1337

> Rome, the common fatherland of mankind,
> the head of all things, the queen of this earth
> and its cities.
>
> —Fam. XXIII 2

> Rome, which was once the world's head and
> is now its tail.
>
> —Boccaccio, Decameron V 3

PETRARCH'S MOUNTAIN MOOD OF EXALTATION
and repentance did not provoke an immediate conversion
to a better life. In the fetid streets of Avignon the old
enemy attacked again with the poisoned poniard of concupiscence. Some time between October 10 and Christmas Day, 1336,
as a simple calculation will show, Petrarch learned that he was due
to become a father.*

Of the mother we know nothing, except that she was unmarried.
Years later, Petrarch, writing to his son Giovanni, refers scathingly
to the dissimilarity of their two natures, which, "if men's suspicions were true," that is, if Petrarch were indeed Giovanni's father,
should be very much alike. These cruel words to a youth already
burdened with illegitimacy suggest that Petrarch was not convinced that Giovanni was his son, and that he had no scruples
about hinting to the young man that his mother was a wanton.

We have no knowledge, either, of Petrarch's response to the

---

* Petrarch recorded in his Virgil the death of his son Giovanni in the night
of the 9th to the 10th of July 1361, in the twenty-fourth year of his age. (Reproduced in Fracassetti, Fam. II 242.) He says in Sen. I 3 that his dead son had not
completed his twenty-fourth year. The phrase would have been inapt if his
twenty-fourth birthday were more than six months distant; Petrarch would
have written something like: "He had barely attained his twenty-fourth year."
Thus the boy was born between July 10 and approximately December 31, 1337,
and must have been conceived between October 10, 1336 and March 31, 1337.
But Petrarch left Avignon on or about December 26, 1336, and there is no
reason to suppose that Giovanni was the product of a Roman escapade. Hence
the boy was conceived between October 10 and December 26, 1336, and, with
normal gestation, was born between July 10 and September 26, 1337.

news of his approaching fatherhood. One may, with many critics, dismiss the matter as one of small importance, and presume that Petrarch did the same. Illegitimacy in the clerical and noble societies of fourteenth-century Europe carried less of a stigma than it does today. But human impulses are still more compelling than the social conventions of time and place. I suspect that the announcement came to Petrarch as bad news indeed. His patron, Cardinal Colonna, was a man of exemplary life, and would probably welcome no clerical bantlings (although there is at least a possibility that the eventual son was named Giovanni in propitiation of the Cardinal). The financial problem of support of mother and child would soon arise. More, Petrarch's fatherhood would accord ill with his role as the enslaved and ever faithful worshiper of Laura. Many an admirer would be grieved, if not shocked, and many a cynical acquaintance would be ready with jokes and mockeries. Indeed, what would Laura say?

These are worldly considerations. The otherworldly considerations reached deeper into his heart. He had prayed, on the summit of Mont Ventoux, for divine help to guide him out of the valley of his sins. Now no sophistry could conceal that divine aid had failed him, that the Devil had played his trump.

What would be the emotions natural to a sensitive, introspective spirit confronted with unwelcome fatherhood? Shame, certainly, before the world, before Laura, before the immaculate image of himself that he was ever striving to erect in his own mind. His private shame was transformed into a horror of Avignon and of all its inhabitants. He was filled with a desire to flee the city and to flee at the same time his own distresses, his own responsibilities.

It seems not too fanciful to accept that in November or December of this year 1336, when the mysterious paramour informed Petrarch that she was pregnant by his work, he employed every device to escape, to put into effect his long-cherished purpose of visiting Rome.

He wrote to Bishop Giacomo Colonna, who had now spent four years in Rome. He dwelt on his longing to see both the ancient city of the pagan past and the holy city of Christianity, "like a heaven on earth, sown with the sacred bones and ashes of the martyrs and bathed in the precious blood of witnesses to the truth." However, he sighs that the visit to Rome must depend on permission from his master, Cardinal Colonna; he hints that the Bishop might obtain this permission from his brother.

Probably it was not permission that Petrarch needed so much as money. His benefice in the poorest of country cathedrals would certainly not defray the costs of a tour to Rome. He needed a substantial gift, or a mission, from his patron.

His prayers were suddenly answered. Whether the Cardinal made him a munificent Christmas present, or, more likely, found some ecclesiastical or family business requiring a courier to Rome, he dispatched Petrarch southward on or about December 26, 1336.

Petrarch took ship in Marseilles, and landed in Città Vecchia, fifty miles from Rome, in early January. According to his instructions, he first turned inland to the village of Capranica, which lies in the hill country northwest of Rome, on the old Via Cassia, or the new Strada Statale No. 2. Many a motorist on his way to Viterbo and the north traverses Capranica without slackening speed.

Here Petrarch was received in the castle of Count Orso dell Anguillara, whose wife was a sister of Giovanni and Giacomo Colonna. The approaches to Rome, he learned, were filled with peril. The permanent feud of the Roman nobles had flared into actual war. Petrarch must not think of venturing into the city without an armed escort. He sent a message to Bishop Giacomo in Rome; and on January 26, 1337, the Bishop, his elder brother Stefano, and a hundred armed horsemen arrived. The party remained in Capranica for a month to settle a family quarrel. Petrarch spent much of the time wandering in the hills, dreaming, and writing poetry. He wrote to Cardinal Colonna in Avignon:

> All about are numberless hills, not high or hard to climb, and affording broad views. In the shady folds of the hills dark caverns open. A leafy wood lies round about, fending off the sun's rays, except that in the north a low hill slopes down to a sunny valley, the flowery home of honeybees. Springs of sweet water babble downward to the lower levels; stags, does, goats, and the wild forest creatures wander over the open hills; every kind of bird warbles by the brooksides or in the branches. I need not speak of the cattle and the gentle sheep, and of the fruits of human labor, the sweet gifts of Bacchus, the rich gifts of Ceres, of the nearby lakes and rivers, of the sea not far away. All that is absent from this country is peace, whether for some crime of the people, or decree of heaven, or fate written in the stars. Can you be-

lieve it—the shepherd, well-armed, stands watch in the woods, not fearing wolves as much as robbers! The plowman, wearing armor, uses a
spear as a rustic goad, prodding therewith the backs of reluctant oxen;
the fowler hides his net under a shield; the fisherman hangs his hooks
with their deceptive bait from a sword; and comically indeed, a man
fetching water from the well ties his rusty helmet to a dirty rope. In
short, one does nothing here without weapons in hand. The night-long
shouting of guards on the walls, voices calling to arms, have taken the
place of those sweet sounds I used to draw from my lute. Among the
dwellers in these regions you can see nothing secure, peaceful, and
human, only war and hatred and devil's work. . . .

But custom rules in all things. Amid the soldiers' clamor and
trumpet-blasts, as the others assemble to an alarm, you may often see
me wandering over the hills and earnestly meditating some poem that
may bring me the favor of posterity.

One of the poems written amid the alarums of Capranica has in
fact brought Petrarch the favor of posterity. It is the beautiful
Canzone L, *Ne la stagion che'l ciel rapido inchina*, with its lovely
series of vignettes of nature and country life:

> It is the evening hour. The rapid sky
> bends westward; and the hasty daylight flees
> to some new land, some strange expectant race.
> An old and weary pilgrim-woman sees
> the lonely foreign desert-dark draw nigh.
> Fearful, she urges on her stumbling pace,
> and to her resting-place
> at last she comes, and knows
> the sweetness of repose.
> The pains of pilgrimage, the road's duress
> fade in enveloping forgetfulness.
> But oh alas, my hurts that ache by day
> are but more pitiless
> when the light sinks into the west away.
>
> When the sun's burning wheels have sped along,
> and night pursues, rolling his deepest black
> from highest peaks into the sheltered plain,
> the hardfist yokel slings upon his back
> his tools, and sings his artless mountain-song,
> discharging on the air his load of pain.

And yet his only gain
is, on his humble board,
rude fare, which poets honor, yet abjure.
Let him be happy, let him sleep secure,
though I no happiness have ever won,
no rest, no ease, no cure,
with all the turning of the stars and sun.

And when the shepherd sees the evening shade
rising and graying o'er the eastward land,
and the sun dropping to its nightly nest,
he rises; takes his well-worn crook in hand;
and leaves the grass, the spring, the beechen glade,
and quietly leads the tired flock to its rest.
He finds a cave, recessed
in crags, wherein to spread
green branches for his bed,
and there he sleeps, untroubled, solitary.
But then, O cruel Love, the more you harry
my breaking strength to that most hopeless chase
of her who flees apace;
and Love will never aid to noose the quarry.

In the sea's bays the sailors on their bark
throw down their limbs on the hard boards to sleep,
when the sun dips beneath the western main.
Oh, though he hide within the farthest deep,
and leave Morocco's mountains to the dark,
Granada and the Pillars and all Spain,
and though the worldwide pain
of suffering man and beast
in the first night have ceased,
there comes no night with mercy to conclude
my ardor, ever in suffering renewed.
My love grows old; soon will my captor see me
ten years in servitude.
And still no rescuer comes with strength to free me!

And as I seek with words my wounds to numb,
I watch at eve the unyoked oxen turning
in from the fields, down from the furrowed hill.
The heavy yoke is never lifted from
my shoulders, and my hurts are ever burning,

and in my eyes the tears are springing still.
Alas, it was my will
to carve the unearthly grace
of her most lovely face
in the immutable matter of my heart.
Now it is carved so deep that strength nor art
may rub it thence until that final day
when soul and body part.
Even then, perhaps, it will not pass away.

O my unhappy song,
my grief has made you grieve.
You will not dare to leave
my heart, to show your sorrows anywhere.
And yet, for others' praise you shall not care,
for all your burden is the weight of pain
left by the flames that flare
from the cold rock to which I cling, in vain.

For the pregnant paramour in Avignon there was no poetry.

Finally, about March 1, 1337, Bishop Giacomo's mission was completed and the way to Rome reported open. The party took the Via Cassia, crossed the Tiber at the Ponte Milvio, entered the city at the Porta del Popolo, and safely reached the towered fortress of the Colonna.

Petrarch was too busy staring about him to record his observations. A poet does not usually record; he transforms. He thrusts his impressions into the subconcious, and there they ripen, or fester, to reappear in some half-recognizable guise. An emotion emerges, aptly arranged, in new settings, unexpected contexts. Petrarch's longing for Rome and his longing for Laura recur, strangely blent, in his sonnet XVI. He assumes the habit of a pilgrim, while Laura is likened to Christ, whose face is imprinted on the famous veil of Saint Veronica:

The ancient graybeard shoulders on his load
and quits the home of all his many days,
under the silent loving-fearful gaze
of eyes forfending what the hearts forebode.
Thence in life's wane his old ambitions goad
his quaking shanks into long longed-for ways.

Only the burning of his will upstays
him, by years broken, spent by the long road.

But so at last his longing brings him nigh
to Rome, to look upon the painted face
of Him whom soon in heaven he hopes to view.
Ah, Donna, Donna, even so go I,
seeking forever in whatever place
some much-desirèd shadowy hint of you.

Rome was enclosed, as it still is, by the third-century Aurelian Wall, making, with the Tiber, a circuit of about twelve miles. A million men had dwelt here under the Empire; by the fourteenth century the population had sunk to a number estimated variously at from 15,000 to 50,000. Old Rome had crumbled, to make an earthly layer lumpy with bricks, potsherds, and bits of carved stone. (Anyone who has seen a bombed-out city knows what a mass of dirt a house makes when it returns to its elements.) On this immense grave the medieval Romans built their castles and their thatched hovels with the materials at hand. Some of the area was feebly tilled; more was a briary waste or a swamp with marble islands. The Roman aqueducts were broken; those who were forced to drink water drew it from the tainted yellow Tiber. The filth, the foul smells, and the fevers of Rome were notorious. The Queen of Hungary visited the city in 1343; she was so revolted, and so assailed by beggars, that she immediately left.

While other Italian cities were building magnificently, Rome was robbing its own past. The nobles raised their gloomy, defiant towers, piling together old marble, brick, and volcanic peperino. Most of the towers were brought down by the earthquake of 1348 or by later rulers, but a few, such as the Torre delle Milizie and the Torre dei Conti, still stand. Ancient greatness was for sale. Many Italian cathedrals, including that of Orvieto, were built of materials from Rome. Even Westminster Abbey got some. Lime-kilns were set up by the great ruins; the imperial palaces of the Palatine, the baths of Diocletian, the Julian basilica, and the marble facings were turned to lime. Even statues went into the kilns. (In modern times the statues of the Vestal Virgins were discovered, ready for cooking, in a kiln set up in their temple. The destroyers must have been suddenly interrupted, perhaps by the old gods.) When the marble shell had gone from the buildings the red brick remained, as we see it today. The Middle Ages reversed Augustus' boast that he had found a city of brick and left it one of marble.

Earth covered the Forum and most of its monuments. The arches of Septimus Severus and of Titus were half buried. The sacred spot had become a public dumping ground and a cattle pasture, *il Campo Vaccino*. Even the churches shared the general degradation, with the abandonment of Christendom's capital by the Popes. The roofs leaked unchecked, the altars were unadorned, and in the lesser shrines ragged priests said the offices.

The people, the remains of the *populus romanus,* had the character of their city. Between the nobility and the mob there was almost no bourgeoisie. Industry was trifling; Rome's business was the feeding, lodging, and fleecing of pilgrims, and begging, and crime. Brigandage, murder, abduction, rape were commonplaces, with justice helpless. "He was in the right who best wielded a sword," said a contemporary. Even the Roman diversions were bloody. In 1332 a bullfight was held in the Piazza Navona, Turnip Square. All the young gentlemen, including three Colonna, performed as mounted matadors. The bulls won, losing eleven of their number and killing eighteen men and wounding nine. The costs were defrayed by a special tax on Jews.

Absurdly, indecently, the Roman mob kept all the arrogance of its ancient forebears. This villainous spawn thought itself, as of right, the world's master. Although it had chased the Popes away by its violence and turbulence, it resented bitterly the migration to Avignon, and demanded that the Popes and their profitable Court return to their proper home. This demand Petrarch ardently supported, as we have seen.

Filled with expectant emotions, Petrarch visited the two Romes, pagan and Christian. In his inspection he had at least two guides.

One was Paolo Annibaldi, one of the nobles who adhered to the Colonna. His family occupied the Colosseum as their town house. Paolo was a worthy companion; he wept tears of shame at the sight of the ruins, and vowed that he would try to check further ravages.

The other guide was Giovanni Colonna di San Vito, uncle of Bishop Giacomo and of Cardinal Giovanni. He was a great

ROMA

traveler, and had been to Egypt and Arabia. He was of a religious
bent, and later became a mendicant friar. He and Petrarch wandered about the city of ruins, a living memorial of dead greatness.
Footways skirted walls of travertine, dodged among decapitated
pillars. Heads of unknown gods and emperors peered down at
street-corners. Horses drank from richly carved sarcophagi.
Every relic, every name had its associations. The Sacred Way, the
Seven Hills, the Campus Martius, the Tarpeian Rock, and the
rest recalled pitiful chaste Lucretia, Virginia's death at the hands
of her virtuous father, Horatius swimming the Tiber, Marcus
Curtius plunging into the abyss, Caesar's triumph and assassination, the melting of Coriolanus at his mother's plea; and Augustus'
sight of the boy Christ at the conjuration of the Sybil, and Peter
on the cross, and Paul beheaded, and Laurence grilled. But oh,
Petrarch cries, how ignorant of their past are the Romans! Nowhere is Rome so little known as in Rome!

"After our long fatiguing journeys through the immense city,"
he says in a letter to Giovanni di San Vito, "we would often halt
at the Baths of Diocletian and climb to the roof of that structure,
once so magnificent, for nowhere is the air fresher, the view wider,
the silence and solitude more grateful. . . . As we sat there, all the
ruined greatness was under our eyes." With the inspiring melancholy of the past about them they talked of history and philosophy, and, at Giovanni di San Vito's surprising request, of the origin of the mechanic and liberal arts. The time, the peace, the
mood, he says, can never be recaptured or repeated. Giovanni
urged Petrarch to put his words into a book, and this, perhaps, is
the origin of his *Rerum memorandarum liber*.

We are told today that Roman antiquarianism did not begin
until the fifteenth century. The examples just given make clear
that some desire to preserve the ancient relics existed already in
Petrarch's time. Add that Bishop Giacomo Colonna was a protector and preserver of antiquities. And Petrarch remembers: "Often a vine-dresser came to me in Rome with a gem of ancient work-
manship or a gold or silver coin in his hand, turned up by his hoe,
to sell it or ask if I could recognize the engraved face of some
hero." We are told also that the sense of ruins, the poetic view of
the humbled past, was an invention of the sixteenth century. Another obvious error.

Petrarch saw the Christian as well as the pagan city, making
the pilgrim round with the standard guide-book, *Mirabilia urbis
romae,* in hand. He follows this guide in his *Epistola metrica* II 5,
recording the miraculous relics, but remarking not at all on the
beauty of the structures, even the splendid original St. Peter's
built by Emperor Constantine. No doubt he prudently took advantage of the indulgences, by which a calculating pilgrim could
get credit of a hundred thousand years against his time in Purga-
tory. The best bargain was offered by St. Julian's, where a shrift
was good for eight thousand years' remission of torture.

Petrarch's worldly experience was enriched by his stay in the
Colonna castle. He learned the quality and manners of those
mighty nobles who for two centuries and more ruled as tyrants in
the Italian cities.

The head of the house was Stefano Colonna the Elder. "My
great Colonna, magnanimous, courtly, constant, and generous,"
Petrarch calls him. He had fought with Popes, and had made
peace with them, without surrender. He was Vicar of King Robert
of Naples and occasionally Senator of Rome. He had fathered ten
sons, three of whom, to be sure, had to be legitimized. Though he
was nearly eighty, his greatest pleasure was in fighting, preferably
fighting the Orsini. These in 1335 captured a Colonna bridge over
the Tiber and broke down two of its arches. Stefano retook it, to
carry on the long War of the Bridges. During Petrarch's visit
(probably) the enemy barons attacked the Colonna church of
Sant' Angelo in Pescheria, of which Cardinal Giovanni Colonna
was titular vicar. The attackers, with a siege machine, demolished
the campanile and the roof, broke the bells, shattered the marble
of the façade and the walls, and amputated the arm of a saint's
statue. But of this battle Petrarch unfortunately tells us nothing.

He tells us, however, of an incident he witnessed. Several of
Stefano's stalwart sons were in the castle courtyard, practising riding down a fixed target with a stout spear. The game was to shiver
the spear; but none could succeed in the trial of strength. From
his window old Stefano shouted abuse at his milksop progeny. The
eldest son, a famous warrior, shouted back: "It's easy enough for
you, father, to sit in the window with your hands in your pockets
and watch us sweat, and gabble about weak young men and how
tough you old boys used to be." The words brought the old man

running down. Shouting: "You think I'm no good, do you!" he leaped on the nearest horse, seized the spear, and charging, shattered it to bits.

Again, Petrarch remembers exactly and vividly a conversation with the elder Stefano. The two were taking a walk; they stopped to talk at a place (on the Via del Piè di Marmo) that can still be exactly located. Petrarch begged his companion to make peace, and the elder asserted, as have so many others, that his whole aim and desire was peace, but that war was necessary in order to make peace secure. Then, with strange prevision, he exclaimed that it would be his fate to be the heir of all his sons.

We do not know how long Petrarch stayed in Rome, or by what route he returned home. Some have supposed that he left Rome toward the end of April, that he paused only a moment in Avignon, and then made, on some unknown mission, his journey to the Britannic Sea. It is possible. All that we can be sure of is that he was in Avignon by August 13, 1337. He found there either a baby boy or a mother big with child. Neither sight can have pleased him. He immediately sought means to escape from the horrid city to a hidden country fastness, to Vaucluse.

X: VAUCLUSE, 1337-1341

That was almost the only time I have known that could really be called life.

—Sen. X 2

"HERE WAS A GLORIOUS WOMAN IN MY LIFE, notable for her virtue and her noble lineage, famed far and wide from my songs," wrote Petrarch to Bishop Giacomo Colonna in 1338.

Still she stands before my eyes, terrifying me, assailing me, nor does she show any sign of leaving me in peace. She had captured me by no feminine guile, but by her simple ways and by her rare beauty. I bore her yoke for ten years, though scorning myself for my subjection. I was wasted by my disease, the fever-glow had penetrated to my very marrow. I hoped to die; and then longing for liberty invaded my afflicted breast and planted there courage to rebel. I rose against my subjection, and strove to cast off my bonds. God aided me, while she, offended, tried to keep her dominance, and prepared even heavier shackles for me. I fled, and went wandering through the great world. I found a kind of peace, and even learned to laugh again. I thought I had gained freedom from my mad love, but my wounds were merely crusted, not healed. Hardly had I returned to her sweet home than they broke out afresh, and again I longed for death. My only hope lay in flight. As the benighted steersman fears the lurking reefs I recoil in terror from her face, from her words that fire the mind, from her gold-clouded head, from her necklaced throat, her quivering shoulders, her eyes delighting in my death.

In this desperate pass I perceived a rock upon a secret shore, a refuge against disaster. And now, hidden among the hills, I weep my past life.

Thus Petrarch makes Laura alone responsible for his retreat to Vaucluse. He enforces his contention in the *Canzoniere,* as in madrigal LIV:

Because she bore Love's mark, a Wanderer
suddenly struck my heart, one youthful day,
and all my praise and honor turned to her.
And hunting her through the green wilderness,
I heard a voice cry, high and far away:
"All your pursuit is vain and purposeless!"
And then I sank in the shade of a beechen tree,
and gazed about, perceiving none too soon
the forest menace that encompassed me.
And I turned back, about the hour of noon.

("The hour of noon" is of course the mid-point of life, set by Aristotle and Dante at thirty-five.)

The poet's motives for seeking a retreat were certainly not so simple as he would imply. There was of course Laura. A casual encounter in the street, or a deliberate rendezvous, would stir the old pain, and, in his favorite metaphor, set his wounds a-bleeding. The situation was intolerable. It could be ended only by decisive action, which must mean, obviously, the reform of his life. This had already been clear enough on the summit of Mont Ventoux. The lesson there stated was strengthened by his reading and by his prayers during his pilgrim round in Rome.

But there were other reasons for a retreat. Avignon was the home not only of Laura but of his newborn son and of his paramour. We do not know if the mysterious woman was vindictive, or grasping, or merely pitiable. In any case she was inconvenient, a reminder and reproach of his sinful weakness, a mockery of his published image and of his private image too. Petrarch never liked responsibility; he much preferred giving advice, praise, and blame to others. His impulse was all to escape unpleasantness. He wrote once: "Harassed by so many obsessing cares, I did as I commonly do in such cases, taking a course congenial to my inertia. I resolved to brush them all aside, and, if possible, to forget them."

There was also a problem about Gherardo. He had been deeply in love; and about this time the object of his affections died. He was so overcome that he blasphemed the God who had sentenced her. The young man was always a trial and a burden on his brother. It would be a good thing, thought Petrarch, to get Gherardo out of Avignon and into a wholesome country environment.

There was still another reason for retreat, and very likely the

most powerful of all. Petrarch was widely esteemed as a poet and
scholar. But what, with his great gifts, had he actually produced?
About eighty of the poems in the *Canzoniere;* a few of those now
assembled under the head of *Rime disperse;* a handful of metrical
epistles in Latin; some songs that have have not survived. Not a
very impressive achievement for a lyric poet at thirty-three. His
various projects for scholarly celebrations of the Roman past had
advanced not at all. In the circumstances, he wanted what every
poet and scholar wants, or thinks he wants—freedom from the
obligations of regular employment, and leisure to capture the
great works glimmering mistily in his mind. And he wanted to
find and possess himself. He grieved that he was not born an ordinary man, content with mediocrity. He was no ordinary man, and
he was conscious that the search for himself and the discovery of
himself would be a thoroughly justifiable occupation. "There are
no riches or treasures worth as much as absolute control over our
own minds," he said again.

Such a purpose was far more original than it would appear
today. The deliberate analysis and construction of a personality
for its own sake was a practice unknown in his time. It has been
said that Petrarch was the first man who—like Rousseau, Byron,
Foscolo—built up such a personality, with no other object than
itself, "by a happy calculation of the most refined vainglory." His
effort, and his success, have been called, again, "the consecration
of a renewed human dignity."

His purpose was still vague in his mind. All that was clear was
that he must escape from the tormenting city to a solitude where
he could work at leisure. He says:

Whether through love of letters I love places friendly to leisured
literary pursuits, or whether perhaps the unlikeness of my habits to
those of the mass makes me hate and flee them, or whether awareness
of the special quality of my own life impels me, I flee the many-
tongued witnesses. . . . How can you estimate these common satisfactions—to live as you wish, to go where you wish, to repose where
you wish (in the spring on purple beds of flowers, in the autumn on
a heap of dry leaves), to cheat the winter by basking in the sun, the
summer by seeking the shade, and thus to neutralize the seasons?
Throughout the year to be your own companion, to lodge everywhere
with yourself, far from evil and from bad examples! Not to be

crowded, pushed, put upon, trod upon, not to be dragged to banquets when you aren't hungry, not to be forced to talk when you'd
rather say nothing, not to be greeted at awkward moments, not to be
clutched and held at a street corner, and not to spend the day, according to fashion's foolish decree, gazing at the passing throng! One
man stares at you as at some kind of monster; one immobilizes himself before you; one, bowing low, follows behind you, asking loud
questions about you of his companion or of passers by; one jostles you
in a crowd, or ostentatiously yields place to you, which is worse; one
thrusts out his hand, one taps his head in greeting; one starts a long
speech when you're in a hurry; one gives you a sour look and purses
his lips. Think what it means not to grow old amid such boredom, not
to be forever squeezed and squeezing in a throng of hail-fellows, not
to mingle your breath with that of a thousand others, so that you
sweat even in midwinter; not to unlearn humanity among men, and
in disgust come to hate men, business, those you have loved, yourself!

In this state of mind his thoughts returned to the enchanted
Fountain of Vaucluse, seen and loved in boyhood. Thither, in the
autumn of 1337, he fled, with his brother.

This was a sensational act. It lay outside the comprehension of
medieval times, proud as they were of their new cities promoting
the interests of the citizens and harboring a relatively refined
social life. Avignon society could not understand why a popular,
successful literary man should leave its comforts for the barbarous
hardships of country life, among boors and beasts. As Tatham
says, had Petrarch retreated to a monastery the world would have
understood, "but this step was so entirely novel as to set people
talking; perhaps it actually contributed to enhance his growing
renown."

Precisely. The world knew well the cenobite, seeking treatment
for his sinful soul in a monastery. It knew also the anchorite, the
hermit, who could find his God only in some high mountain cave.
But Petrarch was not looking for God in Vaucluse; he was in
search of himself. He was the first literary recluse, foreshadowing
Montaigne and the Romantics to come. "Livers of busy lives do
not live," he said. "They talk with others, not with themselves."
He wanted to talk with himself, and he expected that in self-
communion he would find a message for his fellows. Nor would
his solitude be total; he would have the company of his books and
the long visits of congenial friends. His days would be laborious.

He would write, at last, works that would astonish the world he affected to despise.

There is an excellent modern parallel—Thoreau. Vaucluse and Walden would lie close together in a spiritual geography. Petrarch and Thoreau were filled by a similar disgust with the busy competitive society about them; both sought self-knowledge, leisure to read and meditate and write. Neither fled very far. Vaucluse lies twenty miles from Avignon; Walden Pond is only a couple of miles from Concord, and Thoreau often walked into town for human converse and for one of his mother's famous apple pies.

Petrarch did not deceive himself. In his *Secretum*, his utmost effort for complete sincerity, his St. Augustine tells him that his retreat is merely a roundabout way of attaining his ambition, and a means of setting himself apart from the despised *vulgus*.

Those of us who are still bound by the anxious cares of the world must wonder about the expense of abandoning it. Petrarch's only regular income was the small stipend of his canonicate at Lombez. He had to supply his own needs and those of his brother, and probably he made an allowance to the mother of his child. At this point he purchased a small house in Vaucluse, with some land about it. He had two servants and two horses. He had to buy essential furniture and household equipment, and costly books and paper, and he had to entertain visitors, even though frugally. Where did the money come from?

Certainly from the ever kind, the ever gracious, Cardinal Colonna in Avignon. The Cardinal's generosity was the more praiseworthy in that he was supporting a poet in absence, and in that he was depriving his own little court of a useful secretary and of a brilliant celebrity, impressive to visitors. But one supposes that the Cardinal summoned Petrarch whenever a special need arose.

Whoever paid for it, the Vaucluse establishment made a perfect *modus vivendi* for a poet, yielding neither deficit nor surplus. A friend wrote Petrarch a begging letter; he replied by describing his own needs, and ended by asking the would-be borrower for a loan.

The Fontaine de Vaucluse is a geological phenomenon. An underground river, uncharted, unexplored, emerges under over-

hanging cliffs 350 feet high in a nearly circular pool, the source of the River Sorgue. It is a siphon, really. Captain Cousteau and his aqualunged companion plunged down 200 feet, seeking the main inlet, and nearly lost their lives. In the spates of spring and autumn the waters whirl and boil; the flow is estimated at 9,000 English gallons per second. At other seasons the flood sinks, disclosing a cave wherein lies a smaller pool, the Fontaine de Vaucluse proper. The outer pool recedes, laying bare moss-covered rocks. The over-flow descends through a narrow rocky gorge for a half mile to the village of Vaucluse. The waters are of a strange clear emerald green, attributed to aquatic plants in the stream bed. "A liquid grass," a modern writer calls the water. The gorge is today barren and grim, but in Petrarch's time the stream was bordered by cool-shadowing oaks, and there was a giant poplar under which sight-seers would picnic. Petrarch drew in the margin of his Pliny a sketch, not very deft, showing the fountain itself, with its cliff and reeds and flowers, and a crane that has just caught one of the river's still celebrated fish, and the Oratory of St. Victor, a pil-grimage place that has long since vanished.

The little village of Vaucluse stands on the right bank of the Sorgue. Here is still the church where Petrarch did his duties. On a height on the left bank stood the small castle of the feudal lord, the Bishop of Cavaillon. In Petrarch's time it was seldom occupied, and today it is only ruins.

Petrarch's house was on the left bank, at the foot of the cliff surmounted by the Bishop's castle. One had access to it from the village, as one still has, by crossing a bridge and traversing a tunnel under a promontory, dug by the Romans as part of an aqueduct carrying the Sorgue's waters to Arles. Petrarch's home was a mere cottage, with servants' quarters adjoining. The rear was built into a recess of the rock; the front stood only a few steps from the water. The little museum that now shamelessly proclaims itself *la Maison de Pétrarque* stands on the approximate site.

The sentimental visitor today must use his imagination to recall the beauty of Petrarch's solitude. The steady water power from the natural reservoir and the emerald waters of the Sorgue were found to be admirable for paper-making. Mills were set up in the eighteenth century; still their ugly bulks crowd the stream. There is no peace. Vaucluse has become the resort of all the south-

land's *profanum vulgus.* On a bright spring Sunday thousands
come to tread Petrarch's paths and eat the descendants of his fish.
The half-mile walk from the village to the fountain is lined with
shed-like booths, offering food, drink, souvenirs, lottery wheels,
ring-toss games, opportunities to display one's strength for a small
fee. When Henry James visited Vaucluse in the early eighties the
baraques rented brushes dipped in tar, with which to inscribe
one's name on a rock; but advertisers caught the idea, and now
there is no longer room on the rocks for names. Petrarch's Nymphs
of the Sorgue have vanished, to be replaced by boisterous Marseil-
laises in halters and shorts.

Humble as it was, Petrarch's home was the first he had possessed,
and he was mightily proud of it, and happy in his independence.
He engaged a country couple to serve him; by great good fortune
they turned out to be those jewels that have almost vanished from
the world. Raymond Monet, though rough and untrained, was a
tireless worker, and was fidelity personified. He took jealous charge
of his master's finances, and reproved his prodigalities. When the
poet returned from a trip, Raymond would demand an accounting
of his expenditures, and sigh: "You've made a long journey,
master, but believe me, you'll always come back with empty
pockets." Though illiterate, he honored Petrarch's books like
sacred relics, and knew each of them by name. "He was always
overjoyed when I would put a book in his hands. He would press
it to his breast and sigh; and often he would talk in low tones to
the author. He had, curiously, the sense that by merely clasping
and looking at the books he became wiser and happier."
Madame Monet was no beauty.

If you could see that face, so dry and sunburned, so lacking in vital
juices, you would think you were looking at the Lybian or Ethiopian
desert. If Helen had had such a face, Troy would still be standing.
. . . But her soul is as bright as her face is dark. . . . She does not feel
her lack of beauty, but seems to regard it as right and proper. No one
could be more faithful, humble, and hard-working. She works all day
in the fields under a sun so hot the cicadas can hardly bear it, and with
her tough skin defies Cancer and Leo. Returning home at evening,
the old woman puts her indomitable little body to the household
tasks, like a young girl just out of bed. There's never any murmuring,

complaining, or excitement, only an incredible care for her husband
and children and for my guests, and an equally incredible unconcern
for herself. This iron woman has only a bed of brushwood laid on the
floor, and bread as hard as clay for food, and for drink a watery wine
that tastes like vinegar; and if you give her anything more delicate,
she thinks, because of long deprivation, that everything dainty is dis-
agreeable.

This incomparable couple tended Petrarch's home until they
died, forever secure in his affection. In his will he left the small
domain of Vaucluse to their sons, subject only to one prior claim.

The first winter in Vaucluse was something of a trial. The
valley was dank and chill, the house surely ill equipped for harsh
weather. Gherardo appears to have retreated in disgust, and
Petrarch was left alone with his servants and his dog. The Avignon
friends who had promised to visit him refrained, frightened by the
winter weather, the rough journey, and by reports of the poet's
hard fare and Madame Monet's cooking. In place of friends came
the peasants, to ask of the strange wizardy man advice about their
legal rights in property quarrels, about dowries, gain, advantage,
for all the world like the danglers at the Papal Court.

In his solitude Petrarch had his books. He liked to quote Seneca:
life without letters is death, *otium sine literis mors est.* His books
were living persons to him, like his companion Muses and the
woodland nymphs. These secret friends, he tells Bishop Giacomo
Colonna,

> come to me from every part of the world and from every age. They
> are friends illustrious in speech, intelligence, government, war; not
> difficult; they are content with a corner in my humble house, never
> reluctant or boring, eagerly obedient to my command, ready to come
> or go at my call. Now these, now those I interrogate, and they answer
> me at length, telling their tales and singing their songs. Some explore
> the secrets of nature, some give counsel on better living and better
> dying; some tell their own high deeds and those of past heroes, and
> make old times live again in their words. Some drive away my dis-
> tresses with their cheer, and bring back laughter to me with their fun.
> Some teach me to bear all burdens, to hope for nothing, to know my-
> self. They are the artificers of peace, war, agriculture, law, navigation.
> They raise me up in adversity, curb me in prosperity, bid me look to
> the end, remind me of the swift days and of life's brevity. For all these
> gifts they ask a small price—only an open door to my house and heart,

for hostile fate has left them few refuges in the world and only reluctant friends. If they are admitted, they think any lurking-place a man-
sion, and lie trembling until the frigid clouds may pass and the
Muses again be welcomed. They do not require that silken hangings
cover my bare walls or that rich foods perfume my table, or that my
halls resound with the clamor of many servants attending a throng
of guests. My sober troop of books are content with their own provisions and share them with me, as I sit wearily on my rose-colored
bench. They give me sacred food and pour me sweet nectar.

With the coming of the lovely Mediterranean spring he had
the rewards of the solitary. In old age he remembered his delight
in the silent fields, in the stream's murmur, with the cattle lowing
in echoing valleys, with the concert of birds by day and nightin-
gales' solos by night. Often the dusk took him by surprise, far from
home. Often he rose at midnight, recited his office, donned a rough
country smock, and, not to disturb his servants' sleep, slipped out
in the moon's glimmer to the open fields or to the hills, or, with
mingled delight and terror, to the ominous cave of the fountain.
He had no fear of ghosts and spectres, or of wolves, none of which
he ever encountered. Nor did he need to fear mankind. Early
rising field workers, singing at their tasks, and quiet fishermen
would greet him cordially. He became himself a quiet fisherman,
with hook and line, with darting spear, with nets, and with traps
plaited of willow withes. There were no enemies in that happy
time; he thought peace could never depart from his valley.

Inviting Giovanni Colonna di San Vito, his companion in
Rome, to visit him, he tells his friend that he will be waiting by
the Sorgue's bank.

You will see me content with a small but shady garden and a tiny
house, which will seem all the tinier on receiving so great a guest.
You will see me from morn to eve wandering alone among the
meadows, hills, springs, and woods *(solivagum herbivagum montiva-
gum fontivagum silvicolam ruricolam)*. I flee men's traces, follow the
birds, love the shadows, enjoy the mossy caves and the greening fields,
curse the cares of the Curia, avoid the city's tumult, refuse to cross the
thresholds of the mighty, mock the concerns of the mob. I am equi-
distant from joy and sadness, at peace by day and night. I glory in the
Muses' company, in bird-song and the murmur of water-nymphs. My
servants are few but my books many. Now I am at home, now walking,

now halting, now laying my weary limbs on the tender grass or by a babbling brookside. Not the smallest part of my pleasure is that I rarely see a human creature, who will have time to tell me only a modicum of his personal cares. And you will see me often silent, with a faraway look, and often busy talking to myself, and forever scornful of myself and of all mortal matters.

Again, he writes to Guido Sette, who had played with him in boyhood by the Sorgue. He hints that the two might spend their old age together in the peace of Vaucluse. "Silver fish play in glassy pools, far away a few cows low in the fields, health-bearing breezes whisper lightly in the swaying trees, many various birds sing in the branches, and, if you will permit me to quote myself:

> Philomel moans by night, the turtle-dove speaks her woe,
> and from the shining fountain the murmuring waters flow."

The space between his house and the river was occupied by his garden, in which he took great delight. It contained vegetables, grapevines, olive and fruit trees, and flowers—lilies, narcissus, roses, violets. His servants of course did the heaviest work, but he liked to take an active hand, and did much of the planting himself. In his *De remediis* he recommends laborious recreations, "as, namely, some time to graft the tender twig upon the budding stock, or to correct the rank leaves with the crooked hook, or to lay quicksets into the dyke in hope of increase, or to bring the silver streams by new-digged furrows into the thirsty meadows." In the letter to Guido Sette, just quoted, he discusses the best date for planting trees. His worthy farmer and an old countryman have agreed on the sixth of February, especially if the moon is right. His oldest trees, he says, were planted by Bacchus and Minerva, the youngest by himself.

Not content with a single garden, he laid out a second, for flowers alone, in the upper valley, beside the large pool, or just below it. As the site lay among bare, tumbled rocks, it was necessary to roll away the boulders, build a wall against spring freshets, and make a bed of good earth brought from the lower valley. His visitors found themselves summoned to join in the heavy labors as an appetizer before their country repast. The nymphs of the stream took umbrage at all this activity, as we shall learn.

Mostly his joy was in wild nature. His imagination peoples the

countryside with classic forms, the woods with dryads and hunting
Actaeon, the Sorgue with water-nymphs, with staring Narcissus,
with the Muses. At the same time he observed the external world
with a sharp eye. Thus he describes a little bird whose song out-
does the nightingale's; its head is black, its flanks gray, and it likes
to go hopping among the vines; there was never a more beautiful
voice in a smaller body. (This is perhaps the *capinera,* or black-
headed linnet.) Thus again he describes a dreadful thunderstorm,
with the opening of the clouds in lightning, all the stars gone
except pallid Saturn, the swollen river submerging his flowers and
breaking the irrigation barriers, the pattering hail, the pebbles
and loose earth rattling on his roof, the cracking of branches in
the wood, the floundering of cattle seeking their stables, the mother
clutching her babe to breast, the priest in his best vestments pull-
ing frantically at the bell-rope.

Such exactly recorded observation as this is something new in
literary history. The classic poets had of course loved and described
birds and flowers and country labors, but usually with a certain
externality, as disinterested spectators. The Middle Ages were
strangely oblivious of natural beauty. The anthologist has trouble
enough finding examples of awareness of nature in Alcuin, Walther
von der Vogelweide, the Arthurian romances, and popular lyrics.
Even the Provençal poets, celebrating love in the springtime,
settled down to a few stylized examples, stock properties such as
dawn, fountains, undifferentiated birds and flowers.

"With Petrarch reappears the cultured enjoyment of nature,"
says a critic. He communicated his enjoyment by a new direct
awareness and by a new rendering of the pictorial quality of the
landscape and its wild inhabitants, a recognition of the "picturesque." He opened his eyes and ears to sights and sounds which,
however familiar, no writer had thought to record. He describes,
for instance, the peasant silently intent on his labors, as the blows
of his mattock sound dully in the earth and the sparks fly from
struck stones. Dante could have made such a note; no one else of
his times, I think.

It is true that Petrarch's nature descriptions often lack specific-
ity, in comparison with those of our nature-writers. A modern poet
may be botanist and zoologist; he likes accurate lists of flowers in
bloom, and seeks the exact, observed detail. A short numbering

of flowers and birds sufficed for Petrarch, and his adjectives are few and ever-recurring. He was content to call a brook "murmuring," a mead "flowery." His method at least permits the reader to fill in the picture from his own experience of brooks and meads, whereas a modern poet's precise description may escape the reader's knowledge and dull his response.

Petrarch displayed, further, a new emotional participation with nature, what we now call empathy. His intimacy with nature became at times a merging with it. He felt himself to be a tiny voice in the great harmony. He did not merely watch the birds; he tried to feel with them for a moment. The nightingale's lament for his lost love blends with his own. This identification with the wild will reappear in literature only with Wordsworth and Shelley.

Finally, Petrarch perceived for the first time the beauty of wild, forbidding, waste, gloomy scenes. He loved the stony barren hills and the dark foreboding forests; he loved the moonlight. What allured him in the cave of Vaucluse's fountain was its mystery, its horror. "That mixed feeling of horror and delight anticipates the mood of European poetry by more than four centuries."

Opening himself to the inspiration of nature, he pursued his literary purposes. As he watched, he worked. He found his country solitude stimulating, and urged it upon other budding authors, calling on Cicero, Virgil, Plato, and St. Cyprian for support. Mountain poems are the best, he said; they taste of Alpine grass. He composed as he walked, his feet marking the rhythm. (And what are poetic "feet," if not the poet's steps?) Sometimes the Muses were coy, and he had to spend a whole long summer day on a line or two. But sometimes they were kind, and he was filled with an incredible and inexpressible joy.

He wrote many fine poems in Italian to and about Laura, to fill out his *Canzoniere.* He began, apparently, his *Trionfi,* or *Triumphs,* writing a longish poem on the Triumph of Cupid. To these we shall return.

On Good Friday 1338, as he was wandering on the hills, he received an inspiration that he could regard only as divine. (Good Friday was always a fatal date in his life.) He would write a great epic poem on the life of Scipio Africanus, who broke the power of Hannibal and subjected Africa to Rome, and who was distinguished for all the virtues that we think of as Roman. He would write it in noble Latin, Italy's proper language. He would give modern Italy its first proper epic poem (for the *Divina Commedia*, in the vulgar tongue, could hardly be in competition). What a vista opened before him! The name of Petrarch would be forever united in a trinity with Homer and Virgil. Years later he wrote a friend: "There I began *Africa*, with such a gush of fervor that now, when I am filing away at the first draft, I am amazed at my audacity and at the vastness of my design."

Being scholar as well as poet, he devoted his less inspired hours to a project conceived in Rome. He initiated his *De viris illustribus*, a compendium of the lives of great men of all ages and countries, a Universal Biography, indeed. His first version began with Adam and was to end with Julius Caesar. Later he restricted it to the lives of great Romans, from Romulus onward. The book has little to commend it to the modern reader, glutted with encyclopedias and digests. In its time it was, however, a precious manual, drawn from original sources. Petrarch says that his purpose is to provide inspiring examples, recording the habits, domestic life, utterances, physical appearance, ancestry, and death of his subjects. He treats his authorities with a critical spirit rare in his age. Discrepancies among his authors lead him to doubt some old tales of Roman heroism. He says that the story of Horatius at the bridge "has found more to marvel at it than to believe it." The book was to occupy him, off and on, through all his life. On the very night of his death he was at work on the life of Caesar.

So ran his country routine, in high thoughts, in dreams, in labor, in frugality. His fare was simple and rustic; Madame Monet was obviously the worst of cooks. No matter; Petrarch liked coarse food, with no fuss, and was happy with a bit of bread and cheese in pocket to eat in a mountain shepherd's hut. He was naturally ascetic, in the matter of food at least. He was almost a vegetarian, sneering at wolfish carnivores who make living sepulchres of their bodies. In the season he would eat all day nothing but fruit, even unripe. He fasted regularly out of devotion, but without much merit, one would say, since he seems to have enjoyed abstinence. "Feed the brute body once a day," he says. His drink was water, "to follow my nature, which understands what I am and tells me what is good for me." Wine he drank only from social convention; he would have renounced it entirely had not Jesus set a contrary example.

No doubt the Vaucluse cuisine gained a discouraging reputation. Petrarch invited young Agapito Colonna, his former pupil, offering poet's fare, apples, chestnuts, milk, hard half-baked bread, and with great good luck a hare or a crane or a pickled boar's snout. There is no sign that the invitation was accepted.

His best friends conquered their niceness. Guido Sette returned happily to the spot where he and Petrarch had sported in youth. The old friends Socrates and Laelius came, but never, apparently, Cardinal Colonna. Especially there was Philippe de Cabassoles, Bishop of nearby Cavaillon, and tenant, as Bishop, of the castle that stood above Petrarch's cottage.

Philippe de Cabassoles was a gentleman of an old Provençal family, of about Petrarch's age. He was sturdy of build, energetic, ready and eager for any undertaking. He was sincerely pious, and was much beloved by his flock. He rose eventually to be Patriarch of Jerusalem and Cardinal. He loved the classics, and wrote some essays that still remain in manuscript. When they were both old Petrarch wrote him, recalling their happy days in Vaucluse, their tranquillity and leisure, their wandering in the woods, deep in talk of literature, of great deeds of the past, and of their eternal salvation. At sunset they discovered, amazed, that they had passed the day without thinking of food, and they met the reproaches of the servants, who had been hunting them all day in the woods. Philippe, an inveterate reader, would ask for a book, and when offered Cicero or Plato would say that he preferred Petrarch. There could be no higher flattery than this.

One day Philippe called on his friend and found him worn out with work on his *Africa*. He asked Petrarch to do him a favor. When this was granted, he demanded the keys to the cupboard. He then assembled all the books and writing materials and locked them up. "I am ordering a ten-days holiday for you," he said, "and I order you not to read or write anything during that time." He then went away, leaving Petrarch helpless, bored, and angry. That day seemed longer than a year. On the next day Petrarch had a severe headache from morning to night. When the third day dawned he woke with a fever. Philippe returned, and in alarm restored the keys; and Petrarch immediately recovered.

For Philippe Petrarch wrote his *De vita solitaria*, a celebration of retirement from the active world. The perfect solitude he conceived would not be absolute; there would be room in it for a friend. Toward the end of his book he says beautifully: "Not only will you, Philippe, be the support of my quiet, you, only you, will be my quiet, not only the comfort of my solitude, but my solitude; and I will seem to be truly alone when I am with you."

Another visitor was Dionigi da Borgo San Sepolcro, Petrarch's one-time confessor and the donor of his *Confessions of St. Augustine*. He had been stationed for some time in Paris; he stopped in Avignon on his way to Italy. Petrarch wrote him a poetic invitation to Vaucluse, adroitly including fulsome praise of King Robert of Naples, whom Father Dionigi was due to visit. Father Dionigi accepted the invitation; and probably Petrarch dropped in his confessor's ear a hint that it would be a good idea for King Robert or somebody to revive the classical custom of crowning a poet with laurel. What poet? Well—

Still another visitor was Guglielmo da Pastrengo, the scholarly lawyer of Verona, whom we have already seen in Avignon in 1335, making peace with the Pope for his master, the tyrant Mastino della Scala. Mastino again got into trouble in the summer of 1338, by stabbing to death his cousin, the Bishop of Verona, on the steps of the episcopal palace. Guglielmo da Pastrengo and Azzo da Correggio were sent in haste to Avignon, with evidence that the dead Bishop had been organizing a conspiracy against the peace. During his stay at Court Guglielmo came often to Vaucluse, and helped roll the great stones from the upper garden to make a wall against floods. Wearied, Guglielmo and his host watched the water-birds with their fledglings cowering under sheltering wings and reaching for food with trembling mouths. Then the two lay on the grass and for long hours talked of the Muses and of the ancient poets.

Guglielmo had time, in the intervals of business in Avignon, to fall in love. One day Petrarch, strolling by the lower reaches of the Sorgue, encountered a party of gentlefolk. He could not tell at first if they were men or women, "for the new French luxury imposes such a common fashion that you can't tell men and women apart. But as we drew near their faces became clear, as did the delicate head-bands and the jeweled necklaces and the hair-decorations and the fine purple-bordered gowns and the fingers sparkling with gems." In the party was Guglielmo's beloved. They shook hands and talked. Petrarch asked where they were bound. "To the famous Fountain of Vaucluse!" Petrarch speculated that perhaps the lady hoped to find there her Guglielmo.

There were plenty of other visitors to the poet's retreat, which came to rival the fountain as a tourist attraction. Noble and learned eminences traveled from France and Italy only to see him and to ruin his day's work, as he tells us with a mingling of annoyance and satisfaction. Even, he says, a soft, effeminate lawyer came to his valley, not from desire for peace, which he hated, but to imitate the Poet. Soon he bored himself as much as he did Petrarch, and returned to the pleasures of the city. Had Petrarch not foreseen this outcome, he avers, he would have left Vaucluse himself.

In the list of visitors to Vaucluse there is a conspicuous lacuna. We have no clear indication that Laura ever saw the valley. Nor, in fact, is there any word of an invitation to his paramour and his small son.

His peace suffered various interruptions. Probably in Lent of 1339 a man "more distinguished for rank and wealth than for brains," possibly Prince Humbert of Savoy, stopped in Avignon on his way to the shrine of Sainte-Baume. He wanted Petrarch for traveling companion. Cardinal Colonna sent the poet a request which amounted to an order. Unwillingly, Petrarch complied.

The cave of Sainte-Baume lies about twenty-five miles northeast of Marseilles. Here Mary Magdalen, after her miraculous trip to France in an abandoned boat, spent her last thirty-three years. Her shrine was, and still is, a favorite place of pilgrimage. Engaged couples make piles of stones to indicate the number of children they desire, and nubile maidens are promised that if, as they climb the hill above the shrine, a garter comes loose they will marry within the year.

Petrarch's eminent penitent spent three days and nights praying in the cave. This was more than the poet could endure. He went wandering in the magnificent beech-woods, forever sacred from the axe, and held imaginary conversations with his absent friends. He wrote for Philippe de Cabassoles a Latin poem on St. Mary Magdalen, a rather sexy poem indeed, with much tearing of blond hair and beating of the delicate breast with penitent hand. He does not question the story of the Saint's translation to France and her retreat to Sainte-Baume.

The visit to Sainte-Baume has been regarded as a stage in

Petrarch the Pilgrim's progress toward a better life. This does not seem to me very likely.

Petrarch's first stay in Vaucluse made an epoch in his life, and established for all times a convention of literary retreat. He came there in distress of spirit, troubled by unrequited love, by unfulfilled ambition, by remorse of conscience. In his mind was no conflict of faith and doubt; his conflict was between his passions and his ideals.

He made of Vaucluse the perpetual symbol of spiritual and aesthetic hygiene in solitude. His purpose was not religious; it was secular and humanistic. Solitude, in his conception, was an escape from the world's overwhelming foolishness to creative leisure, among great books, noble thoughts, and worthy friends. "No solitude is so profound, no house so small, no door so narrow, that it may not open to a friend." As Zeitlin says, he disavowed the duties toward one's fellow men recommended by the moralists; his renunciation was that of the egotist. His retreat was more like that of Horace than like that of a Christian mystic. Vaucluse was his Sabine Farm, complete with garden, woods, and a never-failing fount of pure water, but lacking the Falernian.

Petrarch himself says that what he seeks in solitude is happiness, not salvation. He would choose a serene, pleasant life in society rather than a sad, burdened solitude, and he has chosen solitude only because in it he can find peace and liberty.

He found, of course, that peace, liberty, and happiness are never absolute. The days, the nights, were very long, and inspiration often laggard. He was irritated by sightseers and untimely visitors, but he was irritated also when no friends came at all. Solitude is dangerous for a melancholy man, he confesses; and "for a soul obsessed with passions nothing is worse than leisured peace, nothing more hurtful than solitary freedom; for lascivious thoughts creep in and lewd imaginations, and fair-seeming evil, and the familiar curse of idle minds—love."

Perhaps the source of his troubles—though a stimulation to achievement—was non-ecclesiastical celibacy. He said: "I feel forever something unsatisfied in my heart." The something unsatisfied resulted from his defiance of nature's simplest injunction, without his accepting the training or obtaining the rewards of the clerical celibate.

Physical exhaustion, frugal diet, and prayer could not banish the lewd imaginations. Nor could they banish the melancholy of the busy mind, racing in solitude without contact or conflict, refusing the monitions of the will. "What good is it for me to enter this wilderness alone, to follow the river-courses, to explore the forests, to sit on the mountain-tops, if wherever I go my mind follows, in the wild just as in the cities? The mind must be laid aside. The mind, I say, must be left at home, and I must humbly pray God to create in me a clean heart and renew a right spirit within me. Then at last I shall have penetrated the secrets of the solitary life."

This is the cry of Childe Harold:

> Still, still pursues, where'er I be,
> The blight of life—the demon thought.

Or, to return to Petrarch: "If the woods and streams could fulfill all our needs, Vaucluse would be enough. But nature requires something more. The mob thinks that philosophers and poets are hard as rocks, but in this it is wrong, as in so much. They too are flesh and blood; they keep their human nature, though they reject fleshly pleasures. There is a limit of necessity for both philosophers and poets, and it is dangerous to transgress it."

Thus Petrarch well recognized the threats of solitude as well as its joys, and he was soon to escape from it as he had escaped from the city's crowds. But in memory the joys of Vaucluse far outweighed its pains. In old age he reflected that only his years in the Closed Valley merited the name of life.

He wrote a lovely little singing poem to his Vaucluse:

> Valle locus Clausa toto michi nullus in orbe
>   gratior aut studiis aptior ora meis.
> Valle puer Clausa fueram iuvenemque reversum
>   fovit in aprico vallis amena sinu.
> Valle vir in Clausa meliores dulciter annos
>   exegi et vite candida fila mee.
> Valle senex Clausa supremum ducere tempus
>   et Clausa cupio, te duce, Valle mori.

To the Closed Valley I came as a boy
    to play in its sun-spotted glades;
to the Closed Valley I came as a youth
    to ponder my books in its shades;
to the Closed Valley I came as a man,
    and happily there labored I.
To the Closed Valley I'll come when I'm old,
    and in the Closed Valley I'll die.

XI: LOVE—MOLTO AGITATO

> The errant, dubious soul finds what comfort
> it may.
>
> —Rime *CXXV*

WHEN GUGLIELMO DA PASTRENGO ARRIVED in Avignon in 1338 he sent a message to Petrarch in Vaucluse that he was in town and would like to see his friend. Petrarch rode into Avignon, a four-hour trot; but once within the walls he was so overwhelmed with revulsion that, feeling like a runaway slave before a looming prison, he turned around and trotted back by night to his refuge. In his letter of apology he admits that the city had already lured him from his security.

> I had decided to endure all the menaces of fortune, if only I might live a little for myself alone, though soon I should die. And gradually I began to attain my wish, and my spirit began to cast off its everlasting shackles, to my unspeakable joy, so that my life seemed almost celestial. But what is the power of long habit! Often I find myself seeking that abominable city, drawn by no hook of necessity, and of my own accord I return to my bonds, and from safe harbor I set out on that sea where I have so often been shipwrecked.

Though drawn despite himself, he looked with a bilious eye on the abominable city, that "inn of grief, mother of error." He has even no word of praise for the new structures, so fascinating to modern eyes, that were to form part of the Palace of the Popes. Benedict XII was beginning the work, with the two square donjons, La Campane and the Tour des Anges, and the Pontifical Chapel. The planning was not very functional. From his apartment high in the Tour des Anges the portly Pope had to descend for his bath more than a hundred steps and then remount them.

Petrarch admitted to Guglielmo, in the letter just quoted, that he returned to the abominable city of his own accord. He thus

hinted that the novelty of his solitary life in Vaucluse was beginning to wear thin. Usually he insisted that his trips to town
were always unwilling. "If some necessity drives me into the city,
I have learned how to create a solitude for myself in the throng
and a harbor in tempest by a device that not everyone knows, that
of so ruling my senses that they do not actually feel what they
feel."

He had occasional peremptory reasons for visiting the city.
Guido Gonzaga, ruler of Mantua, instructed his agents in Avignon
to interview the poet in their spare time and report on his character and activities. Petrarch was summoned, without regard for
his own spare time. He wrote an adulatory letter to the tyrant,
with no indication of reluctance. A Greek monk, Bernard Barlaam,
came to sound out the papacy on a reunion of the Eastern and
Western Churches. Petrarch eagerly sought him out, and, on a
later visit of the monk, tried to learn from him the rudiments of
Greek.

He made also the acquaintance of Simone Martini, the great
Sienese painter, who was brought to Avignon in 1339. Simone was
a student of the classics and a poet in a small way; he was phe-
nomenally ugly, but possessed of much social charm. Petrarch
probably watched him doing his frescoes in the cathedral. These
have now faded to a uniform blur, very unfortunately from a
literary standpoint, for the figure of the maiden being rescued
by St. George was said to represent Laura. Simone and Petrarch
became good friends, as poets and painters commonly do. Simone
painted a frontispiece for Petrarch's fine manuscript of Virgil
(now in the Ambrosian Library in Milan). The poet commissioned also a small portable portrait of Laura, to be his companion
in solitude. The fact is troublesome to those who maintain that
Laura's identity was a guarded secret, for there must have been
sittings, or at least an identification of the subject. The portrait
showed her smiling, kindly, promising peace. Petrarch carried it
everywhere close to his heart. And then he says no more of it. Perhaps he destroyed it, or lost it, or wore it out.

His presence in Avignon brought him into contact with Laura,
by design or by chance. He would go by night to sigh under her
window, or he would happen on her sitting alone on the Rocher
des Doms (*Rime* C):

That window where the sun at midday shows
(another sun may shine at midnight there);
that other window where the gusty air
plays chill and wintry tunes when Boreas blows;
that rocky seat whither my lady goes
to sit alone and argue with her care;
the stones she's trodden; every pavement where
her shadow for a second did repose;

that ambush where Love pierced me with his dart;
the new spring season, opening afresh
my old, old wounds, after these many years;
her face, her words, that wound me in a mesh,
that are today compounded with my heart—
these fill my eyes with a desire of tears.

The streets of Avignon were rich with associations, sweetly painful. Petrarch wrote his friend Sennuccio del Bene, a fellow Florentine exile in the papal city, who knew the real Laura well (CXII):

Sennuccio, would you have me, then, confide
my way of life, the tale of my duress?
I burn, I melt, with all the old grievousness,
and Laura rules me still, for woe betide,
here she was humble, there she walked in pride,
now harsh, now gentle; pitiful, pitiless;
now she was gay; now in her sober dress;
now scornful; now demure; now angry-eyed.

Here she sang sweetly; here she sat awhile;
and here she turned; and here she held her ground;
her eyes here stabbed my heart with a fatal ray.
And here she spoke; and here I saw her smile;
'twas here she blushed—oh, in this helpless round
our master, Love, pursues me night and day.

Wandering in gardens where he had walked with Laura, he
finds peace (CXXV). He does not know the exact spots her foot
has pressed, but he reflects that every flower and shoot had its root
in sources sacred to her; the thought makes him happier than
would a precise location. There was a blissful day when they met
in the street and she saluted him kindly (CX). And a dreadful day
when he went to see her without permission; her anger blazed in
her eyes, and he retreated in fear (CXLVII). But she relented, and

welcomed him, laughing, and he recovered from his "anguished, desperate life." But then desire reawakened, so that he was no better off (CXLIX). When he grew importunate she checked him, calling on reason, modesty, and reverence to restrain his kindled hopes; but inwardly, he knew, she scorned his ardor (CXL). She wept, and he was shaken to the core (CLV and CLVIII). She moved him to tears, singing in her clear, sweet, angelic voice one of his own lost compositions (CLXVII). He thought he saw a ray of pity, but was so flooded with words that he could utter none of them (CLXIX).

Laura's image pursued him to Vaucluse. He had thought that he could escape her by retreating a mere twenty miles into the country. He had thought, fondly, that he could divert his ardor from Laura to Christ, and that Christ would bring peace to his soul. On Good Friday 1338, that great day when he had the inspiration for his *Africa,* he wrote an anniversary sonnet to record his eleven years of subjection (LXII). But even in his prayer his thoughts are fixed less on his Savior than on his captor:

> O Heavenly Father: after wasted days
> and all those hungry nights when my desire
> ran in my veins with new-replenished fire
> at recollection of her lovely ways;
> O Heavenly Father, lend thy hand to raise
> me to the good life whereto I aspire,
> rescue my feet from the encompassing mire
> and from the traps my adversary lays.
>
> Father, today the eleventh year is turning
> since that unhappy hour of desolation
> when the yoke first upon my shoulders lay.
> Have mercy, Lord, on my long shameful yearning,
> lead thou my thoughts to a better destination;
> remind them thou wast crucified today.

He wrote to a friend, later, that in the shades of Vaucluse, that stout stronghold, he had hoped to abate the fever that had so long wasted him. What folly! The remedy turned to his undoing. With no recourse, he says, he burned the more desperately with the consuming cares he brought with him. The flames burst forth from his lips, out of his breast, and filled the valleys and the upper air with his plaint, woeful indeed, and yet, as some alleged, sweet.

In a poetic epistle to his friend Laelius, probably of 1339, he describes the country scenes, and continues:

> All these things stir in my heart the still warm ashes, and I fear that the fire may break forth anew. My love was dead, and high time too; but Cupid, offended, again picked up his arms and his golden shafts. I saw him myself, sharpening his arrowheads on a smooth stone, and with his finger testing the deadliness of the worn points. I saw him gently draw the fatal bow, and aiding himself with his knee bend the curved weapon, guiding the murderous bowstring with his thumb. . . . I am in deadly fear of him, lest he reopen my old wound with his new shaft, for he has many allies. The mere aspect of this place invites him, with the murmur of the breezes mingling with birdsong, the fair colors with sweet odors, the grasses with the foliage, the lilies, narcissi, roses, and violets all in rivalry. And therewith are repose by the green river banks, light sleep, and the prattle of water leaping and softly fleeing. And what of the sweet songs that at night, dawn, or evening, a nymph across the river sings to me with angelic accents?

(By some critics the nymph is taken literally, as a village girl who brought the poet solace, or as Laura herself on an escapade. But this seems an unnecessary supposition. It is enough to regard her as mere background music. Did the poet also see Cupid sharpening arrowheads?)

He had his hours of joy, of pride in his own constancy (CXLV):

> Now put me where the sun's infuriate rays
> bring death to bloom; or where the ice and snows
> outmaster him; or where his chariot goes
> gleaming along serene and tempered ways;
> put me in Fortune's shadow or full blaze,
> under bright skies, or where the twilight glows;
> where the day rules; where nights untimely close;
> in age's ripeness; in green growing days;
>
> put me in heaven or earth or in the abyss,
> in vale or marsh, or on the hills upheaving;
> tethered to body, soaring free in bliss;
> obscure on earth or every fame achieving—
> I'll be what I have been, naught else but this.
> I'll live as I have lived, loving and grieving.

The sight, the thought of Laura could ravish him with pure, unmixed delight (CLX):

Love and I stood agape; we marveled how
no wonder's ever mazed the human sight
like the speaking lips and laughing eyes alight
of our one Lady, who has no equal now.
Under the fair serene of her calm brow
my ruling constant stars are shining bright,
to fire the kindred heart and lead aright
him who would take Love's highest, sternest vow.

It is a miracle, when on the grass
like a flower she sits! Or when her candid breast
is crushed against a bush, without her care!
How sweet it is, in spring to see her pass
alone, and by her lovely thoughts caressed,
weaving a circlet for her golden hair!

Such poems as these have led many to conclude that Laura was familiar with Vaucluse, perhaps as a springtime visitor to some nearby castle. This is going too far. Poets' imaginations are not to be taken as factual records. Often a poet carries an impression, or a phrase, for years before it emerges in finished form. A fervent imagination has indeed little need of facts. Petrarch could people the glades of Vaucluse with nymphs and dryads; why could he not see there as well the beloved form of Laura?

Petrarch's poetry is "non-immediate," says an eminent modern critic, Umberto Bosco. The mood comes first; introspection analyzes it; specific details, memories, turns of speech gather about it; the rhyme and rhythm impose their obligations, and have their effect on the thought. Eventually the poem, the concretization of the mood, takes shape.

The effort to resolve the completed poem into its constituent factual inspirations leads often to absurdity. One of the sweetest of the canzoni is *Chiare, fresche e dolci acque* (CXXVI). It describes his lady's bath in a country pool, and her repose on the bank, as a shower of blossoms descends on her from the branches above. Did Laura actually bathe naked in her desperate lover's presence? The critics have disputed whether Laura *laid (pose)* her fair limbs on the bank or *put (mise)* them in the water, whether she was fully immersed or whether she merely went wading. The safest conclusion is that the whole scene was the product of Petrarch's excited imagination.

In imagination his eloquence mastered her, to his triumphant joy (CXXXI):

> I'd sing such songs of joy that every day
> I'd draw a thousand sighs from that hard breast.
> A thousand high desires that hide unguessed
> would melt and bloom to my impassioned lay.
> And pity upon her lovely face would play,
> and unaccustomed teardrops would attest
> the all-too-late regrets of one distressed
> with new repentance for a mistaken way.
>
> I'd see the snowbound roses of her lips
> quivering; and that glint of ivory
> that marbles the onlooker. Every reason
> I'd see wherefor my joy of life outstrips
> the pain of it. I shout exultantly
> that I am kept unto this elder season.

If in his dreams he was mastering, he was also mastered. If he could pretend a triumph, with the aid of holy Poesy, he knew that he was victim of a relentless obsession, which he ascribed not to his own character but to the god Amor or to Laura herself. He returned often to the figure of the bird-snare, the baited net hidden in the grass (CVI):

> A lovely new-fledged angel, shy and wary,
> came down from heaven above the blossomed shore
> whereon I walked alone my fated way.
> Seeing me there defenseless, solitary,
> she quickly cast the silken snare she bore,
> and in the deep green grassy path it lay.
> So I was taken; and I blessed my capture;
> under the light of her eyes was only rapture.

There can be rapture in subjection, as all the world knows. But rapture must of its nature be brief; it passes, and subjection remains. Petrarch expanded the conceit of the snare in CLXXXI:

> Love made a snare, a beautiful device
> woven of gold and pearls, and this he laid
> twined in the grass, under the sorrowful shade
> of the laurel tree to which I sacrifice.
> Sweetmeats were strown thereon, of greatest price,

though bitter at core. I took them unafraid.
Ever unearthly-lovely music played,
unheard since Adam's hour in Paradise.

The radiance of her eyes outdid the sun,
transfiguring the earth in a holy blaze.
Then with her ivory hand she twitched the rope!
And so I fell in the net, and was undone
by her angelic words, her darling ways;
also by pleasure; by desire; by hope.

He was well aware of the nature of his joyful moments. The
curse of his spirit—and his permanent literary merit—was self-
centeredness, self-examination, torturing introspection. His love
for Laura turned his thoughts at least temporarily outward, to
fix on an object outside himself. He confesses his case in the
canzone *Gentil mia donna* (LXII): "I return to the old familiar
war, thanking nature and the day I was born that they have
destined me to such a boon, thanking her who raised my heart to
such hope; for till then I had been burdensome, obnoxious to
myself, but thenceforth I found an inward satisfaction, filling with
high, sweet thoughts that heart to which she holds the key."

The examination of his contradictory thoughts and emotions
fascinated him (CXXXII):

Can it be love that fills my heart and brain?
If love, dear God, what is its quality?
If it is good, why does it torture me?
If evil, why this sweetness in my pain?
If I burn gladly, why do I complain?
If I hate burning, why do I never flee?
O life-in-death, O lovely agony,
how can you rule me so, if I'm not fain?

And if I'm willing, why do I suffer so?—
By such contrary winds I'm blown in terror
in a frail and rudderless bark on open seas,
ballasted all with ignorance and error.
Even my own desire I do not know;
I burn in winter, and in high summer freeze.

The observed oppositions, the antitheses that were the natural
form of his thought, found expression in balanced verbal antith-

eses. The result was the poem of paradox, which was imitated
by a thousand, nay, a hundred thousand poets, including Shakespeare. For example, CXXXIV:

> There is no peace; I am too weak for war.
> I fear and hope; a burning brand, I freeze.
> I fly o'er heaven, and lie upon earth's floor.
> I grasp the void; the whole world's on my knees.
> I'm jailed without a sentence; at the door
> pauses my captor, balancing her keys.
> Love will not let me live unprisoned, nor
> will he let death bring me its blessed ease.
>
> Eyeless, I see; tongueless, I shout and cry;
> I beg my doom and succor with one breath.
> Loathing myself, another I'd be wooing.
> I feed on grief; I laugh with streaming eye;
> and equally I hate both life and death.
> This is my state, my lady. It's your doing.

Laura served as the agent and stimulus for his self-scrutiny.
Petrarch adored her, of course; he also blamed her, reproached
her, called her names, sometimes even hated her. "Femina è cosa
mobil per natura," he sighed, forecasting one of the world's most
popular songs. Her irritations, her grievances, had their justifica-
tions. He was certainly indiscreet, and he was convinced that fame
was the finest reward a man or woman could gain. But Laura's
modesty was revolted by publicity. "You opened your closed heart
to all the world," she said to him angrily. She thought that no
way to treat a respectable married woman.

He imagined, against all evidence, that his devotion was
obscurely working within her spirit (CL):

> "What are you thinking, soul? And shall we see
> this war forever? Shall no truce occur?"
> "Why, who can tell our fate? But I'll aver
> she likes not our disease, fidelity."
> "Why should she care, if but by glancing she
> can make us fire, or than ice icier?"
> "That is the work of Love; no blame to her."
> "Why speaks she then no word to set us free?"
>
> "Sometimes the tongue is silent, and the heart
> laments in misery; the tearless eyes

laugh, hiding floods of sorrow past belief."
"Little indeed such comfort satisfies
the mind where stagnant sorrows lurk and smart!
Hope is incredible to the slave of grief."

Amor promises that eventually Laura will yield to his endless
constancy (CLXVIII). But Amor is a liar often; and Petrarch sees
in his mirror how he is aging; and Laura is aging too. He fears he
will die before she turns kind. Nevertheless, time will not damp
his ardor or staunch his sufferings (XC):

She used to let her golden hair fly free
for the wind to toy and tangle and molest.
Her eyes were brighter than the radiant west.
(Seldom they shine so now.) I used to see
pity look out of those deep eyes on me.
("It was false pity," you would now protest.)
I had love's tinder heaped within my breast;
what wonder that the flame burned furiously?

She did not walk in any mortal way,
but with angelic progress. When she spoke,
unearthly voices sang in unison.
She seemed divine among the dreary folk
of earth. You say she is not so today?
Well, though the bow's unbent, the wound bleeds on.

He was tired. The word *stanco* keeps recurring in successive
sonnets. He longed for peace; he found beautiful phrases, still,
slow, moving lines, worthy of Dante, to describe peace (LXXIII):

Pace tranquilla senza alcuno affanno,
simile a quella ch'è nel ciel eterna,
move da lor inamorato riso.

("Tranquil, carefree peace, like that which is eternal in heaven,
proceeds from the enamored laughter of her eyes.") He summoned
the ultimate peace of death (LXXXVI):

Oh, I shall always hate the window whence
Love, cruel love, transfixed me with his ray!
Why had it not sufficient force to slay?
It's good to die in youthful vehemence.
No, I must live, in lifelong penitence.

jailed on this earth. What, lifelong, did I say?
My pain will live when life has passed away;
the soul remembers how the heart laments.

Poor soul! You should have learned the lesson well.
In vain earth's mightiest do importune
time to turn back its pages, or suspend
its flight a moment. There's no more to tell.
Begone, sad soul! He cannot die too soon
whose happy days have come to their last end.

He hints, even, at suicide (CLII); but it is only a hint. No poet, so far as I know, has ever committed suicide for love. For literary discouragement, like Chatterton, yes; for publicity, yes, like Larra; from secret tortures, like Hart Crane; but not for love.

These confessional poems of Petrarch's first Vaucluse period constitute a portrait of the artist rather than a portrait of the beloved. His subject-matter is his emotional history; this he explores and discovers by the method of introspection. The image of Laura changes constantly with the poet's changing moods. Sometimes she is real, factual; sometimes she is a dim faraway influence, heavenly or almost diabolical. Says Bartoli: "He objectivates his subjective states. He is angry with Laura because he is ill content with himself; when his black mood discolors all externals, she too is black . . . She is merely the reflection of his spirit."

Introspection was his occupation and joy. Introspection was hardly a new invention; every religious practised it, especially the mystics. However, they were concerned with the preparation of their souls for eternity, whereas Petrarch sought only to know himself. No one before Petrarch examined his own self so thoroughly, so relentlessly as he, nor did anyone after him until we come to Montaigne. (No one, at least, who recorded his explorations in written words.)

The basis of his love, he knew, was sensuality. "The senses reign, and reason is dead," he says (CCXI). He longs to pass a night with Laura in the woods, by moonlight (XXII, CCXXXVII). She bids him keep his desirous hands to himself (Eclogue III). And so forth.

Sensuality is readily transformed into pleasure in pain. "I am

one of those who delight in weeping," he says, and describes how
he even seeks out reasons for shedding tears (XXXVII). As Wordsworth says, the Poet is a man pleased with his own passions and
volitions. "Even sadness may have a delight of its own," Petrarch
avers. His sorrow is sweeter than others' joy. Men will point to
him and say: "There goes the man who wept forever, and in his
plaint was blest more than others in their laughter!" He hoarded
his grief, to enjoy it in recollection, telling a friend that he must
economize on sorrow, in order to have always something to
remember, something to say, some reason to weep. Writing of the
death of a dear friend, he said:

> I have a feeling of woe and calamity, which nevertheless is somehow
> welcome to my mind, for there is a certain sweetness in lamentation,
> on which, in these days, I feed and torture myself and find pleasure.
> For if I found no pleasure therein, what could compel me to these sad
> thoughts? The pleasure, truly, is more grievous than any torment; but
> while memory racks the mind, one's complaints are lightened.

Thus he made a technique of self-castigation, using memory as
the whip. He dwelt forever on remembered sufferings, especially
those inflicted by Laura. By brooding upon them he could lift
himself to a state of excitement, of ecstasy, in which poetry would
naturally flow. The thought of Laura served as a precipitant, as a
trigger. But the real Laura recedes, to become a cloudy symbol;
and no doubt the real Laura was well aware of it.

Did he in fact actually love Laura, according to the world's
understanding of love? Some have denied it, alleging that she was
a mere servant of his egotism, or even a traditional poetic device
and nothing more. Such conclusions seem to me untenable.
Petrarch loved Laura, passionately, desperately, and long. He
loved her in his own way; being what he was, he could love her in
no other way. He loved her in the poet's way, as woman, as goddess, and as Muse. Laura, esteeming her own little personality as
something of value, resented his using her for copy; she did not
realize that he loved her in part because he could use her for copy.
"If my life is to bear any fruit, the seed was sown by you," he tells
her (LXXI): For him the proof of his love was her stimulation of
his spirit to the production of poetic fruit; and indeed that seems
an excellent proof.

Did Laura love Petrarch? No.

The examination of Petrarch's poetic method and concept, of his place in literature, may be deferred to a later page. Here let it suffice that his songs delighted his contemporaries because of their verbal beauty and their exaltation of love, and because they re-vealed the poetic quality of commonplace experience. He sang a recognizable human love against a background of a recognizable city, or against a localized natural décor. Laura is a foreground figure in a realistic stage setting. We see her in the dawn and under brightening skies, in the green meadows and by purling brooks, treading on flowers, and forever accompanied by singing birds. Petrarch invented the blending of pictorial and musical elements to relate the old drama of the human heart, the drama of love, fidelity, and despair.

XII: THE LAUREL CROWN

The poet's reward consists in the charm of personal glory and in the immortality of one's name.

—Coronation Oration

TO PETRARCH, IN HIS COUNTRY MEDITATIONS, came a most wonderful idea.

For a dozen years he had been celebrating Laura, with numberless punning references to the evergreen Laurel, sacred to Apollo, symbol of immortal poetry. In the great past poets were publicly crowned with laurel-leaves on Rome's Capitoline Hill. The custom had to be sure lapsed for over a millennium, but in 1315 the poet Mussato was laureled by the University of Padua. In 1319, the year before Petrarch's arrival in Bologna, that city offered to crown Dante, but the poet, who hated or feared Bologna, rejected the bid.

The idea of a tribute to his Laura, the idea of the ancient Roman custom, the idea of the contemporary revival of laureling, blended to make Petrarch's wonderful idea. He would be crowned in Rome, the sacred spiritual city, the heart of the world. He would restore the broken tradition, standing on the very spot hallowed by the great poets of the Roman past.

Many difficulties stood in the way. He had to implant the concept among Rome's rulers, spur them to establish the laureateship, and then persuade them that he was the fittest living poet to wear the crown. He was almost unknown in Rome. The body of his work, for a poet of thirty-six, was not very impressive. His poems in Italian, widely diffused though they were, were regarded by scholars as mere bagatelles. Petrarch tells us that poetry itself was disesteemed by the learned, and that poets were rare, humble, venal, addicted to the commonplace, and adjudged even infamous. It was to be foreseen that his coronation would provoke sharp criticism and jealous outcries. On the other hand he had a widespread personal reputation as a Latinist, as an acute though unproductive scholar, and as a bibliophile. He was known to have some historical works under way. He let slip the news that he had begun to write an epic poem in Latin on Rome's greatness. But these were projects, not achievements. His qualifications in 1340 for the laureateship seemed, and still seem, on the whole, slight.

To attain his ambition it was necessary to do a good deal of wire-pulling. The details, naturally, are suppressed in the edited correspondence he has left us. He enlisted the aid of the Colonna in Rome, set them talking among their powerful friends. And he began a campaign for the support of the more powerful King Robert of Naples.

King Robert was the grandson of Charles I of Anjou, French conqueror of Naples and Sicily. He was the leader of the Guelf party, and a faithful supporter of the Popes. The city of Avignon was his private property; Petrarch conveniently forgot that Robert had welcomed the Popes to Avignon as his tenants, that he had steadily intrigued to keep them there, and that he was the chief promoter of French policy in Italy. He was now sixty years old. He was tagged "the Wise," because of his prudence in government and because of his interest in scholastic philosophy and theology, perhaps also because of his stinginess.

King Robert loved to preach; Dante calls him "the sermon-king." He was extremely pious, supporting the Spiritual Franciscans in spite of their disfavor with the Popes. He alleged that he wanted to abdicate in order to become a friar; dissuaded, he installed twelve Franciscans in his palace, and, wearing their coarse garb, sang matins with them. He and his queen on occasion served the monks and nuns in the convent refectory. His scholarship was considered astounding, and not quite proper for a king. He composed a treatise on the moral virtues, which those who have read it find uncommonly dull. Petrarch tells us that in all his activities he kept his books by him, by night and day, walking or sitting, and that he was eager to learn and interested in new inventions. His one liberality was the patronage of scholars. He supported the University of Naples, employed a corps of translators, copyists, and illuminators to diffuse Latin versions of Arabic and Hebrew

works, and invited learned men to stay at his court on the equivalent of research fellowships. However, his interest was all in medieval literature and science; he had little concern for the Roman
classics or for contemporary poetry. This was the man Petrarch
chose to be his advocate and sponsor, while the Colonna were
planting the idea of a laureateship in Rome.

Petrarch made an astute and deliberate campaign. We have
seen that his confessor, Dionigi da Borgo San Sepolcro, paid a visit
to Vaucluse in 1338, on his way from Paris to Italy. Certainly
Petrarch confided to him his ambition. Father Dionigi arrived in
Naples before October 1339, received much favor at Robert's
court, and ere long became a bishop. Presumably he inspired the
King to write a courteous letter to Petrarch, expressing interest in
his literary work. Petrarch replied (December 26, 1339) with a letter expressing such adulation as to make his most devoted admirers blush. He crawls and slavers before the monarch. But he does
not mention the laurel, except by noting slyly in his concluding
sentence that King Robert is adorned with the twin laurels of
war and study. Immediately after, he writes to Father Dionigi:
"You know what I think of the laurel-crowning." He continues
that the King's letter was by no means clear, but that he would
take it as a summons to Naples, and that he wished to receive the
laurel from King Robert alone.

No doubt; but if King Robert should prove reluctant or obtuse,
there was no harm in making alternative plans. Petrarch had probably made friends in Paris with Roberto dei Bardi, head of the
theological faculty at the University of Paris. Apparently he sent
to this powerful person a passage from his *Africa,* with a suggestion that coronation by the University would be an appropriate
meed. For such a function there was no tradition, no precedent, in
France. In fact, the suggestion must have seemed more than peculiar to many of the faculty, for Petrarch's poems in Italian could
hardly have been widely known in France, especially among the
scholarly theologians of the University, and his poetic epistles in
Latin were few and personal.

Nevertheless, the wire-pulling worked. On the first day of September 1340, at nine in the morning, a messenger arrived in Vaucluse bearing an invitation from the Roman Senate for Petrarch
to come to Rome and be crowned with the poetic laurel. At four

in the afternoon appeared a courier from Roberto dei Bardi, with
a similar invitation from the University of Paris. Petrarch immediately sent the two letters to Cardinal Colonna in Avignon, asking
his advice. His accompanying letter gives the impression that the
invitations, unsolicited, took him totally by surprise, and that
their almost simultaneous delivery was something of a miracle.
But Cardinal Colonna knew better, and so does posterity. The invitation from Rome had unquestionably been organized by Giacomo Colonna and others of his family in Rome. The Cardinal advised Petrarch to accept the Roman offer.

Petrarch conceived of the crowning as something like a university's award of a doctoral degree, which was symbolized by a
crown or occasionally by a laurel wreath. (The crown has today become a hood, conveying a symbolism which seems more than un-
fortunate.) As Calcaterra says, the laurel meant for Petrarch a
right or license to practice poetry, with all the rights, privileges,
immunities, honors, and insignia appertaining thereto. Thus he
felt that a preliminary examination was essential. Only with proof
in hand that he had passed his examination could he present himself as a worthy candidate to the crowners. And the only person fit
to examine him was King Robert the Wise of Naples.

The decision, says Tatham, "effectually raised the ceremony
from being a municipal honor decreed him by his friends to the
rank of a 'Spectacle,' enacted before the eyes of Christendom in
the world's capital. . . .In spite of the novelty of the project [of a
royal examination], he must have been aware, at least subcon-
sciously, that it would add great éclat to the ceremony, and that it
might help to stifle the murmurs of envy."

The consent of King Robert was soon obtained. Petrarch spent
the autumn preparing for his examination and working on his
coronation address. In February 1341 he set forth. Who paid for
the trip? Surely Cardinal Colonna and Bishop Giacomo, who had
new returned to his diocese in Lombez. King Robert, notoriously
close-fisted, could not be expected to examine the candidate and
pay his expenses too.

Despite his terror of seasickness and of maritime perils, Petrarch
journeyed to Naples by sea. He accompanied Azzo da Correggio,
whose interests (one may remember) he had already defended before the Papal Court. Azzo and his three brothers, rulers of Parma,

were preparing a little rebellion against their nephew and overlord, Mastino della Scala of Verona, and Azzo was obviously laying the ground by visits to the Pope and to King Robert. The
chances are that in shipboard confidences Petrarch was admitted
to the secret.

Naples under good King Robert was regarded as the most agreeable of Italy's, nay, of the world's, cities. Its population was about
60,000. Its noble setting, between Vesuvius and the sparkling bay,
impressed even eyes commonly heedless of scenery. There were
three parts to the city. Along the waterfront crowded the merchants, bankers, artisans, and shippers of every nation, in the sec-
tion that is now Old Naples, picturesque in its poverty. On the
rising ground above, around the Duomo, stood the aristocratic
and ecclesiastical quarter. Westward, between the Castel Nuovo
and the Castel dell' Ovo, was a new-built area of palaces and gardens. The Neapolitans were reputed to be tall, well-dressed, clever,
naturally eloquent. They were also extremely fond of pleasure.
Young Boccaccio, who, though a mere bank clerk, was admitted to
high society and to a liaison with an illegitimate daughter of King
Robert, tells us of bathing-parties, boating trips with beautiful
girls at the oars, picnics, dances, hunting, fishing, and shellfish collecting. Amour was popular. The King had to issue an edict
against abductions and kissing in churches.

Petrarch was cordially received by King Robert, and was lodged
in his Castel Nuovo by the sea. (It was called New, and still is, because it was built in 1280). Petrarch joined the royal party, which
daily adjourned to the high-walled garden for crossbow contests.
At first he regarded the diversion as a waste of time in trifling, but
his scorn turned to respect. "I was often in the number when the
King, measuring the shots, would give his body exercise while dis-
cussing governmental problems."

King and poet had long colloquies on literary and historical
subjects. King Robert urged Petrarch to find the lost books of Livy
(which are still lost). There is some reason to believe that the two
sketched the first modern map of Italy. Petrarch showed the King
some samples from his *Africa*, in preparation. And at Petrarch's
urging the King subjected him to a three-day private examination
on his qualifications for the laureateship. The subject was poetry,
its nature, uses, and devices, a subject on which the examiner was

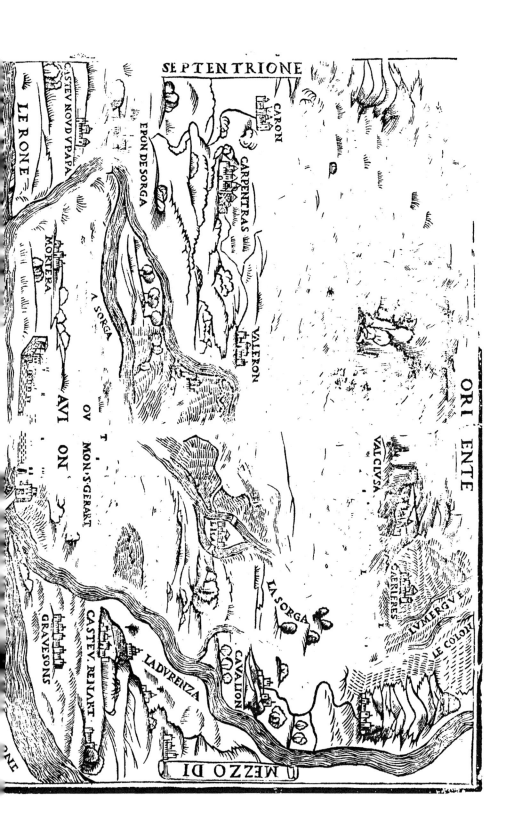

Map from *Il Petrarcha con l'espositione d'allessandro Vellvtello e con molte altre vtilis sime cose in diversi Lvoghi di qvella nvovamente da Lvi aggivnte . . .* (Vinegia, Bernardino de Vidali, 1528). The Lilly Library, Indiana University.

much less informed than the examinee. A public examination followed, which Boccaccio attended, worshiping. Naturally Petrarch passed *summa cum laude,* and Robert formally declared him worthy to receive the laurel. The King asked even that the poet receive the crown immediately from his own hands, but Petrarch, using all his tact, explained that he was bound by the invitation from Rome.

Petrarch was in Naples for about a month. He made there two lasting, faithful friends—Giovanni Barrili and Barbato da Sulmona. Barrili, Royal Chamberlain, was of the highest Neapolitan nobility. Later he underwent a troubled period as Seneschal of Provence. Barbato da Sulmona was of lower rank, a lawyer and bureaucrat. He and Petrarch were congenial from the first, being of like age, character, and habits, and sharing an enthusiasm for classical letters. With these two Petrarch saw the sights of Naples: the fearful cave of the Sybil, who was mute for them; the torpid, evil lake of Avernus, whose sulfurous smell gave proof that Tartarus lay not far below; the squalid marsh of Acheron; Virgil's tomb and the half-mile tunnel below it, which Virgil was said to have magically pierced in a single night. (But the wise King pointed out that there were unmistakable tool-marks on the walls.)

The time came for the candidate to leave for his coronation in Rome. The King, regretting that his years prevented his making the trip, appointed Giovanni Barrili his representative at the ceremony. He took off his royal robe and put it on the poet's shoulders, asking him to wear it at the crowning. The action followed Oriental tradition, symbolizing the conferral of the donor's qualities and powers, absorbed in the fabric, on the recipient. The King kissed Petrarch farewell, and uttered his last wish, that Petrarch would write a poem in his honor.

Petrarch took his humble leave. He rode with Azzo da Correggio to Rome, arriving on Good Friday, April 6, 1341. That fateful day! The fourteenth anniversary of his meeting with Laura, who had stimulated him to become a great poet! Maybe she would be sorry when she learned how everyone except herself rendered him proper honor!

Giovanni Barrili did not appear. It was later learned that he had met brigands on his way to Rome, and had been forced to turn back.

On Easter Day the coronation took place. According to an eye-witness account (which has, to be sure, been impugned by some modern scholars), a procession was formed, headed by twelve noble youths in scarlet, reciting poems composed by Petrarch for the occasion. Then came six principal citizens, in green and crowned with flowers. Then the Senator, Orso dell' Anguillara, Petrarch's host at Capranica in 1337. He wore a laurel wreath, as did his eminent attendants, among them old Stefano Colonna. The procession climbed the Capitoline Hill, the site of the Temple of Jupiter. It entered the twelfth-century Senatorial Palace and mounted to the audience chamber on the second floor.

The officials took their places. Trumpets sounded, and the candidate for the laureateship was bidden to stand forth. He appeared, bareheaded, wearing King Robert's royal gown. He pronounced his Coronation Oration, lasting about half an hour, and concluding with a request for the laurel crown of poetry. He then cried three times: "Long live the Roman people and the Senator, and God maintain them in liberty!" He knelt before the Senator, who after a short speech asked the assembled citizens if they approved the award. They did so, weeping. The Senator took from his head the laurel crown and placed it on Petrarch's, saying: "This crown is the reward of merit." Petrarch recited a sonnet on the heroes of Rome, which has not survived. The audience clapped and shouted: "Long live the Capitol and the Poet!" Petrarch admits that he was in a kind of intoxication, blushing at the applause and praise.

The procession then reformed and marched to St. Peter's, where Petrarch laid his crown among the offerings. Then Stefano Colonna gave a very fine banquet for the chief participants in the ceremony.

Petrarch received from the Senator a splendid diploma, or privilege, which he had helped to compose. The document gave him the right to wear in public a crown of laurel, beech, or myrtle, and the poet's costume. (What is the poet's costume? Dante was buried in one, but no one has thought to describe it.) He received the right to teach, dispute, interpret, and compose on all poetic and historical subjects in all places whatsoever. He was further declared a Roman citizen. This was a matter of great importance, for Petrarch was a stateless man, an exile from Florence and a mere transient without civic rights in Avignon. A stateless man was a helpless unprotected waif in Italy. Petrarch was henceforth to proudly proclaim himself a Roman, with the right to speak for his city and reprove her at need.

His Coronation Oration is an important document in literary history, a significant statement of the nature of poetry and of the poet. It has been printed only once in Latin, once in French, and once in English. It should be better known.

In sermon fashion, he first states his text, from Virgil's *Georgics:*

> Sed me Parnasi deserta per ardua dulcis
> raptat amor.

"A sweet love draws me up on the lonely, arduous slopes of Parnassus." He salutes then the Virgin with an Ave Maria, thus making clear that humane learning is in harmony with faith. He develops his text, noting that literary eminence is high and difficult, and that it can be attained only through love, or impassioned desire. "Study without love and without a certain delight and gusto of the mind does not bring the desired effects."

The poet's task is hard by its very nature. "Whereas in the other arts one may reach one's goal through study and toil, it is quite otherwise with the art of poetry, in which nothing is accomplished without a kind of inner power, divinely infused in the poet's spirit." The poet's task is rendered the harder by the materialism of the surrounding world, and Petrarch has himself suffered from the hostility of fate. But "my desire is so strong that it seems to me that I shall conquer—and that I have conquered."

On the other hand the poet is aided in his arduous ascent by his eagerness to exalt the honor of the Republic, by the charm of glory for his person, and by his stimulation of others to poetic endeavor. "Since others are reluctant I have not feared to offer myself as guide for this toilsome path—perhaps even dangerous to me—and many, I think, will follow after."

He then speaks briefly of his concept of poetry. He quotes Lactantius: the poet "should take things that have really occurred and transform them by means of oblique figures, with a certain beauty, into things of a different sort. But to invent all that one writes is foolish; that is to be a liar rather than a poet." Poets have

set forth physical, moral, and historical truths under the veil of
fictions, and with deliberate obscurity, for "poetry is all the
sweeter as its truth is more laboriously sought, and hence is the
more delightful when discovered." Such is the poet's mission. "I
should like to seem a poet, in order not to be something else."

The poet's reward consists in the undoubted satisfaction of personal glory in his lifetime, and even more in the hope of earthly
fame after death, indeed, of immortality. He may likewise confer
immortality on his subjects; how many mighty men and warriors
have passed into oblivion for lack of a poet to celebrate their works
and spirits!

Petrarch concludes with a statement of the holy properties of
the laurel. It is unwithering and incorruptible; it is immune to
lightning; when a sleeping person is touched by its leaves his
dreams come true.

This little *Ars poetica,* brief though it is, elucidates Petrarch's
high conception of the poet and his work. He insists on reality as
a necessary base for fiction; he warns against the excesses of the
undisciplined imagination. Poetry is for him the transformation
of reality by means of a set of symbols that the reader must penetrate. He demands of the reader intellectual as well as emotional
participation. In this demand he is in complete accord with modern poetic practice and critical theory.

One may notice his offer to help other poets, suggesting that he
foresaw an intellectual renaissance in his times. One may observe
that his symbol of the ascent of Parnassus recalls, perhaps uncon-
sciously, the reality of his climb up Mont Ventoux. And one may
suppose that in his long celebration of the laurel his thoughts
dwelt upon Laura.

Well, it was a great occasion. "From the downfall of Rome,
perhaps even from the time of Plato and Aristotle, a poet and
thinker, a man of words, was never so honored by the general public as was Petrarch." What a contrast was his case to the neglect
and hostility suffered by Dante! Petrarch gained at a stroke an immense and lasting fame, and he established a precedent for the
honoring of poets and for the honor of poetry. "Everyone thought
that the happy reign of Saturn had come," said Boccaccio.

Of course the reaction followed. The jealousies Petrarch foresaw came to utterance. An unidentified critic alleged that he had never heard of the poet until he was crowned, that the ceremony and the laureate were ridiculous, and that anyway poetry is puerile and poets are liars, and mad. Petrarch wrote two furious rebuttals in verse, one ending "Sus nulla Minervem!"—a pig is nothing to Minerva.

The critics and cavilers were, however, unimportant. The coronation remained a supreme event in literary history, the recognition of poetry as a contemporary art and as a civic and public good. It may even be taken to mark the beginning of the literary Renaissance in Italy, as the symbol of the revival of classic culture and of the consciousness of a new culture beginning to bloom.

The coronation was also a supreme event in Petrarch's life. Though later he modestly pretended to put away the crown, his gesture was no more convincing than that of Caesar. The laurel consecrated the work he had already done; it gave him confidence in the value of his own thoughts and words. Does not Bergson say: "We cling to praise and honors in the exact degree in which we are not sure of having succeeded"? (He does.) The coronation gave Petrarch a background of authority—Rome. As Rome's fosterling, he dared to speak as a Roman to Rome and to the world. The laurel forced him to merit his eminence by new and better work. It altered his concept of himself. He could not long be satisfied to dream by the emerald waters of Vaucluse. The laureate had his obligations to Rome, to Italy, and to posterity. He had to do his duty to poetry.

XIII: PARMA—AND *AFRICA*

> *Joy: Yea, what say you unto it, that I write
> books myself?*
> *Reason: A publique disease, contagious, and
> incurable.*
>
> —De remediis (Phisicke against Fortune),
> *I 43*

PETRARCH AND AZZO DA CORREGGIO LEFT
Rome together toward the end of April 1341. After a brush
with brigands just outside the walls they turned back, obtained a sufficient guard, and traveled north to Pisa. On the way
Azzo confided to the poet that he and his three brothers were about
to conduct a quick revolution in Parma that would put them in
absolute control. He urged Petrarch to pay a long visit to the city,
promising him honor and ease and an opportunity to pursue his
literary ambitions in peace. Petrarch was easily persuaded. Parma
bade fair to be more interesting than Vaucluse, the new patron
more openhanded than Cardinal Colonna.

Parma is one of the ancient cities that stand on the Via Emilia,
the Roman road that runs with hardly a curve over the Lombard
plain, along the edge of the Apennines, from Rimini through
Bologna, Modena, Parma, and Piacenza to Milan. For modern
readers Parma suggests Stendhal's Charterhouse and the castle
where Fabrice was imprisoned, but these were not built in Petrarch's time.

The revolution duly occurred on May 21, 1341. Tyranny, in
the person of the Correggi's nephew, Mastino della Scala of Verona, was overthrown, and the reign of justice, liberty, prosperity,
and peace, personified by the four Correggi, began. It is true that
to obtain the aid of Milan they had made a secret pact with its
hated tyrant, Luchino Visconti, promising to hand over Parma
to Milan in four years. But probably none of those concerned expected that the pact would be honored.

Petrarch arrived in Parma on the day after the uprising, and

PARMA

found the city seething with joy. He wrote a fulsome canzone, celebrating the triumph of that Royal Heart, Correggio (*Cor regio*). But later he chose to omit the poem from his authorized *Canzoniere*.

The Correggi were as good as their word. After presenting Petrarch to the local men of mark ("Ser Petrarca, you know, has just received the laurel crown in Rome. You must ask him to recite something"), they offered him a summer retreat in their castle of Rossena, fourteen miles to the south. It stands, half ruined, on a northern spur of the Apennines, above the village of Ciano and the small river Enza. Near the castle lies a sweetly wooded high plateau called Selvapiana, whence one looks afar across the immense plain of the Po even to the faint distant wall of the Alps.

Selvapiana, like Vaucluse, responded to deep rhythms in the poet's spirit. Natural beauty operated on him almost violently, provoking uplifted words to match his uplift of spirit. He was always stirred by the peace of murmuring woodlands and by great rolling views. He describes the plateau, the cool green under tall beech trees, the springing waters, the birds and beasts. He had a special flowery knoll, bird-haunted, inviting to reposeful inspiration.

He sent his thoughts to Laura, far away beyond the plains and mountains. He wrote for her one of the most beautiful and famous of his canzoni (CXXIX):

> From thought to thought, from mountain-peak to mountain,
> love leads me on; for I can never still
> my trouble on the world's well-beaten ways.
> If on a barren heath there springs a fountain,
> or a dark valley huddles under a hill,
> there may the harrowed soul find quiet days;
> there freely she obeys
> love's orders, laughing, weeping, hoping, fearing;
> and the face plays the mimic to the soul,
> now glad, now charged with dole,
> not long in any manner persevering.
> At sight of me a man of subtle wit
> would say: "He burns, and sees no end of it."
>
> In the high mountains, in the woods I find
> a little solace; every haunt of man

is to my mood a mortal enemy.
At every step a new thought comes to mind
of my dear lady, whose remembrance can
turn all the hurt of love to gayety.
I would no sooner be
quit of this bittersweet existence here
than I reflect: "Yet even now Love may
destine the better day.
I, loathing self, may be to others dear!"
So I go thinking, hoping, sighing, now;
May it be true indeed? And when? And how?

And in the shade of a pine tree or a hill
I halt; and all the tumbled rocks near by
are pictured with the beauty of her face.
And tears of tender melancholy fill
my bosom; and "Alas! Alas!" I cry;
"What have I come to? From how far a place?"
But, for the little space
that the uneasy mind thus looks on her,
rapt out of self into another sphere,
then I feel Love so near
that the tricked soul rejoices it should err.
So clear I see her, and so fair and pure,
that I pray only that the fraud endure.

Often I've seen her—who'll believe me now?
treading the grass, cleaving the lucid water,
alive, alive, in a forest beech-tree caught,
white mid the clouds; so fair, Leda would vow
the famous beauty of her lovely daughter
is dimmed as a star when the broad sun beams hot.
And in what savage spot
I chance to be, on what most barren shore,
ever more beautiful she walks with me.
Then when Truth makes to flee
my darling cheat, I find myself once more
a dead stone statue, set on living stone,
of one who thinks and grieves and writes alone.

Now it's my whole desire and all my pleasure
up to the highest mountain-ridge to climb
to dizzy and unshadowed solitude.
And thence I send my flying gaze to measure

my length of woe. I weep a little time;
the mist of grief blows from my dismal mood.
I stare afar and brood
on the leagues that lie between me and that face,
ever so near and yet so far away.
Soft to myself I say:
"My soul, be brave. Perhaps, in that far place,
she thinks of you in absence, and she sighs!"
Then my soul suddenly wakes and gladly cries.

My song, beyond these alps,
in the land where skies are gayer and more clear,
you'll see me soon, where a quick streamlet flows
and where the fragrance blows
of the fresh Laurel that I love so dear.
There is my heart, and she who reft it me;
here you may see only my effigy.

In the heady mountain air of Selvapiana, environed by beauty,
Petrarch was inspired to continue his interrupted *Africa,* and in
Parma during the following winter he worked at it with a zeal
that, late in life, still amazed him.

Africa is the first true epic poem of modern times, unless one
broadens the definition to include *Beowulf,* the *Chanson de
Roland,* the *Nibelungenlied,* and the *Divine Comedy.* Probably
Petrarch planned it in twelve books, like the *Aeneid,* and perhaps
he wrote them, though we possess only nine. His purpose was to
glorify eternal Rome, of which he was now a proud citizen. He
wished also to give the unworthy Romans of his time a sense of
their peerless past and to inspire them by example to reestablish
their city as the spiritual center of Italy and of the world.

The poet begins by invoking the favor of the Muses, Jesus
Christ, and King Robert of Naples. He sketches the historical
background of the Punic Wars, and introduces Scipio, his hero.
Scipio's father, Publius, appears to his son in a vision, reviews the
previous history of Rome, and foretells the future greatness of the
Roman Empire and its eventual downfall. He foresees that even
in disaster Rome will still be queen of the world, like an old lion-
ess whose roar continues to terrify and subdue the forest. Rome
will live till the world perishes!

In the Virgilian manner, Petrarch seizes the opportunity to

make flattering references to his contemporaries, such as Stefano
Colonna, and even to himself. Old Publius says to Scipio:

> I seem to see a young man born in the land of the Etruscans who will
> retell your exploits, like a second Ennius. . . . He will stay the fleeing
> Muses with his songs; he will prolong our life on earth. I love him for
> his services to us; he will be inspired not by force, money, fear, hate,
> ambition, but only by admiration for our great deeds, by love of truth.
> . . . But this too will pass; and when books perish, you will suffer an-
> other death.

Scipio sends his dear friend Laelius to Africa, to enlist King
Syphax of Numidia as an ally. Laelius spends most of his stay in
Numidia relating the history of Rome and of Scipio himself, but
he does not persuade Syphax to join the Romans.

The tragic love of Rome's ally, King Massinissa, and Sophonisba, King Syphax's queen, is then recounted. Massinissa appears
as the doomed, fatal lover of modern Romanticism. To express his
despair Petrarch finds some eloquent and moving lines. Sophonisba, to resolve an intolerable situation, thirstily drinks poison.

The Punic War goes on, following the directions of Livy. (In-
cidentally, Petrarch gives the Carthaginians a magnetic compass.)
We have a scene in heaven, before the throne of Jove. Jove blends
somehow with Jehovah: "I will put on flesh, descend to earth, accept the burdens of humanity, suffer a shameful death! . . . Rome
will be my holy city. And I shall come soon, so captured am I by a
placid Virgin, so allured by her breasts filled with sacred milk!"

Hannibal is defeated, and Scipio pacifies Africa. A Carthagin-
ian ambassador comes to Rome to sue for peace. He is taken on a
tour of the city. We have a picture of Rome in its greatness, with
its palaces, temples, sculpture, aqueducts. Peace is concluded, and
Scipio, accompanied by the poet Ennius, sails for Rome. Ennius
discourses on the art of poetry. He says that the poet must construct his fiction on truth. On this base

> he may hide himself under a varied, agreeable cloud, imposing a long
> but pleasant labor on the reader, that the sense may be the more dif-
> ficult in the search, the more delightful in the discovery. All that has to
> do with history, the practice of virtue, the lessons of life, the study of
> nature, is the realm of poetry, only on condition that things otherwise
> bald and bare be hidden under a shroud, and that they deceive the
> sight by a thin veil, now hiding, now revealing. One who makes up
> everything does not deserve the name of poet, but that of liar.

(Ennius is quoting Petrarch's Coronation Oration.) Ennius adds that the poet is rewarded by the laurel crown, which insures immortality.

Homer appears, and spotlights the vale of Vaucluse. "Who is this youth about to bind green laurel on his brow?" exclaims Ennius. Why, who but Petrarch? "He will recall the long-fled Muses, and will restore the ancient sisters to Helicon! And he will write *Africa!* And be crowned on the Capitol, escorted by the Senate! He will be as dear to Rome as a woman's late-born son! A scholar, he will celebrate ancient Rome and the Romans, especially Scipio. He will write big books on history. Who can tell all that he bears yet hidden in his mind?"

Ennius takes a quiet look at the dreaming bard. He sees a young man, his brow laden with care, seated, pen in hand, on the greensward among trees and limpid streams, cool fountains, beetling crags. Says Homer: "Behold these shady groves. Hence he will raise his spirit to these noble tasks. Later, traveling by land and sea, he will let his projects lie fallow for years. But when freed from the storms of worldly affairs, he will write again."

(Thus the *Africa* is in part a poem about the poet writing the poem. This practice is to be condemned.)

In conclusion, Petrarch proclaims that the *Africa* will long outlive its author, for the Lethean sleep of his country will not last forever. The shadows will lighten, and our descendants will again bask in the pure ancient light! Then you will see Helicon bloom again, its sacred laurels green with leaves. Mighty but reverent minds will appear; literary passion will redouble the love for the Muses.

> Do thou, my *Africa,* remember to keep my name fresh. Thanks to thee, may fame visit my tomb and honor attend my ashes. Life will be sweeter to me among such a people; my glory will defy the grave. Traverse, unknown, the succession of heedless generations, lodging only with some rare, humble friend until the new age shall come. Then assume a new youth, when the light kind to poets shall shine, and an age shall dawn to bless and favor all good men.

It would be pleasant to announce that such an age has dawned, and that the *Africa* is about to burst forth on the world in glory. But the fact is that to this heedless generation the book is balefully, Cyclopeanly dull. It is duller than Voltaire's *Henriade,* duller than the *Faerie Queene.* Even those who are accustomed to reading unreadable books in the line of business have to fight their way through it. And since it is unreasonable to compound dullness upon dullness by dwelling on a great poet's failures, I shall be brief.

The poem has recognizable merits. It makes at least an effort to be realistic in its evocation of history. It eschews magic, monsters, the trappings of medieval romance. It contains some fine Virgilian lines, for example:

> Facili labuntur secula passu:
> Tempora diffugiunt; ad mortem curritis; umbra,
> Umbra estis pulvisque levis vel in ethere fumus
> Exiguus, quem ventus agat.

There are some sustained passages, as on the woes of Sophonisba, wherein private emotion warms the poetic fancy. But mostly the poem is cold, false, and dead. The structure is incoherent, the movement sluggish, the characters crudely drawn. The apparatus of the classical epic is a heavy burden, with the background of mythology, the parades of classical heroes, the prophetic dreams, the apostrophes to Fortune and other abstractions, the endless flash-backs, the long comparisons, introduced by "not otherwise than." The poem is a doomed exercise in scholarly imitation.

Petrarch was trying to write a best-seller. He whipped it up with bloodshed and sex, but the blood is mere paint, and the sex is posed and motionless, as in the neo-classic pictures of Jacques Louis David. Clearly, Petrarch lacked the creative imagination and the narrative gift necessary for his enterprise. He was an introspective, bound within his own experience; he could not penetrate the souls of others. His quality, in short, was that of the lyric, not the epic, poet.

His own attitude toward the poem was ambiguous. Often it seemed to him magnificent. He boasted of it, to himself and others, appealing confidently to the judgment of posterity. He wrote in 1349: "I worked at *Africa* with such ardor that now, as I am polishing it, I wonder at my own courage, and I am almost frightened at the massive foundations I laid." The book had to be good, for he had received the laureateship largely on the promise of a great epic for Italy. To disavow *Africa* would be a disavowal of his right to the laurel crown.

And yet he knew in his heart that the great work was misbegotten. Eager as he was for praise, he permitted only a few of his chosen friends to read excerpts, under solemn pledges of secrecy. He admits that despite the labors of many years he can't find the right path, that his book wanders in darkness toward the grave. His contemporary, Vergerio, says that at the mention of the *Africa* he showed his distress by his look. Another early writer, Beccadelli, says that on hearing the one revealed passage sung, Petrarch wept because he could not suppress it. He threatened to burn the whole; Boccaccio, who had been permitted to read a part, protested, calling the poem divine, Italy's sublimest honor.

Petrarch's reluctance to publish *Africa* was reenforced by circumstance. In Naples in 1343 he allowed his friend Barbato da Sulmona to copy the thirty-four-line speech of the dying King Mago, a bravura passage on death and hope. Barbato violated his pledge of secrecy; the passage was soon in circulation, and was severely criticized, especially in Florence. Petrarch heard that some base listeners had actually laughed! But this is an offense against the holy Muses!

All his life he kept his poem by him, a torturing possession. He worked at it intermittently, especially up to 1349. His friends clamored for a glimpse of it, promising themselves a rare literary delight. But much as Petrarch desired the world's praise, he feared even more its disappointment. He was often on the verge of burning the manuscript, and in fact it is likely that he destroyed about three books, thus leaving gaping lacunae in our text. In the end he left most of it for his vindication by posterity. When it was published after his death, most readers were disconcerted. Leonardo Bruni has a character in one of his dialogues say that Petrarch's labors have brought forth a ridiculous mouse. So far, posterity has been no kinder. But posterity has still a long time to go.

At the summer's end Petrarch returned to Parma. The Correggi put at his disposal a small retired house with a garden and an orchard and a brook between. Nothing could have delighted the poet more. Visitors were instructed to respect his solitude, but when solitude palled he was assured of diversion and adulation at the Parmesan court. He found in the city a congenial group of literary enthusiasts, including a bibliophile physician, two humane schoolmasters, and a scholar-poet, who became his friends and correspondents for life.

He received a picturesque testimony to his fame, which he later
remembered with justifiable complacency. There was an old blind
poet-school-teacher in Pontremoli, near La Spezia on the Ligurian coast. In the spring of this year 1341 he learned that Petrarch
had gone to Naples. He summoned his son to guide him, and made
the toilsome journey thither, hoping only to stand in the presence
of his idol. He came too late. King Robert gave him audience and
was deeply struck by his blind, bronze dignity. "Your poet is in
Rome," said the King. "You must hurry, or you will have to pursue him into Gaul." "If life permits," said the old man, "I will
pursue him even to the Indies!" Leaning on his son, he stumbled
over the rough roads to Rome, and came again too late. The two
had perforce to return to Pontremoli. During the winter the old
man learned that Petrarch was in Parma. He crossed the Apennines, his son guiding the blind feet up through the snows and
down the icy slopes. Overcome by emotion, he embraced Petrarch,
exclaiming: "I have come all this way to see you!" Everyone
laughed loudly at the idea of a blind man seeing, and he rejoined,
affronted: "I see him much more clearly than do these who have
eyes." He remained by Petrarch's side for three days, continually
praising God for according him such happiness.

Petrarch's stay in Parma was saddened by news of death. He
came to the point where he could not open a letter without trembling and paling. Tommaso Caloiro, a dear companion of college
days in Bologna, "without whom I could not move a step," died
in Messina. And his confessor, Dionigi da Borgo San Sepolcro,
who had effectively promoted his campaign for the laureateship.
And finally and most dreadfully, his beloved Bishop Giacomo
Colonna.

Two (or three?) years later, Petrarch, sitting in his Parma garden, described to a friend how Giacomo Colonna had appeared to
him in a prophetic dream. Petrarch had heard of Giacomo's illness, and was anxiously awaiting news. Asleep in bed, he suddenly
saw his friend in vision.

> He was alone, and was crossing the little brook in my garden. In
> amazement I ran to meet him, asking where he was coming from,
> whither going so fast and all alone. He didn't answer my questions,
> but—he was always joking—he said, smiling: "Do you remember when
> you were living with me beyond the Garonne, and how you hated

those Pyrenean thunderstorms? Well, I've got sick of them, and I'm going to Rome, and I won't return." While saying this he had walked hurriedly to the end of the garden. I begged him to take me with him; but he pushed me back gently with his hand a couple of times, and said, with a change of expression and voice: "Stop; I don't want you with me now." I stared at him, and I saw by his pallor that he was dead. Distressed and frightened, I cried out; and waking at the same moment, I heard the end of my own cry. I made a note of the day, and told the story to some friends and wrote of it to others. Twenty-five days later the news of his death was brought to me. I compared the times, and found that he had died on the very day when he had appeared to me.

Petrarch's comment on his telepathic experience is cautious enough. He recognizes the possibility of coincidence, and agrees with Cicero that for one dream proved true thousands are false.

At the end of the winter or in the early spring of 1342 Petrarch left his cordial friends in Parma and returned to Avignon. We do not know exactly why. He had been absent from home for over a year. Perhaps Cardinal Colonna wanted his useful secretary back. Perhaps Petrarch was homesick for Vaucluse in the springtime; perhaps he was worried about Gherardo; perhaps he wanted to see Laura again.

XIV: CRISIS

> *Deep and dark are the hidden places of the*
> *human spirit, and the color of thoughts is not*
> *to be discerned in that gloom.*
>
> —Sen. IX 2

IN THIS SPRING OF 1342 POPE BENEDICT XII WAS
dying of a fistula. Petrarch wrote Philippe de Cabassoles,
Bishop of Cavaillon, a really shocking letter, describing the
ship of the papacy racing to its wreck, guided by an old, incompetent, drunken steersman. The writer rejoiced in the Pope's imminent disappearance, and assumed that the Bishop would rejoice
with him.

He died on April 25. The Conclave immediately met, and
elected another Frenchman, who took the name of Clement VI.
A Benedictine monk, of gentle though not noble birth, he was a
celebrated preacher and theologian and had been Provisor, or Director, of the Sorbonne and Archbishop of Rouen. According to
contemporaries his fault was that he was not very religious. His
memory was phenomenal; Petrarch attributes its quality to a fortunate blow on the head. His Benedictine erudition was balanced
by an aristocratic courtliness of manner and by an equally aristocratic openhandedness. In fact he was so liberal of the Church's
wealth and offices that eventually he exhausted the treasures laid
up by his predecessors. Aristocratically also, he was fond of horses
and women. He had a sort of papal hostess, his niece, Cécile, Vi-
comtesse de Turenne, whom Petrarch calls "Semiramis," and of
whom everybody readily believed the worst. She was accused of
being the chief agent for the acquirement, and even the purchase,
of benefices.

Toward Petrarch the new Pope showed immediate and continuing favor. One of his first acts was to appoint Petrarch to a can-

onry in the cathedral of Pisa, on the recommendation of Cardinal
Colonna. In October he further proved his benevolence by con-
ferring on the poet a priory in the Pisa diocese. Unfortunately it
turned out that the priory was already occupied. Petrarch brought
suit to obtain possession; after two years a papal commission upheld his rival.

An unlearned modern reader may marvel that a wandering
and worldly poet, with no more qualification than a bit of hair-
clipping, could hold canonries in the cathedrals of Lombez and
Pisa and a priory as well, that he could refrain from ever visiting
the scenes of his nominal duties, and that he could draw the revenues with no qualms of conscience. But an abuse, if sufficiently
widespread, is no longer an abuse. Let the inheritor of ownership,
the vacationist on an expense account, the professor gamboling
on a foundation grant, be prepared to cast the first stone.

Soon after the Pope's coronation a deputation arrived from
Rome to beg him to return to the eternal but ravaged city. Petrarch's aid was enlisted; he wrote a long metrical epistle to the
Pope. Clement listened with his usual grace, but declared that,
sympathetic though he was to the idea, the time was not ripe; the
war between France and England obliged him to remain in Avignon, in closer touch than he could be in Rome. He consented,
however, to declare a Papal Jubilee in Rome for the year 1350.

Petrarch presumably lived with Cardinal Colonna and served
him at need. He was busy also with his compilations, especially his
biographical series, *De viris illustribus*. He began his *Liber rerum
memorandarum*, or *De rebus memorandis*, a record of notable and
surprising events in both ancient and modern times.

In the summer of 1342 the Greek monk Bernard Barlaam,
whom Petrarch had met in Avignon in 1339, returned to the city.
He had become a convert to the Roman Church, and was at Court
looking for a job, as converts do. Petrarch arranged to exchange
with him lessons in elementary Greek for advanced Latin. The
two met daily for a time, but Petrarch did not learn much beyond
the elements of Greek. He could hardly have learned much, without a grammar or dictionary and with an unskilled teacher talking bad Latin. Imagine trying to learn Greek by spelling out word
by word a dialogue of Plato! Anyway, the lessons soon came to an
end, in part by Petrarch's doing, for he warmly supported his

teacher's successful candidacy for a bishopric in Greek-speaking Calabria.

All his life Petrarch regretted that he had so generously cast away his one opportunity to penetrate Greek beauty and wisdom. He collected Greek books, and loved to dandle and caress them, imploring them to break their muteness. His effort to learn Greek was a rare novelty in his time. Others, like Boccaccio, imitated him, but not till the arrival of Chrysoloras in Florence in 1395 did the revival of Greek studies in Italy take place.

One recognizes that in this summer of 1342 Petrarch was in Avignon, not in his beloved Vaucluse; and one may even wonder if Vaucluse was actually so beloved after all. He wrote a friend, seven years later, to be sure: "Vaucluse could well offer a very pleasant diversion for a brief time to those who are sick of the tedium of city pleasures, but in the long run it couldn't promise or provide the necessaries of life." Evidently he came to regard Vaucluse as merely a delightful retreat from the compelling urgencies of Avignon. The urgencies were at this time very compelling. He had his court to pay to the new Pope, in the effort to obtain his benefices. He had his Greek lessons. He was worried about Gherardo, who was going through something of a crisis. The sight of Laura after a year and a half of absence opened his old wounds, the hemophilia of his heart. And there were other urgencies, of which, for good reasons, he tells us nothing.

There are hints that he passed through a stage of aroused sensuality. A ballata, *Donna mi vene spesso nella mente,* expunged from the *Canzoniere,* reveals the existence of a rival to Laura; for her he is filled with desires. And some time in 1343 he fathered a daughter, named Francesca after him. The mother is unknown; she may or may not have been the mother of his son Giovanni, who was now five years old. Francesca may have been conceived at any time between March 1342 and March 1343. Psychologically, the most likely time is the summer or autumn of 1342, for this conviction of disloyalty to ideal love, to clerical rectitude, and to his own image as a divine poetic moralist may have worked cruelly on his spirit, bringing him to the tragic self-critical mood of the following winter. Nor are we to overlook the financial strains, which become spiritual strains, upon a poet saddled with an unwanted household.

These are specific, identifiable causes for a state of psychological depression. There were others less tangible. Petrarch was now thirty-eight years old, past the mid-point of life, when a man begins to be conscious of decline and fall, of his own mortality. He had been deeply shaken by the deaths of friends, his contemporaries in age. He was further shaken by the death, in February 1343, of his kind patron, King Robert of Naples. Petrarch had struggled long for fame, and he had gained it officially on the Capitoline Hill. But the attainment of one's ambition is always disillusioning (or so we are told). Most people remained ignorant of his illustriousness, or were unimpressed by it. I suspect that even Laura was more interested in her children's health, or in Avignon gossip, than she was in the poet's crowning. He found himself unchanged; he was still unsure of his actual eminence in worth, and was tortured by his failure to produce the supreme epic that would justify his laurel crown. His love for Laura was as exasperating as ever; the sight of her aroused new tears for old desires (Rime CXVIII). Lust had done its work better than love, and its product provoked him to anguished regret, if not repentance. He was haunted by a sense of unfulfilment, leading him even to melancholia, even to despair.

The crisis was of course the conclusion of a long development. Three years before he had written, in a moment of depression and in a time of pestilence, a poetic epistle to himself. Many are dying, he writes; I am filled with the terror of death; I think of my dear dead friends. I am like a sailor in tempest, a father in a burning house. How shall I save my soul? The world holds me, impetuous pleasures grip me, the violence of habit binds me. But death is at hand, and long plans are useless; now is the time to choose the right way, to renounce the flesh, to find peace.

The mere writing of such words was however sufficient discharge, sufficient solace, for the moment.

Now in 1343 the self-questioning became more acute. He wrote Guido Sette that he did not trust his own judgment of himself, that he was oppressed by human frailty, that he was prostrate in the filth of the flesh and in the bondage of mortal nature; but, though bowed under the yoke of inveterate habit, he was eager to rise clear of it. Probably at this time he wrote the splendid sonnet CLXXXIX with its haunting opening: *Passa la nave mia colma d'oblio,* "My ship is freighted with oblivion." It concludes: "Reason and skill are dead among the waves, so that I begin to despair of reaching harbor."

In whom could he confide, whom could he love, in expectation of return? Most of his best friends were far away or were dead. There was his brother Gherardo, of course; but Gherardo was parting company with him.

For Gherardo had found God. He had never assuaged his grief for the death of his beloved, a few years before. His life had not been very satisfactory to himself. He had not fulfilled his early promise. He may have had some small employment, or he may have lived on alms and patronage. Much though he loved and admired his brother, he must have been irked by dwelling forever in the great man's shadow. I see him as one of those intelligent, amusing ne'er-do-wells who brighten every small city by their rejection of accepted values. Now he found that he could live his own life by renouncing it, and that his renunciation would prove his spiritual superiority to his dominant elder brother. He meditated on abandoning the world and entering one of the severer religious orders. He must have often talked the matter over with his brother during the winter of 1342-1343. And Petrarch must have felt a mingling of repulsion, pain, admiration, and envy at the thought of such a step. In comparison, his own retreat to the sylvan joys of Vaucluse was a mere selfish indulgence.

Gherardo could not quite bring himself to the point of decision. He petitioned for a post as writer in the Curia. The Pope made the appointment on March 13, 1343. Perhaps the prospect of life in that "penitentiary" determined Gherardo to the alternative choice, or perhaps he was moved by the spiritual excitements of Lent and Easter, which fell on April 13. At this time (probably) he made a pilgrimage to the shrine of Sainte-Baume. In the holy gloom of the grotto the divine aid of Mary Magdalen conquered his wanton heart. He proceeded from the shrine (probably, again) over the stony mountains to the Carthusian monastery of Montrieux. There we find him in April 1343. In a farewell letter he adjured his brother to make a full confession of his sins, to say his offices regularly by day and by night, and to renounce the impurities of his life.

Montrieux lies in a well-wooded mountain valley, about twenty

miles due north of Toulon. The old monastic building, Montri-
eux-le-Vieux, established in the eighth century, was used as the
priory's infirmary and barns, the home of its flocks of sheep and
goats, the site of its tiny tannery and glass factory. A mile away
lies Montrieux-le-Jeune, the home of the monks. It was afterwards
pillaged and destroyed in the sixteenth-century wars of religion;
rebuilt, it was pillaged and destroyed during the Revolution. Rebuilt again in the nineteenth century, it was rendered desolate by
the banishment of the religious orders from France in 1901. But
not long ago the old monks came creeping back.

The white-robed, sandaled, head-shaven Carthusians serve one
of the grimmest and most rigorous of monastic bodies. Since their
founding by St. Bruno in 1084, in the Alps above Grenoble, they
have attracted men in extreme revulsion against their own sin and
the world's. Each monk has his little hermitage, where he lives,
works, and eats. He sees his fellows only at the midnight office,
which lasts two or three hours, at High Mass at 5 A.M., at Vespers,
and when, on high feasts, the day's one meal, frugal and meatless,
is taken together. Once a week the monks are allowed to take a
silent walk together outside their enclosure. At Montrieux the
silence was remitted for the conduct of a school and for the recep-
tion of visitors. (Indeed, many medieval monks dodged the rule
of silence by an elaborate sign language. A visitor objected to their
signals and hissings, and said he seemed to be watching a stage
play.)

The mere existence of the Carthusians and their diffusion in
French *Chartreuses,* English Charterhouses, Italian *Certose,* in-
validates the cynical generalizations about monastic behavior that
we draw from Boccaccio and others. All generalizations must by
their nature be partly false. All general rules must contain their
paradoxes. One striking Carthusian paradox is that these auster-
est of ascetics manufacture the sweetest of liqueurs for the feasts of
bons vivants and from its sales support their retreats and their
ample charities.

Gherardo entered the monastery as a novice brother, or oblate.
He sat below the choir monks, the priests. His entry into religion
deeply moved his brother. Again as on the slopes of Mont Ventoux
Petrarch saw Gherardo take the hard straight way to the summit,
while he was tempted to find a circuitous path, which turned out

to lead gently downward. Once more he had to admire his brother humbly, to recognize his own lack of courageous decision. And since he was above all things a literary man, his distress of spirit found its issue not in action but in literature.

In the time of his misery, he says, he composed in a single day of swelling emotion seven penitential psalms, based on the Psalms of David, but expressing his own woe and need. "David," he later wrote, "is my beloved poet; I want to have his Psalms ever in hand and before my eyes, awake or asleep; and when I come to die I want them for my pillow."

His psalms are very beautiful, done in the rolling Latin of the Vulgate. They attained a wide popularity; George Chapman (of Chapman's Homer) paraphrased them in English. They are the appeals of a desperate man, caught by the world's wiles, for divine aid in the salvation of his soul. And they are totally centered on himself; they are all "How I suffer! How I need the succor promised me!"

His First Psalm says, in summary: I have walked care-free in slippery places, and I have flattered myself in my sins. I thought that youth's splendor could not mislead me, and eagerly I followed its promptings. I said: "Why tease yourself about the ends? Every age has its own end. God sees all this, but he laughs at it; he will be ready with his pardon. You can be converted when you will!" But now evil habit holds me its slave. I know not where to flee; I shall die in my sins, unless I have help from on high. Lord, have mercy upon me!

The Fourth Psalm is a thanksgiving, stating his gratitude for God's mercies, and especially for the beauty of this world. It reads, in part:

For me hast thou created the sky and the stars and the succession of the seasons. . . . Thou hast dressed the fields with green grasses and the hills with flowers and the woods with leaves on every branch. Thou hast prepared rest for the weary, shades for the burning, and delightful nooks inviting to repose, and lucent springs for the thirsty, fruits and berries for the hungry. . . . Thou has loved man so far as to give him many pleasures, to me also; nay, with many particular gifts hast thou endowed me. Thou hast adorned man's body above that of all thy creatures; thou hast set his members in marvelous order. Thou has given him a face imperious and serene and a spirit capable of knowing thee and of contemplating heavenly things. . . . When I was falling thou hast sustained me, and hast held me when I slipped, and hast pointed the way when I was in error. Thou hast lifted me up when I lay prostrate, and hast brought me from death to life. Thou hast had compassion on my labors when I deserved not mercy but hate. . . Remember no more my ingratitude, but save my soul, which has no hope in its own power.

One may compare this psalm with St. Francis's *Song of the Creatures,* which similarly celebrates the beauties of our universe. But the Saint's creatures join in a great chorus of praise to God for their existence, while Petrarch's are chiefly sympathetic with the poet's despair.

His despair was, however, genuine and profound, as were his aspirations for a better life. Perhaps at this time, perhaps a year or two later, he wrote his splendid canzone of introspection (CCLXIV), *I' vo pensando,* examining the forces at work in his spirit, trying to understand his conflicts.

I go thinking [he says] in tears and self-pity. I have often asked God for power to escape the prison of mortal limitations. I reflect in terror on my state, on the dishonor of my life. An inner voice tells me: "Root out the impulse for pleasure; you know its false fugitive sweetness. You can master it by right thinking. Cast off your love for Laura; seek a higher love. For earthly love is appeased by a movement of the eyes, a word, a song, but heavenly love is above such enticements." And another voice murmurs of fame. I try to shut it out, in vain, well though I know the vanity of reputation among men. Only God can free me from these shameful passions for love and fame. I see my case clearly. Love is the enemy of honor; it is wrong to love mortal things with the ardor of divine love. Reason, obscured by the senses, proclaims this fact, but old evil habit drowns reason, presenting me forever with the image of her who was born to compass my death. Thus I am ever at war with myself, with shame struggling against a passion so strong that it will make a pact only with death. Let me then try to find a new rule of life, for I see the better way and choose the worse.

In the same mood of dubiety and aspiration he wrote in the troubled springtime of 1343 one of his great contributions to literature, his *Secretum,* his Secret Book.

XV: THE SECRET BOOK

> *You are my Secret Book; and you will recall
> to me in secret what you have recorded in
> secret.*
>
> —*Proem to* Secretum

THE SECRET BOOK WAS WRITTEN IN AVIGNON
in the winter of 1342-1343, before Gherardo's departure
for his monastery in April. Petrarch had been reading
Augustine's *De vera religione* with passion, neglecting the Roman
philosophers and poets. The reading sent him back to Augustine's
Confessions, wherein he found, with tears, not the story of another's pilgrimage, but his own. The Saint, he says, "first raised
me to the love of truth; he first taught me to breathe healthfully
who so long had been breathing poisoned air. May he remain
happy through endless time, who first freely offered me his hand,
and who put a bridle on my roving spirit."

Naturally, then, his own confession took the form of a dialogue
with the sympathetic heavenly spirit who had traveled his own
road through sin and error and had found salvation at the end of
it. Augustine has been well called Petrarch's conscience. Or one
may say that in the *Secretum* Franciscus is Petrarch's natural everyday self and that Augustinus is the secondary self, the Critic.
Petrarch's ability to imagine a dialogue of the two shows that the
Critic was dominant within him.

Since the book has never gained the diffusion it deserves, since
it is not readily available in most libraries, and since it has, or
should have, a high standing in literary history, I shall make of
it a long abstract, reducing it, however, to a fraction of its compass.

PROEM

Bemused, as is my frequent case, in reflections on how I had come into this life and how I should leave it, I was suddenly aware of a woman clothed in light and beauty. She said to me: "Fear not. In pity for your errors, I have descended from afar to bring you timely aid. Enough, and more than enough, have you gazed with clouded eyes at the ground. If hitherto they have found pleasure in mortal things, what may you not hope if you raise them to look at eternal matters?" "Who are you?" I asked, trembling. "I am Truth." Looking at her glorious face, I knew she could be none other.

As I was gazing on her with ineffable delight I perceived a venerable, majestic person by her side. I did not need to ask his name; his religious aspect, his modest air, his grave eyes, his sober bearing, his African dress, his Roman style, identified that most glorious Father. Augustine. His loving regard, sweeter than that of any human, removed all doubt. Truth turned to him and interrupted his profound meditation with the words: "O Augustine, dearest to me of all men, you know this man to be your devotee, and you know how he has suffered, all unaware, a long, dangerous illness. You must look to the life of this wasting man. None better than you could do this work of pity, since he has always worshiped your name, and since his miseries are similar to those you suffered when you were locked in the prison of the flesh." Said he: "I shall obey you, who have ever been my guide." And she: "I shall remain by your side during your colloquy."

Then we sat down, all three. And with Truth sitting in silent judgment by our side, the Saint and I engaged in a conversation that lasted three days. That our familiar talk might not be lost I have written it down in the measure of a little book, not that I wish to number it among my published works and attain glory thereby, but that I may read it over whenever I wish and taste again the sweetness of my experience.* So, my little book, you will flee all the concourse of men and you will be happy to remain alone with me, and you will never belie your name. For you are my *Secret Book,* and that will be your name. And when I am busy with more serious matters you will recall to me in secret what you have recorded in secret.

* If he had been totally sincere with himself he would not have needed to make this explanation.

To avoid the repetitions of "said he" and "said I" I shall represent our words in the form of a dialogue. I learned this style
from my Cicero, and he in his turn had learned it from Plato.*
But let us not digress. Augustine then addressed me as follows.

BOOK I

AUGUSTINUS: What are you doing, poor little man? What are
you dreaming? What do you look forward to? Have you then
forgotten all your miseries? Don't you remember that you are
mortal?

FRANCISCUS: Certainly I remember it. In fact, that thought
never comes to me without bringing a twinge of terror.

AUG.: I wish you did remember it, as you say. You would save
me a lot of trouble. The best way to despise properly the temptations of this life is to remember one's own misery and meditate
assiduously on death. The thought of death should penetrate
to the very marrow of your bones.

FR.: It does indeed. But the thought of death doesn't seem to
banish my distress of mind.

AUG.: Anyone who seriously longs to cast off his distresses
cannot be disappointed of his desire.

FR.: What's this? Everybody wants to get rid of his woes, and
very few have been able to. Most people are unhappy against
their will.

AUG.: I thought you were more intelligent. If you had properly absorbed the true and helpful words of the philosophers
you have read, if in fact you had studied for yourself and not for
others, if you had drawn from the reading of so many books a
rule for your own life instead of seeking vaingloriously the
windy applause of the vulgar, you wouldn't say such stupid
things.

FR.: You make me blush like a schoolboy. But still I don't
know what for.

AUG.: For many things; but first of all for your idea that a
man can be unhappy against his will.

FR.: Ah, I'll stop blushing! Everybody knows that poverty,
pain, ignominy, diseases, death, come against our will and without our agency. Hence it's easy to recognize our distresses and
easy to hate them, but it's not easy to get rid of them. The first

* Nor would he need this interesting fact if he intended the book for his
eyes alone.

two points are in our power, the third is in the power of
fortune.

AUG.: Your impudence makes me angrier than your mistakes.
Idiot, have you forgotten the words of the philosophers and
saints, that no one can be made miserable by such miseries? If
virtue alone renders man happy, the contrary of virtue must
render him unhappy.

FR.: That's Stoic doctrine, more theoretical than practical.

AUG.: Are we agreed on this, that a man becomes unhappy
only through vice?

FR.: Well, I've noticed that many, including me, are chiefly
tormented by our inability to shake off the yoke of vices, although we have struggled all our lives to that end with all our
powers. So one may admit that many are very miserable against
their will, while grieving and hoping for deliverance.

AUG.: I'll tell you the method of deliverance. The first step
is to meditate on death and human infelicity; the second is to
struggle with intense desire to rise.

FR.: It hasn't worked with me.

AUG.: In men's minds there is a perverse and pestilent longing to deceive oneself. You men should fear the frauds you per-
petrate on yourselves. Everyone esteems himself at more than
his worth and loves himself more than is his due. The deceived
is never separate from the deceiver.

FR.: You've said that before. But as far as I can remember I
have never deceived myself. I can only wish I hadn't been deceived by others.

AUG.: Right now you are deceiving yourself, in boasting that
you have never deceived yourself. Do you think that anyone can
sin perforce? Sin is a voluntary action; if the will is lacking, the
act ceases to be sinful.

FR.: I'll have to grant that. I feel it in myself and I conjec-
ture it in others. I suspect that I am being punished, that since
I didn't stand upright when I could, now that I want to rise
from my abjection I no longer can.

AUG.: Instead of "I no longer can," you should say: "I no
longer wish to."

FR.: I'll never confess that. Heaven knows—no man does—
how I have suffered and how I have longed to rise.

AUG.: Conscience may well have made you weep, but it has
not made you change your intentions. Certainly you could have

reformed, if you had really wished to. Look at my own story, in my Confessions.

FR.: I know all about that. Every time I read your Confessions I am moved by two contrary feelings, hope and fear. Sometimes it seems to me, in tears, that I am reading not another's story but the record of my own pilgrimage.

AUG.: You must learn from it to desire your amelioration passionately. Consult your own conscience. It is the best interpreter of virtue; it is the infallible, truthful judge of your thoughts and acts. It will tell you that you have never properly aspired to salvation.

FR.: My conscience tells me that is true. But how can this great desire work?

AUG.: In opening a way through difficulties. The desire for virtue is a large part of virtue. And this desire can arise only through the extinction of other desires. One must dare to say: "I have nothing further in common with the body; I am revolted by all the visible world; I aspire to greater felicities."

FR.: How can one attain this state?

AUG.: First, as I have already recommended, by the constant remembrance of your mortality.

FR.: So I don't meditate on death?

AUG.: Very rarely, in fact, and so limply that your meditation does not penetrate to the depths of your calamities.

FR.: I thought the opposite.

AUG.: I am not talking about what you thought, but about what you ought to think. You ought to think constantly about the fragility of your state and bear constantly before your eyes the image of your mortality. Few think profoundly that they must necessarily die. You must ever aspire to that life wherein you will cease to be mortal. So you must look continually on the picture of a dying man, on the chilling limbs, the burning, sweating breast, the gasping breath, the receding, filming, tear-filled eyes, the livid face, the sunken cheeks, the yellowed teeth, the sharp nose, the foam at the lips, the thick, dry tongue, the strangle in the throat, the revolting smell, and above all the horror of a face without intelligence.

FR.: I see that I must tell myself the whole truth.

AUG.: Think also of the final judgment, when you must give an account of all your deeds and words, when you can put no trust in wit and eloquence, riches and power, bodily beauty or worldly fame. You must think of heaven and hell not as possible but as necessary and inevitable. Then you may be sure that you have not meditated in vain.

FR.: You terrify me. And yet such meditations are familiar to me, especially at night, when the spirit, released from its daytime cares, collects itself within itself. Then I compose myself in the attitude of a dying man, and I picture vividly to myself the hour of death and all its horrible accompaniments, so that sometimes I seem to look into hell; and I am so shattered by this vision that I rise up all trembling, and I frighten anyone who is present by crying: "Alas, what is happening to me? And what will happen? Mercy, O dear Jesus, aid me!" I fall in a sort of fit; and when I tell my friends of it I move them to tears. Such being my case, what holds me back? What obstacle lies in my way, so that my nightmare meditations bring me only terror, but I remain what I was before, like those who have never known such experiences? I am worse off than they, for they enjoy their pleasures, whereas for me every pleasure is blended with bitterness.

AUG.: You should rather be happy because you are aware of your state. There is hope for you. You must reflect forever on the imminence of death, thanking God for his warnings. As for these midnight phantasms, they are not divinely sent, but are the products of a tortured spirit. Your salutary purpose for reform is weakened by the excessive mobility of your mind. Hence your inward discord, the anxiety of a mind that tortures itself and cannot bring itself to wash away its own stains. While it recognizes its own tortuous ways it does not desert them; while it fears the imminent danger it does not conjure it away.

FR.: Alas, wretched man that I am!

AUG.: Good! You are shaken out of your torpor. Now let us repose a little in silence, and leave the rest to tomorrow.

FR.: That is what I need: repose and silence.

BOOK II

AUG.: Did you sleep well?

FR.: Well enough.

AUG.: Let's return to our subject. Many evils assail you, but you don't realize how many and how mighty are your enemies. Let's take the capital sins in their order. First, the most grievous sin of pride. How petty are the superiorities you look on with complacency! You are proud of your intellect, of your reading of many books; you glory in your own high talk and in the

shape of your mortal body. And yet you recognize how often
that fine intellect fails you, and in how many ways you can't
equal the competence of the simplest of men. I'm putting it
mildly; there are mean, common animals whose powers you
could never imitate by any application. And you would glory in
your intelligence! All your reading, what good has it done you?
Of all the books you have read, how much has clung in your
spirit and taken root there, to produce fruit in its time? Examine yourself, and you will find that all you know, in comparison
with what you don't know, is only a tiny trickle compared with
the ocean. And what is the use of knowing many things if, when
you have learned the dimensions of heaven and earth, the measure of the seas, the courses of the stars, the virtues of plants and
stones, the secrets of nature, you still don't know yourself?*
What difference does it make that others applaud your words,
if these are not approved by your own inward judgment? What
can be more puerile, nay, insane, than, in your heedlessness and
sloth, to spend your time in the study of words, to find your
pleasure in talk, not even to perceive your own shame with your
bleary eyes? You are like those birds that, according to the story,
so delight in their own sweet song that they die of it. How often
have I heard you complain that neither tongue nor pen could
express the ideas that were clear enough in your thought! What
then is this rhetoric, so limited and frail that it can't embrace
its own subjects or possess what it has embraced! So much for
pride of mind! And as for your pride of body, what pleases you
therein? Perhaps its vigor and health? Nothing could be more
idiotic. A weakness arising from the slightest of causes, the attacks of illness, the bite of a worm, a poisonous exhalation, may
make an end of body. Or perhaps you think you're handsome,
and you look admiringly on your features and complexion?
Have you forgotten the fable of Narcissus? And the revolting
ugliness beneath the skin? And the approach of age's decay?

    FR.: Hold on a minute! You say I boast of my intelligence.
Well, the only intelligence I claim is that I have never trusted
it. Why should I be proud of reading many books, from which
I have derived little learning but much distress of mind? You
accuse me of seeking glory in fine language when, as you admit,
my chief torment is that it can't suffice to express my ideas. And
when you talked seriously about my beautiful body you almost

* A recollection of Augustine's words that Petrarch, on the summit of Mont
Ventoux, found in the *Confessions*.

made me laugh. So I have put my hope in this wretched mortal frame, which daily warns me of its frailty? Heaven forbid! I admit that when I was a boy I took pleasure in showing off my fine face and licking down my hair, but such vanity disappeared with my youth.

AUG.: There is much I could say in reply, but I prefer to let your conscience shame you. You try to hide your pride, but you reveal it in your depreciation of others. That revelation of self-esteem is more unpleasant than undue exaltation of oneself. I would much rather see you exalt others, even though preserving your own primacy, than watch you trample them down and then haughtily display a shield of humility, made of the scorn of others.

FR.: As you like. I have no very high opinion either of myself or of others. I don't like to say outright what I have learned to think of most men.

AUG.: Well, let's pass on to the other points. Of envy I absolve you. But what about greed for temporal goods?

FR.: Come, come! I never heard anything more absurd. There's nothing I'm freer from than avarice.

AUG.: Not so free as you think. And not so free either from ambition. What are these incessant cares and worries of yours? You may say that you want to be in a position to help your friends. But that would be just a noble excuse.

FR.: I'm not inhuman enough to be unmoved by concern for my friends, especially those who are endeared to me by their virtue and merit. Some I admire, some I venerate, some I love, some I pity. On the other hand I'm not so high-minded as to ruin myself for my friends. I have to think of my own future, provide a competence for old age, and hence combine some material concern with my cultivation of the Muses.

AUG.: A useless labor, and a senseless one. You can get along with very little. You were never so well off as when you were wandering alone and carefree in the hills. Then you thought yourself the richest and happiest of mortals; but now you have abandoned that frugal country peace. You began to despise the berries of your bushes, the rough clothing, and life among peasants, and you have come to learn cupidity amid the city's tumults. You are still hesitant, perhaps because you are caught in the snares of sin, or perhaps because God wills that where you passed your youth under the discipline of others you should, though your own master, drag out a sad old age.

FR.: Well, if I try to provide against poverty in that sad old age, what is wrong with that?

AUG.: The wrong is that you are forever concerned with the ephemeral, and you forget the eternal. Nothing is more senseless than to suffer poverty forever, out of fear of suffering it for a day.

FR.: True; but my desires are modest and limited. I don't want abundance; but I don't want to live in need.

AUG.: Only the gods don't live in need. Don't you know that man is the most needy of all the animals? Cease to hope for the impossible; content yourself with man's lot, and learn to have both too much and too little, to surpass and to be surpassed. You can't shake off the yoke of fortune that rests on the necks of kings. You can be freed from it only when, conquering human passions, you submit yourself totally to the rule of virtue. Then you will be free, needing nothing, subject to no man, finally a king, powerful and absolutely happy.

FR.: I wish that I could wish for nothing. But I am dragged on by perverse habit. I feel forever something unsatisfied in my heart.

AUG.; Let us speak of ambition. Examine your heart and you will find that it has no little place there.

FR.: You think it was nothing that I have fled the cities whenever I could, disdaining assemblies and public ceremonies, seeking the woods and country peace, forswearing vain honors? And I hear myself accused of ambition!

AUG.: You mortals renounce many things not because you despise them but because you despair of attaining them. You haven't proved to me that you haven't desired honors, but only that you hate the trouble of seeking them. Don't hope to hide behind a finger, as the saying goes. This flight from the cities, this longing for the woods of which you are so proud, doesn't excuse you; it's just a shift of blame. All kinds of roads lead to the same goal; and believe me, though you have left the trodden highway, you are trying to reach on a byway those ambitious ends you claim to despise. Your insistence on free time, your solitude, your incuriosity about normal human occupations, your studies, whose purpose is glory, all prove your ambition. But let's get on. I won't mention gluttony; you're free of that. And wrath is no serious fault of yours. But there are more dangerous passions for you.

FR.: Good God, what more dangerous can remain?

AUG.: How great are the flames of lust?

FR.: Sometimes they are so great that I grieve that I wasn't born insensible. I would rather be a motionless stone than feel the upheavals of my body. Sometimes I think I have risen above them; and then I fall again, with bitterness of spirit, into the old miseries.

AUG.: I am not surprised, for I was a witness of your struggles, and I saw you rise and fall; and now, in pity for your prostrate state, I have proposed to bring you aid.

FR.: I thank you. But what human power remains to help me?

AUG.: None; only divine power. A man cannot be chaste without God's gift. You must beg for this gift, humbly and often with tears. He does not deny what is properly asked.

FR.: I have done that so often that I almost fear to bore him.

AUG.: Not humbly enough, not soberly enough. You have always reserved a little place for future desires; you have always set the term of your prayers too far ahead. I speak out of experience; the same thing happened to me. I used to pray: "Lord, grant me to live chaste; but not right away; pretty soon." But a man who prays for tomorrow loses today.

FR.: I shall then pray assiduously, without weariness, shame, or despair.

AUG.: Good. And keep in mind the words of Plato, that nothing hinders knowledge of the divine more than the carnal appetites and the flame of lust. But since we are to return to this subject, I shall deal now with other grievous wounds of your spirit. You are afflicted by a calamitous ailment, which the moderns call *accidia* and the ancients *aegritudo,* or depression, or acute melancholy.

FR.: The very name makes me shudder.

AUG.: I am not surprised, since you have suffered from it long and grievously.

FR.: I admit it. The assaults of the other passions are brief and they contain their modicum of pleasure, but this plague holds me so close that sometimes it tortures me day and night, robbing me of light and life, plunging me into hell. But strangely enough I feed so upon tears and pain with a kind of atrocious black satisfaction that I am unwilling to be torn from them.

AUG.: What is the cause of your depression? Illness, misfortune?

FR.: All kinds of causes. Specific reasons; and in general my abhorrence and contempt for the human condition.

AUG.: What especially afflicts you?

FR.: Everything I see, hear, and feel.

AUG.: Gad! There is nothing you like?

FR.: Nothing—or not very much.

AUG.: All this is what I have called accidia. You loathe all your own concerns.

FR.: Other people's too.

AUG.: Even your advantages, which others envy?

FR.: Only the most wretched of creatures could envy a wretched man.

AUG.: You think that fortune has been unkind to you?

FR.: Very unkind, very evil, very arrogant, very cruel.

AUG.: Well, everybody can't be first.

FR.: I don't want to be first. No one has had more modest ambitions than I, but no one has gained them with more difficulty. I call Truth to witness that I have never desired to stand first. I abhor an existence filled with care and trouble; I much prefer a middle state, Horace's golden mean, *aurea mediocritas.* But even that I haven't been able to attain. Forever doubtful of the future, with my mind in suspense, I have gained no pleasure from fortune's favors. As you know, I have always been dependent on others, and that's the unhappiest of states.

AUG.: You would have it that you alone of all men might live free from care? Very few indeed have been able to live for themselves alone, and the happiest are those who have lived for others. There must be other reasons for your melancholy.

FR.: Don't you know that cruel stroke of fate, which in a single day struck me down, and all my hopes, and my property, and my family and home?*

AUG.: I see your eyes flash. Let's go on, for this is no time to deal with that matter.

FR.: Then there's my life in this most horrible of cities.** Sometimes it seems to me that I have descended into hell. How can I do here anything really good, think honest thoughts, write proper poetry?

AUG.: Plenty of others, and great men too, have suffered in the same way. You came of your own free will to this city and to this state of mind, and by your own free will you can escape. You can train your ears to listen to the city's din with pleasure, as to a waterfall. By such devices you can banish your melancholy.

* See page 37.

** His succeeding description of repulsive Avignon has been quoted in Chapter Three.

FR.: I must yield to you, although I am not entirely convinced. At least, my condition no longer seems so wretched as it
did. Let us now postpone further talk till tomorrow.

BOOK III

AUG.: I haven't yet touched your deepest and most persistent
troubles. You are fastened by two mighty chains. You are like a
miser in prison shackled by golden fetters; you would like to
get free, but you don't want to lose them. But there's a law in
this prison: if you don't throw off the chains you can't go free.
And you love them; you even boast of them.

FR.: What are these chains you're talking about ?

AUG.: Love and glory.

FR.: Gods above, what's this I hear? So you call love and
glory chains, and if I permit it you'll take them from me? You
want to rob me of the loveliest things in life, and condemn to
darkness the fairest part of my being?

AUG.; I'm going to try to, though I doubt if I succeed. Tell
me, don't you think love is the utmost madness?

FR.: The fact is, love depends on its object. It can be called
either the ugliest passion of the spirit or its noblest activity. If
I adore a wicked, contemptible woman, that is madness; but if
a rare exemplar of virtue attracts me and I devote myself to loving and venerating her, what of that?

AUG.: There's no difference. In both cases you bid farewell to
reason and to awareness of truth.

FR.: You're wasting your time. I've never loved anything
foul, anything that was not very beautiful.

AUG.: Even beautiful things can be loved foully.

FR.: Do you know who it is you're talking about?

AUG.: I have thoroughly considered my subject. We are going to talk about a mortal woman, whom you have been admiring and celebrating during a large part of your life. I am amazed
at your long insanity.

FR.: Don't be offensive. Do you realize that you are referring
to a woman whose mind, ignoring earthly cares, burns with celestial desires? In whose aspect, as truth is truth, shines heavenly
beauty? Whose behavior is an example of perfect virtue? Whose
voice, whose eyes, are more than mortal, whose very walk seems
no human action? Think of that, please, and you will realize
what sort of language you must use.

AUG.: Poor fool! So for sixteen years you have fed your flame
with false cajolements! How you have suffered! But in the end,

when those eyes close in death, you will be ashamed that you tied your immortal soul to a mortal body and you will blush to recall what you have so exalted.

FR.: God forbid! I shall not live to see her death.

AUG.: How do you know? She is getting older; that splendid body, worn out with illness and with frequent childbirths, has already lost much of its old vigor. It is folly to submit your soul to any such mortal thing.

FR.: I have not done so. I have never loved her body so much as her soul. My delight was in her character, transcending mortality, resembling that of the angels. So if—the mere utterance makes me shudder—if she should die first, I would appease my grief by saying, with Laelius, wisest of the Romans: "I loved her virtue, which has not been spent."

AUG.: Well, pour all the praise you like on your little woman. I won't contradict you. She's a queen, a saint, if you like, or as Virgil said, a goddess, a sister of Phoebus, a nymph. But her great virtue won't help to excuse your errors.

FR.: I call Truth here by our side to witness that in my love there has never been anything base, lewd, or in any way culpable, except perhaps in its excess. Nothing more wholly beautiful than my love can be conceived.

AUG.: I'm sorry to hear such nonsense from one who ought to think more clearly.

FR.: Whatever I am is due to her. I should never have gained my present reputation, however one may judge it, if she hadn't tended with her noble sympathy that tiny little seed of virtue that nature sowed in my breast. She recalled my youthful spirit from all turpitude, pulled me back, as they say, with a hook, and forced me to look upward. How could I fail to be transformed by her character? Never has any slanderer, however scurrilous, attacked her good name or dared to find anything reprehensible in her actions, words, or even gestures. Even those who leave nothing unsoiled spared her, in admiration and reverence. It is not strange that her good fame inspired in me the desire for fame, and eased my labors to that end. From my young manhood I longed for nothing else than to please her, who alone had pleased me. You know how, to gain that end, I spurned the temptations of a myriad pleasures and subjected myself prematurely to laborious cares. And you order me to forget her or to love her more temperately!

AUG.: You make me sick at my stomach.

FR.: Why, pray?

AUG.: Because to think falsely is a sign of ignorance; but to proclaim the false impudently is a sign both of ignorance and of vainglory.

FR.: How can you prove that I have either thought or said anything false?

AUG.: By everything you have said! First of all when you say that she has made you what you are. The fact is that she has prevented you from developing. What a man you might have been, if she hadn't captured you with her beauty! It is kind nature that made you what you were; she prevented you from becoming what you might have been, or rather you threw it away for her, for she is innocent. Her beauty seemed to you so sweet and attractive that you destroyed your native possibilities in your longings and wailings. And you boast that she preserved you from all turpitudes! Perhaps she did save you from many, but she forced you into greater calamities. For one who drives us to our downfall while keeping us out of various filthy courses, or who inflicts a mortal wound while healing some minor scratches, can hardly be called our liberator, but rather our murderer. So she whom you call your guide has saved you from foul actions only to lay you out on a splendid bier. And as for her teaching you to look upward, to disdain the mass of men, what else is that than making you slave to her alone, forgetful and scornful of all else on earth? There is nothing worse for a man among men. When you recall that she involved you in innumerable labors you are certainly telling the truth. But you got a good deal out of them! And as for your boast that she made you seek for fame, well, that is the worst burden on your soul. In short, this woman you exalt so highly is ruining you.

FR.: What do you mean?

AUG.: She has distracted your mind from the love of the Creator and has turned it to the love of the creature. You have loved the Creator only as the artificer who made that beautif..l body.

FR.: I protest to Truth here present and to my conscience that I never loved her body more than her soul! As she has grown older and her bodily beauty has dwindled I have been the more constant. Although the flower of youth visibly fades with the passage of time, the beauty of her spirit kept increasing, and this has kept me faithful.

AUG.: Are you trying to fool me? If that spirit had inhabited a squalid body, would you have loved it as much?

FR.: I don't dare to assert that, for the spirit is invisible. But if the spirit should make itself manifest, no doubt I would love a beautiful spirit even in an ugly habitation.

AUG.: You are playing on words. For if you can love only what is evident to the eyes, you love the body. However, I won't deny that her spirit and her character have added fuel to your flames, just as her very name greatly increased your passion. You loved body and soul together, and both of them immoderately. And you have fallen into great disasters because of this love.

FR.: That I will never admit, even if you put me to torture.

AUG.: Do you remember your boyhood, your love of God, your meditations on death, your religious feeling, your love of virtue?

FR.: I remember very well, and I grieve that as I have grown older my merits have decreased.

AUG.: When did you lose these good habits?

FR.: I came to a parting of the ways, and I took the downward path. And I have never been able to find the right way again.

AUG.: How old were you when this happened?

FR.: It was in the midst of youth's fevers. If you wait a moment, I can recollect the exact year.

AUG.: And when did this woman's beauty first appear to you?

FR.: Oh, that I'll never forget!

AUG.: How do those two times match?

FR.: Well, in fact her appearance in my life and my steps astray happened at about the same time.

AUG.: That's what I was after. And this glorious woman, this guide to heaven, why didn't she hold you by the hand and show you the right road?

FR.: She did all she could. Unmoved by my prayers and blandishments, in spite of her youth and mine and in spite of certain circumstances that might have moved a heart of stone, she kept her feminine purity and remained firm, impregnable. Isn't that something? She showed me my duty; and when I went my headstrong way she preferred to abandon me rather than to follow me.

AUG.: Ah, then you did sometimes have base desires! You denied that before. Well, that's the familiar madness of lovers, always saying: "Will I, nill I, nill I, will I." You don't know what you want or what you don't want.

FR.: You've tricked me. If perhaps I had such desires at the time, youthful ardor caused them. Now I know better. But she never wavered in her womanly virtue. If at the time I protested against it, now I am glad of it, and I thank her.

AUG.: It's hard to trust someone who has fallen once. That flame of yours may be less intense, it hasn't been extinguished. And in ascribing so much merit to your beloved, in absolving her, you are condemning yourself. Love has made you wretched; that's what I began by saying. Earthly love leads to the forgetfulness of God; it has brought you to the miserable state you have described. In your folly, you were not even content with gazing on her living face, the source of your woes, and you obtained from an illustrious artist a painted image and carried it around with you, to have something to cry over forever. You sought out everything that would provoke and irritate your emotion. And—the final proof of an unhinged mind—you were as much allured by her beautiful name as by her body, and with incredible folly you cultivated every punning significance of it! You loved the laurel, whether of emperors or poets, because it chimed with her name. You could hardly write a poem without dragging in the laurel. And since you couldn't hope for the imperial wreath, you longed for the laurel crown of poetry as immoderately as you had loved the lady. You will be shocked some day when you reflect how much effort you spent in obtaining it, though I grant that you were often borne on the wings of inspiration. Don't speak; I know what is in your mind. I know that you were a poet before you fell in love. But the difficulties and dangers in the way of success would have delayed your effort, if the memory of that sweetest of names hadn't spurred you on over land and sea to Rome and Naples, where finally you gained what you had lusted for so ardently. Anyone who doesn't take this as an indication of notable madness must be mad himself.

FR.: What do you want me to do? Despair?

AUG.: First we'll look for remedies. Cicero says that many think of driving out an old love with a new one, as a nail drives out a nail. That's good advice. A mind dispersed on many objects has the more difficulty in concentrating on one. But the danger is that if you cast off this passion, which I admit is one of the nobler sort, you may get entangled in many, and become, instead of a lover, a libertine. I won't disapprove of your passing from one subjection to another, for perhaps in such excursions you may find your liberty, or a lighter servitude; but I would much reprobate your bowing your neck to a series of sordid involvements.

FR.: May the patient interrupt the doctor for a moment? Let me tell you this—I can never love anyone else. My eyes are so used to gazing upon her, my mind is so used to admiring her, that all that is not she seems dark and ugly. So if you command me to love another in order to free myself from love, you are asking the impossible. It's all over; I am done for.

AUG.: Then you must find some external remedy. Can you persuade yourself to run away?

FR.: Painful though it would be, I could do so.

AUG.: If you can, you're saved. How can you be secure in this place, where remain so many vestiges of your old wounds, where you are oppressed by the present and the past?

FR.: I have often attempted flight, in search of freedom. To obtain it I have wandered far and wide, east and north, even to the edge of Ocean. But wherever I went I bore my hurt within me.

AUG.: As Socrates said, you were always traveling with yourself. You must lay down that old burden of care, and prepare your heart; then at least you will be really fleeing.

FR.: I don't see how that will cure me.

AUG.: I didn't speak of curing or of getting well; I said: "Prepare your heart." You must teach your heart to cast off its burdens; you must go away without hope of return, without a backward glance. But you must beware of a relapse, in revisiting familiar scenes. You yourself have often thought you were cured, and you would have been cured if you had remained away. But walking the well-known streets, recalling old vanities at the mere sight of certain spots, you were struck dumb, you sighed, you stood stock-still and barely refrained from tears. Wounded once more, you fled, murmuring: "I feel that here are still hidden some traps of the old enemy; here remain some relics of death." Is a man ever cured? A look at a comely body arouses lust; a glance from lovely eyes may awaken sleeping love. You must not only quit this pestilential city, you must flee with all diligence whatever recalls your mind to its past occupations.

FR.: I have already been meditating flight, but I am uncertain where to go.

AUG.: Many ways, many harbors are open to you. I know that you love above all Italy and your sweet native soil, and rightfully enough. I therefore advise Italy, for the manners of its people, for its skies and surrounding seas and shores and Apennine hills. Go surely and quickly, and do not turn back. Forget the past, look to what is to come. Too long have you been an exile from your fatherland and from yourself. It is now time to return, for "evening is falling and night is friend of the despoiler."* But avoid solitude, until you feel that no after-affects of your illness remain. When you said that your rustications were of no benefit to you, you were stating the obvious. What remedies could you expect to find in a remote, solitary country place? I admit that when you fled there alone and kept sighing and looking back at the city, I often laughed at you from on high, and I said to myself: "Love has surrounded that poor fellow with a Lethean cloud, and to flee from his disease he is running toward death!"

FR.: Ovid advised forlorn lovers to avoid solitude. I have known that passage from boyhood.

AUG.: What is the use of knowing so much, if you couldn't make the application to your own necessities? I have been the more surprised at your error in seeking solitude, in that you knew the wise verses of the ancients against it, and you have added a few yourself. You have often complained that solitude has done you no good.**

FR.: Have you any other remedies to suggest?

AUG.: To set forth everything one knows is rather to show off than to really help a friend. But Cicero says that three things distract the mind from love: satiety, shame, and reflection. Well, satiety in your case is impossible. As for shame—tell me, and excuse me, have you looked in your mirror lately?

FR.: What do you mean? Yes, I suppose so, as usual.

AUG.: Haven't you noticed that your face is changing, day by day?

FR. Now that you mention it, yes. Men seem to get old faster now than they used to. Of course I have been white-haired since my youth, like Domitian, Numa Pompilius, and Virgil.

AUG.: If you had been bald you would have dragged in Julius Caesar. At any rate, shame should banish passion. You are too old to play the passionate lover. Most men don't reach

* From Petrarch's *Penitential Psalms*
** *Ep. metr.* I 14, *Ad seipsum,* etc.

your present age.* Renounce the follies of youth; extinguish
the ardors of adolescence. Don't be forever thinking of what
you have been; look around you to realize what you are now.

FR.: Do you know what brings me a little comfort? She is
getting old along with me.

AUG.: Perhaps you think it's more decent for you to love her
when you're both old than to fall in love with a girl? As a matter
of fact love is all the uglier as there is less basis for love. You
should therefore be ashamed that your mind never changes,
while the body is continually changing. That is a subject for
reflection, which, as I said, is Cicero's third cure of love. Meditate on your manhood, on the nobility of the human spirit, on
the fragility and filth of the body, on the brevity of life, on the
flight of time, on the certainty of death. Think how revolting
it is to be the world's laughingstock, how improper your behavior is for your clerical profession. Recall all your sufferings
for her sake, all your lamentations and tears. Think, at the same
time, of her ungrateful and supercilious bearing, how, if she
was occasionally kind, it was more briefly than the blowing of
a summer breeze. Think how you have added to her fame, and
how much she has subtracted from your own life, and how you
have protected her own fair name, while she has always been
perfectly unconcerned about your state. Think how she has distracted you from the love of God, how she has interfered with
the completion of the works you have in hand. And finally
think of what she actually is! Few consider with a realizing
sense the filthiness of the feminine body. Repel every recollection of your past preoccupations and all thought of the past.
And besiege heaven with your prayers; tire the ears of the
heavenly king. Let no night or day pass without tears and sup-
plications. But we've talked enough about this. Now I come to
your final fault, which I must undertake to cure. You are unduly desirous of worldly glory and of immortality for your
name.

FR.: I must confess it. I cannot restrain this appetite.

AUG.: But it is to be feared that the longing for vain immortality may block the road to true immortality. Worldly
fame is nothing but the diffuse gabble of many tongues. It is a
gust of air, the breath of many men. You despise the vulgar
mob; but you delight in the silly little words of the very men
whose actions you condemn. Worse, you find the summit of
your felicity therein! What is the purpose of your perpetual

* Petrarch was thirty-eight.

labors, your night vigils, the fervency of your studies? You may answer: "To learn something useful for my life;" but you already know all that is needful for life and death. It would be better for you to apply what you know to your conduct. And I notice that you have tried in most of your works to tickle the public taste, to please the very people you particularly dislike, plucking posies, in your poems, histories, and speeches, to enrapture your hearers. And not content with their ephemeral applause, you have lusted for fame among posterity. Thus you started a big history of Romans, from Romulus to Titus; and without finishing that, you dispatched a poetic craft to Africa. And so, writing of others, you forget yourself. And death may strike you down before you finish either task.

FR.: I have been afraid of that. I once fell seriously ill, and I thought I was going to die. And what tortured me most was the thought that I was leaving my *Africa* half finished. As I didn't want anyone else to edit it, I had determined to burn it with my own hands. That is a bitter memory.

AUG.: You confirm me in my judgment. But suppose you had plenty of time, leisure, tranquillity, without dull periods or physical weakness, that you were spared all those interruptions that have interfered with your writing, that every condition was favorable. What great thing do you think you would accomplish?

FR.: No doubt some brilliant, rare, excellent book.

AUG.: The more excellent it might be, the more it would detract from the care of your soul. And how vain and transitory is earthly fame!

FR.: Oh, I know all that old stuff of the philosophers about the vanity of human wishes and so forth. But I don't expect to become a god and embrace eternity. Human fame is enough for me. That's what I long for. Being mortal, I desire only mortal rewards.

AUG.: What a calamity, if you are telling the truth! If you don't want immortal rewards, if you don't look to eternity, you are condemned to earth. Your fate is sealed; there is no hope for you.

FR.: All I meant was this: I treat mortal things as mortal, and I don't affront the nature of things by vast, unreasonable desires. I don't abandon eternal concerns; I just defer them.

AUG.: Take care! Death may strike at any moment. Time is short; it is dangerous to make any postponement.

FR.: Still, there is some reason in my stand. That glory which

it is permissible to hope for must be sought while we are here
below. The greater glory will be enjoyed in heaven by those
who will be admitted there; they won't even think of earthly
glory. So this is the order: the care for mortal things must come
first in mortal minds; eternal concerns will succeed in their
turn to the transitory.

AUG.: What a foolish little man you are! You think that all
the joys of earth and heaven will shower upon you at your summons! What is earth in comparison with heaven? I hate to hear
you sneer at the "old stuff" of the philosophers. Is the geo-
metrical proof that our earth is tiny, just a long island of land,
old stuff? Is it old stuff that of the world's five so-called zones the
middle one is uninhabitable by men because of the sun's heat,
the extreme one to north and south burdened by intolerable
cold and perpetual ice, so that only the two temperate zones
are habitable? It is doubtful whether the antipodes are inhabited; I don't think so myself.* That leaves only the north temperate zone, which, according to some, is divided into two parts,
one reserved for our uses, the other cut off by the northern
Ocean, which forbids our access to it.** In this tiny world glory
is of small account.

FR.: Do you then order me to give up my studies and live
ingloriously?

AUG.: I will never advise you to live without glory, but I
admonish you not to prefer the quest of glory to that of virtue.
I will lay down this rule: take no heed for glory; the less you
long for it the more of it you will gain. A man would be mad
who would bustle about under the midday sun to show others
his shadow, and no less mad is he who, in the ardors of life, tries
to promote his own fame. Go to your goal, and your shadow
will follow you. You wear yourself out writing books; you're
making a great mistake, for you forget your own advantage in
trying to bring advantage to others, and thus in the vain hope
of glory you waste unwitting this brief span of life.

FR.: What shall I do then? Shall I leave my books unfinished?
Wouldn't it be more sensible to hurry them to a conclusion, if
God grants it, and then, being freed of these tasks, to give myself wholly to higher things? I can't calmly leave half done
works that have cost me so much.

AUG.: I know where the shoe pinches. You would rather

* *De civitate Dei*, XVI 9.
** Historians of cosmology take note.

abandon yourself than your little books. Lay down the burden
of your histories; the deeds of the Romans have been sufficiently
celebrated by themselves and by others. Abandon Africa and
leave it to its inhabitants. You won't increase either Scipio's
glory or your own. He can't be any further exalted; you are just
creeping along behind him. So surrender all these works, and
at last give yourself back to yourself! And, to return to the point
from which we started, begin to think deeply about death,
which little by little and all unconscious you are approaching.
You are part of the great procession; exulting in the prime of
your life, you are treading on the heels of others; but others are
treading on yours. Remember Cicero: "All the life of a philosopher is meditation on death." You can find the right path by
listening to your own spirit, which tells you: "This is the way
home." I pray God that he may accompany you and bring your
wandering steps to safety.

FR.: Oh, may your prayer be granted, and by God's favor
may I come safe out of the maze, free of my own self-deceptions
and delusions! And may the storms of my spirit subside, and
the world be silent, and fortune molest me no more!

Surely there is no need to embark on a long analysis of the Secret
Book. Any reader even of this summary must have recognized its
qualities of dramatic vivacity, of psychological perceptiveness, of
comprehension of morbid states of spirit. It is the revelation of an
abnormally sensitive mind in an emotional crisis, frustrated in love,
in ambition, and in self-esteem, and trying to be utterly honest
with itself. It is the indispensable gloss to the *Rime;* it lays bare
the reality underlying the poetic fiction. It is the first great example of literary introspection, as opposed to the professional introspection of religious seers. As such it has its importance not only
in the history of literary psychology but in the history of the
European concept of human character. And somehow the book
seems to me outside of history, superior to time. Its picture of a
tortured sensibility involved in a maze of doubts, struggling
against its own impotence, is as modern as yesterday's best-seller.

One will notice Petrarch's method. He is trying to locate his
own truth by the device of triangulation, by taking sights from two
separate standpoints. He divides himself in two, in the hope of
reuniting in a more confident whole. Petrarch-Augustinus is bluff,

hearty, and commonsensical, but earnest with holy ardor; Pe-
trarch-Franciscus is bewildered, reluctant, and inconstant. But is
any character really constant? Augustinus has of course the star
role, as he must win in the end, but Franciscus is no mere foil to
the teacher. Indeed, Franciscus has the better of some arguments,
and Augustinus has to pass on without winning his point. The
author is playing fair with the characters he has conjured up from
himself.

To Petrarch himself the Secret Book was an essential record of
his crisis, a *mise au point* of his mind and soul. It was not, however, like Pascal's *Memorial,* the record of a mystical experience
destined to change his life. St. Augustine came to him not in fire
but in cool meditation. The writing of the *Secretum* was a spiritual purge, which cleared his mind of its accumulated poisons and
left him restored in health and free to act in much the same manner as before. He continued to love Laura, to turn his longings into verse, to write his big books, to pursue his worldly ambitions.
He retreated, on occasion, to the solitude of Vaucluse. After all
his condemnation of fleshly lusts he continued to relapse, until at
least 1350, when he was forty-six. He never came to believe Augustinus' contention that scholarship is vain and sinful. In short,
the Secret Book is not a revelation from his higher self but an effort for self-understanding. If we prize it as such, we are giving Petrarch his reward, for we are the posterity to which he looked so
plaintively.

XVI: NAPLES, 1343

> *Naples, gay, peaceful, abundant, magnificent.*
>
> —Boccaccio, Fiammetta, *II 45*

PETRARCH LIKED TO FIGURE MAN'S LIFE BY THE
Pythagorean symbol of the Greek letter rendered by a Y.
One travels up the stem to the fork, where one must choose
the left arm or the right, diverging to infinity.

In his own case the fork was the crisis of 1343. It marks his shifting from poetry toward scholarship, from love toward ambition,
from worldliness toward religion. But the crisis was no sudden conversion, immediately altering his life. He had reached not a peak
but a plateau.

He continued to write love-poems to Laura. After all, he had
a reputation to sustain, and there were plenty of events and circumstances suitable for commemoration. However, most of the
poems written during the rest of Laura's lifetime are calmer, more
resigned, than were the earlier outcries of longing. He had lost the
crowding lyric urge of youth, but he had learned a formula, a
technique, with which to construct a sonnet of conventional passion.

Scholarship occupied him more than poetry. He had several
books in hand: *Africa,* and *De viris illustribus,* his set of biog-
raphies of great Romans; his *Rerum memorandarum liber,* a compendium of remarkable facts from history and his own experience. Other projects were soon to take shape. He was conscious of
a mission to restore to Italy knowledge of its Roman past and
pride in it. He was forming the concept that, as humanism, came
to endow the intellectual history of our world. As Italy's laureate,
he could look for no greater poetic eminence, but the bays of

learning remained to be won. Learned books would, he felt, give
him the authority of a moral philosopher, the schoolmaster of his
times.

His ambition turned also to the active world of affairs. He had
already given unasked advice to Popes, urging them to return to
Rome. Now that he was the friend of kings and city tyrants his
confidence in his own judgments increased. He labored ever more
earnestly to bring about, by timely counsels to the mighty, the
pacification and the unification of Italy, under the headship of
Rome. To this end he accepted diplomatic missions, more willingly than he would confess to himself.

As the *Secretum* makes clear, he was seeking the solace of religion. He had been pious from boyhood; he never knew doubt of
Christian dogma. But from the crisis of 1343 onward he intensified
his formal practices. He was obsessed by the thought of death and
its sequel. His religion was more fear than love; he was afraid of
damnation and was by no means sure of his qualifications for
heaven. He was no mystic. There is nothing in Petrarch to match
Augustine's ecstatic appeal for Christ's love, or Dante's celebration
of *l'amor che muove il sole e l'altre stelle.*

As he crosses the plateau of his life and begins to descend the
farther side he becomes, on the whole, a less attractive human being. Perhaps this is the common case. Elderly reasonableness, good
sense, must be a surrender, a rejection of youthful aspirations together with youth's follies. Disillusion, pessimism, sourness, invade Petrarch's spirit. He becomes at times a cantankerous moralist, pointing his scorn at almost everything in the world of men.
His vanity, fed by adulation, grew monstrous. He has been accused
of selfishness, cruelty, avarice, hypocrisy. The accusations are unfair, but they can be supported by many texts.

The clue is, I think, that he was never sure of himself. His two-
mindedness, so well revealed in the introspections of the *Secretum,*
led him to doubt every impulse. He had to be forever reassured of
his superiority, nay, of his very reality. His lust for fame is born
of this need for reassurance. The applause of flatterers sounded
false in his ears; nothing could satisfy him but the acclaim of posterity. And even that he must surely find insufficient.

King Robert the Wise of Naples died on January 20, 1343.
Petrarch describes his edifying end: "He regarded his body as a

prison, his weakening limbs as chains upon his liberty." Petrarch
thought of writing his biography, but never got around to it.

King Robert left his realm in precarious state. Heir to the kingdom was his granddaughter, Giovanna, barely seventeen. She was
married to a Hungarian Prince Consort, Andrea, still younger.
The government was in the hands of a regency council, headed by
Robert's widow, and including Petrarch's close friend, Philippe
de Cabassoles, Bishop of Cavaillon. "A pack of wolves," Petrarch
called the regents, while excepting Philippe, a lamb in their
company.

It happened that three noble brothers named Pipini, great
trouble-makers, were held in a Naples prison for crimes against
the state. Their ample properties has been confiscated. There was
a relationship, whether of interest or friendship, between the
Pipini and the Colonna. The mother of the Pipini appealed to
the Pope for their release, using Cardinal Colonna as intercessor.
The Pope hearkened to the Cardinal and requested the Naples
regency to release the Pipini; when his request was rejected he
repeated it in stronger terms. And Cardinal Colonna reinforced
the papal summons by sending Petrarch to Naples as his personal
representative.

Petrarch welcomed the appointment. He would travel honorably, with a small suite, and with all expenses paid, to a city dear
to him. He would deal with kings and queens. And he would escape hateful Avignon, rendered the more hateful by the claims and
lamentations of an inconvenient mother with his inconvenient
child, just born or just about to be born.

His reports of his journey illustrate the trials of travel in his
century. He left Avignon in September and rode to Nice, passing
near Gherardo's monastery of Montrieux, without stopping, for
during Gherardo's novitiate all visits were forbidden. At Nice he
found a ship, and, probably in rowing out to its moorings, was
either capsized or in danger of foundering. His precious *Confessions of Saint Augustine* was, he says, under the waves of the sea,
sub fluctibus maris. Foul weather laid him low, and forced the ship
into Porto San Maurizio. Sick and famished, he slept in a detesta-
ble bed in a sailors' tavern. He refused to reembark, but left his
servants and baggage on board. He bought two stout German
horses, and with one companion continued along the coast road
of the Ligurian Riviera. Beyond Spezia he ran into war; the Milan-

ese armies were drawn up before the Pisans, and were threatening
to fight at any moment. Petrarch had therefore to hire a craft to
take him and his horses around the war. He came ashore near
Viareggio, and proceeded by land through Pisa, Siena, Perugia,
Todi, and Narni to Rome. There he was warmly received by majestic old Stefano Colonna, who talked a whole day long of his son
the Cardinal and of his friends the Pipini. He hurried on to
Naples, arriving on or about October 10. There he was lodged in
the convent of San Lorenzo (in whose church Boccaccio had fallen
in love with his Fiammetta, nine years before).

His mission went badly. Admitted to the Council, he was presented to the young Queen Giovanna. (She has since become a
legendary wanton, the subject of many plays and novels.) He
found the Council dominated by a horrible hunched limping libidinous Franciscan, a kind of Rasputin. Only good Philippe de
Cabassoles dared stand out against him. The Franciscan evidently
wanted a bribe, and, receiving none, turned Petrarch's plea for
the release of the Pipini brothers to scorn. Petrarch visited the
prisoners, in chains in the Castel Capuano. The justice of their
cause, he says, damns them; their life is in danger, for the great
of the realm have shared their property and wish to suppress possible accusers.

Petrarch spent two fruitless months in Naples. He was impressed again by the beauty of the city's setting, and by Giotto's
frescoes in the Royal Chapel of the Castelnuovo, which have since
disappeared. He was impressed also by the prevalent gayety and
license, encouraged by the teen-age Queen and her Consort, who,
in fact, soon succeeded in emptying the treasury of all wise King
Robert's savings. But the dark underside of license was all too evident. The Council meetings Petrarch attended adjourned before
dark, for fear of attack by roving gangs led by penniless young
nobles.

Petrarch killed time by making a visit, with his two old Neapolitan friends, Barbato da Sulmona and Giovanni Barrili, to
Baia, sacred for its classical memories. He was thrilled by the remains of villas and temples in this most elegant of Roman resorts.
But in his letter he gives less space to antiquity than to a mighty
Amazon dressed in men's clothes who outdid the soldiers in heav-
ing an iron bar and a heavy stone.

NAPOLI

On November 25 he witnessed a terrific storm, and wrote a
famous description of it to Cardinal Colonna. The weather signs
beforehand were ominous, and a pious bishop read calamity in the
stars and predicted an earthquake.

Night came; a throng of fearful women, forgetting modesty in their
sense of peril, roamed through the streets and squares, with infants in
their arms, and, praying and weeping, besieged the doors of the
churches. I was disturbed by the general alarm, but went home early
in the evening. The sky was calmer than usual, and most of my fellow-
lodgers had gone confidently to bed. I decided to wait for the moon
to set; it was in its seventh day, if I am not mistaken. So I stood at
my window, facing west, until, before midnight, it veiled its gloomy
face in clouds and hid behind a mountain. Then I too retired to take
my delayed repose.

I had hardly gone to sleep when suddenly, with a horrible uproar,
not only the windows but the walls themselves, built on solid stone,
tremble to their very foundations, and my night-light, which I usually
keep by my bed, goes out. We all leap from bed, and sleep is succeeded
by fear of imminent death. While every man seeks his neighbor in the
darkness and calls out trembling encouragements in the dreadful
lightning-flashes, the monks and their sainted prior, David—whose
name I am glad to honor—having risen to sing the midnight praises
of God, seize in terror on their crosses and holy relics of saints, and,
loudly imploring God for mercy, burst into my room carrying torches.
At this I revive a little. We all hurry into the church, and there we
spend the night, prostrate and groaning, and convinced that the end
of all things is at hand and that everything is about to collapse about
us. . . .

What rain, wind, lightning, roaring in heaven, quaking of earth,
bellowing of the sea, despairing cries of men! After a night that
seemed magically doubled in length, we conjectured that day had
dawned, for light there was none. The priests in their sacred vestments served at the altar, and we, not yet daring to look out at the
sky, lay outflung on the bare wet floor. When finally came a day much
like night, the clamor from the upper city diminished but that from
the harbor-side increased. Our desperation turning to audacity, as
often happens, we mounted and rode down to the port, to see or to
die.

Good God, what a sight! The most ancient sailors call it unexampled. In the roadstead, dreadful wrecks; unhappy men, flung into
the sea, had tried to swim to the nearby shore, and their bodies were

shattered against the rocks like eggshells. The shore was covered with
crushed bodies, some still palpitating; the brains of one, the bowels of
another, gushed forth. The cries of men, the wailing of women, outdid the roaring of sea and air. Many a shoreside house had fallen, the
waves having sapped their foundations. The waters that day knew
no bounds and respected no work of man or nature. That great
breakwater, constructed with so much laborious ingenuity,* and all
the region near the sea were submerged by the waves, and now one
had to navigate where one had gone dryshod. More than a thousand
Neapolitan gentlemen had assembled on horseback, as if for the
obsequies of the city. Mingling with them I began to fear less, since
if I must needs die it would be in company. Then suddenly a new
clamor arose. The very spot on which we stood began to sink, under-
mined by the waters. We fled to higher land. One could not look out
to open sea; mortal sight could not bear the angry visages of Jove
and Neptune. Mountainous waves rolled in, from Capri to Naples.
The sea was not blue, not black with storm, but all horribly white
with foam.

Meanwhile the young Queen, barefoot, with hair unbound, and a
great throng of women, overcoming their modesty in the common
danger, emerged from the royal palace and hastened to the church of
the Virgin Queen, to pray for pardon in this extremity. . . .

There were three long ships, called galleys, of Marseilles. They
had just arrived from Cyprus, and they lay at anchor after their
long voyage, ready to depart on the morrow. They sank under our
very eyes, as we cried in horror; but no one could bring them any aid.
Not one of the sailors or pilots was saved. Other ships of all sorts, some
of them bigger, had taken refuge in the harbor, as in a safe stronghold, and these met the same fate. Only one of all the vessels survived. This was filled with convicts who had had their punishments
remitted, to go and fight in the Sicilian wars. They had been spared
by the executioner to die in battle. Their ship was large and stout
and sheathed with bulls' hides. It sustained the force of the waves
until sunset, and then began to open. The men, in their peril, patched
the leaks frantically. There were about four hundred men on board,
they say, enough for a fleet, let alone a single ship. These mighty
men, having once escaped death, had nothing worse to fear; they
fought with obstinate vigor. But in spite of their struggles the ship
kept gradually sinking. They postponed their doom until the following night. They gave up, laid down their tools, and clustered on

* Begun by Charles II of Anjou in 1302 and still called the Molo Angioino.

the top deck. Then, when hope was abandoned, the sky began to clear and the wearied waves to subside. Thus, while all the others died, the worst survived, whether, as Lucan says, Fortune favors the wicked, or, as Virgil opines, the gods make their own judgments, or whether we are to conclude that those who hold their own lives cheap are safest among life's perils.

One thing looms large in my mind. I must ask you never again to bid me confide my life to wind and waves, for in this I would not be willing to obey either you or the Roman pontiff or my own father, if he should return to life. I'll leave the air to the birds and the sea to the fish; I am a land animal, and I prefer roads. I won't refuse to visit the bequivered Sarmates or the perfidious Moors, as long as my feet can touch the ground. Send me where you will, even to the Indies; but if by water, I refuse. . . . I know what learned men may reply, that danger is everywhere the same, that it is only more evident at sea. All right; so be it; but I was born on land, and you will do me a great favor if you will allow me to die there.

A few days later Petrarch had another shattering experience. The Court and the people were inordinately fond of jousts and tourneys, introduced by the Anjou kings. The calamities of the great storm could not induce the Court to postpone a tourney on November 30, St. Andrew's Day, the name-day of the Prince Consort. Petrarch saw the young royal pair presiding, with the flower of Neapolitan society. At a great burst of applause, he says:

> I looked around, and there at my feet lay a very handsome youth transfixed by a sword. I was horrified, and giving my horse the spur, I fled from that evil, hellish spectacle, inveighing against the companions who had tricked me into attending, the cruelty of the spectators, and the madness of the players at that game. This plague has been passed on from the elders to the younger, ever growing worse, and has now reached the point where a license to commit crime is supposed to show merit and freedom. . . . You won't be surprised that your friends still lie prisoners in this city, in which it is a game to kill guiltless men.

Naples, where Petrarch had found such honor and cultured delight only two years before, had become the abode of evil, a City of Destruction. He made a last vain appeal for the release of the Pipini. Early in December, in anger and disappointment, he set out on the road northward.

His stay in Naples was a stage in his lifelong progress toward self-knowledge. Like other literary men, he learned that he was at a disadvantage in the world of affairs. Intellectual superiority is not enough when pitted against the whole-hearted, single-minded devotion of practical men to their own purposes. Eloquence, even inspired argument, has little meaning in diplomacy, where individual or group interests are in play, where actions are determined by pressures and promises. Petrarch found his knowledge, his methods, and himself inadequate. Naturally he turned his spite against the system; but naturally a residual sense of failure remained in his spirit.

A little later, the Pope sent a worldly-wise cardinal with plenary powers to Naples. He obtained the release of the Pipini brothers, who immediately resumed their careers of violence. The eldest Pipini was implicated in the assassination of the young Prince Consort, Andrea. He fled to Rome, led an uprising, and was finally hanged on his own estates.

XVII: PARMA AND VERONA, 1343-1345

The wise fool, wanting peace without war.

—Sen. *XIII 17*

I N PETRARCH'S FINAL LETTER FROM NAPLES TO
Cardinal Colonna, dated December 1, 1343, he tells his master that he will leave for Avignon within three days. He did
not, in fact, reach home for nearly two years. Unless he was lying
to the Cardinal, on his northward journey he must have received
from Azzo da Correggio an invitation, too attractive to turn down,
to revisit Parma. The invitation must have contained promises sufficient to chase thoughts of Cardinal Colonna's displeasure. Probably Petrarch was reluctant to face the Cardinal with reports of
the total failure of his mission. Perhaps there were also domestic
unpleasantnesses awaiting him in Avignon. He did not like to con-
front trouble; he preferred to pass it by with his nose in a book, or
even to deny its existence.

He arrived in Parma in December and was greeted with incredulous joy. A story had spread that he had died in Naples. A
poetic physician had written a threnody, representing the poets
and scholars of all times and Minerva herself attending his funeral
on Mount Parnassus. Doubting Thomases had to touch him, to
make sure he was not a ghost. Such rumors of his extinction were
to recur often. Petrarch professes himself unable to understand
them, as no one could gain materially by his death. But perhaps,
he says, there were jealous creatures who would like to see his living fame ended and who transform their fantasies into fact, as a
spectator in a theatre accepts as true what he knows to be fiction.

Azzo da Correggio, kindest of tyrants, put at the poet's disposal
his former house and gardens. What is more, Petrarch bought and
rebuilt the house. The funds could have come only from Azzo.

He describes in a metrical epistle to Guglielmo da Pastrengo his pleasure in the task of rebuilding. He dreamed of magnificence, and then checked his ambitions with philosophical counsels. He would have liked to adorn the house with marble, which was too expensive. A crack appeared in the reconstructed wall. He upbraided the masons; they replied: "The ground here is too soft, the house too heavy. New foundations need a little time to settle; we mortal men can make nothing enduring, nothing for immortality. The walls will stand long enough, as long as you and your descendants will live." The poet was shamed. He ordered the work to continue, though with a sinking heart. And in fact the masons were right; their foundations and at least part of their walls still stand.

One wonders naturally about his financial affairs. He was always boasting of his poverty, but clearly it was only relative. He defines his poverty as not absolute, sordid, sad, burdensome, but tranquil, peaceful, decent. In other words, poverty meant having enough money. It is fair to say that he eagerly accepted gifts and grants from noble patrons, like any professor today; it is not fair to accuse him of cupidity or sycophancy. His noble patrons were all men whom he genuinely honored and admired, like Cardinal Colonna and Azzo da Correggio, though modern historians may not share in some of his admirations.

He was happy in his pleasant house and in his country walks, and happy in his friendship with Azzo, with whom he engaged in long, frank conversations. In the autumn of 1344 he received a reproachful letter from "Socrates" in Avignon. Could it have been sent at the instigation of Cardinal Colonna? Socrates told Petrarch that the Pope was asking for him and hinting that he might give him a lucrative post at Court. Socrates spoke further of his amazement that Petrarch could remain so long absent from Laura. Petrarch replied that he was going to stay where he was, that nothing would drag him back to pestilent Avignon. He has put aside his youthful follies, in the number of which he includes his great love. He is looking to higher things. In Parma he has found peace, despite alarming rumors of war round about. In Italy he proposes to die, and when at length his tomb will be broken by time his ashes will blow away on the soft Italian breeze.

It is commonly written that Petrarch had his seven-year-old son

Giovanni brought from Avignon to Parma, to be educated by a brilliant young schoolmaster-poet Moggio de' Moggi, who was tutor to the sons of Azzo da Correggio. The supposition rests on a phrase in a letter of Petrarch to Moggio: "The boy learned to admire you from infancy, and to love you before he loved anyone else." But for reasons that are not worth detailing I think it more likely that Giovanni did not go to Italy till 1347.

Petrarch's stay in Parma was fruitful. He worked at his *Rerum memorandarum* and probably at his everlasting *Africa*. It is reasonably conjectured that he then wrote in Italian his *Triumph of Modesty*, a pendant to the *Triumph of Love*. In spite of his alleged renunciation of love he added a number of poems to the *Canzoniere*.

However, no scholar in that Age of Tyrants could long live secure in productive peace. Two aggressive powers were rising in northern Italy: Milan under Luchino Visconti and Verona under Mastino della Scala, nephew of the four Correggio brothers. The Correggi had gained control of Parma with the aid of Luchino Visconti (does one remember?) and had secretly promised to turn over the city to him in four years. But Azzo had a better idea. Without informing his brothers, he sold the lordship of Parma to Obizzo d'Este, commander of the Veronese troops, for 60,000 gold florins, and decamped. This was about November 1, 1344. The three Correggio brothers gave up, and Obizzo entered Parma, with the usual acclamations and announcements that mercy, pity, peace, and love had at length begun their reign. But Obizzo fell into an ambush by the Milanese, who then laid siege to Parma. Naturally Mastino della Scala of Verona was shocked at the outrage. He sent an army to besiege the besiegers. In the circumstances, life in Parma, within its double blockade, was very uncomfortable during the winter of 1344-1345.

I had already been possessed for some time by the desire for liberty [Petrarch wrote to Barbato da Sulmona]. I had already begun to long for my transalpine Helicon [Vaucluse], since my Italian Helicon was ablaze with war. But what could I do? The road to the west had become impassable, so I looked to the east. Although this region swarmed with enemy troops, it seemed safer than the long roundabout way through Tuscany. So at sunset on February 23 I ventured forth from the city with a few companions. We succeeded in dodging the

hostile pickets. About midnight we got near Reggio, held by the
enemy. Suddenly a band of marauders burst out of ambush, loudly
threatening us with death. It was no time for deliberations; the time,
the place, the ring of enemies were too terrifying. Few in number, un-
armed, unprepared, what could we do against so many armed men,
practised in violence? Our only hope lay in flight in the dark. "The
comrades scatter, and black night covers them," as Virgil puts it. I
too fled, escaping death and the whistling arrows.

But when I thought that I had got safe—when, pray, is man ever
safe?—my trusty horse stumbled into a hole or against a tree-trunk
or a rock—I couldn't tell what in that black night. I was thrown to
the ground, shattered and almost unconscious. But I assembled my
wits and stood up. And, though for some time now I haven't been
able to raise my hand to my mouth, fear gave me strength to remount
my horse. Some of my companions had turned back to Parma, but
some, after vain wanderings, remained fixed in purpose. Our two
guides, tired, fearful, and totally lost, forced us to halt in a retired
spot, where, to add to our terror, we could hear the voices of enemy
sentinels on unidentifiable walls. Add to this a heavy rain mixed
with hail; amid the lightning flashes our fear of a dreadful death increased. [Curiously, the peasants of Reggio still tell how Petrarch, *il
Patriarca*, saved himself by conjuring up a tempest.]

The story is much too long to recount in detail. We spent that
really hellish night in the open, lying on the ground, while the swelling and pain of my injured arm increased. No grassy turf invited us
to sleep, no leafy boughs or rocky cave gave us shelter. We had only
bare earth, foul weather, Jupiter in anger, and the fear of men and
wild beasts, and I had my injuries into the bargain. There was one
comfort in our distresses. We stationed our horses across the path,
and used their backs as tents against the storm. Though before they
were shying and nervous, now they became quiet, as if they were aware
of their own sorry pass; and so they did us a double service that night.
Thus in toil and terror we reached daybreak. When the dim, dubious
light showed us a way among the underbrush we hurriedly left that
ominous region. Received within the walls of a friendly town named
Scandiano, we learned that a large force of horse and foot had been
lying in wait outside the walls to seize us, and shortly before our arrival had made off, driven by the storm. . . .

I then revealed my accident to my companions, who were moved to
tears. And since it did not seem safe to stay there, I took a mountain
path to Modena, and the next day went on to Bologna. From there I
am dictating this letter, to inform you of my own case and of the

general situation. My body will receive all the care humanly possible;
cure is certain, though it will be slow. The doctors promise recovery
by summer; I look for aid from Almighty God. In the mean time
my stiff right arm will not obey orders, but my mind is strengthened
by adversity.

As soon as Petrarch could travel with comfort he set out again,
not westward to his transalpine Helicon, but northward to Verona. Why the change of plan? No doubt he was summoned by the
irresistible Azzo, who had patched up his quarrel with Mastino
della Scala and had established himself in Verona. (He was now
very rich, of course.) Or perhaps the wars made the route by
Verona and the Alps the safest way to France. In Verona Petrarch
lingered, reunited with Azzo, with Guglielmo da Pastrengo, and
with other good friends.

Soon after his arrival in Verona he made his greatest literary
find. Rummaging in the cathedral library, he turned up a manuscript of Cicero's *Letters to Atticus,* hitherto unknown, except in
extracts quoted by other writers. Finding no competent scribe, he
devotedly copied the entire manuscript, into a codex so large that
it had to stand on the floor. His method was to write as he read,
without forward glances, thus obtaining infinite delight. His crippled right arm must have fully recovered.

The discovery was a capital one, both for the scholarly world
and for Petrarch. The Cicero he had known and worshiped had
been the orator and moral philosopher, the complacent utterer of
eternal verities, including not a few eternal platitudes. In the revealing letters to Atticus Petrarch discovered the incorrigible active politician, the none too scrupulous intriguer, the shameless
courtier of young Octavius. The letters did not reach the conclusion of Cicero's political activity, when his severed head was nailed
to the Roman rostrum and Fulvia, wife of Mark Antony, thrust
a hairpin through the famous eloquent tongue.

Petrarch was deeply pained to make the acquaintance of this
venal Cicero. He wrote his master a letter, dated "from the Upper
World, on the right bank of the Adige, in the city of Verona beyond the Po, on the 16th Quintile Kalends, (June 16), in the 1345th
year since the birth of that God whom you did not know." The
letter, he says, is not a counsel but a lament. Why, he cries, did you

involve yourself in so many vain contentions and quarrels? Why
did you abandon the retirement proper for your age, profession,
and fortune? Why did you let the false dazzle of glory bring you
to a death unworthy of a philosopher? Forgetting your own precepts, you stumbled and fell on the very road that you have lighted
for others. If you honestly sought liberty, why did you become a
familiar of Augustus? I pity you, my friend; I grieve for your errors. Like Brutus, I can have no confidence in those arts in which
I know you were so skilled. What avails it to teach others, to be
forever uttering golden words about the virtues, if you don't heed
them yourself? How much better it would have been for a philosopher to grow old in rural peace, reflecting, as you yourself said,
on immortality, not on this petty life, without concern for the
consular fasces, or triumphs, or any Catilines? But this is all useless! Farewell, my Cicero!

Not long after, Petrarch, remorseful, wrote Cicero a second letter, filled with apologies and praise. And finding conversations
with dead authors pleasant, he wrote several more, to Virgil, Horace, Homer, and others. These are really brief critical appraisals
of their work, in a familiar personal style, expressing Petrarch's
own estimates and moral judgments. Thus he inaugurated a minor
literary subspecies, the Letter to a Dead Author.

The discovery of the precious volume otherwise inspired Petrarch. In the *Ad Atticum* he met the everyday human Cicero,
telling of gardens and dinner parties, of the collapse of some of his
shops, of his need for a couple of library slaves to glue pages, of
trouble with the steam-pipe in his bathroom, which overheated the
bedroom above. The example of these familiar letters suggested to
Petrarch that his own might also be Literature. He began seriously
to collect and edit his own Familiar Letters for the edification of
posterity. Thus he provided us with the third (with the *Canzoniere* and the *Secretum*) of his important contributions to the
world's literature.

The reading of the *Letters to Atticus* further affected Petrarch
in a way that has only recently been defined. Hans Baron tells us
that the typical medieval Cicero was a teacher of misogyny and of
flight from active life. The new-discovered Cicero was civic-
minded, an active participant in public affairs. When Petrarch's
dolor at the loss of his serene, unworldly counselor had passed he

took to heart Cicero's lesson. Hitherto he had regarded his studies, his knowledge, as a selfish private satisfaction. From now on we are to see him, following Cicero's example, trying to impose his judgments on the world's rulers, and accepting, on occasion, a part in the world's business.

He did not, for all that, renounce his taste, and his search, for solitude. But he came to conceive of solitude as less a retreat than a means of service to others. A scholar should use his retirement to keep alive and to pass on the accumulated wisdom of the past. Petrarch thus defines the scholar's duties:

> to devote oneself to reading and writing, finding alternately labor and solace in each, to read what the first men wrote and write what the last men may read, and since we can't thank our elders for their gift of learning, to show our gratitude by passing them on to posterity, to keep fresh their names, whether unknown to the masses or fallen into oblivion, to dig them out of time's ruins, to transmit them clothed in honor to our children's children, to guard them in our hearts and keep them sweet on our lips; and in short by loving, remembering, celebrating them in every possible way to render them the gratitude which, though not adequate to their merits, is their due.

This would be a good motto for a Graduate School of Humanities.

Petrarch's discovery of Cicero's letters is an important event in the history of Humanism. This seductive word, distorted to fit numberless modern uses, means to the historian a combination of a revived passion for classical antiquity with respect for human worth and dignity, a secular justification of man's life in this world by his works in this world.

Petrarch was not the inventor of humanism. In the late thirteenth century signs of the coming spirit are discernible in several Italian cities, including Florence, Verona, Bologna, and Naples. In Padua a group of learned lawyers fought the prevalent scholasticism, hunted ancient manuscripts, and wrote long Latin poems on recent history. One of them, Mussato, wrote the first secular drama since classic times, a tragedy in Latin verse, in the manner of Seneca, on the bloodthirsty tyrant Ezzelino da Romano. Petrarch was therefore carrying on a tradition already formed. He became, however, dominant in the literary-scholarly group of his day. His great example inspired the eager young poets of Italy, and indeed it has not yet lost all its force.

Petrarch justified his primacy and attested his theory of the poet-scholar's duty toward society by formulating the concept of Italian patriotism. There are glimmerings of it in Dante, but Dante's patriotism was more Florentine than Italian. It remained for Petrarch, the exile, the cityless man, to conceive and express Italian nationalism. To this he was led in part by his profound conviction that his contemporaries were inheritors and continuers of the Roman Empire, in part by the spectacle of Italy's miseries.

The miseries were dreadful indeed. Petrarch's own life has afforded many examples of the prevailing violence, injustice, insecurity, want. The Holy Roman Emperor, Louis of Bavaria, under permanent excommunication, exercised his nominal guardianship of Italy only to exact trifling blackmail. The Popes in Avignon played Italian politics, chiefly to safeguard their own possessions in central Italy. In the north, tyrants ruled their cities with strong hands, and reached out for neighboring cities until they perished, commonly by assassination. The commercial city-republics, Florence, Pisa, Genoa, Venice, struggled bloodily to keep their independence.

The splendor of the Middle Age had disappeared, and the splendor of the Renaissance had not yet come. The Hundred Years' War began in 1337, devastating France and dimming its art and literature. Under the rule of force the common mind was invaded by materialism and skepticism. Trade dwindled, with the insecurity of the roads, and the commercial prosperity of Florence and other manufacturing cities dwindled in consonance. When the kings of England and France defaulted on their debts many of the great banking houses were bankrupted. The Turks advanced in the east, upsetting the lucrative trade of Venice and Genoa with the Levant. Agriculture suffered, and grain scarcities became common. Minor plagues appeared, premonitory of the Black Death of 1348. In the universal woe and dislocation, new state and power systems arose, the origins of modern European states.

A new scourge came to afflict Italy—the condottieri. The Italian city-states had never supported regular armies; in an emergency the citizens were supposed to rush to arms, which they did with much reluctance and little competence. German knights began drifting into Italy and taking service where they could find it. How, in fact, could a poor noble prosper, except by war, pillage, and ransoms? Pisa, in 1342, took the decisive step of hiring a force of German mercenaries, under the notorious "Duke" Werner von Urslingen. The Pisan war ended, and the mercenaries found themselves without employment. Some were hired by Luchino da Visconti of Milan, who established a standing army, regularly paid and reasonably loyal. Most of the unemployed joined Duke Werner, who thus became the *condottiere* or "conductor" of a band known as "The Great Company." He had inscribed on his doublet, in silver letters, the words: "Duke Werner, the enemy of pity, of mercy, and of God." He was also the enemy of humanity. He developed a technique: the Great Company would invade an unsuspecting region, rob, burn, rape, and kill; then it would threaten the capital city with attack, unless it would pay an enormous ransom. Thus he obtained vast sums from Siena, Perugia, Florence, and Bologna. In 1343 the Great Company worked its ravaging way to the gates of Parma. Having by that time all the booty it could transport, it was persuaded by bribes to return to Germany. Petrarch, arriving in Parma at the end of the year, heard many a tale of the condottieri and of wicked Duke Werner.

The memories of the condottieri, the calamities of Italy, and his own experience inspired Petrarch to write one of the greatest of his canzoni, *Italia mia* (*Rime* CXXVIII). Its noble summons to Italian unity and its bitter hostility to the Teuton have spoken vibrantly to every Italian heart, through centuries of division and subjection, through the Risorgimento and the two World Wars. It is the great classic of Italian patriotism.

It runs, in summary, thus:

My Italy, I grieve for the mortal wounds in your beautiful body. Christ, take pity on her, suffering such a cruel war for so slight a cause! Melt the hard hearts, and let me proclaim thy truth!

What are these foreign swords doing here? Why is our green land soiled with barbarian blood? Lords of Italy, you compass your own destruction! Nature built the Alps as a barrier against German rage, but short-sighted interest has brought this plague upon us! Heaven is angry; the predators are let loose among the flocks! Italy's divisions are laying waste the world's fairest land; and we are paying foreigners to shed our own blood! Don't you realize German duplicity? Noble Latin stock, cast off these oppressions and the superstition of German invincibility!

Is not this the land where I saw the light and was cherished, my homeland, my benign, devoted mother? Arise, Italians, take arms, for ancient valor is not yet dead in Italian hearts!

My lords, death awaits you; soon you must lay down hate and scorn. Turn to some better employment, that the way to heaven may be opened to you!

My song, be humble, for you are addressed to haughty folk, ever hostile to the truth. Speak then to those few high hearts that love virtue. Say to them: "Who gives me strength to speak, as I go crying: 'Peace! Peace! Peace!' "

Petrarch's work rings with the cry for peace. But there was no peace, and there is no peace.

XVIII: VAUCLUSE, 1345-1347

> *I want a solitude not utter, a leisure not inert and useless, but a retreat which may be profitable to many.*
>
> —De vita solitaria, *II 14*

PETRARCH LEFT VERONA IN AUGUST OR SEPtember 1345 (probably) and on arriving in Avignon received a cool greeting (certainly) from Cardinal Colonna, for overstaying his mission to Naples by nearly two years.

Bad news came from that city. The young Prince Consort, Andrea of Hungary, was assassinated, apparently at the instigation of some of the Queen's relatives. Among the participants was one of those Pipini whom Petrarch had labored to set free from prison. Hungary took fire, accusing the Queen and all her house of complicity, and proclaiming that the murder was a *casus belli*. The Pope, nominal overlord of Naples, tried to appease matters through his agents, including Philippe de Cabassoles. But matters were not appeased. Two years later a Hungarian army, including a corps of mercenaries under wicked Duke Werner, attacked Naples and shed a great deal of blood, though not that of the movers of Andrea's murder.

Petrarch meanwhile retired to Vaucluse, finding bliss in his dear valley and in the speaking solitude of his library. He brought surely many books from Italy to introduce to his old companions in their repositories.

He had also a living companion, a young relative from Florence, Franceschino degli Albizzi. The boy was a poet, of winning character. He prized the privilege of living with the great man; he must have been a considerable solace when Petrarch would fall into one of his fits of *accidia*, or when the solitude of Vaucluse would change its friendly face to hostile.

Philippe de Cabassoles returned to Provence from Italy in January 1346. Petrarch sent him a sweet poetic invitation to share the rustic delights of Vaucluse, pointing out that the gardens and shrubbery needed their attention. Philippe came for a happy fortnight, and inspired Petrarch to write his *De vita solitaria*. Good "Socrates" came also from Avignon to spend Christmas of 1346 in the valley, and the two walked over the hills, in their country clothes, to call on Philippe in his Bishop's Palace in Cavaillon. The loving commerce continued. Petrarch sent the Bishop a gold-and-silver-colored fish (a chub? a tench?) and a fat wild duck caught by his dog.

This dog was large, white, and noble, a present from a Spanish king to Cardinal Colonna. While in Avignon he was taken to the Papal Palace to look at a caged lion; he flew at the cage, barking enormously, and tried to tear down the bars. The Cardinal, finding him an uncomfortable pet, sent him to Petrarch, with a collar, a disk on his breast, and a jacket in the Colonna colors, red with embroidered white columns. He passed happily from high condition to low, from palace subjection to the frugal freedom of a country cottage. He regained his health and spirits, carried his head high, and, washed in the pure waters of the Sorgue, lost his mange. He undertook his duties with joy, guarding the house by night, protecting Petrarch's fields from shepherds seeking free pasturage. If Petrarch overslept in the dawn he would scratch reprovingly at the bedroom door. Then the two would set out, the dog bounding ahead, constantly turning to catch the master's eye. Petrarch would lie down on the streamside grass, and the dog would carefully examine all the neighborhood before coming to rest against his master and ward.

Among the chilly springs is a rockbound spot familiar only to the birds. I seek it out; he bars access to others with his great body. He announces, barking, any intruder, and attacks unless I bid him "Down!" Fierce with an enemy, he is gentle with a friend, drooping his ears and wagging his tail. . . . He goes bounding through the woods and into the stream, and comically imitates the voices of singing children. He is a bitter foe of wild geese, chases them over the rocks, plunges after them into the water, and brings them back, a dripping offering for my rustic repasts. . . . With weaker creatures he is meek as a lamb. He would not touch a sheep, a kid; he pretends to be frightened of a

hare, yet he will bite a pregnant sow and seize marauding cattle by the
ear. . . . A puppy may attack him with impunity, but he would not
quail at an angry lion.

The gallant dog once did Petrarch a great service. An aggressor
drew his sword with hostile intent, and the dog tore it from his
hands.

Petrarch devoted himself earnestly to flower-growing. He had
tried to build beside the pool of Vaucluse a garden where he might
welcome the exiled Muses. But the Nymphs of the stream took offense that he should prefer nine old women to them. A host of
Nymphs attacked, and tumbled his garden into the roaring waters.
Now he set to work again, hired a band of peasants and shepherds, chopped at the cliff, rolled a barrier of great stones to the
waterside, and built an all-weather walk down the valley to his
home. It was in vain; the war ended in total victory for the
Nymphs.

Very unmedievally, Petrarch watched his peasant neighbors
with sympathetic pity. He wrote Laelius:

Under my eyes I have the fishermen, worn out with cold and hunger.
It seems almost incredible. They labor all day, stripped and fasting,
and all night long until dawn, casting their hooks and nets, with one
constant result; to catch nothing, but to waste time that might be
more usefully spent. Yet their minds are so fixed on their task that
they can't be torn away from the fatal stream. The longer their harsh
labors last the better they like them. Scraping the very river bottom,
they find among the rocks and waters the poverty they would avoid,
and never obtain what they so eagerly seek. . . .We have an eagle in
our hills. A common swineherd, rougher than his own beasts, nay
rougher than the hirsute wild boar, has laid a plot against her, and
counting his life at its true worth, has let himself down by a double
rope from the lofty cliff that overhangs the Sorgue like a cloud. It
frightens me even to think of it. The bold pillager reached the eyry
and robbed the solicitous mother of her fledglings, the hope of her
race. He did this not once but twice or thrice, until finally the eagle
left her ill-starred home and moved her bushy bedding to another
part of the cliff, hoping to raise there a new family. But I think she
won't be any luckier there, for her stony-hearted enemy, eager for a
small gain and careless of his life, is busily knotting his ropes, with
which, suspended over the void, he will seize the prey as usual in its
new site.

Why did the peasant want the eaglets? Not for food, surely; probably to sell to some noble lord, to be trained to falconry.

On one occasion at least Petrarch was not content to watch the simple countrymen at their tasks; he intervened to prevent injustice. The lord of the nearby village of Thor, having failed to gain the good graces of a beautiful village girl, was incensed when she proved to be pregnant by her rustic lover. Though lover and lass prayed for permission to marry, the lord clapped the young man in jail, and promised to have him executed. The indignant villagers appealed to Petrarch, their wizard friend with powerful friends. Petrarch wrote earnestly to Laelius in Avignon, asking him to use his influence at Court. "We too have burned with love in our time, brother, and we ought to help lovers. . . .We should not suppose that country folk love less ardently than we; the blind bow-boy rules over every rank of mankind." We do not know how the case turned out; but if Petrarch's appeal had failed we should probably have heard more of it.

In the winter of 1346-1347 Petrarch paid a visit to the Montrieux monastery to see Gherardo for the first time in four years. Though his stay lasted only for a day and a night, it made a profound impression on him. The midnight offices in the candle-lit chapel, the harmonious chants without accompaniment, the smell of incense, the austere silence relaxed only out of courtesy to the visitor, stirred his romantic senses. He shared in a life that he must have at least imagined as possible for himself, a retreat from the world to a refuge of prayer and praise. And this retreat was total and irrevocable, a scaling of heights, whereas his own was full of compromises and equivocations and descents into seductive verdant vales.

When the time came to leave, Gherardo assumed a new authority and Petrarch a new humility. Gherardo laid three commands upon him: to be scrupulous in confession; to make his devotions by night as well as by day; and to abstain from commerce with women, "without which I had once thought I could not live."

Sobered and uplifted, Petrarch returned to Vaucluse.

His solitude there was laborious. He wrote a friend, Cola di Rienzo:

> The place is most suitable for my studies from morning to night, with its shadowing hills, sunny valley, hidden nooks, and the delightful

solitude that reigns everywhere. One finds there more tracks of animals than of men. The grave silence is broken only by the murmur of running waters, the lowing of cattle pastured along the shore, and the singing of birds. I say no more, because it has already become well known for its own sake and through my verses, so widely diffused. I came here eagerly, partly because my ears were battered and my mind afflicted by the city's tumult, partly to finish certain works which were half done or merely projected.

This was one of the most fecund periods of Petrarch's literary life. He worked at his compilations and moral essays, rifling his library and his capacious memory for pertinent examples. He did not desert Euterpe and Erato for Clio; he wrote poetic epistles and a series of Latin eclogues, and from time to time he added to the collection of poems to Laura in Italian. Many an author has found that a state of heightened tension provoked by labor in one literary field finds simultaneous outlet in another field. What an author needs is not so much leisure as stimulation by activity.

Petrarch's visit to Montrieux inspired him to write for the monks a small treatise, *De otio religioso*, On Monastic Tranquillity. It is in effect a sermon in praise of religious retirement, on a text from the 45th Psalm in the Vulgate (the 46th in the Protestant Bible): *Vacate et videte quoniam ego sum Deus,* "be still, and see that I am God." Petrarch celebrates monastic peace and silence as a means of liberation from the world, the flesh, and the devil, and as a way to the knowledge of God. He enforces his homily with literally hundreds of quotations. I find the book very tiresome.

The *De vita solitaria* is much better. It was suggested in conversations during Philippe de Cabassoles's long visit to Vaucluse in 1346. Petrarch worked at it off and on for years, and what with one thing and another did not deliver it to Philippe till twenty years later. As the *De otio religioso* deals with religious retirement, the *De vita solitaria* treats of the satisfactions of a layman's solitude as a way of life on this earth, in contrast to the miseries and subjections of cities. The theme forecasts the Return to Nature of Rousseau and the eighteenth century. The book is likewise significant in implying that self-cultivation is a proper end of man, and that a superior man is justified in abandoning the world in order to train and tend his personality. Again, this is a humanistic concept.

The book begins with a long description, really a caricature, of the day of a successful city businessman. However exaggerated, and however dependent on classic satirists, the description includes many details that might brighten a historical novel, as indeed they may well have done. The businessman, surrounded by flatterers, sits at dinner on cushions under an unsteady canopy. Filthy cooks prepare menacing concoctions; the rarest of wines are defiled with honey, sugar cane, blackberries. Serpents are kept in containers on the board, as protection against poison. A "pregustator" plies his perilous trade, tasting all dishes and proving their innocence by his survival. Opulence upon the table contrasts with horror below. "The floor stinks with upset gravies, it is slippery with wine and grease; bones and blood lie about."

The value of the book depends on what one seeks in it. It contains an abundance of wise and eloquent passages, and many a curious anecdote. For the delver into Petrarch's life and spirit the book offers many revelatory notes. It betrays a sour monastic attitude toward women, destroyers of men's peace of mind; for the moment, the poet denies Laura and his master Amor. The body, he says, is the domestic enemy; one should keep it so exhausted that one will long rather for food than for lasciviousness. But these ascetic counsels he promptly belies. His lasting ideal was frugal scholarly retirement, the *otium literatum* of the ancients. He admires, broad-mindedly, the Brahmins, their retirement to woods beside a stream, their serenity and silence, their refusal of fear and desire, but he cannot approve their nudity, their inhuman disregard of food and sleep. He applauds Ciceronian moderation. "Let your sleep be short, your food light, your drink simple, your dress modest; but there should be some difference between a man's dress, bed, and food and those of cattle. . . .In all things I seek for measure. . . .To spend one's whole life outdoors is more proper for bears than men."

As for his scholarly compilations, he seems to have put aside his *De viris illustribus* in favor of the *Rerum memorandarum liber*. He had worked at it fitfully since 1337; he never finished it, since by its nature it could never be finished. It is a collection of remarkable facts, from his reading and experience. The genre was already well known; there were many medieval *factorum et dictorum memorabilia*.

The book contains little to interest a modern reader, unless per-

haps some new compiler of old anecdotes. One must however remark the author's very unmedieval skepticism about the miraculous. He tells us to regard prophecies with distrust; "who believes
the prophecies of the mad is himself mad." More reasonable is the
contention that the dying may foresee the future, for their souls
are half freed from the body. But don't listen to old wives' tales,
don't heed dreamers and snorers! People aver that the sun shone
at night? Well then, it was day. They say that the shields hanging
on the walls of a besieged city miraculously fell down? Probably
the leather straps were gnawed by mice. "If you told me that the
mice were gnawed by the shields, that would be a real portent."
Do not confuse the miraculous with the rare. A mule gives birth;
that is rare, but not miraculous.

Cicero had proposed in his *De divinatione* rules for the circum-
spect observer: in the case of a reported wonder, investigate the
cause if you can, and if you can find none, still be assured that it
exists, for nothing can occur without a cause. Petrarch goes further, to erect a dogma of critical method: "This rule is to be laid
down: nothing happens contrary to nature, even though things
may seem contrary. In fact nothing is a portent among men. This
is very important: in men's minds, so well constituted by nature,
many various errors have pullulated, and in the realm of reason
many ancient follies and superstitions rule, but finally reason
holds its place there, by which we can be distinguished from other
animate creatures."

This trust in human reason is a component of the humanism to
come. It is also a forecast of the rejection of miracle by Diderot
and others of the Enlightenment.

The *Rerum memorandarum*, like Petrarch's other books, is
marred for the modern reader by his abuse of quotations. But we
live in an age of reference books and of libraries. Petrarch's readers had no place to look anything up. Many of his citations come
from obscure or newly-discovered authors, like Plautus, and were
certainly welcomed by his contemporaries more than they are by
ours. However, even some of his contemporaries found that he
overdid his quotations. He replied to critics: "I could use fewer; I
could even not write at all. . . .But there is nothing that moves me
so much as the examples of great men. It's useful to uplift oneself,
to test one's mind to see if it contains something solid, generous,

firm, and constant against ill fortune, or if one has lied to oneself about oneself. To do this there is no better way than to measure oneself against these great men."

The writing down of old wisdom was for him a method of communion with the noble spirits he loved. He continues, in the letter just quoted:

I talk much, I write much, but less to benefit these desperate, wretched times than to relieve and unburden my own mind. . . .I write to please myself; and while I write I associate eagerly with our ancients in the only way I can, and I happily forget those among whom an evil fate has forced me to live, and I employ all my strength of mind to flee the moderns and seek the ancients. As the very sight of my contemporaries offends me, the recollection of the glorious names and noble deeds of men of old fills me with such an unspeakable joy that, if it were known, many would be amazed to learn how much more delight I take with the dead than with the living.

His joyful friendship with the great dead moved him constantly to repeat their words. To quote is to recognize another's wisdom and to share it. "I was born to better things than to be the slave of my body. You say: 'Seneca said that!' Certainly he did; and I say it too, and many will say it after me, and perhaps many said it before him, and whoever may say it, if he's sincere, will say a very fine and splendid thing."

(Does a critic reproach me for quoting too much? I quote Petrarch in defense of quotation.)

Petrarch varied his prose composition by writing a series of Latin Eclogues, inspired by Virgil. They are collected under the title *Bucolicum carmen*. They are puzzling and often exasperating works. The poet takes a subject of private concern, transports it to a pastoral setting among nymphs and shepherds, and puts two or more interlocutors with classical names to talking. Useful information and ideas often gleam amid the gloom. Thus in the First Eclogue Silvius (Petrarch) discusses with Monicus (Gherardo) the merits of the classic poetry of Virgil versus those of the Psalms of David. This is interesting to the literary historian.

The allegory in the Eclogues is so thick that, as Petrarch proudly proclaims, they are totally incomprehensible without the author's key. Following medieval doctrine, he believed in the poetic value of allegory. Thus he found an allegory, a moral sense, in

Virgil: the subject of the *Aeneid* is the perfect man; the storm released by Aeolus represents the attack of passions and appetites on reason, and so on. Petrarch did his best to incorporate allegory in his *Africa*. In the Eclogues it is overwhelming.

It is only a step from the prizing of allegory to the prizing of obscurity for its own sake. Petrarch recommended literary difficulty, alleging that the labor of the reader to understand brings him a sweet delight. "What we have sought with difficulty becomes dear and lingers the more clearly in the memory." His defense of hard poetry is very apt today.

But his taste for obscure allegory passed as he grew older. He abandoned ambiguity for clarity, being less eager to dazzle by mystery than to convey his thought entire to others. It is much easier to be obscure than to be clear. Obscurity is our natural state; clarity is a victory.

Thus during his stay in Vaucluse Petrarch was busily writing in various styles. He was occupied also in building up an informal association of book-hunters. He wrote to a cousin in Florence:

> Divine favor has freed me from most human passions, but one insatiable lust remains—I can't get enough books. Perhaps now I have more than I need; but with books as with other things, the more one gets the more one wants. And books have their own special quality. They thrill you to the marrow, they talk to you, counsel you, admit you to their living, speaking friendship. And they introduce you to other books, their friends. Some people, to be sure, accumulate books with no intention of using them, but just from lust of possession; not to nourish the mind, but to ornament their rooms. So if you love me, put this charge on a few trusty scholars: let them ransack Tuscany and look through the book-cases of the monks and of other studious men, to see if anything may turn up to sate, or better to irritate, my thirst.

With his letter Petrarch enclosed a list of Books Wanted, and remarked that he had sent the same list to friends in France, Spain, and England. He was establishing himself as the moving agent in the great work of recovery of the classic past.

All this book-buying was very expensive, and possibly Cardinal Colonna's generosity was strained. For all his praise of poverty, Petrarch wanted more money. He petitioned the Pope, in 1346, for a vacant canonry and an archdeaconry in the cathedral of

Parma. His Holiness granted the canonry, which apparently bore
a comfortable income, but not the archdeaconry. He went farther;
he suggested an Apostolic Secretaryship, a high and important
post, putting its incumbent at the nerve-center of European politics, in constant intimacy with the Pope himself. But it was very
exacting and would demand all a man's time and thought. Petrarch succeeded in declining it without offending the generous
pontiff. This Pope Clement VI and others several times hinted
that Petrarch might qualify for a bishopric; but obviously the
ecclesiastical obligations and the duties of a bishop had no charm
for him.

In 1347 the Pope granted a greater kindness to the poet. He
legitimized his son Giovanni, in answer to a petition. Legitimation
was important, for it made the boy eligible to hold a benefice and
enjoy its revenue. The Church has always insisted that its clergy
be physically and morally whole and that they be of sanctified
origin, even if the santification be an afterthought.

The Pope's favors could not allay Petrarch's dislike of the
Papal Court. He wrote three blasting sonnets against its wickedness and lewdness. To these "Babylonian sonnets" we shall return, noting here only that while he was seeking and obtaining
favor from the great he was penning venomous attacks on his
benefactors' institution and way of life.

After two years in Avignon and Vaucluse Petrarch decided to
return to Italy. His motives, as usual, were mixed. His congenital
restlessness made even Vaucluse seem a bore. His young relative
Franceschino degli Albizzi left him, apparently to travel in northern France. His relations with Cardinal Colonna were strained.
The Cardinal had become distrustful and demanding, and
wounded him by introducing him to proud prelates who treated
him with disdain. And most importantly, Petrarch was lured to
Rome by the rebellion of Cola di Rienzo, of which we shall tell
in its time.

Petrarch wrote, in defense of his remove, his Eclogue VIII, a
mingling of affection and rancor toward his master, the Cardinal.
It is couched in the form of a dialogue between a poor shepherd
and a rich one. The poor shepherd, Amyclas, asks leave to depart,
complaining of his poverty and of the bad weather and foul water
of his home. "Love of the homeland draws me. The savor of
Italian grass is the sweetest." When Ganymede, the rich shepherd,

asks how he can bear to quit his friends, Amyclas replies: "The land has become hateful to me. At first I was bound to it by habit, by your friendship, by the fair form of an enticing girl. But youthful passion is unfitting in an elder. I have served you for twenty years. Now I want to be buried in my homeland; let me go. A friend is summoning me." Ganymede: "So I have cherished you from youth and formed you by my teachings only to have you seek another host? I have labored for another's benefit. You were poor in youth, you will be poor in old age, and poor you will die. I shall enjoy my wealth alone." Amyclas: "And I shall go singing, alone, in the hills and forests, under Apollo's frondage, and I shall labor in the flowery fields like the honeybees. You will dwell in your rich wood, but burning cares will trouble your repose."

This was an unpleasant leave-taking from a kind master, with its reference to a rival patron (perhaps Azzo da Correggio, perhaps Cola di Rienzo). It was also an unpleasant end to a friendship that had filled half Petrarch's life. Cardinal Colonna could regard the poet as ungrateful and self-seeking, and so can certain modern commentators.

The outward, the published reason for Petrarch's departure was that he should be installed in his Parma canonry. The Pope made the journey official by appointing him a papal envoy, with an important letter to deliver to Mastino della Scala in Verona. Petrarch bore also a commission from the papal librarian to establish in the Italian libraries a bibliography of the works of Cicero.

Petrarch had hoped to take as traveling companion a young musician friend who sang more sweetly than a nightingale or a dying swan, but the young man seems to have disappointed him. It is likely that he was accompanied by his ten-year-old son Giovanni, happy in his new legitimation. Petrarch proposed to give him a proper education under a superior Italian schoolmaster. They left for Italy on November 20, 1347.

But first Petrarch had a sweetly painful farewell to make. He called on Laura. She received him among her attendants. She was strangely somber, oppressed as by a premonition. As he remembered (Rime CCXLIX):

> I am in terror when I scrutinize
> the mind's clear record of our parting day.
> I left my heart with her and came away,
> and yet my thought to her forever flies.

Still like a rose I seem to see her rise
'mid lovely ladies, lesser flowers were they.
Humbly she stood, nor sorrowful nor gay,
as one whom fear entirely occupies.

Her usual elegance was laid aside,
her pearls and garlands and her colored dress;
she did not laugh and sing and talk again.
And so I left my darling to be tried;
and now black thoughts and dreams and omens press
hard on my soul; please God it be in vain.

XIX: LOVE—ADAGIO PATETICO

> *Now blessed be the songs of many years*
> *that I have uttered in my lady's praise,*
> *and blessed my desire and sighs and tears.*
>
> —Rime *LXI*

I WOULD OFTEN FLEE TO THE SOLITUDE OF VAU-
cluse as to an impregnable fort, hoping to quell in its shades
the youthful fever that wasted me for many years. But alas
for my fond hopes! My very remedies worked to my bane, for I
burned the more desperately with my smoldering woes, with no
one at hand in that solitude to help quench the fires. So the heart's
flame issued from my lips and filled the valley and its skies with a
woeful murmur indeed, though some called it sweet. Thus were
composed those songs in Italian of my young distress, of which I
now repent with shame, although they seem to be very welcome to
those who suffer from the same disease." Thus Petrarch wrote to
Luca Cristiani in 1349, with genuine shame for his subjection,
but with honest complacency also. In the chemistry of the spirit
the emotions do not neutralize each other.

In Vaucluse and Avignon in 1343, in Parma in 1344, he had
written occasional love-poems to Laura, as inspiration visited him
or a happy conceit came to mind. These he later fitted into the
Canzoniere in appropriate places, according to a scheme partly
chronological, partly psychological.

On returning to Provence in 1345, he called on Laura. He observed that she was growing older; she bound her hair with pearls
and gems, in middle-aged style. He hoped in vain to learn that she
had missed him during his long absence. On the contrary, she received him with a storm of anger and prideful scorn. Undaunted,
he visited her again, and gazed so greedily at her eyes that she

shielded them with her hand. He seems even to have ventured a
caress unduly bold (CCXL):

> Already I have asked Love's intercession
> with you, my lady, and I'll ask again
> (my bitter joy, and my delicious pain!)
> pardon for my unpardonable transgression.
> I'll not deny it, reason and discretion,
> which properly the upright soul restrain,
> are impotent when winds of impulse reign
> that put me in carnality's possession.
>
> Your heart, it is so surely comprehending,
> and with such heavenly virtue does it brim
> as never rained from any star in air.
> Say then, in undisdainful pity bending:
> "What help was there? My face obsesses him
> because he is so greedy and I so fair."

She alone of all the world was unmoved by the poetry that, he
assured her, would render her immortal. She was ice; flowers
would sooner bloom in winter than love in that frozen heart. But
her purity was admirable and beautiful. He importuned her with
too frequent visits, but it was beyond his power to absent himself
from her. She was infuriated by a gossiping tale that he used the
name of Laura in some poems to cover a base attachment for another lady. Despite his frantic denials, there are in fact indica-
tions that he wrote some poems to this mysterious rival, and that
he either excluded them from the *Canzoniere* or adapted them to
fit Laura. Though the supposition is unsure, we may readily accept that the fleshly poet was involved with a woman or women
more responsive than Laura, that he paid them in poet's kind with
poems, and that eventually he found the poems too good to be
denied to posterity.

His love for Laura was still sensual in essence. He had always
felt a certain satisfaction in the deplorable vigor of his passions.
"Desire spurs me, Love guides me, pleasure draws me, habit transports me, hope cajoles me," he wrote (*Rime* CLXI). "The senses
reign, and reason is dead." His desire was sinful, as he well knew,
as he had acknowledged in the *Secretum*. However, the recognition of sin is by no means equivalent to its cure. Reason told him
to abandon Laura, to break loose from her agonizing scorn and

seek the way to Heaven. But the second thought immediately followed, that her very mistreatment was sweet. He returned to her
therefore, well aware of the dangers to his peace and life.

His sufferings were real, however much he found pleasure in
their analysis and expression and in the portrait of himself as the
greatest despairer of all time. He wrote (CCXXIV):

> If constancy, a heart that cannot feign;
> if sweet-repining honorable desire;
> if longings burned in chastity of fire;
> if the hunt through the labyrinth, in vain;
> and if the thoughts writ on the visage plain
> but strangled on the lips, when fears conspire
> with shame to make them silently retire;
> if pallor, violet-tinct with lover's pain;
>
> and if the holding of another dear,
> more dear than self; if tears and sighs and woe,
> ardor and wrath are all one's meat and wine;
> if burning far away and freezing near
> are reasons that in love I suffer so—
> Lady, the fault is yours. The hurt is mine.

(One may notice the form of this sonnet: a fourteen-line sentence, a succession of correlative subordinate clauses leading up to
the conclusion, the message, the punch, in the last line. The structure was one of Petrarch's favorites, and after him it was used by
many thousands of successors, including Shakespeare.)

The solitude of Vaucluse he found hostile to his peace of mind,
whereas he could submerge his troubles in activity, even in the
bustle of cities (CCXXXIV):

> O little room, my harbor from the sea
> of stormy's day tempestuous concerns,
> now all the day's constraining but adjourns
> my griefs, to spring nocturnally in thee.
> O little bed, once my security
> from woe, upon thee Eros overturns
> the gathered pain of tear-collecting urns,
> tilted by two fair hands of ivory.
>
> So now I flee my outraged sanctuary,
> but most myself, the thoughts of my own mind,

those very wings on which I once have flown.
In the hateful, hostile mob (O strange vagary!)
my only port and refuge can I find,
such is my fear to find myself alone.

His commonest device was one familiar to every modern poet. He would brood on an actual incident of the endless courtship, perceive in it a drama of meaning, a generalization, and this he would transform into a conceit, or coherent rounded thought fitting tightly in his fourteen lines. Laura dropped a glove, perhaps one of those very gold-embroidered silk gloves inventoried among Laura de Sade's possessions. Petrarch picked it up and thrust it in his bosom, proposing to keep it as a precious relic. Then, shamed at his mean presumption, he gave it back. The result is *Rime* CXCIX:

O lovely hand that lightly holds my heart,
that needs but close to press my life away;
hand in which nature and heaven's self display
in their own honor, all their craft and art;
nails, of the rarest pearls the counterpart;
delicate, slender fingers, which today
naked I've been permitted to survey
(they're not too frail to set my wounds a-smart!)

O white and dainty and belovèd glove
in which the ivory and rose has lain,
never was any spoil so sweet as this!
I'll steal as well the veil that hides my love!
—No, I'll not steal. Here is your glove again.
How quick the vanishing of human bliss!

He encountered a group of ladies, Laura's friends. He asked for her, and was told that she was housebound by a jealous person, whom one is tempted to identify with Hugues de Sade (CCXXII). He saw twelve ladies in a river boat, with Laura in the middle (CCXXV). (The apostolic number, one notes.) They came to shore and climbed into a triumphal chariot, and Laura sang with celestial sweetness. No doubt this was one of the episodes of a country festival, of a sort still common in Provence.

At a party, an eminent visitor singled out Laura, though she was not the youngest or the richest, and bestowed on her a public kiss (CCXXXVIII). "The sweet, strange act filled me with envy."

The identity of the noble visitor is a subject of furious controversy. Again, Petrarch and Laura visited an old gentleman's celebrated rose-garden (CCXLV). He picked the two most perfect blooms and gave one to each, saying, with a laugh and a sigh: "The sun never saw such a pair of lovers!" Oh blessed eloquence! Oh happy day!

More of his days were unhappy. Laura's occasional illness filled him with terror and pity, and pity, he observed with interest, increased his desire. Her glorious eyes were afflicted by some malady, natural enough amid the blowing filth of Avignon. Petrarch caught the disease (pink-eye?) from her, to his great satisfaction.

He was resigned to his hopeless pursuit, finding in it a *modus vivendi* or a *modus amandi*. He wrote (CCXVII):

> Once I besought her mercy with my sighs,
> striving in love-rime to communicate
> my pain, to see in that immaculate
> unmelting heart the fires of pity rise.
> I longed the freezing cloud that round her lies
> in the eloquent winds of love to dissipate—
> or else I'd rouse against her all men's hate
> because she hid from me her lovely eyes.
>
> But now I wish no longer hate for her
> or for me pity; for I know at last
> in vain against my fate I spend my breath.
> Only I'll sing how she is lovelier
> than the divine, that, when my flesh is cast,
> the world may know how happy was my death.

The thought of death, hers and his, was much in his mind. Her gathering illnesses no doubt provoked the splendid CCXLVI, beginning "L'aura che'l verde lauro e l'aureo crine/soavemente sospirando move." One notes the triple pun in the first line and the onomatopeia of the second, which defeat the translator.

> The gentle airs, breathing a little sigh,
> lift the green laurel and her golden hair;
> and Laura's face, so delicately fair,
> sets free the vagrant soul from body's tie.
> She is the candid rose, thorn-compassed, shy,
> and yet our age's glory and despair.

O living Jove, grant me this single prayer:
grant only that before her death I die.

So I'll not see the sun go out, to bring
the world's disaster, and to leave behind
my eyes, no other light discovering,
my soul, to one unending thought confined,
my ears, that never hear another thing
but the sweet language of her virtuous mind.

Forebodings of her death increased, perhaps intensified by certain epidemics that foreshadowed the Black Death of 1348. He
wrote (CCXLVIII):

You seek the best that Nature can confer
upon our universe? Then come and see
that beauty shining like a sun on me
and on the world, virtue's disparager.
Only, come soon; Death ever is astir
to seize the best, leaving the wicked free.
She is too lovely for mortality;
the gods are looking eagerly on her.

Come soon, and you will see all comeliness,
all virtue, and all gentle-mannered ways,
sweetly conjoined past any power to sever.
And you will vow my rimes are valueless,
you'll stand so dazzled in delicious maze.
—But if you linger, you will weep forever.

Before his departure for Italy in November 1347 he arranged
a farewell meeting, in the presence, of course, of some sympathetic
lady friends. She was unwontedly sombre. Brooding on the moment, he reflected (CCL):

Madonna once would come in dreams to cheer
my slumbers with angelical delight;
but now she brings foreboding in the night,
nor can I drive away my grief and fear.
And in her phantom-face I see appear
her own hurt mixed with pity for my plight,
and I hear words that cry above my fright
that the final term of joy and hope is near.

"Does our last evening not return to you?"
she says. "Your eyes were wet and shining when

for the lateness of the hour I had to flee.
I could not, nor I would not, tell you then,
But now I tell you, it is proved and true,
never again on earth you'll look on me."

When he had got to Italy, what with lack of communications, what with the outbreak of the Great Plague, the poet's forebodings turned to terrified conviction (CCLIV):

There is no word of my adorèd one,
my lovely and belovèd enemy,
and frantic hope and fear alternately
rowel my reason, and my spirit stun.
Beauty ere this by beauty's been undone,
and she's all beauty and all modesty.
Perhaps God wants such virtuous radiancy
to take from earth, and set in heaven, a sun

and no mere star. Why then, I'll soon behold
the end of my few joys and many tears.
Why did we have to part, that unconsoled,
far from her side, I fill my heart with fears?
The fable of my life will soon be told;
my time is done in the middle of my years.

"Petrarch's originality," said Edgar Quinet, a nineteenth-century French critic, "consists in having realized, for the first time, that every moment of our existence contains in itself the substance of a poem, that every hour encloses an immortality." These are good words, and true. Petrarch was the first to recognize that the picking up of a lady's glove, a gift of roses, an eye-inflammation, could provoke thoughts that do often lie too deep for tears. He discovered that the smallest incidents of everyday life could be transformed into poetry, that they are themselves poetic. However commonplace his discovery may seem today, it was momentous for literature and for man's awareness of the holy wonder in his existence.

His second great novelty is that for the first time since Catullus he sang a completely human love. He rejected the stylized posturing of the troubadours, the philosophical and allegorical tendencies of Guinicelli and Dante, the mystic idealism of the stilnovisti. In short, as Adolfo Bartoli says, he brought woman down to earth. While Beatrice is lost in high heaven, a far dream, more angel than woman, a reflection of divine light, Laura is a real woman, living in the routine of the petty Avignon nobility. Bartoli continues:

> This descent into his own spirit, with its seizing of its griefs and joys, its making of a fleeting moment an immortal poem; this self-scrutiny, turning every impulse into art; this abandonment of medieval symbolism and transcendental idealism; this seeing of humanity plain, feeling it in all its truth—this is what makes Petrarch the first lyric poet of the new time, the heir of antiquity and the herald of the great art of the modern world.

Why, indeed, should this discovery have been so novel? The poetic impulse has always existed; there have been poets since language emerged from the stage of grunts and barks. The Middle Ages are rich in poetry, lyric, epic, devotional, humorous. But the poetic spirit, tense and oppressed with strange emotions, had no established, acceptable form of release. It was Petrarch who found, for his own and future times, a way to convert private emotion into adequate verbal form. In so doing he created the Italian poetic language, still standard. He created our concept of what lyric poetry is. He created also the conventional character of the poet, a man of intense feeling, whether ardor, joy, or woe, whose feeling turns to song as naturally as does that of a courting bird. He showed the would-be writer how a poet should look, act, think, feel.

We may smile at his excess of emotion, and find in it a share of self-deception. We may find the total devotion of the *Rime* even a little ridiculous. Still, we should wonder at total anything, and especially at total devotion. If we say that his love was exaggerated, we can only mean exaggerated for us. We admit our own incapacity to exaggerate thus. Maybe we are condemning ourselves, not Petrarch.

XX: COLA DI RIENZO

Truth is the mother of hatred.

—Fam. *XV 12*

T THE OUTSET OF THE FOURTEENTH CEN-
tury a certain Lorenzo, or "Rienzo" or "Rienzi" in the
Roman dialect, kept a tavern beside the Tiber. His wife
helped out as laundress and water-carrier. The couple produced in
1313 a son, Nicola or Cola di Rienzo, a handsome, imaginative,
brilliant boy. His mother died, and he was put in the care of a
relative at Anagni, in the shadow of the old Papal Palace. He must
have had some good schooling, for he was steeped in Livy, Cicero,
and the Roman poets, and he learned to write Latin with classical
felicity. On his father's death in 1333 he returned to Rome,
studied the notary's trade, and married a notary's daughter. He
developed an emotional antiquarianism, and collected antique
gems. He was the first person in 600 years, so far as we know, to
copy and preserve Rome's mossy, chipped inscriptions. He loved
to translate and expound them for the benefit of passers-by. His
collection is said to be incorporated in Pope Martin V's fifteenth-
century handbook.

Cola's antiquarianism developed into a passionate devotion to
ancient Rome, and a no less passionate indignation at the city's
degraded state, with the papal rulers far away and with the local
barons engaged in noble gang warfare. An avowed dreamer—he
called himself *tribunus somniator*—he came to picture his own
petty self as the cleanser of modern Rome and the restorer of
ancient greatness. To explain and justify his illustrious emotions
he conceived a pretty theory, that he was in fact the son of Emperor Henry VII, who was in Rome being crowned from May to

July 1312, and who must surely have fallen in love with the pretty laundress, wife of Lorenzo.

Cola was deeply influenced by the prophecies of Joachim of Floris, twelfth-century illuminate, whose doctrines were dear to the Spiritual Franciscans. Joachim alleged that the Age of the Father was long past, the Age of the Son was near its close, and the Age of the Holy Spirit was at hand. A dreadful period of catastrophes, comets, meteors, earthquakes, hurricanes, floods, plagues, under the temporary rule of Antichrist, would presage the coming of the Age of the Holy Spirit. To Cola, God's evident anger at the Popes, the Emperors, and the miserable world plainly proved that Joachim's prophecies were correct.

When Petrarch was laurel-crowned in April 1341, Cola would hardly have absented himself from that glorification of Rome's past, that declaration of hope in its future. But we have no proof that the poet and the visionary met.

In 1342 Clement VI received the papal tiara. A delegation of eminent Romans came to Avignon, praying His Holiness to return to his seat in Rome, and in any case to proclaim the Papal Jubilee not a centennial but a semi-centennial, with the next Jubilee to occur in 1350. A Jubilee, with its promise of unheard-of-bargains in indulgences, would attract pilgrims from the whole world and would go far toward relieving the business depression in the Holy City. Cola di Rienzo, representing the tradesmen and workmen of Rome, was sent as a late supplementary delegate to Avignon. He arrived only in January 1343, but he wrote the delegation's official report, announcing that the Pope was unable to return to Rome in person, but that he graciously authorized a Jubilee in 1350. Cola signed himself "Roman consul, and sole legate of the people, of the orphans, widows, and the poor."

Unfortunately Cola, in an address to the Pope and Consistory, went out of his way to assail the Roman nobles, calling them, probably with entire justice, highway robbers, assassins, grafters, and adulterers. The Pope seems to have been rather pleased than otherwise; Cola was justifying by inference the settlement of the papacy in Avignon. But the Italian cardinals, Roman by birth, relationship, or sympathy, froze with disapproval. Cardinal Colonna wanted to have the upstart jailed. In Rome the nobles responded to the news of Cola's denunciation by confiscating his small property. Therefore Cola prudently remained in Avignon when the delegation returned to Rome. He was in hard straits, destitute and sick, apparently forced for a time to take shelter in a charity hospital.

Cola and Petrarch inevitably met. This spring and summer of 1343 were for Petrarch, as we have said, a period of crisis, with the writing of the *Secretum,* the retreat of his brother to a monastery, the birth of a daughter combining to provoke a deep spiritual upheaval. His friendship with Cola fits in this period of sharpened sensibility, when he was in a mood to reject old ways, to hunt new directions for his spirit. The two were immediately bound by liking and mutual respect, by a common ardor, a romantic patriotism, a mystical Romanism. They shared a pious enthusiasm for ancient Roman writers and a dream of what Rome might again become. "There was a psychic affinity between the two men, which would draw them together at once," says Tatham. "Each was an idealist; each rested his hope in the revival of a glorious past without much practical knowledge of present conditions; each was apt to be blinded by his gift of exuberant rhetoric to the hard facts of the existing situation."

One day the two met by chance in the old church of St. Agricol. They emerged, eagerly talking. Petrarch wrote Cola two days later:

> When I think of our earnest, sanctified conversation before that holy ancient temple I feel afire, as if an oracle had issued from its recesses. I seem to have heard the voice of a god, not a man. You depicted to me the present decadence and ruin of the divine Republic, and with your moving eloquence you touched our wounds to the quick, so that the sound of your words, still ringing in my ears, brings renewed distress to my mind, tears again springing in my eyes, flame bursting from my heart.

Petrarch was always ready to intervene against injustice, especially toward one to whom he was emotionally bound. He pleaded Cola's case with Cardinal Colonna, and the Cardinal relented, doubtless perceiving no menace in the penniless and rather grotesque enthusiast. The Cardinal spoke to the Pope, and the Pope appointed Cola (though not till April 1344) Notary of the Capitoline Camera, with the adequate salary of five gold florins a

month. Petrarch had of course left for Naples on his diplomatic
mission in September 1343.

Cola returned to Rome, probably in the summer of 1344. He
soon made himself heard. At a public meeting he arose and
shouted to the noble officials: "You are no good citizens, who suck
the blood of the poor and won't help them!" One of the Colonna's
knights strode down and struck him a resounding blow in the
face, and a senatorial secretary made an obscene gesture.

Undaunted, Cola built up his reputation and power among the
discontented commoners, merchants, and artisans. He promised
that with the government by the people and with the humbling
of the barons peace and order would reign and the Popes would
return. He had large symbolic paintings made, like billboard car-
toons, picturing Rome as a sinking ship or as a desperate woman
assailed by noble brutes. From a tribune in St. John Lateran's,
dressed in outlandish robes of his own design, he harangued the
citizens. He discovered an ancient bronze tablet (now in the
Capitoline Museum) that conferred the rights of rule on Ves-
pasian. He had it incorporated in a giant picture and lectured on
it, deducing, very unwarrantably, that all sovereign rights reside
in the Roman people alone. The Roman people were impressed,
but the nobles found him merely comic. They invited him to dinner and bade him speak; they roared with laughter when he proclaimed: "I will be a great lord, and Emperor; and I'll bring you
barons to justice; I'll have *you* hung, and *you* beheaded!"

It is a very curious episode in the history of class struggle, of
proletarian revolution. The idea of popular sovereignty was of
course drawn by Cola from his reading of Roman republican history. The idea was developed by others in Italy before Cola,
especially by Marsilius of Padua. The medieval *populus romanus*
had its recognized rights, even to crown Emperors. But certainly
Cola's driving force derived not from theory but from emotional
need, from the hatred of the innkeeper's brilliant son for the rich
and well-born, from the sufferer's desire to teach the happy higher
caste what suffering means. Add to this his sense of destiny, of being God's chosen instrument, which can so readily end in
paranoia.

The 20th of May 1347 was Pentecost, when the Holy Ghost
descends to earth to bless his favorites. By luck or by heaven's dis-

positions old Stefano Colonna had taken Rome's militia into the
country to collect food, and the two noble senators were absent.
On Saturday, the eve of Pentecost, Cola assembled his partisans
and occupied the buildings on the Capitoline without meeting resistance. On Sunday, with great blowing of trumpets and ringing
of bells, the people marched to the Capitol behind the red banner
of freedom, the white banner of justice, and St. Peter's banner of
peace. The Pope's Vicar was in the van, for the Church had every
reason to desire the overthrow of rule by the great arrogant families. Cola spoke eloquently of the misery and servitude of the poor
Romans and read his code of reform, and all the people acclaimed
him their lord. Two days later he summoned his Parliament. He
assumed the power to reform administration and justice, the right
to decide foreign policy, the right to impose capital punishment.
He took the title of Tribune, which recalled the defenders of
democracy in old Rome.

The barons remained strangely inert. They had no rules for
conduct in such an overturn of all familiar sureties, and their old
family hostilities made union difficult. Can it be that they were
afraid, in view of the overwhelming popular enthusiasm for Cola?
Could their callous consciences have been touched? Were they
troubled by recollection of Cola's after-dinner speeches? At any
rate, most of them swore loyalty to the new government.

The Pope recognized the new regime, in the interests of peace
and order, but he preferred to call Cola Rector, rather than
Tribune.

The news of the *coup d'état* filled Petrarch with joy. He found
a hero in his mean century. "I think of you day and night," he
wrote to Cola. He reveals that he was informed of Cola's dream;
he foresees that Rome will rise again to its ancient greatness. He
promises to write daily, with inside news of the Papal Court. He
proposes to compose Cola's history, and also a great poem that
shall fire all Italy.

One of his letters of this period may be taken as typical. It is a
paean to liberty. He urges Cola to die rather than to surrender
liberty. Forget your old affection for Rome's masters, ravishers and
plunderers, interlopers, foreigners! The Orsini came from Spoleto,
the Colonna from the Rhine. They rose by theft and rapine, seizing Rome's wealth, suppressing its liberty. Such is their insanity

that they wish to be held not men but gods. You are another Brutus, avenger of the state. The tyrants, or rather bandits, have grown fat and rich on public misery. They even wreaked their vengeance on ancient marbles! They have broken down the triumphal arches and sold the stones; they send columns and inscribed gravestones to Naples. You Romans have done nothing! You were sheep! But now you are awake. Drive out the ravening wolves! Arise! They can do nothing against you if you are united. Traitors must be punished by the sword! And do you, O Tribune, rush to combat! If you must die in battle, do so courageously, for you will assuredly be rapt to heaven! Be sure to take communion regularly, and read the great examples of Roman history. And you, O Romans, bethink you that this man was sent you from heaven. Dare all for love of country; die with joy! Unfortunately my clerical state and my circumstances prevent me from joining in your holy war, so I send you only words. But I shall recall the Muses from their exile, and sing strains that shall ring through the ages!

Now Cola sent a circular letter to the princes and rulers of Italy, summoning them or their representatives to a conference on August 1. He promised liberty, justice, and peace to all Italy, *sacra Italia*. (This is the first recorded use of the expression.) Thus he makes clear the height of his purpose, to unite the Italian nation under the headship of Rome. He signs himself "through the will of Jesus Christ Niccolò severe and clement, tribune of liberty, peace, and justice, liberator of the sacred Roman republic." Very few of the princes answered the letter.

Meanwhile, true to his promises, he reformed the administration of his city. He formed a popular militia and had his own bodyguard of a hundred picked youths, who swore to die with him. He raised money by strict tax collection; previously very little of the levies had reached the treasury. He reorganized the judiciary and the courts, decreeing that no case should last over two weeks. He established a Family Court, with the duty of settling disputes privately. He conceived even a rudimentary social welfare program, with provisions for housing and food distribution. At the same time he enacted blue laws against adultery, blaspheming, and gambling. Everyone was required to take communion annually or or suffer confiscation of one-third of his property.

On the last day of July he attained his apotheosis, being dubbed knight under the auspices of the Holy Ghost. Preceded by a bearer with an unsheathed sword, he led a great procession to his head-quarters, the Lateran Palace. He wore a white silk gown embroidered with gold, and carried a sceptre. Over his head fluttered a pennon emblazoned with the sun. In the Baptistery of St. John he took the ritual bath of purification in the porphyry tub wherein, it is said, Emperor Constantine was cured of leprosy by Pope Sylvester. Then the vigil, the sleep in a bed of state, which ominously collapsed. The next day, dressed in scarlet, he appeared on the balcony of the Lateran Palace and received the golden spurs. He proclaimed Rome the capital of the world and all Italians Roman citizens. He summoned the two contenders for the emperorship, for him to decide between them. He summoned also Pope Clement and the College of Cardinals. He made three sword-cuts to east, north, and west, exclaiming: "Questo è mio!" The Pope's Vicar began to protest, but Cola had him drowned out with a flourish of trumpets. Below in the Campo Lateranense the people assembled around the equestrian statue of "Constantine," which is now on the Capitoline. It was ingeniously equipped to spout red wine from one nostril, water from the other.

Two weeks later Cola was crowned as Tribune in Santa Maria Maggiore, with a silver wreath and sceptre. A Roman senator presented him with an orb, symbol of sovereignty. Cola, in his harangue, compared himself with Jesus Christ, who at thirty-three ascended to heaven, crowned with victory.

Now all this was very picturesque (and strangely proto-Fascist), but it revealed the growth of inordinate pride, which has undone so many reformers. The ceremonies alarmed the Pope, who saw his claim to Roman rule flouted. The rulers of other Italian cities were outraged by Cola's assumption of overlordship. And the more sober of his Roman hearers trembled at his presumption and whispered that he was mad. The fickle populace began to fall away from his banner.

Cola wrote to Petrarch, dating his letters in the First Year of the Liberated Republic, thus superseding the years of Our Lord, and providing a precedent for the Fascist calendar. He may have made the poet a dazzling offer. A recently discovered letter from Barbato da Sulmona to Petrarch suggests a duumvirate in Rome,

Petrarch to be the theorist, Cola the executive. We do not know if this idea echoed one of Cola's, but unquestionably Cola invited Rome's poet laureate to come to his city and partake of its restored glory. Petrarch was sorely tempted. But he was in a very awkward position; to pay his way he would need either an official mission or a subsidy. His loud advocacy of Cola while the Pope was withdrawing his favor debarred him from appointment as an emissary. A subsidy could come only from Cardinal Colonna, and the Cardinal was turning very cool toward his protégé. Perhaps he was informed by the postboys, great readers of letters, that Petrarch was accusing the Cardinal's father and family of every crime and urging their extermination by the sword. Perhaps Petrarch's conscience troubled him. It should have.

In August came the news of Cola's elevation to the knighthood of the Holy Ghost, of his coronation as Tribune, of his blasphemies and infringements on papal rights. Petrarch found himself very uncomfortable in the Palace of the Popes. He retired to Vaucluse and wrote his Eclogue V, designed to uplift the spirits and stay the morale of the Roman people. But its symbolism is so lofty that in spite of the author's appended explanation still no one is quite sure what it means.

In Rome matters moved swiftly. King Louis of Hungary, preparing a punitive expedition against Naples, found it politic to send an embassy to Cola. The Tribune summoned Hungary and Naples to appear before him; he then pronounced Hungary in the right. Thus he enraged not only Naples but the Pope, that city's guardian. Cola learned the idealist's lesson, that high abstractions like justice had best be left shining in the realm of the ideal. The sword of justice has a dull blade; it always lets some innocent blood.

A rebellion broke out on the northern approaches to Rome. The Orsini plundered the country up to the city's walls. The barons plotted busily. The citizen army and Rome's new allies proved very reluctant to fight.

In early September a messenger from Cola to the Pope, bearing a silvered wand for obeisant people to kiss, was held up not far from Avignon; his captors broke his sacred wand and his letter box over his head. Petrarch, assuming that the outrage was committed on orders from the Papal Court, was horrified. He informed Cola that at a conference of high prelates in Avignon the question was soberly discussed whether the union of Rome and Italy in peace would be advantageous to the papacy, and the conclusion was reached that a unified Italy would be disadvantageous. Petrarch interpreted the decision as meaning that Italian discord brought to the Curia numberless appellants with their hands full of gold. "Let the wolves be called, that the sheep may have more need and fear of the shepherd!" he wrote, in ironical elucidation.

On September 14 Cola assembled in the Capitol for a conference all the barons he could reach, then treacherously arrested them all and confined them in the Capitoline prison. Friars Minor prepared them for decapitation on the morrow. Old Stefano Colonna alone refused confession and communion, treating his captors with sarcastic contempt. The barons begged the Parliament for mercy. When the moment came for the shedding of so much noble blood, Cola hesitated. He announced that the barons repented and bowed to the People. He bestowed on them rings and curious titles, then marched with them to Mass. Thus the coup ended in a parade and in universal anger. In the popular view the bold, decisive, though treacherous, stroke had turned into foolish softness. It would have been much better, said the mob, to kill the nobles rather than to shame them. The nobles were furious at the remembrance of their own pleas for mercy, anxious to make amends for their poltroonery. They recognized that their only hope of survival lay in the destruction of Cola.

On September 19 Cola issued a manifesto announcing that all Roman citizens would have a hand in the election of the Holy Roman Emperor. The next Emperor should be Italian; the name of Cola di Rienzo was suggested.

The nobles retired to their country castles and openly organized rebellion. The Colonna even made peace with the Orsini. Cola contented himself with writing manifestoes and letters to the Pope and with displaying on the Capitoline a large painting of the two chief rebels hung by their feet. He entered on what the historian Theseider calls his "verbose-mystical" phase, apparently losing contact with reality. His health suffered; he was subject to insomnia, nightmares, manic and depressive moods, alternations of activity and aboulia. The morale of his people sank, with hard times, food shortages, disorder.

When news of the arrest of the Roman nobles and of Cola's
support of the Hungarian attack on Naples reached Avignon,
papal policy toward the Tribune hardened. The Pope called Cola
a usurper, threatened him with an interdict, accused him of
heresy. Petrarch's disquiet and indignation grew. There was no
peace for him in Vaucluse. It is very likely that he felt that if he
could only join Cola in Rome he could persuade the Tribune
to follow a more reasonable and successful course. But to get permission and funds for a trip to Italy he would need an effective
excuse.

As we have already recorded, he found his excuse in his desire
for formal installation in his Parma canonry. At the same time, the
Pope made him an official envoy to Mastino della Scala in Verona,
and gave him an urgent letter calling upon Mastino to oppose the
passage of Louis of Hungary into Italy. Delayed by illness, Petrarch, probably with his son Giovanni, left Avignon on November 20.

On the same day the counter-revolution in Rome began. The
Colonna, in concert with the other nobles, arranged that secret
agents in the city should be stationed at the Porta San Lorenzo
and should open the gates to the attackers. But Cola was warned
by his counter-intelligence corps. The traitorous guards were replaced by loyal defenders. The assailants appeared outside; old
Stefano Colonna shouted that they were a group of Roman citizens returning home. The gates opened to entrap them. A few
leaders charged impetuously in; the gates swung shut, and the in-
truders were massacred. Two sons and a grandson of Stefano Colonna fell.

Two days later Cola, who had taken no heroic part in the action, brought his son to the bloody pool wherein the Colonna had
died, and with its red waters consecrated him Knight of the Victory. This ceremony, says Theseider, was regarded as in very bad
taste, even for those times.

Thus old Stefano's prediction, made to Petrarch ten years before, that he would survive all his sons, came close to the fulfil-
ment that was reached in the following year, with the death of his
last son, Cardinal Colonna. Stefano refused to weep for the victims of the ambush. He said only: "God's will be done; it is better
to die than to live in servitude to a clown."

On December 15 came a determined uprising of the nobles and their sympathizers. They marched to the Capitol, shouting "Death to the Tribune!" Cola's militia responded only limply, the populace not at all, and Cola, instead of rousing his partisans with eloquence and vigor, fell into weeping despair. He fled to the Castel Sant' Angelo, held by his friends, and then to Naples. There for the moment we shall leave him. Rome promptly relapsed into its familiar anarchy.

Petrarch had arrived in Genoa on November 25, 1347. There he received news of Cola's extravagances, of his open alliance with the King of Hungary, and of the battle of the Porta San Lorenzo. He recognized that any hope of a Rome reborn, under the enlightened guidance of a Tribune and a Poet Laureate, was ended. He wrote a sorrowful letter to Cola, reproaching him for his misdeeds and chiefly for his truckling to the worst elements of the populace—for with all Petrarch's glorification of the Roman people he was no democrat; he had only contempt for the vulgar herd. "Shall the world then see you fall from being the leader of the good to become the partner of the vile? . . . I cannot alter matters, but I can flee them. . . . I was hastening eagerly to you; now I change my course. Certainly I shall not see you transformed into a different man. A long farewell to thee also, Rome, if these stories are true."

It was a sad waking from a beautiful dream. Petrarch fell back on his alternative plan. He went to Parma, where presumably he was confirmed in his canonry. He then delivered the Pope's urgent message to Mastino della Scala of Verona. He had taken plenty of time. The message, adjuring Mastino to oppose the passage of King Louis of Hungary, arrived some time after the King had passed through Verona without hindrance.

During 1348 the trace of Cola is hard to follow. Evidently he tried to join Louis of Hungary in his attack on Naples; he found Louis in retreat, not from Neapolitan might, but from the dreadful plague, advancing from Sicily. Before the end of the year Cola took refuge among the Celestine monks who dwelt in the stark folds of Monte Maiella, in the Abruzzi, and who, light-headed with hunger and self-castigation, cultivated mystic experience. Adepts of Joachim of Floris, they saw in the plagues and earthquakes proof that the reign of Antichrist had come and that the Age of the Holy Ghost was at hand. It appears that one of Cola's companion monks convinced him that God was trying him, preparing him for new and greater tasks as agent of the Holy Spirit, to persuade the Emperor to a universal reform, in accordance with the Joachimite prophecies. The Emperor, notice, not the Pope. The Pope had issued an order for Cola's arrest and deliverance to the Inquisition. Cola lost his confidence in the papacy as the savior of the world.

In the summer of 1350 Cola, anonymous in his black Celestine gown, attended the Jubilee in Rome—where he must have felt many a sharp dazzling memory rise—and then joined a band of Bohemian pilgrims, with whom he crossed the Alps to Prague. There he announced his presence to Emperor Charles IV, who had held his exalted status for only a year. The Emperor gave him three interviews, and was tempted by Cola's eloquence, by his proposal of an assault on Rome that would render the Emperor temporal ruler of the city, in preparation for the promised coming of a new Angel-Pope and the Age of the Great Universal Reform. But Cola fell into his old error of excess and lost the Emperor's confidence. As ecclesiastics claimed him on the ground of heresy, Charles had him put in a secure though comfortable prison.

The Pope demanded him, and Emperor Charles, after long delay, yielded. Cola arrived in Avignon, under guard, in August 1352. As he entered the city gates he inquired if Petrarch was at Court; he learned that the poet was in his retreat at Vaucluse. Cola was confined in the Tour de Trouillas of the Papal Palace. Shackles on his leg were attached to a ring in the ceiling, but he could move, he had his bed, food from the papal table, plenty of books.

Petrarch made no effort to visit the prisoner. Perhaps such an effort would have been fruitless. He describes Cola's state in a letter to Francesco Nelli—a rather cool letter. He is not even sure if Cola is actually to be pitied, for he should have died a glorious death on the Capitoline, instead of submitting to shameful imprisonment. "I loved his virtue, praised his purpose, wondered at his courage. I congratulated Italy, I foresaw the rule of the kind city and peace over all the world." So, he continues, he had urged Cola on with inspiring letters, of which he was in no way ashamed. Returning to the present, three cardinals have been appointed to

try his case. "In a way, I admit that he is worthy of every punishment, because what he wished he did not wish with sufficient per-
severance, as the need and status of affairs demanded; and, having
undertaken the defense of liberty, he let the enemies of liberty depart with their arms when he could have crushed them all together
—an opportunity which fortune had granted to no other ruler."

The reference is to the night of September 14, 1347, when Cola
held at his mercy, by trickery, most of the great Romans, including three of the Colonna. The passage in Petrarch's letter has been
sharply criticized, as worse than Machiavellian. After all that the
Colonna had done for him, Petrarch regrets that Cola could not
bring himself to crush (*opprimere*) them. And what can "crush"
mean, if not murder or imprison? To such criticism one may answer that Roman history is full of examples of the supremely virtuous man's rising above the obligations of friendship, gratitude,
and affection, in devotion to the state's interest. Nevertheless Petrarch rises above such obligations almost too easily, with no indication of moral struggle.

He sought to help Cola's case by writing an appeal to the
Roman people. He insists that Cola is accused not of neglecting
but of defending the cause of liberty. "This is the greatest crime
that is charged to him, a crime judged worthy of the gallows: that
he has presumed to state that even now the Roman empire is in
Rome and in the hands of the Roman people." After a long celebration of Roman glory Petrarch concludes that the empire ceases
to be Roman if it is established elsewhere. He begs and beseeches
the Romans to come to the aid of their defender, to send an embassy demanding that he be carried to Rome for trial on the scene
of his alleged crimes.

The committee of cardinals decided that Cola was not a heretic.
The final disposition of his case was delayed by the death of
Clement VI in December 1352 and by the accession of Innocent
VI.

The new Pope recognized that something must be done about
Rome. He appointed Cardinal de Albornoz his legate, to restore
the authority of the Church in Italy. Aware of the nostalgic memories clustering about Cola's name, he released him, on September 15, 1353, and sent him to Rome to promote the papal policies.

Cola delayed nearly a year on the way; he had got fat and lazy in his Avignon prison. He reentered Rome in triumph in August 1354. In a general burst of enthusiasm he was made Senator. But soon his old faults of character appeared, even in aggravated form. He angered many by beheading a popular noble. He showed signs of mental trouble, now weeping, now displaying delirious gayety. After a bare two months the public, angered by a new tax on wine, turned against him.

Early on October 9, in his lodgings in the Capitoline palace, he heard the shouting mob approach. He donned helmet and armor, appeared on the balcony with the gonfalon, tried to speak, but was overcome by clamor. Arrows and stones flew; he was struck on the hand. He opened the banner, and pointed to the eternal letters SPQR, the Senate and People of Rome. The shouting redoubled. He retreated to his room, quickly cut off his beard, blackened his face like a charcoal-burner, donned a worker's smock, put a bed-cover over his head as if he had just looted it, knotted some towels together to make a rope, and slid down to the empty inner court of the palace. He mingled with the throng and joined in their curses and shouts. But he had overlooked his gold bracelets. He was recognized; the mob, demanding blood, stabbed him, cut off his head and paraded it with joy. The headless body was dragged to the Colonna houses near San Marcello and hung by the feet to a Colonna balcony. Then it was burned and the ashes were thrown into the Tiber, the sacred river beside which Cola had been born.

Well, *sic semper tyrannis.* The tragedy of Cola di Rienzo is both melancholy and familiar, the tragedy of generous ideals defeated by flaws of character. With a little more moderation, a little more hard sense, Cola might have been one of the great popular heroes of history, one of the makers of a new concept of government and social justice. But no doubt the great demagogue cannot be moderate, and the reasonable man cannot be great.

XXI: THE BLACK DEATH

Ubi dulces nunc amici, ubi sunt amati vultus,
ubi verba mulcentia, ubi mitis et iocunda
conversatio?

—Fam. *VIII 7*

E HAVE SEEN THAT PETRARCH WAS IN GENOA at the end of 1347, that he renounced his purpose to join Cola di Rienzo in Rome and went instead to Parma and Verona. He was in Verona on January 25, when a great earthquake shook much of Italy and Germany, but nothing worse happened to him than the tumbling of his books to the floor. He returned soon to Parma, and fulfilled his unexacting obligations as canon of the cathedral. The disputed archdeaconry again falling vacant, he asked Pope Clement for it, and was rewarded in the following August. The archdeacon stands second only to the bishop in his diocese. Fortunately for Petrarch, the post did not seem to require residence, or in fact any serious duties.

Now for the first time he was actually well-to-do. He owned his Parma house; he could afford a corps of secretaries and servants; he could buy books and succor his friends. He had such ease and freedom as few poets attain.

He installed himself in his pleasant home with its brook and gardens. The house was as dear to him as his Vaucluse retreat, perhaps dearer, for a certain miasma of pain hung in the Closed Valley. He worked happily in his garden; when asked his profession he liked to reply: "gardener." He was much flattered to be asked by Luchino Visconti, tyrant of Milan, for shoots from his trees. He kept a garden-journal on the end papers of a collection of Latin miscellanies. He took note of the weather, the moon's phase, the temperature, the time of day of his operations. In the spring he had his flowers and early vegetables. In June he dug up a willow

grove to make a meadow, and sowed grass. In November he tried
an experiment; he trimmed the vine-stocks, replanted some shoots,
turned the rest under. He was not very hopeful, because of the
lateness of the season, the north wind, the unfavoring moon, and
the adverse counsels of Virgil in his *Georgics*. But in the spring the
shoots had fair success. He transplanted an apple tree and a peach
tree, which died; but a transplanted hoarhound did well, as did
his salvia, hyssop, and rosemary. He grafted foreign vines success-
fully on old stocks, and trained them from tree to tree to make an
arbor. An entry reads: "February 4, 1349, sixteenth day of the
moon, between nones and vespers, cloudy and damp; but still I
transplanted a fruit tree several years old, but not too old, from a
snady spot to an open one, exposed to the sun, in a deep hole,
but without any manure or other outside encouragement except
for black, fat earth, worked just right. We'll have to see how it
succeeds." In fact it withered away. But *placet experiri*, he repeats; I like to try things out. Thus consistent is character, even in
little things. In his garden as in his study Petrarch was a creative
spirit, an innovator, always eager to try things out.

The garden was also his workshop. He wrote best outdoors,
among the flowers and birds. He informed Luchino Visconti, in
March 1348: "While the gardener is busy with his plants and trees
I shall devote myself to words and poetry, as the stream that divides
my orchard hurries past, softly complaining."

His garden was a refuge not merely from the world's busy distractions, but from the world's sickness, the Black Death.

The Black Death is the bubonic plague. It is caused by bacilli
that inhabit the parasites of rodents, especially the rat-flea. It is
most virulent in hot climates, for fleas are likely to be dormant in
cold weather. It commonly appears in humans only when the rat
population is reduced, when the multiplying fleas seek new hosts.
But infection may be caused by inoculation, inhalation, ingestion,
or the settlement of the bacilli on abraded skin. The bacilli enter
the blood stream, pass to the nearest lymphatic glands, multiply,
infect other glands. They act against the walls of the blood vessels,
producing hemorrhages and the dark patches that inspired the
name of the Black Death. The tongue turns black; swellings and
carbuncles, the "buboes" that give the plague its proper name,
appear under the arms and in the groin. Special sequelae may be

gangrenous inflammation of the throat and lungs, like our malig-
nant pustule of the lungs, with violent pains in the chest, vomiting
and spitting of blood, and a foul smell.

The triumph of the Black Death was prepared by years of excessive rain, short harvests, human hunger, and lowered vitality.
It arrived in western Europe in October 1347, when an infected
convoy of Genoese ships from the Crimea staggered in to Messina.
"Sickness clung to their very bones." The people of Messina would
not let the crews land, but evidently the rats came ashore, for soon
all Sicily was plague-stricken. The disease reached the mainland
and the French ports early in 1348 and traveled rapidly inland
with the fleas of merchants, refugees, and animals.

The cities, of men and rats, suffered worst. Normal life was at
an end. The physicians were powerless; the clergy had no time to
say the last rites. The doors stood open, for no one dared to rob.
Criminals released from jail and hardy peasants from the mountains threw the dead in great common pits, with only a curse for
viaticum.

People thought Judgment Day was at hand, our world at an end
—and indeed the medieval world was *in extremis*. They supposed
that God was inflicting some savage, though incomprehensible,
chastisement on his creation, punishing innocent and guilty alike.
A moral breakdown ensued; those still healthy gratified every
secret longing, for virtue, prudence, public reputation, wealth became suddenly meaningless. Men embraced vice, says Egon Friedell, with a consumptive's sensuality.

Boccaccio has left us the classic description of the plague in
Florence. Many a man, he says, dined heartily with his friends on
earth and supped with the departed in Paradise. People avoided
each other; brother abandoned brother, parents children. Sick
women negligently exposed their bodies to servants. "People cared
no more for dead men than we care for dead goats." The dead
were tossed in huge trenches, like bales in the hold of a ship. Many
of the living spent their time in mirth, jesting, and feasting.
Peasants neglected their farms, thinking only of enjoying what
they had. Animals wandered unchecked through the wheat; but,
Boccaccio notes with interest, many beasts returned voluntarily at
night to their pens and stables. Sheep and hogs caught the disease
and died unheeded where they fell.

The insatiable plague traveled north. It reached England in
August 1348, and then Scandinavia, and then Russia, as it receded
in Italy, as troops of flagellants lashed themselves in the streets to
attract God's attention, as a considerable number of Jews were
burned to appease His wrath.

How many died? No one knows. Various estimates put the
mortality at one-fourth to three-fourths of Europe's population.
Many villages were totally wiped out; many cities became standing
ruins, inhabited by bewildered troglodytes.

The social and economic effects were revolutionary. With the
extinction of families and heirs, ownership of land and houses
lapsed and fell into the hands of lawless squatters, often into the
hands of the Church, still alert to its worldly advantage. Land
went untilled for lack of laborers; the cities emerged from the
reign of disease to find themselves under the reign of hunger.
Church-building and the luxury trades, such as stained-glass
making, came to a stop. In England the workers and commoners,
recognizing their advantage, gained new power. In governments
and the Church, survivors moved up to fill the numberless
vacancies.

Morally and spiritually, the effects of the destruction of half
humanity were strangely slight. One would expect an overturn of
the world's conscience in one way or another, whether a rejection
of the old faith or a deepening of it. One would expect that art,
literature, philosophy, conduct would bear the indelible scars of
the plague. But no; God's lessons did not teach humanity anything much. As soon as recovery began, even before, men reverted
to their previous concerns. The new post-plague world was little
different from the earlier one. The great war between England
and France paused briefly for lack of combatants; it then resumed
for another hundred years. Italian principalities again began
killing as many as possible of their surviving neighbors. Most people seemed determined to banish the plague from memory. Even
Petrarch rarely refers to it, once it is safely in the past.

The plague seems to have spared Parma, relatively to other
Italian cities. To be sure, Petrarch met terror and tears everywhere; he could not walk the streets without meeting a funeral.
But he tells us strangely little of the plague in Parma, perhaps
because his correspondents needed no descriptions of familiar

woes, perhaps because he avoided them by retreat to his silent
library and his gardens, where, in fact, the evil bacilli would not
hunt him out. Evil thoughts could still seek him there, as he hints
to "Socrates": why has God punished us and not our fathers,
equally guilty? Can it be that God has no concern with human
affairs?

His greatest grief was the loss of dear friends. There was Laura,
of course; and Cardinal Giovanni Colonna, smitten in Avignon.
"Fallen is the high Column and the green Laurel," begins an
elegiac sonnet (Rime CCLXIX). His engaging young kinsman,
Franceschino degli Albizzi, fell in Savona on his way to join
Petrarch in Parma. And Roberto dei Bardi, Chancellor of the
University of Paris; and faithful Sennuccio del Bene; and many
and many other friends.

Some time later he had news of his brother Gherardo's heroism
in the monastery of Montrieux. When the pestilence struck, the
prior advised him to save himself by flight. He replied: "I'd gladly
accept your counsel if you would point out to me some place in-
accessible to death." "Here you will find no one to bury you," said
the prior, but Gherardo was resolute. Soon after, the prior was
stricken, and Gherardo buried him. One by one the monks fell, as
many as three a day. Gherardo received their dying kisses, a heroic
act indeed, prayed over them, washed their bodies, dug their
graves, and carried them on his back to their ultimate home.
Thirty-four companions died, and he was left alone, with only a
dog alive. He had to watch all night against the robber bands
roaming the country, and with God's aid and by inspired eloquence
succeeded in holding them off. Anyway, there was not much to
rob in Montrieux. Finally he got relief from neighboring monasteries. He visited the annual assembly of the Carthusians at the
Grande Chartreuse; the humble monk was received with the highest honor among eighty-three priors. He returned with recruits to
refound Montrieux.

The plague struck Avignon with particular fury, suggesting to
many that God was displeased with Christendom's management.
On the pestilence's course we are well informed, through an
account by the papal physician, Guy de Chauliac, and a long letter
from Petrarch's Socrates to correspondents in Flanders. Three-
fourths of the population died, 1,500 in three days, seven cardinals,

a hundred bishops, 358 Dominicans. Seven thousand houses stood empty. Guy de Chauliac says that the affliction began in January 1348 and lasted seven months. Its first form was marked by fever and spitting of blood; death was usual in three days. A second form displayed the buboes in the armpit and groin. This lasted up to five days. "The contagion was so great, especially when there was blood-spitting, that not only by remaining with the sick but even by looking at them people seemed to take it; so much so that many died without anyone to serve them, and were buried without priests to pray over their graves. A father did not visit his son, or the son his father. Charity was dead, hope lost." Socrates adds that the sick were served like dogs by their kin, who put food near them and ran. Many, dying, were buried alive. Even cats, dogs, and chickens shared the general doom. The Jews were accused of bringing the plague by poisoning wells, and many were burned, without effect.

Pope Clement VI remained immured in his Palace, with a giant purifying fire roaring in his hearth. He wore an emerald ring that when turned east reduced the chance of infection, when turned south abated poison. He retreated after a time to a country castle, but endowed Avignon with a new cemetery. It is said, though on dubious authority, that he consecrated the Rhone so that it could serve for the disposal of bodies.

The depleted Curia remained in Avignon. Such is the power of routine that the Court business was somehow carried on, while clerks sickened and fell at their *scriptoria*. In June the Pope bought the dying city from its feudal owner, Queen Giovanna of Naples, for a bargain 80,000 florins. Petrarch's archdiaconate is dated in August of this dreadful year.

It was at the height of this terror that, as we have told, Laura died in the morning of the sixth of April, and was hurried to her grave in the Franciscan church. Socrates' letter reached Petrarch in Parma in the morning of May 19. It may well be that at this time he wrote the first of his sonnets on Laura dead (CCLXVII):

> Alas, that gentle look and that fair face!
> Alas for the body's beauty when you wended
> your gracious way! Alas, your words that mended
> the brutal, and taught honor to the base!
> Alas, that smile of yours, whose wounding grace

has come to death, and all my hope is ended!
You'd have been queen of earth, had you descended
to a younger world, to a less evil race!

Still I must burn in you, in you respire.
I was yours utterly; my stricken heart
can feel no other hurt, after today.
You showered hope upon me and desire
in our last moment, ere we came to part.
And then the wind blew all your words away.

He had already written two parts of a long poem in Italian
terza rima, a Triumph of Love and a Triumph of Chastity. Now
he wrote at least part of a third, a Triumph of Death. In a flowered
valley of Provence Laura meets Death, who plucks a golden hair
from her head. As a great throng of dead and living acclaim her,
she dies:

Not like a suddenly-extinguished light
her spirit left its earthly tenement.
She dwindled like a flamelet, pure and bright,
    that lessens in a gradual descent,
keeping its character while waning low,
spending itself, until its force is spent.
    Not livid-pale, but whiter than the snow
the hills in windless weather occupying,
only a mortal languor did she show.
    She closed her eyes; and in sweet slumber lying,
her spirit tiptoed from its lodging-place.
It's folly to shrink in fear, if this is dying;
    for death looked lovely in her lovely face.

XXII: ITALIAN JOURNEYS, 1349-1351

> *I can't be safe unless the past perishes. . . .*
> *Often a change of position has relieved the*
> *weary, a change of air the sick. Grafting*
> *sweetens fruit trees, transplanted vegetables*
> *gain health.*
>
> —Fam. *IX 3*

FOR ALL PETRARCH'S CLAMOROUS DESIRE FOR peaceful solitude he could not bear it long; for all his philosophic contempt of worldly dignities he could not resist an invitation from the great. In 1349 and 1350 he was away from his Parma house and garden, his beloved books, his archdeaconry, a good half of the time. In Parma were none of the close friends on whom he so much depended. He was on bad terms with the Bishop, who may have been jealous, or maybe irritated by the constant absences of the archdeacon of his diocese. And he was evidently just restless. There was an external reason for his displacements—pressures from men of power who wanted him to ornament their little courts; and internal reasons—dissatisfaction with his unrewarding life and with himself, and the last assaults of the demon of concupiscence. He seemed to be hunting an end in existence by mere movement from place to place.

Importuned by Jacopo da Carrara, benevolent tyrant of Padua, Petrarch paid him a visit in March 1349, and was received not as a mortal but as if he were a blessed soul entering heaven. Jacopo obtained for him a canonry in the Paduan cathedral. "If Jacopo had lived longer, this might have been the end of my journeys and wanderings." But Jacopo did not live long; he was murdered just before the following Christmas by his illegitimate half-brother. This was a family custom; Jacopo had gained the rule of Padua by murdering his cousin in his bed. Petrarch composed for Jacopo an epitaph celebrating his more than human virtues.

Evidently Petrarch's benefices and the favors of the great permitted him to live very much at his ease and free from any tiresome obligations. He had his houses in Vaucluse and Parma, and now the occupancy of a house in the cathedral close in Padua, with a pleasant garden. The servant staff in the three houses was considerable; he had his secretaries and copyists, as many as six at one time; he had his horses, and funds for continual travel and for book-buying. He insists of course that he was always in straits for money, which may be true, and that money and favor always took him by surprise, which may not be quite so true. Wealth, he said, was a slavery; but poverty was a slavery too, and on the whole a worse one.

He returned from Padua by way of Venice, Treviso, and Verona, arriving in Parma in May 1349. He learned that he had just missed a visit from two old friends, Mainardo Accursio and Luca Cristiani. Both had been his college mates in Bologna and fellow servants of Cardinal Colonna in Avignon. Luca was a scholar, Mainardo a man of cultivation and charm. They were returning to Italy after the Cardinal's death. They brought affectionate messages from Socrates. After vainly waiting a day in Parma they pushed on over the mountains toward Florence.

Petrarch was inconsolable. He wrote them long letters, suggesting that they join Socrates and himself in a common establishment in Parma. He offered them his house, gardens, books, possessions, himself. They would spend their days in the tranquil study of arts and letters, in the preparation of their souls for eternity, and in delightful excursions to Bologna, Milan, Genoa, Venice, and the Alpine lakes. "We would have been four bodies in a single soul," he wrote later. The dream of living with a group in studious harmony was a familiar one; he propounded it at least five times. This has been called a proposal for a humanistic lay monastery, an Abbaye de Thélème. In this lay monastery Petrarch would indubitably have been Abbot.

He sent his cook, Gebelino, to pursue the two friends and deliver his packet of letters. A week later Gebelino reappeared, dripping with rain, convulsed with sobs, to report that the friends had been waylaid by mountain bandits. Mainardo was killed, and robbed of 2,000 gold florins; Luca had fought off ten assailants, until some countrymen had run to his rescue. His trace was now lost. The attackers took refuge in a castle, whose noble lord was the protector and director of brigandage. Petrarch devoted himself for a full fortnight to grief, which he describes with a certain complacence. He then wrote an angry exhortation to Florence to avenge Mainardo's murder; and in fact the city sent a successful punitive expedition against the bandit prince.

At some time undetermined, but most likely in the autumn of 1349, Petrarch paid a long visit to Ferrara, the home of the great Este family. Here Cupid made a last desperate assault on his heart, by the agency of a pair of lovely eyes. He admits his temptation in two poems of the *Canzoniere* and in several excluded therefrom. Love and hope were reawakened in his heart; but fortunately the lady died.

From November 1349 to May 1350 Petrarch was in Padua, hobnobbing with the great. In May he visited Mantua, dear to him as the birthplace of Virgil. He wrote Virgil an epistle in verse, describing the beauty of his countryside. He spent a restless summer, journeying to and fro between Parma and Mantua. On one of his trips he was marooned by high waters and mud in the dank village of Suzara. The local lord received him enthusiastically, with the best of food, wine, and company, but the banquet was marred by an assailing host of flies and mosquitoes and by an army of frogs that croaked and hopped unhindered on the floor.

During these years he was intermittently occupied with the collection of his letters in book form. The idea of an *epistolarium* probably arose with his discovery of Cicero's Familiar Letters in Verona in 1345. If Cicero's letters, and Pliny the Younger's, could make a book, why not Petrarch's? The conception of a volume of letters as a literary entity had disappeared during the Middle Ages. Aside from business and official letters, the epistolary genre permitted only rhetorical exercises in a rigidly prescribed form. Once more Petrarch rejected the current mode to return to classical freedom.

He carried his project long in mind. In Vaucluse, a little earlier, he had busied himself in sorting out his old papers, consigning most of them to the flames. His habit was to keep drafts or copies of outgoing correspondence. As he examined the moldy mice-gnawed piles of letters he wondered why he should not use them to review his life's course, as a traveler looks back from a high tower on his road. In January 1350 he wrote to Socrates, disclosing his purpose. He tells how the deaths and terrors of the plague years moved him to think of what he himself would leave behind; he decided then to assemble his old letters and to dedicate those in prose to Socrates, those in verse to his Neapolitan friend, Barbato da Sulmona. He admits that his letters are couched in "a common-place, domestic, familiar style;" but so were Cicero's. He adds that he is preparing a truthful portrait of his own character, no Minerva by Phidias, as Cicero puts it.

He set to the agreeable task of rereading, editing, discarding, rewriting, perhaps even composing supposititious letters to put in appropriate places. In those days letters were written on paper sheets folded in three, guarded by a cord passing through holes in the side margins, and sealed with wax and an impressed symbol. Envelopes did not become standard until the nineteenth century. A bundle of letters was wrapped in waterproof canvas for transport. Professional couriers traveled between the large cities as business offered, the Church and the big merchants employed their own messengers, and friars and officials could be persuaded to carry letters for a small fee. But there was no postal system, and delivery was very uncertain. Petrarch once kept a letter from Italy to Socrates in Avignon for twenty months before finding an emissary. A letter from Emperor Charles IV to Petrarch was delayed for two years—such at least was the imperial apology for not answering Petrarch's message. Border guards and soldiers opened correspondence, for intelligence purposes or out of curiosity. Fine literary style and fine calligraphy tempted thieves, who would sell their prizes to collectors. Petrarch complained that his own missives were often abused, like severe matrons violated by foul adulterers.

Petrarch eventually divided his Familiar Letters in prose into twenty-four books, like the *Iliad* and the *Odyssey*. In the modern Latin edition they run to 1,300 large pages; a translation into our diffuse tongue would double the wordage. The collection begins with a prefatory letter to Socrates and concludes with a series of letters to dead authors, Cicero, Seneca, Livy, Horace, Virgil, Homer, and others. Within the body of the text Petrarch followed a generally chronological order, which aesthetic and other considerations frequently caused him to infringe. He was conscious that he was making a structured book, not a mere assemblage of miscellanies.

He was one of the world's great letter-writers. "I can't stop writing letters unless I stop living," he said. He put a high value on his messages. When one was ready, a secretary was put to copying it, and woe to him if he erred or blotted! He could not bear to have his missives disregarded. He wrote to Laelius: "You've been idle about answering my letters. Well, dukes and monarchs answer them." A letter was mislaid; the whole house was in a turmoil for a day while everyone hunted it in vain. "It was sweet to write, sweeter to read over, and very bitter to remember."

The contents are extremely varied, in both substance and style. Some are cheery anecdotes of daily life, comic incidents, news of his doings, his friends, his garden, his reading. Some are reflections on current events, and some political exhortations to Emperors and Popes. Many are moral essays, satires, portraits, having little to do with the concerns of his correspondent. Indeed, they may have been written with no correspondent in mind, and have been sent off when a messenger turned up on his way to some city where a friend dwelt. Most of them are deliberately literary in character and style. The writer was looking beyond the immediate addressee to the ultimate recipient, posterity.

For the modern reader, temporary posterity, his work has many faults. He is often intolerably garrulous, repetitive, sententious, obtuse. Some of his letters of consolation, recommending stoic insensibility, must have caused angry tears to flow. He even tells Philippe de Cabassoles that the death of his brother should be rather an occasion for rejoicing than grief. He stuffs his letters with quotations from the Roman classics, which fortunately are easy to skip. But of course such quotations were more honored and less accessible then than now.

In spite of all, his letters make one of the most precious possessions of European literature. They reveal to us a total man, a great poet and scholar, wise, absurd, penetrating, vain, uncomprehending, cruel, introspective, self-conscious, enlightened, ancient, modern—one may add a whole thesaurus of adjectives. No other book displays so well the intimate life and thought of a medieval man. No other pictures so thoroughly the background of commonplace or startling reality, during the painful preparation of modern times. Through his letters we may know the man Petrarch, his inward and his outward selves, as we can know no other human being until we come to Montaigne.

Giovanni Boccaccio was now thirty-seven years old. He was tall and stout, with a round face, plump lips, and a humorous expression. He was agreeable in conversation and a great story-teller. He had been trained to be a businessman and a canon lawyer, callings for which he had little taste. All the time he could spare was given to literature. He had written a series of epic poems and prose romances in Italian, and he was engaged in setting down the tales of his immortal Decameron. He had long worshiped Petrarch from afar; in Naples in 1341 he had witnessed Petrarch's triumphant public examination in poetry by King Robert, but he had not dared to kiss the hand of Italy's glorious bard.

Now in the summer of 1350 Boccaccio, domiciled in Florence, ventured to write to Petrarch, lamenting that he could only with much difficulty obtain copies of the master's works, and enclosing a poem of his own for criticism. Petrarch responded cordially, and thus a famous literary friendship and correspondence began.

In October Boccaccio learned that Petrarch was due to pass through Florence on his way to Rome. Boccaccio went to meet the approaching poet and insisted on bringing him home as house guest. The two took an immediate liking to each other.

Petrarch was prepared to dislike Florence, *iniqua urbs*, which had ill treated his father, which had taken no official notice of his own poetic eminence. In Florence dwelt his hated stepmother, and he probably felt nervous about meeting her in the street. But in Florence existed a kind of Petrarch Club, to which Boccaccio introduced him. Among the members were Zanobi da Strada, a poet who had already corresponded with Petrarch, Lapo da Castiglion-chio, poet and law scholar, and particularly Francesco Nelli, prior of the Church of the Holy Apostles. Nelli was the perfect disciple, the perfect organizer of disciples. He was to write Petrarch a whole volume of letters, and Petrarch was to reply, addressing him as "Simonides," because he was both priest and poet.

The club received Petrarch with an adulation that would have embarrassed any ordinary man. "I see you as perfect; you do not seem a mere man," Nelli later wrote him. "You are for me in heaven, and I long to have you descend to me on earth. These words bear no blemish of heresy, but express my ardent love. You are in heaven for me, not as a god, but as a guide to God. . . . You are Parthenias, the virtuous one. You have no avarice, pride, ambition, anxious concern for earthly things." Another admirer, the Venetian Benintendi de' Ravignani, tells Petrarch that he is a healer of souls, fountain of milk, golden river of virtue and eloquence, inestimable treasure of our times, superior to Aristotle in knowledge, to Seneca in eloquence, the equal of Cicero, Plato, Socrates, a god in a human body.

One may imagine the tone of the after-dinner speeches, leading up to a few words by the distinguished guest, with recitation of some of his poems. Nelli describes his platform style, his big, resonant, pleasing voice, varying with the thought, dwelling on the quality of the vowels. He used wide, full gestures, swaying his body to right and left, to the rhythm of the verse. He was bard as well as poet, holding his auditors spellbound.

In later years, whenever Nelli or another received a letter from the master the club would immediately assemble for a banquet. The happy recipient would read the letter aloud, and all would discuss at length the style and substance. If a question arose, it would be communicated to the master himself for his resolution.

After a brief stay in Florence, Petrarch continued on his way to Rome, to attend the Papal Jubilee. This had been broached in 1342, with some poetic encouragement from Petrarch. Pope Clement VI approved it, with a bull ordering the angels to take to Paradise the souls of pilgrims dying on the way. The world's woes —floods, storms, fires, plague, wars, banditry, revolution—pointed to God's anger and the need of world-wide penance. Thirteen forty-nine was a year of earthquakes. In Rome many ancient buildings came down. A large part of the Basilica of St. Paul and the roof of St. John Lateran fell.

Immense numbers responded to the offer of plenary indulgences to those who would visit the three essential churches. Villani says that 1,200,000 came, but this seems physically impossible. The pilgrims had to survive the attacks of brigands on the way and the disorders of Rome itself. Every Roman became an innkeeper, usually a rapacious one, aided by a ban on the introduction of foreign food. Princes and nobles harbored professional footpads in their strongholds. Pilgrims were robbed and killed in the streets, while the canons of St. Peter's fought over the indulgence money collected. When the veil of St. Veronica was shown in St. Peter's a number were usually trampled to death.

The Pope did not attend his own Jubilee. He was represented by two cardinals, one of whom became very unpopular. He had for some reason brought a camel with him. The mob, ordered to stand off and not torment the camel, attacked the Cardinal's palace in resentment. A crossbow bolt traversed the Cardinal's hat; thenceforth he always appeared in public wearing a helmet and with armor under his vestments.

Why did Petrarch, hater of crowds, lover of tranquil solitude, join the pilgrim throng? He gives Boccaccio a sufficient clue, writing from Rome that he hoped by grace to put an end to the errors of his life. Years later he told Boccaccio that he was delivered from the lusts of the flesh, "especially from the time of the Jubilee onward;" that he hated the sin, and was filled with shame and horror at the memory of it. He wrote to Gherardo in 1352 that he was trying to take shelter from the storm by means of frequent confession, which he had long avoided. "The hidden filth of my sins, which festered in silence and in evil torpor, I brought into the open by the aid of wholesome confession. . . . Commerce with women, without which I had sometimes thought that I could not live, I now fear more than death; and although I am often distressed by fierce temptations I reflect on what woman is, and all temptation quickly vanishes and I come again to liberty and peace." And in 1357 he tells Guido Sette that he is still assailed by the enemy, but with Christ's aid he will bridle the rearing ass and prevent lewd dreams from troubling his repose. It is true that in his Letter to Posterity he puts at his fortieth year, or 1344, his rejection of "that obscene act, and even all recollection of it." But in dealing with posterity he could fudge a little with the dates. He had not reckoned with modern scholarship. At any rate, there is no good reason to doubt that after the Jubilee he kept his ecclesiastical vow of chastity.

We have left him in Florence, feted by the Petrarch Club. He bade the members farewell, to make his journey to Rome. For safety's sake he joined a band of mounted pilgrims, a tiresome lot, unlike the immortal group bound for Canterbury. They took the great highway south through Siena. At Lake Bolsena, seventy miles from Rome, the horse of an old abbot delivered a kick at Petrarch's mount, and the iron-shod hoof caught Petrarch just below the knee, with a crack as of breaking bone. He kept on to Viterbo, but finding there no medical aid continued for three days more, in great pain, to Rome. The doctors probed, and concluded that the bone was not fractured. But the wound was horrible and badly infected, so that he could not bear his own smell. How vile and wretched is the body, wherein lodges the soul's nobility!

When Francesco Nelli, in Florence, learned of the accident, he wrote a terrible invective against the criminal horse that had dared to kick the poet. "Wickedest of noisy-foot steeds, never will you gain such fame as you have done by your evil actions! You smell of manure! The farmers of that old abbot will incessantly belabor your back with sticks, throw you stalks and ashes for your dinner, and will sing of you forever and everywhere with rude songs!"

Petrarch must have limped, or have been carried, to the obligatory churches. He must have watched the street sights with interest —the Frenchwomen with their beaked hats, *chapeaux à bec,* the Florentines with unbound hair, the English in their short tight coats, the Germans in their long, severe gowns, the flagellants performing twice daily, bloodying themselves with knotty sticks studded with iron points. But Petrarch was always scornful of the vulgar manifestations of religion, relic-worship, easy miracles and visions. He wrote Barbato da Sulmona that if he had come to Rome the two would not have made the round of churches but would have walked the ancient streets with the curiosity of poets. He did not look up the Colonna family. Giacomo and Giovanni were dead; and no doubt Petrarch was conscious, and the surviving Colonna were too, that he had urged Cola di Rienzo to exterminate them for Rome's good.

By December he was able to travel again. He went north by way of Arezzo, his birthplace. Noble citizens met him outside the walls, and led him, as a surprise, to the house of his birth, "not big or rich, but fit for an exile. The owner wanted to restore and enlarge it, but was forbidden to do so by the magistrates, to keep it intact. Arezzo was more generous to a stranger than Florence to a son."

In fact, Arezzo honored its living poet-son as today San Francisco and St. Louis have not honored theirs.

He stopped briefly in Florence, to see his new friends, and was back in Parma before Christmas. There he remained only a month before returning to Padua.

His visit to Rome, his view of the sorry state of the holy city, left him oppressed and indignant. Renouncing hope of persuading Pope Clement to return to his proper seat, he turned to the Emperor.

This was Charles IV, King of Bohemia. He had been chosen Emperor by the German Electors in 1349, at Worms. He had gone broke buying his emperorship. The story went that when he left Worms he was stopped by his unpaid butcher and an angry throng of creditors and sympathizers. The new Emperor was obliged to borrow from the Bishop to pay his butcher's bill. He retired to his capital of Prague to recoup. But old custom decreed that the election must be ratified by his receiving the Iron Crown, representing political suzerainty, in Milan, and the Golden Crown, symbolizing spiritual regency, in Rome. Charles showed no disposition to undertake the journey, which might be dangerous and would certainly be expensive.

In February 1351 Petrarch wrote a long letter to the Emperor, on a rather hectoring note, reproaching him for his delay in visiting Italy, exhorting him to come speedily to restore Rome's health and grandeur. "If your fame is dear to you, do not delay." He takes no account of the Emperor's difficulties, of the hostility he would meet on his way to Rome, of the political implications of a powerful German overlordship in Rome, challenging that of the Popes. He seems even to have forgotten his own outbursts against the *tedesca rabbia*, German rage. One fears that Petrarch's head was turned by adulation. He dreamed even of being the moral director of Italian, and world, politics. He had already sent unsolicited advice to Popes Benedict XII and Clement VI, to Cola di Rienzo, to various cities; now he would point the right course to the Emperor. Later he told Pope Urban V that he was proud of having scolded the Emperor; he had done so simply because no one else dared to speak. "Silence seemed to me infamous. I wanted posterity to blame him, not me, his sloth, not my silence." Thus he felt himself to be a responsible public figure, whose actions and whose abstentions would be brought before the bar of history.

The Emperor did not, for the moment, reply.

Enjoying his role as a volunteer arbiter of great affairs, Petrarch sent an exhortation to Venice, trembling, in these months, on the edge of war with Genoa. He urged peace on the enemies for the general good of Italy. "I thought myself blameworthy if, in the midst of warlike preparations, I should not have recourse to my one weapon, the pen."

In these mighty matters he could with assurance indicate the proper course of others. He was less assured, and less successful, in dealing with his own domestic matters, and particularly with the education of his son.

Giovanni, now nearly thirteen, was proving a great trial to his father. Hating books and study, he brought only the worst reports from his masters, and would stand sullen and shy under parental reproofs. Giovanni never had a chance to state his own case. Taken early from his mother, sent to a succession of schools in Parma, Verona, and Padua, mocked by his comrades as a bastard, haled occasionally before his austere, ascetic, unloving father in his forbidding study, he had every disadvantage in the world. The best of his teachers was Giberto Baiardi of Parma, whom the boy, robbed of all other affection, dearly loved. To him Petrarch sent his son for a second term, with instructions to beat him soundly if necessary.

Petrarch had on the whole a poor opinion of schoolmasters and schoolmastering. He wrote Zanobi da Strada, his new Florentine friend:

> Let them teach boys who can do no better, who possess a laborious and dutiful, though sluggish, mind, a murky brain, a slow wit, chill blood, a body enduring of labor, a soul scornful of glory, avid for small gains and proof against boredom. . . .Leave this trade to those who enjoy reverting to childhood, who are shy of dealing with grown men and ashamed to live with their equals, who love to parade before minors, to have always someone to terrify, torture, afflict, and rule, though they be hated and feared. . . .Those will best teach boys who are most like them; there is a quick and easy communication between like creatures.

Zanobi took the advice so much to heart that he left teaching and became a government official and poet, and was crowned with the laurel in Pisa in 1355, to Petrarch's disgust.

In March 1351 Boccaccio came to visit Petrarch, who was again in Padua. Boccaccio bore ardent messages from the club members, and also an official invitation from the Priors of Florence to become Professor in the University of Florence, just established. Petrarch might teach anything he pleased. And the Priors had voted to restore to the poet the property confiscated from his father fifty years before.

But at about the same time he received an urgent and cordial letter from two cardinals in Avignon, conveying a message from the Pope exhorting him to return to the Court, with a strong but vague hint of his advantage. Petrarch was much torn. It would be pleasant to be established in high honor in Florence, in vindication of his father's banishment. But the Pope, after all! And he alleges that he was tired of seeking fame, that he was bored by his celebrity in Italy, that he wanted peace and the chance to get some work done among his books and letter files in the sweet solitude of Vaucluse. Also, certainly, he had in mind the advisability of obtaining a benefice for his son Giovanni.

Perhaps even he dreamed an unreasonable, unacknowledged dream. Could the Pope have in mind making him—a cardinal? Could his public letters to Italian rulers have so impressed His Holiness that he would be called to the summit of honor and power? The excited tone of some letters of this period, and his author's vanity, give color to this supposition.

At any rate, he decided to go to Avignon, expecting to be back in Italy in the autumn, unless something unforeseen should occur.

Boccaccio spent a delightful week with Petrarch in the canons' garden of Padua, talking of art and wisdom. We may be sure that Boccaccio showed the master no samples of the *Decameron*, on which he was actively engaged. He returned to Florence with the poet's polite refusal of the university chair. The Priors of Florence then reconfiscated the Petracco family property.

Petrarch left Padua to spend a month in Verona and then returned to Parma. He picked up Giovanni, and in June, in spite of foot trouble—probably the result of the horse's kick—he pressed

rapidly west to the Alpine pass of Mont Genèvre. In the high
mountains he composed one of his horseback poems, *Linquimus
Italiam*, Farewell to Italy.

> The burdened horses strain; angry Jove descends in a whirling storm;
> snow hides the earth from our eyes. We cross the icy soil and the high-
> est pass of Mont Genèvre. Now the water begins to flow forward with
> our steps. The frozen Durance, rockbound, points our way, as it jour-
> neys toward the Rhone and our well-known fields. The wind blows
> loud against us, and whips our faces with turbulent snow. Italy, love-
> liest of lands, lies behind us; a lofty peak hides her from us, while, far
> away, the hills and fields of France are outspread. This was always the
> bound of peoples, so is it now, so will it ever be.

Petrarch and his son arrived in Vaucluse on the 27th of June,
and were joyfully welcomed by the bailiff, Raymond Monet, and
his leathery wife.

XXIII: LOVE—DOLOROSO

> Pur chi non piange non sa che sia amore.
> *Who does not weep knows nought of love.*
> —Fragment of canzone, 1349

> Il cantar che ne l'anima si sente.
> *The song that is felt in the soul.*
> —Rime CCXIII

ETRARCH SPENT THE SUMMER OF 1351 AND
long periods thereafter at Vaucluse. He fell immediately
into his old routine; "I rise at midnight, leave the house
at the first dawn; and in the fields I meditate, read, and write, as
long as I can keep sleep from my eyes, ease from my body, pleasures
from my spirit, torpor from my acts. Every day I wander on the
bare mountains, in the dewy valleys, among the caves, alone with
my thoughts."

He called at the country house of an old friend of Bologna days,
Matteo Longo, Archdeacon of Liége. He found the house tight
closed and the archdeacon gone; an abandoned black dog was
jumping at the door and whimpering. Petrarch was touched.
Knowing how to deal with dogs, he disregarded the menacing
growls and soon had him wagging his tail and welcoming a new
master. The dog, named Zabot, became Petrarch's inseparable
companion. He was swift and tireless, could catch a bird in flight,
a wild duck in the water, or a hare in mid-leap. When he died the
poet wrote for him a charming epitaph:

> Care Zabot, tibi parva domus, breve corpus habebas,
> et tumulus brevis est; et breve carmen habe.

> Zabot, your house was small, your body was not long,
> and little is your grave; so take this little song.

Petrarch had intended to spend his time putting the finishing
touches to several books, his collection of letters, the *De viris illustribus*, the *De otio religioso*, the *De vita solitaria*, even the *Africa*.

But touches seldom turn out to be finishing; as he shook the worms
and dust from his papers he realized that he had a good two years'
work ahead of him.

And he was immediately distracted from scholarship. The
woods and valleys of Vaucluse were filled with the presence of
Laura, or rather not Laura herself, but his own love for her and
his pain. The emotions, the setting, the impulsions of poetry were
present. He turned to the celebration of Laura dead as he had
acclaimed her living. (To be sure, the poems on Laura's death
can often not be dated; some were certainly written earlier, some
later.)

He climbed to the high hill whence he could look down on the
valley and the Avignon plain (*Rime* CCCI):

> Valley, my sorrow's refuge and retreat;
> river, whereto my tears are tributary;
> wild birds and beasts; and fishes, shy and wary,
> within the green walls of your narrow street;
> air, that receives and soothes my passion's heat;
> pathway of grief, where once I was so merry;
> hill, joyful then, and now pain's sanctuary,
> whither Love still compels my docile feet—
>
> your dear familiar forms I recognize,
> but not myself. I am no longer gay,
> I am an inn for everlasting dole.
> Here, where we walked, I see her spirit rise,
> naked and pure, to take the heavenly way,
> leaving on earth the garments of her soul.

The phrase "where we walked," *per queste orme,* has been taken
as proof that Laura visited Petrarch in Vaucluse. This is too bold;
the poet's imagination could put her by his side.

His imagination summoned her to be his kind companion
(CCLXXXI):

> How often to my dear retreat, in flight
> from all men, from my own self most of all,
> I come, to breathe upon the air my plight
> and let my tears incessantly down fall!
> How often, solitary, touched with fright,
> under the grim and shadowy forest pall

I go to dream again the high delight
which Death has taken! And answering my call,

now like a river nymph in silver showers
of Sorgue's bright waters does she rise; I see
her calmly sitting in the streamside bowers
or treading the young grass composedly,
like a real woman pressing down the flowers!
Her face betokens that she pities me.

Inspiration can work in many ways. One of the best is for the
poet to observe an occurrence, a circumstance, and to capture its
meaning within the strict limits of his poem. Thus he affords the
reader the pleasure of working back from the outcome to the
occurrence, and of sharing in the poet's recognition of it. In the
autumn Petrarch heard a bird's melancholy song, and made the
immediate application to his own case (CCCLIII):

O lovely little bird, I watch you fly,
and grieving for the past I hear you sing,
seeing the night and winter hastening,
seeing the day and happy summer die.
If you could hear my heart in answer cry
its pain to your sad song, you'd swiftly wing
into my bosom, comfort you would bring,
and we would weep together, you and I.

'Tis no equality of woe, I fear.
Perhaps she lives whom you bewail; from me
have greedy death and heaven snatched my dear.
But the dark autumn evening hour sets free
the memory of many a banished year;
so let us talk of the past then, tenderly.

Laura appears to him in many guises, as companion, as lover, as
patron saint in heaven, even as mother (or di madre or d'amante).
She is earthly and celestial, realistic and symbolic. She is disem-
bodied purity and she confesses human frailties, affection and
jealousy. Among the angels she does not spend her time glorifying
Deity; mostly she looks down in sweet concern for her faithful
adorer on earth. But in heaven she is happy (CCLXXIX):

If I do hear regretful birds complain,
or the leaves ruffling in the summer light,

or water whispering huskily toward the plain
from my resort, where streamside flowers are bright,
and where I sit, and dream of love, and write—
then do I see and hear her once again
whom heaven vouchsafed a moment to our sight.
Her far voice comes in answer to my pain:

"Why do you waste away in such advance
of time? And why—" so, gently, does she chide,
"do you walk always in a tearful trance?
Weep not for me; out of the death I died
I rose immortal; and in radiance
my eyes, that seemed to shut, have opened wide."

To his poet's imagination she returned so vividly that her
phantom became real. He could not distinguish the seeming
truth of her presence from the witnessed truth of her death
(CCCXXXVI):

Undimmed, unfading in my mind is she,
returning o'er oblivious Lethe's bed,
seeming again a radiance to shed
as in her flowery age, unceasingly.
And so demurely beautiful I see
her feature that I cry, bewilderèd:
"It is her very self! She is not dead!"
I clamor to her that she speak to me.

Now she replies; now she is obdurate.
I catch at reason, lost a little time,
and make the mind repeat the truth it knows:
'twas the year thirteen hundred forty-eight,
the sixth of April, in the hour of prime,
that from the body that blest soul arose.

Dead! That horrible monosyllable, which tolls so dully in English,
is paralleled by the hollow sound of *morta*, which clinks of the
grave-digger's spade. Laura was dead, and her lover's impulse was
to seek the liberation of death. But no—suicide was damnation
(CCLXXII):

Life hurries on, a frantic refugee,
and death, with great forced marches, follows fast,
and all the present leagues with all the past

and all the future to make war on me.
Anticipation joins with memory
tearing my soul in torment; and at last,
did not damnation set me so aghast,
I'd put an end to thinking, and be free.

The few glad moments that my heart has known
return to me; and now I watch in dread
the winds upgathering against my ways,
storm in the harbor, and the pilot prone,
the mast and rigging down; and dark and dead
the lovely lights whereon I used to gaze.

He did not die; he turned the death-wish into beautiful words.
His poetic impulse had been dwindling, as it commonly does when
poets reach their forties. Now the emotional stir aroused by
Laura's death caused poetry to flow again, but only elegiac poetry
(CCXCII):

Those eyes in which I used to put my trust,
those arms and hands and feet that would beguile
my spirit from its fleshly domicile,
until I seemed from the gross world outthrust;
that crisping gleaming golden hair; the gust
of angel-laughter tinkling in her smile
that used to make earth paradise awhile—
these are now dust in the unfeeling dust.

And yet I live and breathe! I know not why!
Life fills me all with self-reproach and scorning.
No shore-light guides my bark; the storm is high.
I'll sing of love no more. The needless warning
comes when my wonted vein is sere and dry.
My harp, it shall be turned alone to mourning.

He saw his duty clear—to assemble and revise his love-poems,
to write new ones to complete and conclude his story, and thus
to make the name of Laura immortal on earth. Then, his duty
done, he might look forward to an eternity of companionship
(CCCXXXIII):

Go, grieving rimes of mine, to that hard stone
whereunder lies my darling, lies my dear,
and cry to her to speak from heaven's sphere.

Her mortal part with grass is overgrown.
Tell her I'm sick of living, that I'm blown
by winds of grief from the course I ought to steer,
that praise of her is all my purpose here
and all my business; that of her alone

is my discourse, that how she lived and died
and lives again in immortality
all men may know, and love my Laura's grace.
Oh may she deign to stand at my bedside
at my near death! And may she call to me
and draw me to her in the blessèd place!

His thoughts ran all on death, his own as well as Laura's. He
recognized the danger of a morbid cultivation of grief, distracting
him from a proper concern with his soul's salvation (CCLXXIII):

What are you doing? Why do you backward peer
still at the days that vanished long ago,
my soul, disconsolate? Why do you throw
wood on the fervent flames that scorch and sear?
All her soft words, her gentle gaze and clear,
which you have limned and celebrated so,
are reft from earth away. And well you know
it is too late. You will not find them here.

Rouse not again that fatal agony,
follow no more those thoughts that lead astray,
take the sure road. Our only heed shall be
heaven. There's nought on earth to make us stay.
Oh all that beauty was calamity,
if living or dead it takes our peace away!

Calamity or not, bringer of woe, destroyer of peace, his love
was, he knew, stronger than death. Come, death, he cried; Laura
and I were bound together all our lives, and in death we shall not
be separated (CCCLVIII):

Death cannot sour the sweetness of her face,
her sweet face can the sour of death dispel.
She taught me the good life, and now she shall
teach me to die the good death, in its place.
And He who shed His blood to give us grace,
Who with His foot broke ope the gates of hell,

> comforts me by His blessèd death, as well.
> So come, dear death; come, with thy kind embrace.
>
> And it is time, O death; do not delay.
> It was high time after thy cruel power
> had made Madonna from the world ascend.
> We'd walked together all along the way;
> together did we come to the utmost hour;
> and where she halted is my journey's end.

The penultimate poem of the book, bearing the fatidic number of 365, symbolically closes a normal year or a normal life. It was probably written a few years after the others, in 1358. The poet concludes his long love-drama by the renunciation of love. Or rather, he turns his love from the creature to the Creator, as the St. Augustine of the *Secretum* had commanded him, long before (CCCLXV):

> Now I go grieving for the days on earth
> I passed in worship of a mortal thing,
> heedless to fledge the spiritual wing,
> careless to try the measure of my worth.
> Thou who dost know my every sin from birth,
> invisible, immortal heavenly king,
> help Thou my soul, so weak and wandering,
> pour Thy abundant grace upon its dearth.
>
> Out of the battle, out of the hurricane
> I come to harbor; may my passing be
> worthy, as all my dwelling here was vain.
> And may Thy hand be quick to comfort me
> in death, and in the scant hours that remain.
> Thou knowest, I have no other hope but Thee.

After this provisional conclusion the poet adds a 366th poem, the leap-year number. It is a canzone of prayer and praise to the Blessed Virgin. She alone is all pure, all wise, all compassionate. She will understand and forgive his sins and errors, of which his worship of mortal beauty, of Laura, is the chief. In his concluding lines he conjures Mary to intercede for him with her Son, true man, true God, "that he may receive my spirit at last in peace." The last word of his book is "peace," the peace that he had begged through all his life, and had not gained because he had not really wanted it. This final poem is in a way an infidelity to Laura, although the attributes of the Virgin strangely resemble those of his earthly love. The conclusion is however logical, representing an ultimate passage from profane to sacred love, an opening out to a new world, not the closing in of an old one.

During Petrarch's last fruitful stays in Vaucluse, between 1351 and 1353, he practically finished his *Rime* in praise of Laura. A few poems may be dated later, such as the last of the anniversary poems, CCCLXIV, written in 1358, thirty-one years after the fateful meeting in the Avignon church. Mostly, however, the elder Petrarch restricted himself to critical revision of what he called, with aggressive modesty, his *rerum vulgarium fragmenta*. This was never finished. Late in life he put his scribe to copying out a definitive edition, then took over and set down many of the poems, with revisions, in his own hand.

The *Rime* are Petrarch's book of love, the tragic romance of Laura. But not alone in the *Rime* does she appear. There are a few important references to her in the *Secretum* and in the letters. A Latin Eclogue and a Metrical Epistle celebrate her. She is also the heroine of a long and pretentious poem in Italian, the *Trionfi*, Triumphs.

According to Wilkins's authoritative studies, Petrarch wrote the first three sections of the *Triumph of Love* in 1338, when his love for Laura was only twelve years old. He returned to the task intermittently, writing a part of the *Triumph of Death* soon after Laura's own death in 1348. He added sections from time to time, with much revision, and in his last years, from 1371 to 1374, produced the final triumphs, of Time and Eternity.

The medieval Triumph was an ecclesiastical ceremony, a parade of banners and relics, with masked figures on foot or in chariots. The Middle Ages loved opulent symbolisms, such as the marriage of the Doges with the Adriatic. (In 1342 the new Bishop of Florence formally wedded the Abbess of San Pietro Maggiore; he gave her a horse; she gave him a bed.) Kings and princes took over the Triumph, with recollections of old Rome, to celebrate their magnificence, and poets, such as Dante, described it lengthily and gave it supernal meanings.

Petrarch's *Triumphs* are cast in *terza rima*, the form Dante in-

vented. They follow a clear story line. In the *Triumph of Love*
the poet, one April morning in Vaucluse, has a vision of Amor, or
Cupid, passing in a fiery chariot, followed by his devotees and victims. An endless procession of history's unhappy lovers passes in
review. At sight of a maiden purer than the candid dove
Petrarch is smitten, and joins the bemused throng. The way leads
to Cyprus, Venus's domain. Briefly he rejoices in the flowery, bird-
loud glades of eternal spring, and then realizes that the road leads
on, down to the chambers of hell.

In the following canto Love's Triumph is undone by the Triumph of *Pudicitia*, Modesty, Chastity, Feminine Virtue. Laura
and other great exemplars of Virtue seize and bind the malefactor,
Love. The procession moves to Rome, where Laura deposits the
spoils of Love in the temple of Pudicitia.

The next canto depicts the triumph of Death even over Virtue.
Laura and her cheery band of chaste ladies leap to the green fields
of Provence. A somber woman, black-robed Death, meets them,
and offers Laura an immediate escape from pain and the griefs of
age. Death plucks a golden hair from Laura's head, and Laura
gently expires.

She appears to the poet in a dawn-dream, to tell him that she is
happier in death than in life. Petrarch seizes the chance to ask her
if she had ever thought of taking pity on his long martyrdom. She
laughs, and then says, sighing:

> My heart was never divided from yours, nor will it ever be. But I tem-
> pered your ardor with a look, for there was no other way to save you,
> to save me, and to preserve our young reputations. A mother who
> chastises is none the less loving. How often have I said to myself: "He
> loves me, he is afire; I must see to this. How can I, if I show my fear
> or love? He sees only my outward manner, not my heart." And so I
> curbed you like an unruly horse. Often I put on anger when love
> burned within me, but my desire never bested reason. If I saw you
> overcome by pain I looked upon you gently, thus saving your life and
> our honor. And if your suffering was too severe, I greeted you with
> look and speech, timid or grieving. These were my devices, now a
> warm welcome, now scorn; you know it well, who have so often sung
> of them. Often I saw your eyes so filled with tears that I exclaimed:
> "This man is done for unless he has help!"

"Can this be true?" cries Petrarch; and Laura replies that she was happy to have his devotion and his public honor, but what he lacked was moderation and measure.

> You opened your secret heart to all the world! Hence my coolness, which still makes you suffer. Otherwise our harmony was such as honest love may bring. The amorous impulse was almost equal in us two; but one proclaimed it, the other kept it hid. You were ever demanding your satisfaction, and I said not a word, because my modesty, my fear, made my great desire seem very tiny. Pain is not the less for being suppressed, nor is it greater for noisy lamentation; fiction does not change the truth of things. But did I not lift the veil, that day when we were alone and I replied to your plaints by singing "Our love dares say no more"? That day my heart was yours, but I kept my eyes downcast, and you did not understand. And you complain, though I gave you the most, and denied you the least!

Thus when all was over, when Laura had long moldered in her grave, the poet extorted from her a post-mortem confession. Her coquetries became repressed love; her reluctance became the desperate shifts of virtue at bay. The Triumph of Death is strangely blent with the Triumph of the Poet. He takes, surely, unfair advantage of Laura dead. But, as he says, full justice to lovers is a great offense.

Death, in Petrarch's poem, is vanquished in the next canto, the Triumph of Fame. Another tortuous procession passes, of the immortals of Rome and of other lands, from the Greeks to the Assyrians to the moderns. Petrarch comments on them as they file by, especially on his personal favorites and friends, such as King Robert of Naples and Stefano Colonna.

Fame itself, in the next canto, yields to the Triumph of Time. The sun speeds faster and faster round the world; spring, summer, winter pass in a twinkling; and men's lives and fames are enveloped in oblivion. "Greedy Time conquers all, takes back all to itself. Man's Fame? It dies a second death, as certain as the death of man's body. Thus Time triumphs over the world!"

But even this triumph is not the last. The sun and stars, and earth and sea, collapse; a new, happier, more lovely world arises. Time itself comes to an end. There is no past or future; it is the Triumph of Eternity. In the everlasting heaven shines Laura, her celestial beauty magnifying her earthly beauty. "If he was blest who saw her on earth, what will he be who sees her again in heaven!"

Petrarch's *Triumphs* gained a popularity that for centuries surpassed that of the *Rime*. They pleased the medieval, and Renaissance, taste for pageants, for external, and verbal, magnificence. They lent themselves to illustration, by illuminators of manuscripts and by Renaissance painters. They lent themselves also to learned annotation by literary scholars. Today the *Triumphs* have sadly faded. The endless parade of classical figures bores us. How can we recognize Laodamia and Protesilaus and Argia and Polynices? Their gold and silver is tarnished; their ox-drawn floats pass all too slow. All that remains for the average modern reader are a few fine passages, and suddenly sonorous lines, and the long interlude just quoted, wherein Laura dies and returns to join the poet in a final duet on love confessed but misunderstood, on earthly happiness lost but heavenly beatitude gained.

This is the last of Laura, or almost the last. In his later years Petrarch was inclined to wave her away as a youthful aberration, and to dismiss his love-poems in the vulgar tongue as mere trifles, *nugellae*. We know, however, that his secret life often belied his public face, that he recopied and reordered his poems almost till his death; and in the recopying and reordering he must have felt again the old sweet anguish. In his manuscript copy of *Rime* CXCIX, "O lovely hand that lightly holds my heart," he notes in the margin: "May 19, 1368; Friday. After lying long awake at length I arose; and this very old poem, written twenty-five years ago, kept running in my mind." Laura came to him in dreams and in hours of insomnia. He could not banish her from his deeper, his essential life. He had written truly:

> Together did we come to the utmost hour,
> and where she halted is my journey's end.

But in Petrarch's outward, active life, this is the end of Laura. It is also the end of his serious poetic activity. We may then make a brief review of the quality and importance of his poetry.

Poetry is fitting for ardent souls, he says. It is the most liberal of the arts, the one that comprehends and embraces them all. It makes the mind beautiful and perfect. It derives from the effort of primitive men to use lofty words of praise, in a manner artful and

carefully elaborated and a little strange. It is heightened speech.
It is close to theology; indeed theology is nothing but poetry concerning God. The poet, like the saint, is divinely inspired. Some
may think him mad; but did not Plato warn the man who is
wholly sane to forbear knocking at poetry's door?

He wrote, in answer to a detractor, a letter in defense of poetry.
He says, in summary:

> You call poets liars and fools? No, they sing truth, even to despicable
> deaf ears. You call our labors childish? Ah, look at the noble utter-
> ances of the ancients! A certain divine power of spirit lodges in
> poets; they cover the beauty of things with a teasing veil, which only
> a sharp eye can pierce. Thus they please both children and elders.
> You call us mad? Well, our madness is divine. Dreaming is the singer's
> right. Only when it soars can the soul, escaping mortality, sing of ex-
> alted things, leaving the vulgar mob far below its feet. You would
> drive us from your cities; but we love the woodland solitudes! Who
> will remain to teach you the ideals of the past, valid for the future?
> If poets were mute, man would be mute also, and virtue would hide
> unknown, lovely only to itself, and all the great past would vanish,
> and even the fundamentals of our language! True, Aquinas warns
> that praise of poets will bring worthless ones to the fore. But that is
> the common case; it is no argument against the sublimity of the great,
> such as Virgil, who hide sublime truths under a deceptive clarity.

From Petrarch's writings an entire Art of Poetry has been
drawn. To reduce his conception to a phrase, he believed that
poetry is an inspiration in the soul, given by nature, ordered to
perfect form by the conscious mind. "The law of poetry permits
nothing to be invented except by the concurrence of nature," he
said in a memorable aphorism—nihil nisi naturae consentaneum
lex poetica fingi sinit. "If nature wouldn't give the word, neither
would a thousand Athenses and Romes." When nature has given
its impulsion, the poet is bound to endless, even lifelong, rework-
ing of his form, to bring it as nearly as possible to perfection.

Petrarch had a high view of the poet's mission. His duty is "to
create by imagination, to treat of the nature or order of moral matters, to embellish truth with beautiful colors, and to cover it with
a veil of pleasing invention." Among the numberless definitions
of poetry, this one is still sound, still impregnable. Imagination,
he says, authorizes the poet to alter facts to attain a higher truth.

As to the question if art is for art's sake or for men's profit he seems to waver. Now he says that poetry serves no need; its purpose is beauty and delight. Now he claims for poetry a civilizing function, teaching man to discover the nobility of his nature and to raise general culture. Poetry serves also to preserve the sense of the past, thus compensating for the ephemeral quality of mortality. It lasts forever, while memory grows dim, paintings fade, statues crumble. A poem grows sweeter with age, like wine.

The poet is born to poetry, though he must make himself by his own effort. "Many things are required for good writing: innate ability, discipline, a knowledge of many and memorable things, and—especially for poets—some impulse or ardor in the mind."

The poet will naturally accept and build on past achievements, traditions, forms, techniques. Petrarch's sources have already been reported—his Provençal and Italian predecessors, and the classic poets, especially Virgil. He adopted the current verse-forms, sonnet, canzone, sestina, and the rest, and in writing Latin verse he followed the Roman rules of quantity and imitated the structure of epics, eclogues, and epistles.

If one follows poetic tradition, one must imitate. Do not fear to echo the Romans, who themselves echoed the Greeks. Imitation is the source of all invention. Thus one may borrow old subjects and thoughts, but not words. What is condemned as plagiarism is often unintentional, for books much conned become part of oneself. The resemblance of one's work to that of an original must not be that of a portrait, but rather that of a son to a father. This is what our painters call an "air," visible in the face and especially in the eyes, so that on seeing the son's face we recall the father. Strive for a similarity in dissimilarity, half hidden, revealing itself only to the reflective reader.

The practice of poetry is a burdensome task. The poet must be willing to labor forever on his lines. Sneering at a cardinal who boasted that he had written 370 lines of verse in an hour, Petrarch said that he reviews his own work at least ten times. One must study forever the ancient masters, but one must not be overawed by them; they were men too. Despite old despairers, there are plenty of new things under the şun. Meditate long before setting down your words, then sing them aloud, and listen to yourself with as much detachment as possible.

Thus Petrarch worked and reworked his poems until the end of his life, as appears in his precious manuscript, with his marginal notes, in the Vatican Library. He strove to intensify his harmony, elegance, and energy. An example: beside CLV he notes: "I thought of transposing the order of the quatrains and the tercets, but gave it up because then the fuller sound would have been in the middle and the hollower sound at the beginning and end, which would be bad practice." A fragment of a canzone on the death of Laura is abandoned with the note: "The opening doesn't seem sad enough." Again: "I must remake these two lines, singing them; and I must transpose them. 3 A.M., October 19." It is clear that he was conscious of what we call tone-color.

His conception was musical; sound must accompany sense, the two must blend into one. He sang his poems to the lute, no doubt to some fixed sonnet-tune in his head, and in his singing he was aware of awkward or ugly consonant-groups or vowel-successions. Ugo Foscolo notes that in the canzoni the cadences are so placed as to allow the voice to rest at the end of every three or four lines. No reasonable reader stops to analyze the sound-patterns of the poems, but he must feel that they are somehow satisfactory, that joy, contemplation, woe escape in appropriate verbal music. To hear a fine voice reciting Petrarch is a rich aesthetic experience. Said his contemporary, Filippo Villani: "His rhythms flow so sweetly that not even the gravest people can withstand their declamation and sound."

Poetry, further, requires ornament, to make beauty. Accept then the traditional rhetorical figures, tropes, metaphors, and the rest. Rejoice in allegory, that "beautiful veil," which is no more than an extended metaphor, a sustained symbol. It is a challenge that the worthy reader accepts eagerly. "The more difficult the search, the greater the delight of discovery." Obscurity protects truth from becoming common and obvious.

But let your style be simple and direct, and above all natural. Every man has the style of his own character and thought. One's style should be like a gown, made to the measure of one's own mind. "Every man has by nature something individual and his own, in appearance, gesture, voice, and utterance, and it's easier and better for him to develop and correct what he has than to try to change it."

Petrarch's own great style is individual and natural, a gown cut to fit his own person. A new-discovered sonnet could be assigned to him as readily as a painting can be ascribed to a certain master. He adroitly used the simple style, made of the components of speech in the word-order of prose, but set to the rhythms, rhymes, and harmonies of verse.

He had also, to fit his theories of obscurity, a riddling style, most evident in his Latin Eclogues, impenetrable without his own explanations. He loved to play with recondite classical mythology. His personified Amor, with his bow and arrow, is a limp-winged figure in a tired ballet. He added to his difficulties, and to ours, in his exercises in Provençal ingeniosity. CCVI, for instance, is a canzone of fifty-nine lines, all on the same three rhymes, with no repetition of the rhyme-words. It is an astounding *tour de force,* but it is nothing else.

Especially his fine-spun *concetti,* conceits, overpass sublimity to fall into absurdity. A conceit is like a modern mobile, fantastic, elaborate, delicately balanced to swing with a gust of air. It is a fancy, or a comparison, or a coherent rounded thought, carried to its extreme development. Thus Petrarch compares himself to a midge that flies into Laura's eye, there to die, much to her annoyance. Thus he sends his sighs across the mountains, fears they have gone astray, but thinks they must have arrived, because he hasn't heard them return. Thus during Laura's absence on a visit Avignon suffered from rainy weather; she returned, but the rain continued. Obviously the sun in its storm of tears had not perceived her return.

Such conceits, outdone and overdone by Petrarch's successors, implanted themselves in the poetic tradition of Europe for centuries. Petrarchism ruled until the sixteenth century, when Ronsard, Du Bellay, Shakespeare, though deeply affected by Petrarchism, rebelled. ("My mistress' eyes are nothing like the sun; / Coral is far more red than her lip's red.") The universal vogue of the Petrarchan conceit-sonnet brought it to nearly universal scorn.

Petrarchism itself gained a bad name, until eighteenth-century sensibility rediscovered the original. The Romantics found in Laura's lover the congenial *vague dans les passions.* Petrarch, haggard with despair in his Vaucluse solitude, was the ancestor of Rousseau's Saint-Preux, of Chateaubriand's René, of Werther and Childe Harold; and indeed something of him remains in the tortured heroes of Thomas Wolfe, J. D. Salinger, Henry Miller, and Jack Kerouac.

Petrarch's services to poetry and to literature were enormous. He created the Italian poetic vocabulary and style, which have endured to our own time. He was the first modern poet, says Benedetto Croce, the ancestor of the modern poetic state of mind. "He was the first to express a visible aspiration for beatitude in the love of the creature, who has beatitude to give; the first to seek felicity in sentiment and passion, the first to utter the melancholy of failure, with its sense of caducity, death, undoing." These are qualities of all later poetry, in every European language.

His is great poetry, or there is no such thing. The test of great poetry lies not in literary-historical-critical studies, it lies in the ordinary cultivated reader, you or me. If poetry can still make us feel old joy and pain compounded in beauty, it lives again in us. Said Ugo Foscolo: "The representation of the passions of others is agreeable, because it renders us conscious of our existence by exciting but not distressing us, and conveys to us at once the pleasures of agitation and repose."

Today we judge Petrarch according to the quality of our own times, our training and sets of values. We respond to the reality of his sufferings, we recognize the perfection of his poetic form. Scholarship has revealed the real man, fallible but great, as he has never been known since his own day. We cannot accept the image he tried to present to posterity, the image of the poet faithful to his unrequited love until his death. We know that the image is arranged, that he was not faithful, that he was undone by his human failings. But his very humanity may make him the more dear. He longed to make us conscious of his existence; he has succeeded by making us conscious of our own.

XXIV: WAR WITH THE PAPAL COURT

> *What I want I can't; what I can I don't want;*
> *I seek and do not find what I both can and*
> *want.*
>
> —Fam. XV 11

PETRARCH, ARRIVING IN AVIGNON IN THE SUMmer or early autumn of 1351, found the city greatly changed in the four years of his absence. Half of his old friends were dead of the plague; a swarm of newcomers had rushed in to fill their places at the Papal Court. Pope Clement VI had created twelve new cardinals at a stroke, nine of them French, two Italian. Four were the Pope's relatives; his nephew, or as some said his son, Pierre Roger, later the excellent Pope Gregory XI, was only eighteen.

The great Palace of the Popes that we visit today was near completion. Froissart called it the most beautiful and the strongest house in the world. It was fortress, prison, and monastery, as well as papal residence. There was and is something magnificently sinister about it, with its suggestion of strength and fear. It was a gloomy dwelling, with windows few, narrow, and high. Many corridors and stairways ran in the walls, depriving the rooms of light. To Petrarch its darkness was symbolic.

A cynic mood pervaded the darkness. Pope Clement himself set the key. He had many merits; he was learned, charitable, and strong. He deposed one Emperor, got another elected; he enforced his will on the Kingdom of Naples, on the Visconti of Milan, on Poland. But his magnificence was excessive. With lavish gifts he reduced to nothing the treasures laid up by Benedict XII. "No one should retire dissatisfied from a prince's presence," he said. "My predecessors didn't know how to be Popes." Well, he knew how. His niece, Cécile de Turenne, was hostess of the Palace, and presided at tourneys and splendid hunts. The cardinals followed

their master's example of easy, magnificent life. They were
haughty, turbulent, and inclined to abuse the Beaune wine that
was always at their elbows. We read of fist-fights in the Conclave,
of strange characters and manias. Petrarch recalls a cardinal who
at sight of a rose would run screaming through all the rooms of the
Palace, ready to throw himself down. Venality filtered down to
the lower levels. A poor petitioner had to tip a series of guards to
gain entrance; he then found himself at odds with secretaries who
lived by bribes.

One remembers that Petrarch was lured to odious Avignon,
which of all the world's cities he hated most, by a mysterious
message from the Pope that some great advantage awaited him
there. He may well have seen in vision a cardinal's red hat. Then
his patrons, Cardinals Gui de Boulogne and Talleyrand, "mighty
bulls of the ecclesiastical pasture," revealed that the proposed appointment was the high, confidential, and burdensome post of
Apostolic Secretary, in which he would become rich, through labors and fatigues. They spoke in the name of the Pope himself.
Petrarch was bitterly disappointed. Once already he had dodged
such an offer from Clement. He protested that he had no desire
for wealth, that one should reckon one's travel money according
to the length of the journey, that he had passed the noon of life
and had covered the hardest part of his way, that he should give
more heed to the night's lodging than to the road. His protests
were vain; the princely bulls bellowed him down. They led him
before the Pope, who regarded the appointment as settled. However, the notion was expressed that perhaps Petrarch's style was
too lofty for papal humility. At first he thought this was a joke.
But when he was told that he must "humble his genius and lower
his style," he saw his chance. He felt like a prisoner at the sight of
a liberator unlocking his cell.

> They asked me to write something that would indicate that I could
> skim the ground and adapt myself to the expression of humble
> thoughts. They gave me a subject to write on; and I made every ef-
> fort to spread my wings and fly so high that I would escape the range
> of vision of those who were leading me captive. I could hear the
> Muses and Apollo applauding. Although my exercise was perfectly
> clear it was hardly intelligible to many, and to some it seemed written
> in Greek or in some barbarian tongue.

The Pope, conscious of the dangers of the high style in business, withdrew the proposed secretaryship but not his favor. He offered Petrarch a bishopric, and this too was humbly declined, for a bishopric, the most demanding of the Church's administrative posts, would mean the end of the poet's peace, the end of literature.

Had Petrarch indeed dreamed of the cardinalate? He had certainly made the journey to Avignon in expectation of some high appointment, and the Church has little to give above the bishopric that he refused with disgust. He said later that he would rather be beheaded than wear a cardinal's hat, but it is easy to renounce what has not been offered. As a cardinal he would have been above ordinary burdensome administration; he would have been one of Europe's rulers, in a position to enforce his political theories, to sway kings and princes, to quell war and invite peace, to lead the papacy back to its home in Rome.

If he did dream such dreams, he had now to banish them and to pitch his hopes lower. He petitioned for a canonry in Verona for his son Giovanni. He obtained for Italian friends some ecclesiastical favors. He wrote more appeals to Emperor Charles IV to present himself in Italy for his double coronation. He gave unsolicited advice to four cardinals charged with reforming Rome's government; he urged them to banish forever the Orsini and his old patrons, the Colonna, guilty of intolerable pride, greed, and wolfish violence. He corresponded with Niccolo Acciaiuoli, Grand Seneschal of Naples, who proposed to establish a new Parnassus between Salerno and Naples, probably in the Amalfi region. What a pity that this literary-artistic colony was not planted! He gave good counsels of moderation to the Genoese, temporarily triumphant over the Venetians, excusing himself for interfering "because every man is properly concerned with human misery and every Italian with Italy's woes, and should intervene, if it is possible." This is very fine.

During this period he lived with his old schoolmate, Guido Sette, who had become an important man at court, greedy and ambitious. Petrarch was restless and uncomfortable, even physically. He could hardly persuade his tailor and shoemaker not to make their wares too stylishly tight. He found, to his amazement, that he had made himself many enemies in that city of jealous men. His direct ecclesiastical superior, the Bishop of Parma, thought Petrarch was in Avignon only to do him harm, perhaps to oust him from his seat. Petrarch was charged with avarice, thievery, rapacity, with hiding buried treasure, with being a legacy-seeker. (What can this refer to?) He was accused of being a magician, because he was known to read the works of that old necromancer, Virgil. He laughed, but it was no laughing matter. One who believed the accusation of necromancy was Cardinal Étienne Aubert, soon to become Pope Innocent VI.

Petrarch treated his enemies with a lofty scorn that sharpened their rancor. He wrote: "In the words of Seneca, I regard their words as no more than a fart. If the sound is ugly, what difference does it make whence it emerges?"

His well-wishers could importune him as much as his ill-wishers. Letters, poems, songs, poured in on him from France, Greece, Germany, England. "If I criticize them I'm called jealous; if I praise them, mendacious and false." A plague of verse-writing possessed Avignon.

> Never in Athens and Rome, in Homer's and Virgil's time, was there so much talk about poetry as now on the banks of the Rhone, and never was there so little knowledge of it. . . .The contagion has spread to the Roman Curia. What do you think the jurisconsults and doctors are doing? They give no heed to Justinian and Aesculapius; they don't hear the appeals of their clients and the moans of the sick: dazzled by the names of Homer and Virgil, they are deafened by the noise of the Aonian fount. . . .Carpenters, dyers, and farmers leave their plows and tools to prate of the Muses and Apollo. . . . But poetry, so sweet to the taste, is accessible to few. . . .You may laugh, but I find it painful, to see the streets full of poets, while Helicon remains empty.
>
> My conscience bothers me, because I myself have largely contributed to their ravings and I have done harm by my example, which is not the least agent of harm; and I am afraid that the leaves I plucked of the unripe laurel may inspire in them unhealthy dreams. . . .Even in Vaucluse an old peasant of mine has caught the contagion, and if this goes on you'll hear shepherds, fishermen, hunters, plowboys and the very cows low in numbers.

An old gentleman, in tears, came with his son to visit the poet. He said: "You are the cause of my only son's undoing." Petrarch was stirred and felt himself blushing. He said: "But I don't know you, or your son either." "What of that?" said the old man. "He knows you all too well. I had put him to the study of civil law, at great cost; and now he says that he wants to follow your example. So all my high hopes of him have come to nothing, and he won't turn out, I'm sure, either a lawyer or a poet." Petrarch and the others present laughed, and the old gentleman went away none the happier. "But now," the poet writes, "I recognize that he didn't deserve laughter, but sympathy and good advice, and that his complaints were by no means unreasonable."

Others beside fledgling poets and reproachful parents importuned him.

> The remains of our old misdeeds weigh upon us [he writes]. We would like to make profession of virtue, and we can't. No one puts confidence in our present character if we suffer from a past reputation. A pestering woman friend besieges the door; however often one drives her away she returns, and lies in wait all night. You swear that you want to live chastely; she thinks that you have merely found another girl. As she can't conceive of continence she is convinced that you won't give up women till you give up life. A mob of old friends crowd in, call and shout, summon you noisily to parties and gatherings of noble ladies. If you say you aren't interested, first they look at you in amazement, then they laugh at you and lay hands on you and drag you off to some place you don't want to go to, and they can't believe that one's tastes may change and that old age may affect you.

This is a very curious passage. It was written on September 25 of either 1351 or 1352. Although it is discreetly worded in impersonal form, it must be a record of fact and of those scapegrace friends and misdeeds that Petrarch was usually at pains to conceal. One is surprised to find it among Petrarch's letters, where, perhaps, it was left by inadvertence. It provokes many a question. Who was the pestering woman who haunted his door? Was she the mother of Giovanni, who was now fourteen, or of Francesca, who was eight, or of both? At any rate, she seems to have been presuming on what she felt to be her rights. And what of Giovanni? Was he permitted to see his mother? And did Petrarch take any care for the education of his daughter? Did he even see her? To these questions we have no answer. In his chastened legacy to posterity we have only the faintest of hints that he was still troubled by the demon of lust and that he recognized his harshness toward the mother or mothers of his children. He wrote to Philippe de Cabassoles, in November 1352, that he planned to visit his friend "to lie hid and flee, if I can, not only others but myself—that is, my vices and errors, which have followed me from boyhood to maturity." Again, in his copy of Quintus Curtius, where the author remarks that cruelty and lust often go together, Petrarch writes in the margin: "Audi, et tu!" Listen to this, you!

At least, Petrarch furthered his son's career. The Pope, at Petrarch's plea, kindly granted the boy a canonry in Verona cathedral, in March 1352. The prospect of a life in clerical orders could have brought little pleasure to Giovanni. Petrarch packed him off in June, with letters to his Veronese friends.

He is not ill endowed by nature, I think, but I am hardly able to judge. Whether he is embarrassed by my presence or by consciousness of his own ignorance, when under my eye he always keeps an obstinate silence. One thing is unmistakable; I have never seen anyone with such a loathing for letters. There is nothing he hates and fears so much as a book; that to him is the one great enemy. . . .Often I say to him sarcastically: "Look out that you don't dislodge Virgil from his high place!" And he just casts down his eyes and blushes.

Certainly the great man, the adviser and censor of mankind, was unwise, uncomprehending, unjust with his own son. Five years later Francesco Nelli came to know Giovanni well, and became very fond of him.

Troubled family affairs, disappointed ambition, the annoyances of hateful Avignon, and natural restlessness combined to put Petrarch in an ugly mood. His bile overflowed in anger, and anger found its mark in the Papal Court. He conceived a blasting book of denunciation, to outdo Jeremiah and Juvenal. The book never took form, but its mood is expressed in three Italian sonnets, in some Latin poems, and in a series of letters, the *Epistolae sine nomine*.

The sonnets are in the *Canzoniere*, CXXXVI, CXXXVII, CXXXVIII. They are startling indeed in the midst of the idyll of Laura and love, and they require a great deal of exculpatory footnoting for the use of pious Italian youths today. They are accumulations of scarifying epithets against the Avignon Court, greedy

Babylon, fountain of grief, inn of wrath, school of error, temple
of heresy, shameless whore, whose gods are Venus and Bacchus.
Rima CXXXVI will serve as an example.

> May fire from heaven rain upon your locks, since you rejoice so in
> evil-doing, foul creature, risen from past simplicity to be rich and
> great by impoverishing others! Nest of treachery, wherein lurks all
> the world's evil! Handmaid of wine-bibbing, sloth, gluttony, in whom
> lust does its utmost! In your chambers young girls and old men hold
> their orgies, and Beelzebub in the midst blows the bellows, building
> fires and displaying mirrors for wantonness! Of old, you were not
> nurtured in such softness; you went bare to the blast, unshod among
> thorns. Now you live so that your stink rises up to God!

The *Epistolae sine nomine,* Nameless Letters, are nineteen letters on the same theme. The names of the addressees were suppressed, if indeed they all existed. One at least he sent to Bishop
Philippe de Cabassoles, asking him to return it immediately without copying it. "We'll decide whether to burn it or put it with the
others. I wouldn't dare to show it to anyone but you." Ten years
later he edited the series, removing compromising names, destina-
tions, tell-tale references, providing that the letters be revealed
only after his death. "Then let men rage as they please. What do I
care? *Quid ad me?*"

His preface begins: "Although truth was always odious, now it
is a capital crime." He describes the ugly, sinful city of Babylon-on-
Rhone, ruled by a race of fishers, now marvelously forgetful of
their origin (Letter 5). The Galilean nets are replaced by traps for
the silly, despoiled populace. Mortal sins have become venial; God
is mocked (Letter 6). Give us back Nero and Domitian! Their per-
secution was more open, but lighter and briefer. What monstrous
things I have seen—incest, evil unions, discord between bloated
brothers, hostility to innocence, the murder of wives and mothers.
Wickedness that elsewhere must be sought out are here offered on
street-corners. Christ, right the intolerable wrongs of the world
(Letter 7)! You are omnipotent, aren't you? This is the horrible
Labyrinth of old (Letter 8). Every imaginable horror is here; it is
the home of ghosts and goblins! It is the city of confusion (Letter
10)! Here is Nimrod (Clement VI), the mighty hunter before the
Lord, the tower builder. Here is Semiramis (the Pope's niece, Cécile de Turenne) with her quiver. From this labyrinth the only

hope of escape lies in gold, by which the horrendous Minotaur may be appeased, the prison bars broken, the stones leveled, the jailer placated. For gold Christ is sold. No Noah will survive from this flood, no Deucalion (Letter 11). I see the turbaned Semiramis, disguised as a man, bedazzling the onlookers' eyes with her shrewdness, polluted by her incestuous embraces, treading mankind underfoot (Letter 13). (Does this mean that Cécile de Turenne kept her papal trysts in men's clothing?)

He tells of an observed incident (Letter 14). Two high clerics, descending from the Palace, were assailed by petitioners. One amused himself by giving elaborate, false, cruel answers. Said the other: "Aren't you ashamed to mock these poor people?" The first: "You ought to be ashamed of being so slow-witted that you haven't learned the arts of the Curia." Petrarch was shocked, but the others laughed, appaluding the deceiver.

Letter 17 tells us that Avignon is a rebel against Christ; under His banner it fights for Satan. It has on its lips the words of Judas— *Ave Rabbi.* Like the Jews, the papal courtiers spit upon and buffet the thorn-crowned Christ, adore Him with mocking words. They buy and sell Him, crown him with the thorns of evil deeds, wound Him with the shafts of their wickedness, drag Him to Calvary, nail Him anew to the Cross. Judas will be welcome at Court if he brings thirty pieces of silver, and penniless Christ will be barred out.

Petrarch recalls that when John XXII sent his armies to destroy Milan, as if the region were a land of unbelievers, he put a cardinal in charge, said to be his son, and indeed like the Pope in appearance and savagery. The cardinal came not as an apostle but as a predator, not as Peter but as Hannibal. But God defeated him.

One of his aides I knew, and hated, young though I was. He brought news to the Pope that his armies were repulsed before the city, and said: "I know you desire nothing more than the ruin of Italy, and are spending the Church's wealth to bring it about. We are halted by Milan's defense. There is a better way—take the papacy and the empire and transfer them to Cahors in Gascony, our homeland. With a word you will triumph over your enemies." The Pope replied: "You fool! In that way the Popes would become mere Bishops of Avignon and the Emperor become Prefect of Gascony, while whoever rules Rome would be Pope and Emperor. You would only exalt the name of Italy, whereas our purpose must be to keep Italy from claiming its due."

Avignon is the home of infidelity (Letter 18). The future life is regarded as an empty fable, and hell likewise. The resurrection of the body, the world's promised end, Christ's coming to sit in judgment, are treated as old wives' tales. License to sin is taken as liberal open-mindedness. The city is the habitation of demons. Prostitutes swarm on the papal beds. Aged striplings, white-haired, wide-gowned, foul-minded, abandon themselves to every lust. Satan urges them with every stimulant for failing powers. Husbands of ravished women are driven from their homes to keep them quiet; they are forced to take back wives pregnant by the courtiers, and then, after childbirth, to return them to their unholy unions. Everyone knows this, but few dare speak, or they are deterred by shame.

There was an old cleric, lustful as a goat; for fear of ghosts, or perhaps of mice, he dared not sleep alone. He made new marriages daily, and his embraces were full of novelty, though his years were many and his mouth contained only seven teeth. In his corps of fowlers was one his equal in lust, who spread his snares in every street, especially in the houses of the poor, bestowing money here, there ornaments and rings, and caresses too. He would sing—for he was an excellent cantor, who had transferred his art from the altar to dances and lupanars. "I knew him; he was pointed out by everyone, with stories of the victims he brought to the wolfish fangs of the old man." One story of many: he had allured by his promises a poor girl to do the bidding of the old man. But when the time came she was revolted by his age and ugliness, saying that she had come for a high prelate, not an old deformed priest. At last he put on his red hat, crying: "Cardinalis sum!" And thus he triumphed, with his hat on.

Are these terrific excoriations of the Papal Court true? And are they just? These are hard questions. Not much, aside from Petrarch's work, remains as evidence, though clerical reformers and even saints, Catherine of Siena and Bridget of Sweden, deplored the relaxations of Avignon. No one knew the seamy side of the city's life better than Petrarch. The recipients of his letters did not, so far as we know, contest his allegations. Even Bishop Philippe de Cabassoles, eminent papal diplomat, seems to have accepted them. No one in Petrarch's time made a rejoinder to Petrarch's accusations, and we cannot disprove them now.

Nevertheless, mere common sense revolts at his lurid picture of papal and clerical villainy. Clement VI was an efficient and laborious statesman. Some at least of his cardinals were earnest and hardworking, far too busy to sink themselves in drink and debauchery. When Petrarch says that only by bribery and influence can one gain posts at Court he forgets his own case. Poor and uninfluential, he had received every favor from the Popes. He lived on the benefices they accorded; he had seen all his requests granted. One hears uneasily in the *Nameless Letters* echoes of Horace's and Juvenal's *Satires*. One may relate the letters also to the familiar medieval attacks on clerical morality; one need think only of the *fabliaux* and Boccaccio. Here, as in all Petrarch's work, one may suspect that life is inclined to yield to literature. One recalls his alarming advice to Philippe de Cabassoles: "If true facts are lacking, add imaginary ones; dissimulation in the service of truth is not to be called a lie." And one may agree with the gentle words of an eminent French historian of the Avignon Popes: "Petrarch was endowed with a very vivid imagination."

Petrarch's diatribes were not, I think, entirely true or just. They were, in a way, courageous; yet he impugned his own courage by his caution in making them known, by his consigning them to posterity, which could right no wrongs. The letters were provoked by anger arising from wounded self-esteem. They also embody a certain duplicity, for at the very moment that he was writing his blasts he was courting favor at the Curia, expressing public adulation of Pope Clement and importuning him for favors. And the Pope, who may very well have been informed of Petrarch's subterranean attacks, never relented in his generosity.

Petrarch's purpose was the reform of the Church's conduct at its center. He was no rebel, no schismatic. He makes no criticisms of doctrine or of the priesthood in general. His enemy is only the Avignon court. Some Protestants, hearing a sound like Luther in his philippics, have claimed him as a predecessor and a brother. But Petrarch would have rejected with horror the sixteenth-century Reformation.

Why, if Petrarch so hated Avignon, did he remain in that inn of wrath, that school of error? There are two clear reasons. He had to watch over his petition for a canonry for Giovanni; this was approved by the Pope in March 1352. And Petrarch's patron, the Cardinal Gui de Boulogne, cherished a project to crown Charles

IV Emperor in Rome, and promised Petrarch a place in the papal delegation. But this fell through in April, thanks to Charles' reluctance.

Petrarch was busy, of course, with his books and endless letters. In one long polemic he was engaged by circumstance. The Pope fell ill; Petrarch urged him, orally and by letter, to beware of the swarming doctors and their pretensions and to choose one only, distinguished for competence and not for eloquence. The letter became public. A physician, who was probably the learned and distinguished Guy de Chauliac, replied with a defense of doctors and an attack on poets in general and on Petrarch in particular. This was not to be borne. Petrarch replied in his turn with a small book, the *Invectivae contra medicum*. It consists chiefly of abuse, general and personal, of doctors, and displays an unamiable arrogance and touchiness. The book is of some small interest for medical history, revealing the persistent rationalism, even materialism, of the profession. The physicians of the time were deeply influenced by Arabic medicine and astrology, which led them into unorthodoxy and infidelity. Remember Chaucer's Doctor of Physic, who diagnosed by astrology, whose "study was but little on the Bible." The *Invectivae* contain also some interesting passages on poetic theory, particularly a defense of obscurity in poetry. They offer, however, little reward for the explorer of Petrarch's mind and achievement.

The winter of 1351-1352 amid the trials and broils of Avignon irritated Petrarch almost beyond endurance. To an invitation from Andrea Dandolo, Doge of Venice, he replied that he longed to give up his wandering life, but he was always restless; he could not settle down.

> I confess that in my youth my purpose was to follow the Homeric maxim, to observe the cities and customs of many men, to see new lands, the highest mountains, famous seas, lauded lakes, secret fountains, notable rivers, and all sorts of remarkable places. This I thought a way to become learned without much trouble, nay, with great pleasure. I thought I could banish ignorance by this agitation of body and mind. But I have wandered enough; my desire is sated. It's time I told my soul's standard-bearer what the Roman centurion said to his: "Sergeant, plant the banner; here we shall remain." . . . If I should find under heaven a good place, or at least one not actually bad, I

should gladly remain there permanently. But now I keep turning over and over like a man on a hard bed, and I can obtain no rest in spite of my desire; and since I can find no softness in my bed I try to ease my weariness by constant shifting; and so I stray hither and yon and I seem to be a wanderer forever. Tired of the hardness of one place, I try another; and though it's no softer it seems so because it's different. Thus I am tossed about, well aware that there is no place of rest for me, but it must forever be sought through pain and labor. . . .If one thinks that reward is to be found not in the spirit but in some place or other, if one calls immobility constancy, then the gouty must be extremely constant, and the dead are more constant still, and the mountains are the most constant of all.

A letter to Boccaccio in April 1352 expresses the same itching mood. "Nothing is certain for me except that I have to die. I am like those provisionally freed slaves, neither alive nor healthy nor dead nor sick; I won't begin to live in health until I find the way out of this labyrinth."

To find his way out of the labyrinth was not easy. He was a cleric, under discipline. He had been released by the Pope from direct obedience to his Bishop in Parma, but he was put evidently under the orders of Cardinal de Boulogne. The Cardinal for one reason or another required him to remain within reach of the Court.

He could at least retreat to Vaucluse. There he took refuge in the spring of 1352. He writes pleasantly to Lapo da Castiglionchio, who had sent him a volume of Cicero: "Fleeing the tumult of the abhorred city I came lately to my transalpine Helicon, along with your Cicero. He marveled at the place, which was new to him, and admitted that he had never been so well off in his Arpinate villa, with its icy stream, as at the Fountain of the Sorgue in my company. . . .Cicero and I spent ten happy days together."

There Petrarch remained until late autumn, working on his books, editing his old letters, writing new ones to his affectionate friends and to men of power and place who, he thought, needed moral guidance. Giovanni, now fifteen years old, was sent off in June to take up his canonry in Verona. As we have already told, Cola di Rienzo arrived in Avignon in August and was clapped in prison, and Petrarch wrote some sounding letters in his behalf.

In November, having obtained sufficient permission, Petrarch decided to leave Vaucluse for Italy. He packed his voluminous manuscripts and the most essential of his books. With a train of servants and pack-mules he set out, on November 16, on the dusty road to Cavaillon, where he would take leave of Bishop Philippe de Cabassoles. The season had been very dry; but now the rains began to fall with southern violence. The cavalcade took shelter with Philippe. The rains increased, beating even through the roof of the episcopal palace. A report came that brigands were holding the coastal road to Italy. Petrarch, fearing that his books would be stolen by bandits or ruined by rain, sent some trusty servants ahead to report on affairs in Italy, and, when the weather relented, returned to Vaucluse.

On December 6 Pope Clement died, of an abscess of the spine or perhaps from the rupture of an internal tumor. He had heeded Petrarch's advice to the extent of having no physicians in attendance at his deathbed. The conclave met and elected as his successor Étienne Aubert, Bishop of Ostia. He took the name of Innocent VI. He was French, a lawyer from the Limousin, old, sickly, honest, and high-purposed. He put an end to the abuses of the previous regime and established the reign of austerity. Petrarch called him dull and heavy, and said that he repaired the faults of his over-generous predecessor by the harshness of his refusals. Petrarch had his own grievance against the new Pope, who remained convinced that Virgil-reading Petrarch was a magician.

The reports of his messengers proving favorable, Petrarch decided to return to Italy as soon as the Alpine passes should be safe in the spring. But first he wanted to see once more his brother Gherardo in the Chartreuse of Montrieux.

He has preserved a charmingly vivid travel incident.

On the nineteenth of April, as I was on my way to see my brother again, I happened to encounter between Aix and St. Maximin a large party of Roman ladies. Curiously enough, I could tell from far off their nation and class, by their appearance and behavior. However, I wanted to make sure, lest I should perhaps be in error. When I had come close and heard their speech no doubt remained. I stopped, and as if in ignorance I asked them, in Italian, but using Virgil's expression: "What is your race? And what your home?" At the first sound of an Italian voice they stopped, in high glee; and the eldest of them answered: "We are Romans, and are going to the shrine of St. James

in Spain. But you are perhaps a Roman? And are you going to
Rome?" "Indeed I am a Roman at heart," I said, "but now I'm not going to Rome." Then they all gathered around me familiarly and
talked of all sorts of things very freely.

They told him the gossip of common friends and the exciting news
of Rome, such as the stoning to death of one of the Orsini.

Petrarch found Gherardo happy and in good health. But the
little isolated monastery suffered grievously from the depreda-
tions of nearby gentry, who thought their property rights in-
fringed and who set their men to stealing the monks' sheep, ravaging their vineyards and gardens, and beating their servants.
Petrarch promised to intervene directly with the ultimate gover-
nor of the region, Seneschal Niccolò Acciaiuoli of Naples. As a
result, the marauding gentry were soon called to account.

Gherardo accompanied his brother as far as his rules permitted,
and bade him an affectionate, and, as it turned out, final farewell.

Now Petrarch could begone to his dear Italy. He went in to
Avignon to take leave of his friends, Socrates, Guido Sette, the
Cardinals de Boulogne and Talleyrand. Cardinal Talleyrand
tried to persuade Petrarch to pay his respects to the new Pope, but
Petrarch refused, "because I didn't want to offend him with my
magic, or to be offended by his credulity."

In May or June, with his papers, his collection of Roman coins
and medals, and the best of his library secure on pack-animals, he
took the familiar way up the Durance valley to the pass of Mont-
Genèvre. He said farewell to France, forever. At the summit he
paused to write, or at least to sketch out, a Latin poem, *Ad Italiam,* which still sounds in the hearts of Italians far from home or
homeward-turning:

> Hail to thee, land most holy, of God beloved,
> kind to men of good will, and foe to the prideful,
> generous land, over all that are noble and rich,
> land more fertile, land more lovely than any,
> bound with a double sea, and splendid with mountains,
> holy with feats of arms and with sacred laws,
> home of the Muses, abundant in wealth and men,
> land that nature and art have equally blest,
> destined to be the mistress of all the world!
> Eagerly now from exile I come to thee,

never to leave thee more! Thou wilt give me rest
after my labors, and, when my term shall come,
thou wilt cover my bloodless limbs with a gift of thy soil.
Italy now I behold, from pine-leafed Ginevra!
The clouds are behind me; the warm home-breezes caress me,
rising from far below to bid me a welcome.
This is the land of my fathers. I gladly greet her.
Hail, O beautiful mother, creation's glory!

XXV: MILAN, 1353-1361

> Sorrow: *I am thoroughly old.*
> Reason: *Thou art rather thoroughly ripe. If apples could feel and speak, would they complain of their ripeness? Or rather, would they not rejoice, that they are come to the perfection for which they were made?*
> —De remediis (Phisicke against Fortune), *II 83*

PETRARCH CAME DOWN INTO ITALY, LOOKING for a home. As he descended the Alps, the exaltation of his poem *Ad Italiam* fell with the altitude. Italy offered no welcoming face. Everywhere, he testifies, were war and slaughter, cities in ruins, pirates on the seas, brigands and marauders on the roads. The land had become a gloomy solitude, a fearful desert. We are degenerate in our customs, clothing, manner of life, he said; cruelty and barbarism reign, and liberty is dead.

In such a world the rise of the tyrants was inevitable. The tyrant was originally a paid mandatory of the people. He promised peace and order in exchange for the loss of liberty, and found most men eager to accept the bargain. Once in office as dictator he could not be dislodged except by war or assassination. He tended to establish the continuing rule of his family, which frequently, in impatience, requited him by murder. As Symonds says, he was the enemy of all, including his closest kin; he lived in a gloomy fortress, protected by foreign mercenaries, ever alert against poison, associating with artists, men of letters, astrologers, and buffoons.

Petrarch, followed by his train of pack-mules, came to Milan in June 1353, to call on his excellent friend Gabrio de' Zamorei, vicar to Archbishop Giovanni Visconti, tyrant of the city.

Milan had been a republic until the Visconti family gained

control of it in 1277. Luchino Visconti ruled in the 1340's. He was always accompanied in his city by two savage dogs, which would worry and destroy a man at his signal. Petrarch was on the best of terms with him, wrote him obsequious letters, exchanged with him shoots of fruit trees. He died in 1349, perhaps of poison administered by his wife. He was succeeded by his brother, Archbishop Giovanni. The Archbishop was said to be an excellent ruler, imposing equitable laws, patronizing the arts. He reformed the Church administration and repressed ostentatious luxury. He was also resolutely expansionist, and was hence constantly at odds or at war with other Italian states and with the Popes. Ordered by the papal Legate to choose between spiritual and temporal rule, he celebrated mass pontifically, then took the cross in one hand and with the other drew a sword from within his robes, and told the Legate: "Here are my spiritual and temporal; tell the Holy Father that with one I shall defend the other."

The Archbishop summoned Petrarch to his presence and offered him every inducement to remain in Milan as an ornament to the court. It is not clear whether the offer took Petrarch by surprise, or whether it had been secretly sought. The alternatives were a return to Parma, where his Bishop was hostile, or to Padua, which seems to have no longer attracted him. The Archbishop promised him a quiet house, complete independence, and no duties. Petrarch says that he demurred, and no doubt he did, but not quite enough. He could be extremely dishonest with himself.

At any rate, he yielded, and was established in a pleasant house on the edge of the city, near the church of St. Ambrose. From his front window he looked up at the noble basilica, already over two centuries old; from the rear he regarded the city's walls, open country, and, far away, the Alps. It was a country house in the city, he said, and a city house in the country. True, there was no space for a garden, but he was welcomed in the St. Ambrose close. There he planted spinach, beets, fennel, parsley, olive trees, and the inevitable laurel.

The news of his settlement in Milan shocked the literary-scholarly world of Italy. The reasons were partly political; Milan was the autocratic state *par excellence,* bent on subduing its weaker neighbors, and particularly republican Florence. There was a deeper reason. Petrarch had made himself the symbol of the free scholar-philosopher-poet, the independent servant of truth and wisdom, the uncommitted moral guide. Now he tarnished his own symbol by accepting, for his ease and advantage, subjection to the most tyrannical of tyrants.

Faithful Francesco Nelli, in Florence, had his faith deeply shaken; the Petrarch Club almost disbanded. A Florentine composed a sonnet of reproach, and sent a minstrel all the way to Milan to sing it to Petrarch. Boccaccio wrote an angry, incredulous letter, quoting a friend as saying that Petrarch, from being a Castalian shepherd, had become a Lombard swineherd, imprisoning with himself the Peneian Daphne and the Pierian sisters. You will be spat upon by your once faithful friends, said Boccaccio; what ideal is left in the world?

Petrarch replied lamely to these reproofs, comparing them to the contumely heaped on Christ. He retold the fable of the miller, his son, and the ass, which La Fontaine has made familiar, with its moral that one cannot satisfy everybody and his father. Losing himself in a mist of generalities, he came close to confessing error. "I am shifting and uncertain, and I find no brief and clear reply to abate your amazement—or my own. Don't think that anyone is more surprised than I at my ability to wish in one way and to act in another. . . .We all want to be happy; we can't possibly want anything else. . . .But very few want to follow the one narrow way that leads to happiness, nor do they fully wish to do so; they rather think they wish it than wish it."

His best excuse he does not formulate, perhaps even to himself. His accusers were local patriots, Florentine first of all. Petrarch had no such ties. He was an Italian patriot; his dream was of a united Italy, at peace under the benevolent hegemony of the Popes in Rome, or, failing that, of an enlightened Emperor. Archbishop Giovanni Visconti, absorbing one by one the little states of northern Italy, was moving in the direction of Italian unity. Perhaps even, if he had lived, he might have achieved it.

Petrarch asked of the Visconti only peace, leisure, and support, and these they loyally gave him. He wrote Boccaccio, years later: "In appearance I lived with princes; in fact it was the princes who lived with me." He said that he was rarely in their councils, very rarely at their banquets. He reckoned that in eight years he had lost only seven months in their service. But when all is said and

MILANO

done, his subjection to the Visconti is a moral blot on his record. He revealed that when his principles were at odds with his convenience he was ready to reorganize his principles.

His services were at least high, noble, and exciting. He stood godfather to the son of the Archbishop's nephew, Bernabò, a savage creature who threw a peasant to be devoured by his dogs for killing a hare, and who invented what he humorously called his "Lenten treatment," forty days of slow torture. Petrarch was summoned to write official letters, when his lofty style and talent for scholarly abuse were in demand. He entertained some Genoese envoys who came to offer the lordship of their city to Milan. Most importantly, he was sent as orator of a mission to Venice, to urge peace between that city and Genoa. The mission was a failure, but it brought Petrarch personal acquaintance with the Doge, Andrea Dandolo. To him Petrarch wrote a splendid condemnation of war in general and in particular.

The Archbishop died in October 1354, and Petrarch was called upon to deliver a commemorative oration, when the Archbishop's three nephews were to receive the symbolic staffs of office. When Petrarch was at the very height of his laudation of the deceased the court astrologer stepped forward, to insist that the exact moment had come for the ceremony of investment. Petrarch was at first as angry as a tenor halted in mid-solo, but later he was amused. In a campaign against Pavia in 1359, this astrologer checked the attack to await the fateful hour; but when the hour arrived the drought of months was broken by a terrific rain that flooded the camp and forced the lifting of the siege. Petrarch asked the astrologer what had gone wrong. "Well," he said, "it's very hard to predict weather." Petrarch despised astrology but liked the astrologer, a scholar with a large family to support. When Petrarch asked him how he could believe his nonsense, he answered only: "A man's got to live."

Most important to Petrarch, during his Milan years, were his relations with Emperor Charles IV, to whom he had already addressed two unanswered letters. At length, after nearly three years, the Emperor's reply arrived, a sensible and cordial letter, pointing out that Italy's disorders rendered a coronation in Rome inadvisable. Petrarch answered, speaking very plainly, that the Emperor must come to Italy and restore the Empire, for in his absence tyranny ruled, liberty was dead, justice was prostituted in the brothel of the rich. The Emperor must use force; Italy was too rotten to resist or to cure itself.

The Emperor did in fact come to Italy for crowning, though one may doubt if Petrarch's adjurations moved him much. He was in Mantua, seventy-five miles from Milan, in December 1354. He sent word that he would be glad to receive Petrarch. The poet of course immediately complied, although it was one of the coldest winters ever known. The roads were of steel and diamond; the snow was a blessing, permitting the horses to travel off the icy roadways, past deserted villages and the smoking ruins of war. Petrarch's impatience was such that he insisted on starting before daybreak, in spite of the anguished protests of his companions. He was conducted on the way by Sagremor de Pommiers, an imperial courier whose trade lent itself to fruitful meditations on horseback. To him Petrarch became devoted.

The interview, which lasted from lamp-lighting till deep night, was a wonderful experience. A Tuscan soldier took him by the hand, and said boldly to the Emperor: "Here is the man who will make your name immortal if you achieve something worthy of praise; and if not, he will know how to speak or be silent." The Emperor received his guest warmly, complimented him on his *De viris illustribus,* led him to tell the story of his career. The Emperor asked what life he would like best to lead. "A solitary life," Petrarch replied; "that is better than an Emperor's life. In fact, I have already composed a book on that subject." "I knew that," said His Majesty with a smile, "and if it should ever fall into my hands I would throw it in the fire." "I shall take good care it never does reach your hands." The Emperor asked his guest to join him as guide to the monuments of Rome, but Petrarch was unwilling. On leaving, he presented the Emperor with a set of gold and silver coins of the Roman Emperors. And thus a pleasant, friendly, joking mood was established between poet and mighty ruler.

In January 1355 Charles was crowned King of Italy, in Milan, with the iron crown of the Lombards. He then proceeded, with many long pauses, to Rome, where he received the gold imperial crown from the papal Legate. Fulfilling an old promise to the Pope, he left Rome on the very day of the ceremony. Petrarch was

bitterly indignant that thus he renounced any effort to make
Rome again the world's capital.

The Emperor reposed for a time in Pisa. There, since corona-
tions were in order, he crowned Zanobi da Strada with the poetic
laurel. Zanobi had been a poor Florentine schoolmaster and
poorer poet, whom Petrarch had aided to become a functionary
in Naples. His qualifications for the laureateship were nil, except
for the desire of the Neapolitan Seneschal to have a laureate in his
court. Petrarch took very hard this laureling, which sharply diminished the value of his own. Later he again admitted Zanobi
to his friendship, though scolding him often and high-and-might-
ily, even for reading a cheap book entitled "How to Get Rich."

The Emperor, pursued by angry letters from Petrarch, left Italy
in actual flight from his Italian enemies and returned to his capital in Prague.

In the spring of 1356 the Visconti chose Petrarch to head a diplomatic mission to the Emperor, who was supposed to be in Basel.
His guide was the scholarly courier, Sagremor de Pommiers; he
had also his faithful traveling companion, the *Confessions of Saint
Augustine.* He found Basel a splendid city, its inhabitants cultivated and amiable. He had delightful reunions with some Bologna alumni whom he had known in college thirty years before.
But the Emperor had gone to Prague, and it was necessary to seek
him there. With Sagremor and an armed escort he made the 300-
mile journey through the forests and mountains of southern Germany. The trip was toilsome and dangerous; often the party traveled with swords drawn and crossbows cocked. Petrarch was unsure even of his guards.

We do not know of the formal outcome of his mission, though
Petrarch says that he made himself the spokesman for Italy, and
"warned, urged, and reproved the Emperor, to his advantage." He
had at least a personal success. Charles and his young Empress
were more than cordial to him; he formed lasting friendships with
scholarly statesmen and ecclesiastics. The Emperor made him a
Count Palatine and a Councilor, and asked him to live at his
court, but Petrarch declined on the ground that he could not leave
his books in Italy.

Petrarch returned to Milan in midsummer, probably over the

Tyrolean passes. He continued to exhort the Emperor to fix his seat in Rome, to bring peace to Italy, by the sword if need be. The Emperor continued to return gracefully evasive answers, and to send presents, such as a gold cup. We must think the Emperor justified in his reluctance. His power was clearly insufficient to impose peace on Italy, and Italian unification was far less important to him than the health of his German estates and his own.

Again the Visconti sent Petrarch on a mission, though rather for display than for statesmanship. In January 1361 he represented Milan at the festivities in Paris celebrating the release of King John the Good from four years' captivity in London, on the payment of a properly regal ransom. Petrarch's journey, by the same route he had taken in 1333, was a shocking experience. France was undone by war; everywhere were solitude, woe, ruin, fields abandoned, houses destroyed and deserted. Devastation had crept up to the very walls of Paris. The student throngs had disappeared from the University, and all wealth and gayety were gone.

Petrarch made a fine Latin harangue to the King on the nature of Fortune. His Majesty would have liked to continue the discussion in private, but was prevented by his official duties. The King tried to detain him in Paris, honoring him even by a friendly clutch at his gown. Petrarch was forced, however, to return to Milan, making a very hard and uncomfortable crossing of the Alpine passes in midwinter.

His diplomatic adventures were sops to his vanity, but they were, after all, brief interruptions in the normal course of his days. Since he was a writing man, his constant occupation was writing.

A funny thing [he said]; I feel a need to write and I don't know to whom, or what about. It's a grim sort of pleasure; paper, pen, ink, and midnight activity are more welcome to me than rest and sleep. I suffer and languish unless I write, so that—and this is funny too—rest is toilsome to me, and in toil I rest. . . . When I have bent long over the paper and have tired my eyes and fingers I don't feel heat or cold. I seem to be covered with a soft blanket that I fear to have removed; and if my members refuse to do their duty, I insist. If I am forced by overwhelming necessity I take a break in my labors, like a lazy ass under a heavy load driven up a rugged path, and afterward I pick up my task no less eagerly than the ass seeks the stable, and as it is restored by food and rest so am I by my long nocturnal labors.

He puttered with his *Canzoniere*, revising and correcting the poems, adding few new ones, for the Muses have little love for sober elderly men. He caressed a project of writing his autobiography, "something that I think has not yet been done by anyone." He copied and annotated a manuscript of Terence. He wrote an unimportant booklet, a guide for travelers to the Holy Land, with descriptions of the Italian coast from Genoa to Naples drawn from his own memory, and with the course to Alexandria and Jerusalem drawn from books and maps. And he wrote one of his major works, the *De remediis utriusque fortunae*, translated in the sixteenth century as *Phisicke against Fortune*.

The concept of Fortune always fascinated him. He called it a paltry power, an empty name to which nothing real corresponds. "It's generally believed that when something happens without apparent cause (though really nothing can happen without a cause), it's due to Fortune." But even such seemingly chance occurrences as a rediscovery of buried treasure, or the murder of a wayfarer, are due to specific causes. "All one can find in the events is the events themselves." He says further that although he treats Fortune according to common usage, in fact he is trying to find out what makes men happy or unhappy, and is trying to allay his own passions and those of his readers.

The book consists of 254 dialogues, between Reason on the one hand and Joy, Hope, Sorrow, or Fear on the other. Each dialogue treats of one of life's little recurring events or problems; each ends with the triumph of reason over emotion, and points the stoic moral of impassiveness. The first part indicates (in James Harvey Robinson's words) "the vanity of all earthly subjects of congratulation, from the possession of a chaste daughter to the proprietorship of a flourishing hennery. The second part brings comfort to those in affliction, as to those who have lost a dear one, or suffer from toothache, or are growing too fat."

The book is pervaded by a querulous pessimism; it is always self-assured, superior, inhuman. It is the least amiable of Petrarch's works. He bids a man who has lost his wife dance with joy, and him who has a barren wife rejoice, because she weeps and holds her peace. Better a crocodile in the house than a noble, gossiping wife. He despises art, and calls its admirers mad. "What delight is to be conceived in looking upon faces made of wax or

earth I do not understand." He complains of city noise, of bird-
chattering, of dogs baying the moon, of cats on housetops, of the
ants that have driven him out of his Milan house, of scabs, insomnia, bad dreams, mice, fleas, and flies. The *De remediis* is the
work of an aging man indulging his insufferable petulance.

On the other hand the curious reader is rewarded by many
picturesque glimpses of medieval life and customs. Here, for instance, is the inaugural sermon of a young theologian candidate
for the doctorate:

> There cometh a foolish young man to the church; his masters praise
> and extol him, either upon love or ignorance; he swelleth, the people
> are astunned, his kinfolk and friends rejoice at him; he being willed,
> getteth up into the pulpit, and overlooking all from on high, con-
> fusedly murmureth I cannot tell what. Then the elder sort extol him
> with praise to heaven, as one that hath spoken like a god. In the mean
> while the bells jangle, the trumpets rattle, rings fly about, kisses are
> given, and a piece of a black round cloth is hung on his shoulders.
> When this is done, the wise man cometh down that went up a fool.

One meets also in the book occasional happy flashes of insight
and phrasing: "Only the dead man is free; for the tomb is a castle
that fortune cannot assail." "There is given unto you a body,
which although it be frail and transitory, yet notwithstanding in
show is imperious and beautiful, fashioned upright and convenient in contemplation to behold the heavens." "The power of
shame has often outdone the power of the mind; to chase coward-
ice a spectator has availed more than inward virtue."

The *De remediis* is the most medieval of Petrarch's works, in
its form and structure, in its monkish misanthropy, in its theme of
de contemptu mundi. It was also, for more than a century, the
most popular, being often copied, printed, and illustrated, and
translated into Italian, French, German, and English.

Petrarch was also busy collecting and editing his letters and
forever adding to their mass. He prized them highly, believing
that they could have an almost magical effect in changing the lives
of others. He was in constant fear of plots to divert them from
their proper destination. Others shared his view of their literary
destiny. Guido Sette asked to be mentioned in them, so that his
name might pass to posterity, and indeed he has had his wish.
Francesco Nelli was well aware that his correspondence with Pe-

trarch lifted him from obscurity to be a marked man in Florence. "I was naked and thou didst clothe me with thy glory."

Petrarch was occupied as well with literary scholarship. He was the initiator of linguistic historical criticism. The Emperor sent him copies of imperial privileges said to have been granted by Julius Caesar and Nero. Petrarch pronounced them false, pointing to their anachronisms, as in the use of weekdays in dating; to their errors of fact, as in a reference to Caesar's uncle; to their medievalisms of style, such as the use of the first person plural instead of the singular.

Petrarch was one of the rare men of his time, perhaps the only one, who had learned to read critically. He read an ill-written life of St. Simplicianus and said flatly that he did not believe a word of it. He rejected attributions of works to Ovid and to Church fathers, St. Ambrose and others. He suspected, rightly, that there were two Senecas, not one. He impugned even his beloved Virgil, calculating that the historical Dido lived 300 years after Aeneas.

Thus his life was one of incessant activity. Even his study was active, for, as he said, whoever ceases to learn forgets what he has already learned; we should study as long as we live. He continued to store facts in his prodigious memory, which Boccaccio called rather divine than human. "He seems to have possessed himself c.̇ all history, from the world's creation to the present day. He can see the entire past as if before his eyes." He was no foe of society, provided it be intelligent and polite, and he delighted in listening to music. He could be persuaded to recite his love poems to ladies. And if the old enemy, never despairing, assailed him, he turned on it with the weapons of philosophy.

Materially, he was at ease in his rent-free house, with his horses and servants. His friends wrote that he was regarded as a rich man; he protested that his expenses had increased in proportion to his income, and at the end of a year he had not a penny. Like many another, he thought it a great virtue to want no more money than he wanted.

His life was more happy and serene than that of most men of his years, as he readily confessed. To Guido Sette, who asked an account of his daily routine, he replied that he was hurrying to get his work done while there was still time. He hoped that his name would pass to posterity, but if this was not to be, he would be con-

tent with the respect of a few worthy contemporaries. His body was
still vigorous—too vigorous; he was not able even yet to bring it to
heel. Were it not for Christ's aid he would succumb again, as in the
past. "By his aid I shall conquer my enemies, who so often over-
came me in youth. I shall put a strong bridle on body, that sullen
ass, that he may not lasciviously interrupt my sweet dreams and
my soul's repose." He continued to be frugal in diet and sparing of
rest, for sleep seemed to him a kind of death and his bed a coffin.
He would rise usually at midnight, invariably before dawn, and
escape into his library as into a castle-keep. In the summer he
would often move into country quarters. He was honorably welcomed by the city's rulers and beloved by the commonalty. He
would never leave Milan, he asserted. In a letter to Nelli he adds
that he reads, writes, and dictates at meals, on horseback, and
while being barbered. Sometimes even he wakes by night and
writes, in the dark, thoughts that turn out to be hardly decipher-
able by daylight. He admits also that he has found it hard to overcome his liking for good clothes, but has reconciled himself to in-
conspicuousness.

We may picture him in his study with the aid of Renaissance
paintings, such as the St. Jeromes of Carpaccio, Ghirlandaio, and
Dürer. Clad in his clerical gown, he sits before a sloping writing-
desk, with a stand above it to hold an open book. A fat candle
lights his page; beside it are ranged inkhorn, spare reed or quill
pens, ruler, scissors, pumice, knife for pen-pointing and scraper
for erasures, wax and seal, spectacles, and hourglass. Before his
face hangs a crucifix, and near by stands a brazier and a *prie-dieu*.
A dog or cat watches with admiration.

His health, during the Milan years, was on the whole good.
About 1355 he contracted a tertian fever, the form of malaria that
recurs every other day. He complained later of night pains, pre-
venting sleep. He suffered a grievous accident in 1359. He kept the
big volume of Cicero's letters, which he had copied in Verona,
standing upright by his library door. He brushed against it several
times, and each time Cicero fell and wounded his leg above the
ankle. "Why, my dear Cicero, do you do this to me?" he exclaimed
in reproach. Perhaps, he thought, Cicero was offended at being
kept on the floor. The wound became infected and the leg swelled

painfully. Doctors treated him long and futilely, and opined that he might come to an amputation. He dismissed them, had his servant apply poultices, went on a rigid diet, and got well.

His celebrity tickled his vanity, but brought him many inconveniences and disturbances. Grafters abused his reputation; he was forced to write to Barbato da Sulmona, who had been taken in: "Don't give money to anyone who makes free with my name." A literary goldsmith of Bergamo importuned him for a visit until he yielded out of weariness. He was treated to a sumptuous banquet, which of all things he loathed, and was put to rest in a new, magnificent bed, which, the goldsmith promised, would never be slept in by any other mortal.

He suffered also from his servants, whom he calls lazy dogs and domestic enemies, while women servants are devils incarnate. He ruled them with a high hand, and was requited with idleness, scamped work, and insolence. Once they threatened him with knives; again they robbed him of everything but his books. One suspects that he needed a woman to run his household.

There were other griefs. He had word that a gang of robbers had attacked the village of Vaucluse on Christmas Day, probably of 1354, carried off everything of value, and burned the houses. Robbery, in the troubled times, had advanced from furtive thievery to become an organized military operation. Petrarch's own house, being fire-resistant, suffered little. By great good luck his caretaker, son of old Raymond Monet, had previously stored his books, about thirty in number, in the Bishop's castle on the hill above. These he eventually received, through the kind offices of friends. But, he says, they were badly battered, and still pale and trembling from their ordeal.

The best of his life in Milan was given to work and to friendship, which he elevated to the emotional status of love.

> Every word of my friends is as acceptable to me as my own, and not their words only but their silences and gestures. . . . Virtue is the base of friendship, and for its preservation nothing is needful but mutual charity. . . . I chose my friends prudently, loved them fervently, cultivated them diligently, gave them my total confidence. . . In a word, nothing should be sought in friendship but friendship itself. A true friend thinks of nothing but his friend.

Again, he wrote: "What I love in a friend in his inner beauty, the face of his soul. What my eyes see is not the friend, but his habitation."

He found a number of congenial people in Milan and its neighborhood, though none to replace the friends of his youth, Socrates, Laelius, Guido Sette, Philippe de Cabassoles. He sought out a Greek, Leontius Pilatus, in his eagerness to gain access to Greek learning. He received from a Greek diplomat a fine manuscript of Homer in Greek. He would embrace the inscrutable book, sighing, and exclaim: "Oh thou great man, how gladly would I listen to thee!"

During a happy month, from mid-March to mid-April 1359, Petrarch was host to Boccaccio, who had become reconciled to Petrarch's choice of residence. The guest was forced to participate in garden-labors and laurel-planting, but as he had grown very fat he probably provided more facetious comment than manual aid. Boccaccio hinted delicately that Petrarch was secretly jealous of Dante's widespread fame. Petrarch repelled the suggestion. He wrote Boccaccio, a little later, to reiterate his love and admiration for the great poet. He recognized that Dante's work stood first in the vulgar tongue, and complained that commentators were already mistreating Dante's verse and style; if he hadn't more serious cares he would restore and edit Dante's text. He explained that he had avoided possessing a *Divine Comedy* in youth, only for fear of its undue influence on his own style. But he made clear that he now regarded all writing in Italian as inferior to that in Latin. "I'd like to see my critics write something in Latin, and not mouth their inspiration in the rough vulgar tongue for silly women and artisans." He regarded the ignorant acclaim of the mob as offensive; he did not envy Dante the applause of innkeepers, weavers, and athletic trainers. By implication he assumes a position of superiority.

The suggestion that Petrarch was jealous of his predecessor is very old. A story, unquestionably false, ran that Petrarch had in his study a picture of Dante hung by a foot, as thieves were punished, because Dante had robbed him of his primacy. And one may still suspect that as Petrarch's elderly vanity and lust for fame increased he may have felt stirrings of unlovely jealousy.

If Petrarch could be happy with his friends, he derived only pain and anger from his son Giovanni. He had thought the boy safely lodged in a Verona canonry; but alarming reports came of Giovanni's laziness and uncanonical conduct. He wrote a harsh letter, telling his son that while he was too far away to give the young canon a whipping, he would at least cut off his allowance. A revolution in Verona in 1354, which removed Petrarch's old friend Azzo da Correggio from rule, permitted the Cathedral chapter to oust Giovanni from his living. The seventeen-year-old boy naturally took refuge with his father in Milan, and naturally he soon made life in the quiet house intolerable. One may suppose that Petrarch's midnight orisons would often coincide with the end of Giovanni's day.

Three years later Guido Sette asked news of Giovanni. Petrarch replied that he had good manners and natural intelligence, but fled a book as if it were a serpent. Petrarch had tried prayers, caresses, threats, and the whip, but all in vain. Well, not everyone could be a scholar, but anyone could be good; and the father's utmost hope was that Giovanni would become an honorable and and worthy man.

The hope was soon defeated. Petrarch was infuriated, whether by some particular misdeed or by an accumulation of irritations. He speaks of Giovanni's "frenzied lewdness," of his "character impelling him to crime," and also of his sloth, his mocking manner, his contempt for his father's achievements and opinions. In what must have been a moment of high passion, Petrarch showed his son the door.

Giovanni went over the mountains to Avignon. It is commonly assumed that Petrarch sent him to the Papal Court to solicit an ecclesiastical living in that cess-pool of sin and vice. There is another possible reason. Perhaps he wanted to see his mother.

Now as it happened, faithful Francesco Nelli was sent on Church business from Florence to Avignon in this year 1357. He wrote to Petrarch, imitating his master's diatribes, calling Avignon the world's sewer, populated by wolves and foxes, echoing with the howls of savage lusts. But in fact he did not seem to find it so bad; indeed, he accepted an appointment at the Curia. He looked up Giovanni, found him pleasant, well informed, and well mannered. He wrote to Petrarch in March 19, 1358: "You don't expect him to be born an old man, do you? Please don't open your ears to

every rumor against him. His star will show him to be almost what
you want him to be, fate permitting. As he conducts himself constantly so as to merit my affection, I urge that he receive your
kindness."

Giovanni, in his turn, loved Nelli, from whom he received un-
wonted affectionate understanding. He thought Nelli the greatest
man on earth. If in public he heard another man rated higher
than Nelli, he would cast down his eyes and smile in modest dis-
agreement, and if good manners permitted he would proclaim all
his esteem and love.

In two years at Avignon Giovanni failed to gain the Church
post he sought. His position was a hard one. Trained only for
clerkly labors, for which he had no taste or skill, he was too old
to study law, the notariate, or medicine, or to be put apprentice
to a merchant or artisan, and no other livelihoods were open to
the middle class. His only recourse was to throw himself again on
his father's cold mercies. He wrote an appeal for pardon, and his
father, though highly suspicious of any real amendment, was impelled to grant it.

Giovanni joined Petrarch's old friend Laelius, who was on his
way from Avignon to Italy. One night in January 1360 the two
appeared on Petrarch's doorstep. Petrarch was more than chill;
he expressed no confidence in Giovanni's promises of reform. But
in the end he was moved by tears to tears. He granted his pardon
and permission for the boy to live in his father's house, where he
would have the status neither of a friend nor of an enemy. The
father of the Prodigal Son did better.

Petrarch's opinion of his son did not change. In December
1360 he wrote to Guido Sette that his son had brought him only
trouble, shame, and grief, though he was capable of knowledge
and virtue, had he any wish for such. He was ill-mannered, idle,
envious, insolent, rebellious, the slave of passions and lusts. "But
I must bear all, lest the patience which I praise in others should
appear to be lacking in my case."

He pointed the moral to himself as well as others here and
there in the *De remediis utriusque fortunae*: "JOY: I rejoice in my
young child. REASON: Rejoice as if thou shouldest be sorry, for that
it may of a most pleasant child become a most untruthful and dis-
obedient young man." Again: "REASON: Thou knowest not what

cause of sorrow thou hast purchased by begetting children, what entrance thou hast made into thy house for tears, what power thou hast given unto death and misery over thyself. 'O wretched mothers!' saith Horace; but 'O wretched fathers!' say I.''

Troubles with his son, with his servants, with his masters, with himself, gradually compounded the restlessness that was a constant of his character. In 1353 he had confidently expected to live out his life in Milan. Only two years later we find him inquiring about a possible establishment near Naples, under the patronage of the Seneschal, Niccolò Acciaiuoli. He complains of the constant pounding on his door, of the interruptions of authority and of visitors. In the spring of 1359 some Avignon friends, who must have been ignorant of the *Epistolae sine nomine,* tried again to get him appointed Apostolic Secretary. He wrote that he would on no account accept such a post, but he would indeed like a minor position at Court that would give him leisure to study and write. He was dreaming again of dwelling in Vaucluse.

In the summer of 1360 the plague broke out again, and began creeping up to the walls of Milan. To a friend who offered him a retreat at beautiful Cannobio, on Lago Maggiore, he wrote a val- iant, stoic letter, insisting that as death may find us whenever and wherever it chooses, it is the part of the sage to await it, serene and unterrified; and he would never flee in fear of death, for that fear is worse than death itself.

The threat of plague faded in the winter, as the rat-fleas fell comatose. In January 1361 Petrarch made his trip to Paris. In the spring the rat-fleas awoke. Avignon was hard hit; seven thousand victims are reported, including nine cardinals and seventy bishops. The plague entered Milan. The Visconti, the nobility, the rich took refuge in their country castles. Some time before mid-June Petrarch, forgetting that he would never flee in fear of death, fled to Padua.

Giovanni was left behind, and in a month he was dead of the plague. Petrarch wrote on the guard leaf of his Virgil: "My Gio- vanni, born to bring me grief and toil, afflicted me in his life with heavy and perpetual cares, and with bitter pain when he died. Having known few happy days in his lifetime, he died in the year of our Lord 1361, in his twenty-fifth year, in the mid of night be- tween the ninth and tenth of July, Friday and Saturday. The news reached me in Padua, in the evening of the fourteenth of the month."

Nelli wrote a letter of condolence for the loss of "that very beloved youth." He tells of their mutual affection, and supposes that Giovanni's future would have been bright. "How much firmness there was in the face of that unhappy youth, what elegance of manners, what vivacity of the beginner in the field of eloquence! You will suspect flattery, but all I say is very true, the result of my experience. . . . You have lost a wonderful boy. . . . Without him I find life almost hateful."

Petrarch had spent eight years in Milan, his longest stay anywhere since his youth in Avignon. In these years he reached the summit of his worldly importance. He was adulated by scholars and men of letters, honored by the rulers of Milan, greeted as a friend by a king and an emperor. He was an eminent public figure, entrusted with weighty diplomatic missions. He made valuable contributions to literature and to the world's available fund of knowledge. As he had tried to be the modern Catullus and the modern Virgil, he played the modern Cicero.

But as a person he becomes less engaging than in his younger days. His vanity grew monstrous; his humanity was tinged with inhumanity. He is to be excused; he could hardly doubt the testimony of praise chorused about him. Assuming the role of statesman, sage, and moral philosopher, he denied his own past of error, suffering, and struggle, and with it the ardor and despair of Laura's lover. He was trying to destroy his own best meaning. He was in his fifties, to be sure, already old under the stresses of medieval life. Old men are not very lovely until they can replace their touchy vanity by serenity. We would rather have known Petrarch a little younger, or a little older.

XXVI: PADUA, VENICE, AND PAVIA, 1361-1369

*Everything in life is difficult; the most diffi-
cult thing is knowing how to live.*

—Sen. VI 2

THESE WERE PETRARCH'S MOST RESTLESS YEARS.
In spite of war and brigandage in the countryside, in spite
of age and gathering illness, he spent no more than a year
continuously in any one place. He proclaimed forever that he was
hunting a peaceful retreat where he could do his great work, but
when he found one such he left it rather than affront the great
work to be done. The fact is that his great work was behind him;
all that remained was letter writing, editing, and polemics. Refusing to admit this, he gave himself the illusion of achievement by
rapid displacement of the body.

He looked sourly on his world, ridden by plagues and earthquakes and by the pillaging condottieri, especially the famous
White Company under Sir John Hawkwood. Injustice ruled
among men. "One builds the house, another occupies it, and the
architect sleeps under the stars. One sows, another reaps, the sower
starves. A sailor brings from afar rich garments for another, and
the sailor goes in rags." In this evil world men themselves are
getting worse. "Manners are corrupted, studies depraved, every
bad habit becomes a matter of course." Petrarch breaks out even
against current masculine fashions, hats with horns and feathers,
hair in pigtails, ivory hairpins, immodest, effeminate dress, with
torturing corsets, squeezing the viscera in their cavity. Especially
he reproved the short jackets affected by young men and old, "as
if it weren't enough to have dirty minds, if they can't shock the
eyes of onlookers."

In disgust with the world and in fear of the plague Petrarch

fled from Milan in June 1361 and took refuge in the house in the
cathedral close of Padua, his by right of his canonry. He was
warmly welcomed by the city's ruler, Francesco da Carrara, a good
tyrant, a great builder and stimulator of agriculture, industry, and
the arts. Patron of letters, he solicited Petrarch to make Padua his
official home. Petrarch yielded, and managed to avoid offending
the Visconti of Milan, with whom Francesco da Carrara waged a
desultory war.

However, his Avignon friends renewed their efforts to get him
appointed Apostolic Secretary. He refused again, but proposed
Nelli or Boccaccio for the post, and offered to come to Avignon to
advance his friends' candidacies. Boccaccio's candidacy would
have needed a good deal of advancing. He thought of retiring once
more to Vaucluse. He wrote Nelli: "It may well be that before
long you will hear that I have returned to my transalpine retreat.
I have had my fill of Italy."

We find him in Milan in January 1362, on his way to France.
But news of wars and troubles deterred him. A flattering invitation came from the Emperor in Prague. At first he accepted; *ecce
venio;* and again he changed his mind. In May he was back in
Padua, having transported there his precious library.

Now shining Venice, only twenty-five miles from Padua, looked
to him, as it has to so many others, to be the perfect home. He conceived a brilliant idea. He proposed to bequeath his famous library, probably the best outside of a few great Church centers, to
the city of Venice, to make a public library, a *bibliotheca publica.*
Nothing of the sort existed in his world. In return he asked that
the city grant him a house, fireproof and weatherproof, in which
he could live with his books until the time for the bequest's ful-
filment should arrive. He uttered the hope that his example would
inspire the city and private citizens of good will to add to the collection and make of it a great and famous library rivaling those of
antiquity. The Venetian Council replied in words of which Giu-
seppe Fracassetti, the great editor of Petrarch's letters, says:
"May God save all faithful Christians from such Latin." The tenor
of the missive was better than its Latin. Petrarch's proposal is
warmly accepted; he is named the greatest moral philosopher and
poet within man's memory.

What Venice did, it did magnificently. It offered Petrarch a

VENEZIA

.

splendid twin-towered palazzo on the Riva degli Schiavoni, over-
looking the harbor, and only a few steps from the Doge's Palace.
The palazzo stood on the site of the present Caserma del Sepolcro.
   Petrarch moved into his new home in September 1362. He was
very happy, for a time, in Venice, "noblest of cities, sole refuge of
humanity, peace, justice, and liberty, defended not so much by its
waters as by the prudence and wisdom of its citizens." He became
as proud as any Venetian of the city's worldwide commerce. "Our
wine goes to bubble in British cups, our honey goes to tickle the
taste of the Scythians, the lumber from our forests is carried to the
Egyptians and the Greeks. Thence our oil, linen, and saffron are
borne to the Syrians, Armenians, Arabs, and Persians, and in turn
their goods come to us."
   He loved to gaze out of his window at the harbor activity. Two
great ships, their masts overtopping his towers, wintered at the
marble quay below him. One stormy night in early spring he sat
writing late. He heard a great shouting below, and ran to look
down from his highest window. *Deus bone, quod spectaculum!*
The ships were casting off.

> At this moment, with all the stars hidden by clouds, as my walls and
> roofs were shaken by the wind, as the sea roared hellishly below, the
> ships cast loose and set forth on their journey. One, perhaps, was
> bound for the river Don, with passengers for the Ganges, the Cau-
> casus, the Indies, and the Eastern Ocean. My heart bled for these un-
> happy men. And when I could no longer follow the ships with my
> eyes, moved and stirred, I again picked up my pen, exclaiming, "Oh,
> how dear to men is life, and how little account they take of it!"

   In Venice he received every honor. The highest officials took
him for promenades in their state gondolas. At the tourneys in
the Piazza San Marco celebrating a victory in Crete he sat beside
the Doge himself. The jousters, clad in purple and gold, seemed to
him flying angels; he could almost hear the great bronze horses
stamp and neigh.
   But in spite of all he could not be happy in repose. In just a
year he was back in Padua; thence he went to Pavia, where he
spent two months as a guest in Galeazzo Visconti's mighty new
palace. He returned to Venice for the winter of 1363-64, and in the
spring he was off again for a trip to Bologna and then to the Cas-
entino, the upland Apennine valley east of Florence and north

of Arezzo. Thenceforth for several years he shifted uneasily to and fro between Venice, Padua and its nearby Baths of Abano, sovereign for the itch, Pavia, and Milan. He particularly liked Pavia, because of its beauty, its healthy air, its gentle weather. He journeyed once to Udine, at the foot of the Alps eastward of Venice, to meet the Emperor.

All this time he was, of course, living on the bounty of autocrats and of the Church. Boccaccio and others perceived some discord between his principles and his conduct. Petrarch assured Boccaccio that while he might seem to be an outsider subject to another's rule, in fact he had preserved all his liberty. "Wherever I may be, I shall try to keep my thought free, even though I may have to submit to superiors with regard to my body and external circumstance—whether submitting to one person, as I do, or to many, as do you. I think it's easier to bear one man's authority than that of a tyrannical populace."

If his conscience troubled him at all—as is unlikely—he could appease it by the reflection that he was giving the best of counsel to his noble masters, as he did to Emperor and Pope. To them he hammered on the necessity that both return to Rome, whence they would harmoniously rule Italy and the world.

Emperor Charles, dubious about the harmony, preferred to remain in Prague. But there was a new Pope, upon whose spirit Petrarch could labor.

Innocent VI, old, sour, and sickly, died in September 1362. His pontifical years had been unhappy. Avignon had been twice attacked by mercenary soldiers, and twice he had had to pay them a huge fee, with full absolution for their misdeeds, to persuade them to attack someone else. To ransom the Holy See he had been forced to sell its silver services, jewels, and works of art. Innocent was unlucky even in death. His tomb in Villeneuve-les-Avignon served for many years as a rabbit-hutch.

Innocent was succeeded by Urban V, earnest and pious, French but well acquainted with Italy. No ermine-trimmed coverlets for him; he slept on the stone floor of his palace.

His rule was just but filled with trouble. In 1365 the famous Bertrand du Guesclin, one of France's warrior-heroes, stopped outside Avignon's walls with 30,000 men, mostly riffraff of the wars. He announced that he was leading a crusade against the

Moors in Spain, and that he would have a subsidy from the Pope
of 200,000 florins—or else! The Pope raised the enormous sum by
desperate efforts, and, raging, gave the army plenary absolution.
Du Guesclin then led his assoiled crusaders into Spain, where they
confined themselves to attacking Christians.

Petrarch learned that Urban was very discontented in ill-de-
fended Avignon, and that he publicly admitted that the proper
seat of the papacy was in Rome. Petrarch felt it his duty to convert the Pope's conviction into action. He wrote a letter, really a
long essay, remarkable for many reasons, perhaps most for its freedom of speech.

He begins with hyperbolic flattery, praising the Pope for his
many sweeping reforms. He assumes then the right to speak for
Italy, as he had done to the Emperor. He reproaches the Pope for
his continued residence in Avignon. Rome needs her spouse! Hear
her bitter cry! The Lateran is falling in ruins, the mother church
of the world has a rotten roof, the houses of Peter and Paul and
the Holy Apostles are tottering. It is time to act! It was God who
chose you Pope; you were just an abbot of a humble convent; no
one would have thought of you had not God's finger pointed to
you. The objections to a return of the papacy are invalid. Italy is
the most beautiful of countries; Rome is secure and tranquil,
whereas Avignon is the prey of armed brigands. It is true that we
have in Rome no Beaune wine, but we can import it, and our own
wines are excellent. The Turks are advancing in Greece—and you
sit idle in the west! Why do you not declare a crusade? All Christians would rush to arms! We don't need you in Avignon, but on
the Aegean, the Ionian Sea, the Hellespont, the Bosphorus, the
Propontis! Compel the Emperor to return to Rome! And beware
of God's demand for your report, when he summons you to an accounting after your death!

Pope Urban took Petrarch's plain speaking without offense (if
indeed he read the fifty-page letter through). He decreed that
the papacy would return to its ancient seat. Petrarch, and many
of his biographers, assumed that his eloquence moved the Pope
to his decision. Others are inclined to give more credit to the
armed attacks on Avignon and to a general restoration of order in
Italy by Cardinal Albornoz.

The great remove began in April 1367. The Pope went by sea;

many of the cardinals and immense trains of court officers and stores journeyed overland. The Italian prelates were delighted, like that earlier Cardinal who, pausing for a symbolic act at the summit of a mountain pass, looked over his shoulder at France and exclaimed: *"Aspice nudatas, arida terra, nates;* bare land, behold my bare behind." But the French clerics, deprived of Burgundy wine, which they called the fifth element of nature, were inconsolable. Their welcome in Italy was ambiguous, to say the least. In Viterbo a servants' quarrel developed into a riot, the people shouting: "Long live the people! Die the Church!" Two cardinals were manhandled. But the riot was quelled and the cardinals mollified by seeing the ringleaders hanged before their lodging.

The officials of the Curia found themselves inadequately and uncomfortably quartered in Rome. The French cardinals were embittered; "O bad Pope, O impious father!" they cried. Many of them fell ill, no doubt from what is still known as Roman stomach. The all-healing Beaune wine did not arrive. Petrarch, disturbed by such reports, wrote the Pope another letter urging a complete reform of the Sacred College.

Urban wrote cordially to Petrarch, asking him to visit Rome and making vague promises of advantages. Petrarch replied that in spite of ill health and age's debility he would comply. After many postponements he set forth from Padua in the spring of 1370. On the way he fell in a faint, and remained for thirty hours in a cataleptic state resembling death. He was carried to the ducal palace of Ferrara and tenderly cared for by the Este family. At length he was returned to Padua, prostrate in a boat. He renounced all thought of a Roman visit.

Three years in Rome convinced Pope Urban that the Holy City was a worse home than Avignon. The last straw, apparently, was an alliance of the city's government with Perugia and the eminent condottiere, Sir John Hawkwood, against the Church. In September 1370 the papacy moved back to Avignon, and in December Urban died, by poison, if Petrarch's suspicions are well founded. Petrarch was in despair. "If he hadn't died, he would have read the letter I was preparing, in which I spoke freely of his departure from Rome. It might have worked marvels." Later, Petrarch was persuaded that the Pope had promised him a post of great power and had reneged. Well, the Pope is a man, he said, and the Bible tells us that all men are liars. Even St. Peter lied; why not his successor?

"Nothing is so proper to man as work," wrote Petrarch. "For this he was born, as is the bird to fly and the fish to swim." Restless as he was, he never really rested, except perforce.

He was forever seeking manuscripts. He wrote a friend: "No matter how often I've been unsuccessful, I can't give up book-hunting, so pleasant is it to hope for what one wants. I shall never renounce it from base indolence." He was the first Western scholar to seek Greek manuscripts, much though their muteness distressed him. He resented the ownership of books by ignorant collectors, who keep them prisoner and rob scholars of their use.

His library he called his daughter. A true bibliophile, he loved the physical beauty of books. All the extant volumes from his library are on fine parchment, none on paper, and many are richly decorated. He liked noble bindings; the best, he said, are of silk with silver clasps. The actual writing, he insisted, should above all be clear. He abhorred narrow columns, impeding clarity. He liked the *littera antiqua*, the minuscule of the tenth and eleventh centuries, and disliked the "angular, heavy, massive" lettering of the early fourteenth century. His own handwriting is admirably clear and elegant, readable even for amateurs. But the old story that his handwriting served as the model for the first italic type is clearly false. He was endlessly at war with copyists, who were idle, incompetent, and unreliable. "We make cooks take examinations, not copyists," he complained. Young copyists especially follow the fashion, crowding tiny characters together without spacing, so that they themselves can't read what they have written, and the purchaser finds too late that he has bought a device for blinding him.

But it was the content, not the clothing, of books that brought him his chief joy. The number of one's books is unimportant, he said. The thing is to lodge their contents not in a bookcase, but in one's head; otherwise one will always be inferior to a bookcase. Receiving a new book, even of a familiar text, he would read it for its variations and corrections; he could not leave it until, like a swollen leech, he was filled to bursting; he could not stop to eat or sleep. He read emotionally, identifying himself with his auth⸗

He quotes Cicero in praise of solitude; "as often as I read this sentence I mentally fall in with it as though I myself and not another had written it."

His enthusiasm made him the leader of a scholarly revival. Boccaccio wrote him that through his influence many in and out of Italy had begun to pursue studies in abeyance for centuries. He was the acknowledged master of the book world, the center of the great movement for the recovery of the classics. His versions, says Billanovich, were taken as authoritative and standard for succeeding generations. "If Petrarch's own copies have been lost, one can often reconstruct his texts, even his notes, by the codices descended from them."

Much as he prized critical exactitude, he was preserved from pedantry by his stout common sense (although he could be roused to poetical fury by the accusation that he had used in verse a short syllable in place of a long). He was more amused than angry when, in a group of scholars, they spoke ill of that bright star, Virgil. "I asked one of these pedants what Virgil had done to deserve such censure. With a sneer he replied: 'Virgil uses too many conjunctions.'"

He knew well that substance is better than form, thought better than style, truth better than literature. He wrote his brother Gherardo: "Some of us scrape parchments, write books, correct them, illuminate and bind them, adorn their surface; superior minds look higher and fly above these mean occupations."

Though aware of writing's vanity and doomed fate, he could not stop. Boccaccio urged him to take things easy, to write less. He replied: "There is no burden lighter than a pen, nothing pleasanter. Other pleasures are evanescent and injurious; a pen in hand is soothing, and when it is laid down it still gives pleasure. It is useful not only to the writer but to many others, often far away, and perhaps even to those who will live thousands of years from now." Again, Boccaccio expressed wonder that the old man could still find things to write about. He answered: "How can one say so, if one has present to one's eyes and ears the sky, earth, and sea and all that in them is, and man especially, most marvelous work of mother nature, best and worst of animals, now like unto the angels, now worse than the most venomous serpents?"

As he had long since proposed, he assembled his Familiar Letters, 350 of them, into a volume. But as he could not renounce the pleasures of letter writing, he proposed to start a new series, the *Epistolae seniles*, dedicated to faithful Nelli. By the time of his death this series grew to 124 letters, many of them essays of considerable length. In the modern Italian translation they occupy over a thousand pages.

He put the final touches on his *De vita solitaria* and sent it off to Philippe de Cabassoles, to whom it had been promised twenty years before. He thought of writing a book on the active life to balance it. He began a biography of Julius Caesar, to add to his *De viris illustribus*. However, this period of his life is marked by little in the way of original composition. His one work that still struggles for life is the *De sui ipsius et multorum ignorantia*, On His Own Ignorance and That of Many.

The book was thus conceived: four scholarly gentlemen of Venice were his friends and frequent visitors. They let fall the remark, which soon reached Petrarch's ears, that he was a good man but uncultured. No single sentence could worse wound a scholar. Their surprising judgment was prompted by their adherence to the popular school of Aristotelianism and Averroism, whereas Petrarch was an old-fashioned Augustinian Platonist.

This calls for a little definition. Most of Aristotle was not known in the West until the thirteenth century, when translations of the Arabic versions and commentaries by the Arab Averroes began to disturb and delight philosophers. Fundamentally, Aristotle represents the scientific, positivistic attitude, in opposition to the poetic transcendentalism of Plato, as developed by Augustine. Aristotle and Averroes were therefore welcomed especially by physicians, who deal in scientific fact. Averroism asserted the eternity of the world, thus rejecting Judgment Day, and denied the immortality of the individual soul. It accepted astrology, which, being deterministic, rules out free will and the intervention of divine Providence. To avoid the practical consequence of these dangerous doctrines the Averroists proclaimed that there are two truths, one philosophical, one theological, that what is theologically false may be philosophically true, and vice versa.

The tendency of Averroism, and of the contemporary nominalism of William of Occam, who asserted that God could have embodied himself in a donkey as well as in a man, was toward skep-

ticism and on to heresy, and still further on to Renaissance philosophy. Pietro d'Abano, who practised medicine in Padua, wrote in
1310 a commentary on Aristotle in which he sneered at New Testament miracles, especially the resurrection of Lazarus.

Petrarch was horrified at the new philosophic skepticism. He
had in any case no taste for dialectics and scholastic logic. He
called dialectics a proper amusement for babes, not adults. Again,
he termed current philosophy "a prostitute who worries delight-
edly over vain verbalisms; she is useless and perhaps harmful."
Augustine tells what true philosophy is—a moral and ethical guide
to a better life. Petrarch would not be silenced by a reference to
the holy name of Aristotle. He said that he was anti-Aristotle
whenever Aristotle was anti-common-sense. For instance, Aristotle says that wrath is sweeter than honey. Nonsense! And as for
the Arabs, Petrarch abhorred the whole race of them, and especially that mad dog Averroes.

Petrarch brooded long over the contemptuous remark of the
Venetian Averroists—"a good man but uncultured!" In May 1367,
riding comfortably up the Po to Pavia by barge, propelled by oars,
sails, and towing-horses, he wrote a blasting reply, the *De ignorantia*. "My mind is growing old and cold," he sighs, and then dis-
proves his words by raining fire on his critics.

He berates his philosopher friends for their learned ignorance.
They know all sorts of useless facts out of Aristotle, how many
hairs on a lion's head, how many feathers in a hawk's tail, how
elephants couple backwards, how the phoenix is burned on a pyre
of aromatic woods and is then reborn, how the crocodile is the
only animal able to move his upper jaw. "How could Aristotle
know these things, since neither reason nor experience reveal
them?" he had inquired of his visitors, shocking and surprising
them. Even if the zoological statements were true they would serve
no reasonable end of man. Man's purpose is his ultimate felicity
and of this Aristotle knew less than any poor old peasant woman.
It is far better to be good than to be learned. But these inquisi-
tive men are trying to penetrate, with superb arrogance, the secrets of nature and God's high mysteries, which we accept with
humble faith.

His opponents, he continues, deny Catholic faith and Christ's
teaching. Professing to support the faith, they undermine it with

ogling hints, sophistical blasphemies, impious, nauseous jokes.
They dare even to term Christ simple-minded! And ever they
muffle their statements in pretentious obscurity. They do not even
understand themselves. Their obscurity betrays them, for whatever is clearly understood can be clearly expressed; clarity is a
proof of understanding.

True knowledge, he holds, must bring man to the good life.
But Aristotle merely explains what virtue is, he does not impel
us to love it, nor does he inspire in us any hatred of sin. To know
is one thing; to love is another. "It is better to will the good than
to know the truth. Those are much at fault who spend their time
in knowing God, not in loving him." It is impossible to know God
fully. The demons know God well, but they hate him.

The book closes with a long defense of his devotion to Cicero,
who was almost a Christian.

The *De ignorantia* is often taken to be a representation of the
modern mind, or at least of the humanist return to classic wisdom,
at odds with medieval scholasticism. It is said to represent the conflict of two epochs of Italian and European culture, with Petrarch
upholding the coming times. I do not understand this very well.
It seems to me that the four friends were trying, in however clumsy
a fashion, to understand and explain the external world. They
were sustaining the scientific attitude and freedom of thought,
which are certainly the mark of modernity, against Petrarch's acceptance of theological dogmatism, his preference for moral to
rational judgments, his espousal of the simple faith of old peasant
women. I would conclude that the four friends were on the right
side.

To a friend, asking an account of his state, Petrarch replied in
1361:

> What am I? A scholar? No, hardly that. A lover of woodlands, a soli-
> tary, in the habit of uttering foolish sounds in the shade of beech
> trees, and used, presumptuously, to scribbling under an immature
> laurel; fervent in toil, but not happy with the results; a lover of let-
> ters, but not fully versed in them; an adherent of no sect, but very
> eager for truth; and since that is hard to find and I am clumsy in my
> search, often in self-distrust and in fear of error I accept doubt in
> place of truth. Thus I have gradually become academic, and after so

many others I have rallied to that humble band that claims nothing, holds nothing certain, doubts everything—except what it is sacrilege to doubt.

His fame was widespread. He was besieged by visitors, including minstrels eager to get some unpublished poems with which to make their fortune. He was perhaps better known to the general public in his lifetime than any other poet except Victor Hugo. Returning by boat from Pavia to Padua in 1368 he passed the battle lines along the river Po without a stay; all said that he alone could have thus journeyed freely. Where anyone else would have been slain or imprisoned or robbed, he saw his boat loaded by the soldiery with wine-bottles, game, and fruits.

Fame was certainly a solace. But he was growing old. Age is man's necessity, and, he said, the only thing to do about necessity is to yield to it. He watched the process of aging with utmost interest. He found himself happy, even gay. Age bends the back, but it raises the mind to noble heights. "Let only those complain of aging who have put all their hope, the sum of their felicity, in the body." He told some friends that he had lost his florid complexion, his bright eyes were clouded, his skin rough, his snow-white hair thin. He kept his memory, though it was not so prompt in response as of yore.

> I feel no decrease in my powers in life's honest operations. For those dishonest I am incompetent, and glad of it, and I strive to become more so, aiding the work of time with fasts, vigils, and toils. And when by such means I succeed in banishing everything base from my thoughts I think myself stronger than Milo or Hercules. I feel that I have triumphed over my body, that old enemy, which waged many a cruel war on me, and I seem to be driving a laureled chariot up the sacred way to the Capitol of my soul, dragging at chariot-tail my conquered passions, the insidious foes of virtue firmly bound, and pleasure in chains. . . . Life never seemed so beautiful as it does now. . . . Better a day of this life than a year of troubled youth! Oh, dear old age, unworthy to attain you is he who fears and accuses you! I have always longed for you, without fear; and as you drew nearer I went forth to meet you. I bid you welcome, conqueror of lust and evil passions! You have brought me at last to self-mastery, to liberty! The loss of liberty saddened my youth; its recovery gladdens my old age.

This was his happy mood, which could yield to fits of depression. "I am tired in body and soul, tired of everything, tired of

affairs, tired of myself," he wrote the Emperor in 1362. But he
recognized that a man's opinions change with his moods, and his
moods change with the body's humors. To Philippe de Cabassoles,
who pointed out an inconsistency with an old letter, he wrote:
"I am different from what I was, not merely when I wrote that
letter thirty years ago, but when I began to write this letter."
   He was oppressed by the thought of time and its doomed flight.
The eminent modern critic, Umberto Bosco, sees in Petrarch's obsession with temporal flow, which Bosco calls "lability," a chief
clue to Petrarch's thought. Petrarch believed that he lived in the
last of the six ages of the world, and he thought, with much justification, that his age was a very bad one. He brooded on the pre-
ciousness of the present moment, on our inability to capture and
hold it. "Killing time" seemed to him a dreadful sort of murder.
"How common is the expression: 'Let us chase away this day, let
us do something to make the day pass!' The day ought to be re-
tarded and not urged on its course." The dropping sands of the
hourglass, the very taking of breath, should warn us of lost time,
lost time. "I had got this far in my letter and was wondering what
to say or not to say next, and as my habit is I kept tapping the
blank paper with my pen. This made me think how, between one
tap and the next, time slips on, and I slip too, fall and fail, and
die a little. We are always dying. I while I write this, you while
you read it, others while they listen or stop their ears, we're all
dying." The present is all we have, but there is no present; there
is only past and future. "In human affairs whatever is is hateful.
As the past was hateful when it was with us, the future will be
hateful in its turn. Only memory and expectation are sweet. Thus
you may judge what price to put on things, for they give pleasure
only when absent. Oh how happy, how ever unchanging, is our
heavenly home, where there is neither past or future, where everything is the present!"
   With such powerful thoughts to communicate, and with the
aid of his correspondents in many cities, he became an authoritative moral philosopher, a lay leader of *docta pietas*, learned piety.
As G. A. Levi points out, the Church's ideal was ascetic, monastic;
the rising class of merchants and officials called for an ideal more
adapted to their daily lives. Petrarch aspired to provide such a
doctrine. He tried to show how one may attain to virtue while remaining in the world. But he offered no easy way to reconcile

worldly success with salvation. "No one has got rich in my school; but some who have got poor wouldn't become rich again if they could."

His moral system was based securely on Christian orthodoxy. Christ was the center of his theology, a Christ with a slight humanistic overlay. He calls Christ "our Apollo, son of sempiternal Jove, true god of wisdom." He loved and trusted the Apostles and the early Fathers, Augustine, Ambrose, and Jerome. He did not attempt the later theologians. He mentions Aquinas only once, I think. An Averroistic cleric à la mode visited him. Says Petrarch: "I quoted Scripture; he said, in a rage: 'Keep your little Doctors, yours and the Church's! I know whom to follow, whom to believe!' Said I: 'You have just used the words of the Apostle [Paul]; would you had also his faith!' 'That Apostle was a mere wordmonger, and mad into the bargain! . . . Paul and Augustine and all the rest were a lot of gabblers! Read Averroes!' 'Go to the devil with your heresies, and never come back!'" Petrarch seized his interlocutor's clerical gown and pushed him out the door.

Orthodox Petrarch was, but with a qualification. He was skeptical of inherited superstitions and legends and applied the tests of common sense to his pious readings. He told Boccaccio that often lies and follies hide under the veil of religion, and fraud and deception cloak themselves with God's judgments. He accepted miracles with reluctance. He explains the stigmata of Saint Francis of Assisi—in whom he showed otherwise no interest—as due to autosuggestion, or perhaps to a traumatic psychosis. "His meditation on Christ's death was so intense, his mind was so occupied with it, that it seemed to him that he was crucified with Our Lord. Thus the force of that thought could pass from his mind to his body and leave the visible traces impressed upon it."

In his private life he intensified his pious practices, his midnight prayers, his fasting. He continued to live ascetically. His furnishings were decent, not rich. On his floor lay straw mats, not silk carpets. But he had his little indulgences. His olive oil was sent him from Vaucluse, from trees he had planted with his own hands.

Music was the chief of his pleasures. North Italy was at this time the center of polyphonic music. Most of the princes kept lay composers and performers in their employ. Orchestral instruments were the violin, flute, double flute, tambourine, mandore or small lute, and psaltery. Petrarch, with his strong voice, no doubt joined in informal exercises. He speaks of "the delight I have always felt in musical concerts, which was always so great that sometimes, thinking about philosophers' arguments concerning the celestial harmonies, I was inclined to agree with those who don't envy the gods for hearing the music of the spheres, being well repaid by the sweetness that ravishes the human ear."

His health worsened. The tertian fever that had smitten him in 1355 recurred in following Septembers. He complained of languor and night pains. In 1364 he suffered dreadfully from the itch, or scabies, caused by a mite that lays its eggs under the skin. (The Middle Ages were the heyday of skin diseases, aggravated no doubt by coarse underclothing or its absence.) For about six months he took the ancient hot mineral waters and mud-baths of Abano, near Padua. During that time he could not write or use his hands for eating. He had no help from doctors, mere spectators of his illness. But he recovered, and forgot.

The Middle Ages regarded man's sixty-fourth year, in Petrarch's case from July 1367 to July 1368, as the grand climacteric, most dangerous to life and the mind. Petrarch passed it triumphantly, and wrote Boccaccio that he had had an excellent year, in perfect health. But the Middle Ages were not far wrong. Petrarch's tertian fever recurred in 1368, and was occasionally violent. The year 1369 was a bad one, with forty days of fever in Padua. He could not get to the cathedral adjoining his house without the aid of servants or friends. He lost hope of regaining even moderate health. But in the spring of 1370 he felt well enough to accept Pope Urban's invitation to Rome, and, as we have told, he collapsed in Ferrara in a strange thirty-hour coma. The doctors applied various remedies, but his body made no more response than a statue by Phidias. He was thought dead, and the final offices were ordered. But he rose from his semi-death to confound the physicians.

In his weakness he leaned more and more on his friends. Saddest of his experiences was the disappearance of old friends, some of them bound to him from their common youth. In 1361 died Socrates, "my friend, my comrade, my best of brothers." Then came word of the passing of Zanobi da Strada, and Azzo da Correggio, and Laelius, killed in a mob rising in Rome, and faithful

Francesco Nelli, and Barbato da Sulmona, and Guido Sette, the oldest friend, the school companion. Sagremor de Pommiers, weary of riding on the Emperor's errands, retired to a living death in a Cistercian monastery. Petrarch tried to tell himself that death is natural, that there was no reason for tears; he wanted none shed for his own death. But stoic resolution failed him. "I feed on my troubles; with cruel pleasure I make my food of groans and sighs."

New friends appeared, however, to take the places of the old. Tempting Boccaccio to visit him in Venice, he told of the new and splendid friends. The Chancellor Benintendi came nearly every evening in his gondola and took him for delightful trips on the lagoon. If Boccaccio would come the two would make an excursion to Trieste, Capo d'Istria, and beyond.

Boccaccio was the closest of Petrarch's later friends, though they met seldom. Petrarch was the dominant; Boccaccio, younger, regarded him as the master, and imitated his doctrines of life and literature. In return, Petrarch gave the pupil strength and support. He offered the distressed Boccaccio half his fortune, if he would come and live with him. In 1362 an officious cleric brought Boccaccio a message from a saintly visionary that he had only a few years to live, and that he must give up poetry and get rid of his books. Boccaccio was impressed and frightened. Wonderful, if true, commented Petrarch, but the prophecy is certainly a fraud; don't be a fool. If Boccaccio must sell his books Petrarch would buy them, combine them with his own, and bequeath them to some holy establishment that would perpetually preserve their common memory. At another time Boccaccio proposed to burn his poems in Italian because they were inferior to Petrarch's. The master lectured him sharply, proving that his alleged humility was merely disguised vanity. For himself, he would gladly yield his place among Italian poets, second after Dante. But the important thing is to remain united. Love is all; there is no precedence among friends.

Boccaccio paid two long visits to Petrarch during these years. The first was a three-month stay in Venice in the spring of 1363. The visit was marred by the presence of another house-guest, Leontius Pilatus, the Calabrian Greek, whom the two friends had commissioned to translate Homer into Latin. Boccaccio had established him as Professor of Greek in Florence. He was "a great beast," horrible of aspect, with long tangled beard and hair, dirty, ill-mannered, abusive, always hungry. "The concierge of the Cretan labyrinth," Petrarch called him. His Latin version of Homer is said to be very bad. He hated Italy and Italians, and finally succeeded in escaping to Constantinople. But once there he wrote Petrarch a letter "longer than his beard," begging the means to return. He took ship, and in a terrible storm, clinging to the mast, he was killed by lightning. He was insufferable, but he loved us, said Petrarch; he was truly ill-starred.

Boccaccio's second visit was in Padua in the summer of 1368. Boccaccio spent much of the time making copies of Petrarch's works. We may safely suppose that their conversations dealt much more with Petrarch than with Boccaccio. Boccaccio's letters are full of Petrarch; Petrarch's show no concern with what his friend is doing and writing. Petrarch never mentioned any of Boccaccio's work until, a year before he died, he received a copy of the *Decameron,* of which he read little but the beginning and the end. The curious incomprehensions of the great!

During these years something new came into Petrarch's life—paternal affection.

His son Giovanni had died of the plague in Milan, on July 9, 1361. His passing filled Petrarch with unsuspected sorrow and regret. He wrote to Nelli: "When he was alive I spoke to him in hate, and now that he is dead I love him with my mind, hold him in my heart, clasp him in memory, seek him with my eyes, alas, in vain."

There was another to whom he could perhaps compensate for his rigor toward his son. His daughter Francesca, born in 1343, was now eighteen. Of her mother and of the milieu of her youth we know nothing, but clearly she was gently bred, perhaps in an Avignon convent. Nor do we know when she joined her father. It seems unlikely that she was in Milan with him before June 1361, for he would hardly have left her to brave the plague alone, and if she had accompanied him in his flight to Padua we should expect to find some reference to her. It is tempting to suppose that Giovanni's death and Petrarch's distress and self-reproach turned his thoughts to Francesca, and that he summoned her from Avignon.

He arranged, as a father should, his daughter's marriage. The spouse was Francesco or Francescuolo da Brossano, a Milan gentleman, a good and trustworthy man, very tall, with gigantic hands, placid but cordial in manner, slow but sensible of speech. Everybody liked Francescuolo. The marriage took place before the summer of 1362. There must have been a dowry, but Petrarch does not mention it. The couple lived for a time in Milan; after Petrarch received his palazzo in Venice they moved in with him. In 1367 Francescuolo obtained a position in the city government of Pavia and his wife joined him there. Their first child, a daughter, was named Eletta after Petrarch's adored mother. She immediately captured her grandfather's heart.

Boccaccio visited Venice in 1367, hoping to see Petrarch. He called at the palazzo, but found the great man absent on a trip to Pavia. Francesca greeted him warmly, and, blushing, embraced him in her father's place. She urged Boccaccio to stay in the house, but he feared that in spite of his age, white hair, and obesity his presence might provoke gossip. He joined some friends conversing in the garden, and Francesca played the hostess to perfection. Then little four-year-old golden-haired Eletta was brought in, dressed for company. Boccaccio felt a pang; she was so like his own daughter, lost in childhood. She looked at Boccaccio with a timid smile; he took her in his arms and kissed her.

> Your Eletta's face is like that of my own little girl, and so is her smile, the sparkle of her eyes, her mannerisms and walk, although my bambina was somewhat older and taller; she was five and a half when I saw her for the last time. If they had talked the same dialect, the sound and naïveté of the words would have been the same. . . . As I kissed her tenderly, taking great joy in her talk, the memory of the little girl reft from me brought tears to my eyes.

Boccaccio does not mention Francesca's second child, born early in 1366. Probably he remained in his crib. He was named Francesco, after his grandfather and his father too. He was the image of Petrarch, who loved him with a grandfather's intensity. But he died when barely two years old. Petrarch wrote for him an epitaph and had it carved in gold on a marble plaque in the Church of San Zeno in Pavia. "A beautiful and innocent child, I lie here. Briefly a guest in this world, I had barely touched its stony threshold with my tender foot. Now my parents' grief alone clouds my joy in eternity."

Petrarch, who had often counseled his friends to bear their losses stoically, could not contain his woe. He wrote that he had loved the boy more than a son, because he was the child of Francesca and Francescuolo, both dearer to him than his own soul. Little Francesco was the delight of all, the hope and treasure of the family. His beauty and intelligence were extraordinary; he seemed a child of royal stock. He would have been as handsome as his father, intellectually his superior. He was "the sole comfort of my life, the only light remaining for my eyes. . . . I never loved anything on earth as I did him."

Thus Petrarch set the love of his own flesh and blood above his still-resounding love of a woman. Thus the great moral philosopher learned at length, and in pain, one of the simple truths that everyone knows. He accepted the lessons of humanity. He found an escape from his own intolerable self by means of love for others. He was passing through a spiritual cure.

XXVII: ARQUÀ, 1369-1374

> *Evening is falling; and before night comes we must think of our inn.*
>
> —Fam. *XI 15*

PETRARCH SPENT JUNE 1368 IN PAVIA. HE RE-
turned to his canon's house in Padua in mid-July; he then
decided not to return to Venice, but to make his home in
Padua. Why did he abandon his fine palazzo and his Venetian
friends? No doubt there were accumulated irritations, perhaps
with a new Doge who did not appreciate him at his proper worth;
certainly the blandishments and promises of Francesco da Carrara,
ruler of Padua, were powerful; fundamentally the reason was
perpetual restlessness, weariness with the familiar. One suspects
that Venice, the bitter enemy of Padua, took ill this rejection of its
very lavish bounty, particularly since the bequest of Petrarch's
books to form a Venetian public library seems to have been
abrogated.

Francesco da Carrara made to Petrarch a splendid gift. Very
likely it fulfilled a promise made as temptation. He gave Petrarch
land for a country home, and evidently funds for house-building.
The land lies above the village of Arquà, fifteen miles southwest
of Padua, in the Euganean hills. These are the misty blue hills
that one sees from Venice, looking west across the lagoon. They
are warm and welcoming, disposing themselves naturally in
beautiful forms, in the manner of Italian landscapes. The land is
fruitful; in poetic terms, Bacchus, Ceres, and Pomona dwelt there.
awaiting only the coming of Minerva. The village of Arquà, which
poets struggled to derive from Arcadia, has changed little since
Petrarch's day. A haphazard collection of stuccoed stone houses
surround a small piazza, halfway up the hill. Here is the village

church where Petrarch worshiped, where he lies buried. From it one climbs a narrow lane between flowered walls to the house that Petrarch built. Thence one looks down on his vineyards, the village roofs, and away to hillsides silvery with olives and to the broad yellow and blue Lombard plain.

Petrarch planned his house and gardens with delight. The construction progressed through the summer of 1369. A young literary-minded Paduan friend, Lombardo della Seta, supervised the planting of vines, bushes, and the inevitable laurel. The house is small and cramped, of wood and stone, no architectural shrine. But it is beautifully set, bird-beloved, flower-bedecked, and ringed with vines and fruit-trees, descendants of Petrarch's own plantings. We are shown his desk and chair, which have survived the enthusiasm of six centuries of souvenir-hunters. We may also see his horrible stuffed cat, completely bald; it had lost all its hair by 1650.

He occupied the house by March 1370. He soon added quarters for his daughter and her family. Francescuolo da Brossano gave up his post in Pavia and thenceforth devoted himself to the care of his illustrious father-in-law. The house was gladdened by the presence of Eletta, who was then nine or ten years old.

The sweetness of life in Arquà and failing powers could not still in Petrarch the old impulse to travel. It was in the spring of 1370 that he made his disastrous effort to revisit Rome. In the following spring Philippe de Cabassoles invited him to Avignon; he began to pack, and then yielded to body's weakness. In 1372 Philippe, now a cardinal, was sent as papal Legate to Perugia. Petrarch's desire to see the last remaining of his early friends was so intense that he proposed to ride to Perugia, 230 miles away. As a precautionary experiment he tried riding a mile on horseback, and was forced to recognize that his long journeys were ended forever. The failure was the sadder, for Philippe died in August. Petrarch wrote in his Virgil the last of his obituary notices, ending: "Alas, I am now all but alone!"

He had of course plenty of new friends, though these could hardly replace the old. Lombardo della Seta became his disciple and secretary, lived with him, planted his trees, and after his death served as his literary executor and continuer of his unfinished work. He was a collector of Greek vases, and had examples from

Corinth—though Petrarch pronounced them wares of Samos, of less worth.

Swarms of visitors called to see the great man. They usually arrived at about dinner time, eager for food and conversation. "I can hardly avoid them unless I am willing to appear prouder and stingier than I am in fact. As God loves me, I seem often to see around me those suitors who besieged Penelope, except that they were enemies and these are friends." One is reminded of Voltaire at Ferney and Goethe at Weimar, with Francesca playing the roles of Mme. Denis and Ottilie.

As in the case of Voltaire and Goethe, his visitors gained prestige by proudly reporting their interviews. A scholar wrote Luigi di Gonzaga of Ferrara, in 1371, that he would call on Petrarch in order to find a work rumored to be written by Julius Caesar. "There is the casket and tabernacle of antiquity's monuments. No one can hope to discover what he hasn't got. I will go and see him in Arquà. No refusal is to be feared. Obliging always and to all, he has been particularly so to me." Another scholar, working on Cicero's rhetoric, sought out the master, "that bright light without smoke," and was received with the utmost amiability and with every encouragement. Others describe his serenity and cheerfulness, his forth-streaming (redundans) voice, like that of many waters, his snowy hair, like white wool, his flashing eyes. A cleric who knew him both in Padua and in Arquà tells of his pious practices, of his fasting four times a week. In Holy Week he lived only on bread and water, holding the body in hatred for the health of his soul. His chastity was so great that he never slept naked, to be always ready for prayer. Praying, he was rapt out of himself. "I sometimes saw him in his library in an ecstasy, as we read of Augustine, whom he followed above all other holy teachers." Another acquaintance records that he would take meditative walks, and when a thought occurred to him he would write it on his leather coat. (Presumably with pen and ink-bottle, for lead-pencils were not yet, and the inscribed leather coat was an admired relic two centuries later.)

Building, keeping an open house, supporting a large household, were expensive. In addition to his daughter's family he had an elderly priest as semi-permanent guest. He kept usually five or six copyists, the necessary servants, and always at least two horses. He wanted to build a chapel to the Blessed Virgin. He dropped hints to Pope Gregory that he would welcome a benefaction, not a prelacy or a cure of souls, but something involving no duties. The Pope in Avignon, who had perhaps heard echoes of Petrarch's trumpetings against unholy Babylon, stopped his ears.

The peace of Arquà was marred by war and threats of war. Venice invaded Paduan territory in October 1372. In the following May Padua, having hired an army of barbarous Hungarians, defeated Venice. In July Venice, with an army of even more barbarous Turks, defeated Padua. During the general disorders Petrarch was obliged to quit unprotected Arquà and take refuge in Padua. He joined the peace-making commission sent to Venice in September, and made the introductory speech in a trembling voice. While it seems very untactful of him thus to revisit the city that had treated him so well and that he had requited, on the whole, so badly, his speech on the theme that lovers' quarrels only strengthen love was unexceptionable.

He was still writing. A French cleric was angered by Petrarch's blasts against France and the French, and replied with a counterblast against Italy and Petrarch. Petrarch retorted with an *Invective against One Who Spoke Ill of Italy.* The duel reminds one of a battle between armored knights on horseback, with mighty slow-motion swings of broadsword and mace that seldom find their target.

Petrarch wrote for Francesco da Carrara a long letter that is in effect a treatise on the character and conduct of the Good Prince. Francesco was in fact a good prince, although he did keep in prison his uncle, with whom he was supposed to share the city's rule. A bad prince would have murdered his uncle.

The first principle of the good prince, says Petrarch, should be love, and the second justice. The prince must love his citizens if he is to draw their love. He must reject the desire of some rulers to be universally feared, for one who is much feared must fear much. Love then your subjects like your own children. The republic is a body of which you are the head. But wicked men abound, and these you must treat with stern justice. Show your beneficence by building splendidly, by public works, by repairing the walls and streets. (The roadways have been ruined by those diabolical carts, which I wish Erichthonius had never invented, so do they shake the house to their foundations and destroy the peace and repose of the citizens.) Drive out those swarms of pigs that root in the streets and offend visitors. Keep strict accounts, make sure that no one goes hungry. Eschew public amusements, banquets, theatres, shows of strange animals. Justify new taxes, prevent graft. Visit the citizens, sympathize, console, aid. Don't give a post to anyone who is more bound to others than to yourself. Keep absolute control, for nothing is worse for people than to have to obey many, especially if these are not worthy to command. ("I have myself observed how marvelously patient were peoples under the command of one lord, though harsh and cruel, and how rebellious when more than one required of them obedience and respect.") Be both magnificent and humble, modest in clothing and ornament. Honor men distinguished for character or achievement, in general-ship, science, letters, law, medicine, theology. And try to check the ritual of public mourning for the dead, which has become a holy show.

This is an excellent little commentary, full of wise counsels. It well represents the attitude of the enlightened Italian of the time toward his rulers. Petrarch has no objection to absolutism, but he insists that the prince is the servant of the state, and that he justifies his rule by his devotion to the people, by his ability, and fundamentally by his moral qualities. Unfortunately Petrarch is led astray by details and by his grievances. Had he developed his principles on the level of generalization he would have given us a political treatise to be classed with those of Dante and Machia-velli.

From time to time, during these latter years, Petrarch returned to his *Canzoniere.* Much as he affected to scorn these youthful trifles, *nugellae,* much as he protested that "the common people possess them and ruin them," he loved to work over them and to find in them again Laura and his own young self. He wrote, as a proper conclusion to the book, his beautiful canzone to the Virgin, a prayer, a hymn, a confession. "My life has been only weariness; mortal beauty, actions, words, have encumbered my soul." The poem, and the book, end with the word *peace.* "Intercede for me with thy Son, true man, true God, that He may receive my spirit finally in peace."

He was busy also with a *Life of Caesar,* to be added to his series on illustrious men. It grew enormously under his hands, and became an entire book. He picked up and added to his *Letter to Posterity,* which is both an autobiography and a self-portrait. And he wrote a Latin version of Boccaccio's story of Patient Griselda.

Boccaccio, ashamed of his loose tales in the vernacular, had never lent or given his collection to the master. But the book came somehow into Petrarch's hands, probably in 1373. He dipped into it, finding much to reprove. He applauded, however, the introduction, the extraordinary description of the plague in Florence. He admired also the final story, that of Griselda. This is the tale of a noble who married a peasant girl. Having some peculiar doubts about her patience, he put her to a thirteen-year-test of torture and humiliation. He took away her children and told her he had had them murdered. He repudiated her in order to marry a noble child-bride, and charged her with supervising the wedding feast. She bore everything with a patience approaching imbecility. He then revealed that the child-bride was Griselda's daughter, and that the wedding and his long course of cruelty were a kind of noble joke. Even this revelation Griselda accepted with patience.

Petrarch was deeply moved by the story. One wonders if Griselda suggested his own Francesca, disregarded in all her childhood and youth, and if he saw Eletta in the description of the winsome child-bride. He wrote a free version of the tale in Latin, to make it accessible to the world. His rendering gained an extraordinary success. Some Paduan friends were unable to finish it for weeping. It had a wide diffusion, and when printing came it appeared in many forms and languages, including Bohemian, Hungarian, and Icelandic. Chaucer's Clerk of Oxenford tells the story

> which that I
> Lerned at Padowe of a worthy clerk . . .
> Fraunces Petrark, the laureat poete,
> Highte this clerk, whos rethorique swete
> Enlumynd al Ytail [Italy] of poetrie.

(Chaucer was in Florence in the spring of 1373. He could have made a trip to Padua or Arquà to see Petrarch, but there is nothing to prove it.)

Petrarch became very conscious of the approach of death. He

was an old man, nearly seventy; he says that most men were dead by fifty. Looking forward, he made his will, on April 4, 1370. His estate was not large; he had consistently lived up to his income. He asked that his funeral be humble, without pomp, without tears. He professed to have small interest in his place of burial, but specified several possibilities, including Arquà. He made a series of money bequests, to the Cathedral of Padua for the endowment of masses for his soul, to Christ's poor, to servants; and a hundred florins to his brother Gherardo; and fifty gold Florentine florins to Boccaccio, to buy him a warm winter dressing gown for studies and lucubrations by night. (This is tact; Boccaccio could have bought twenty dressing gowns for fifty florins.) He left his painting of the Virgin Mary by Giotto to Francesco da Carrarra. (It is now unknown.) He bequeathed a horse and a silver cup to Lombardo della Seta, and to Messer Tommaso Bombasi of Ferrara his good lute, to be played not for the vanity of the fleeting world, but to the praise of God eternal. His house in Vaucluse should go to the descendants of his former caretaker, Raymond Monet, or to the village hospital. His residuary legatee would be his son-in-law, Francescuolo da Brossano, who is instructed to divide the property into two halves, to keep one as his own, and to give the other "to that person to whom, as he knows, I wish it to go," who is, of course, Francesca.

No mention is made of the Arquà estate. Perhaps it was included in the residuary property, destined for Francescuolo and Francesca; perhaps it reverted to Francesco da Carrara. Nor is there any mention of the library, which Petrarch had long since promised to Venice, in return for his occupancy of the palazzo in that city. Whatever may have been Petrarch's intentions in these last years, the books did not go to Venice, but fell into the hands of Padua's rulers, and thereafter were scattered all over Europe, from London to Naples. Petrarch's ambition to form a public library was frustrated. The first public library in the modern sense is credited to Niccolò de' Niccoli, who left his collection of books to the city of Florence for such a purpose in 1436.

The approach of death signaled itself in other ways. Petrarch wrote touching final letters to his friends, one breathing affection to Gherardo in Montrieux, one to Boccaccio ending: "Farewell friends, farewell letters." He gave to a young Augustinian monk

of Padua his precious *Confessions of Saint Augustine,* given him
many years before by another Augustinian, Dionigi da Borgo San
Sepolcro. It had accompanied him everywhere, to the summit of
Mont Ventoux, to Rome, to Prague. Though it had grown old
with him and was battered and worn, though the script was too
small for his tired eyes to read, his parting with it was a sign that
the old life was ended, a new one about to begin.

He tried to put on a face of classic serenity, and often succeeded.
"Why should it shame me to be old, if it does not shame me to be
alive?" But he was tired, tired to death.

> I have lived long enough [he wrote]. If I have told my tale to the end,
> I shan't object to stopping; and if the Stage Director wants to break
> off in the middle, very well. I am tired; and even if I should die to-
> day, I couldn't complain that my life has been too short. If everybody
> should reach my age, the world would be too narrow to hold us all.
> Instead of yearning for a longer life, I fear I have already lived too
> long, when I think how many fine friends and great men I have seen
> die, how the world jogs on and today repeats yesterday, only a little
> worse, and what dangers menace us, and what threats and jests of fate
> loom in the Northland, source of eternal woes, and how Italy docilely
> imitates those barbarous customs that I could bear otherwise but
> not here, and what, finally, is the current exile of virtue, the domin-
> ion of vice, and my weariness of men and things! You think that amid
> such distresses life should be sweet to me? On the contrary, it's harsh
> and bitter. But I know that one should bear harshness and bitterness
> with resignation and patience, so I accept life without desiring it.

His health grew worse; he became so thin that he was afraid of
vanishing. But his distrust of physicians did not alter. He hated
their philosophy, and their pride and presumption, their purple
gowns bedizened in various colors, their brilliant rings and gilded
spurs. Chiefly he hated their false pretensions; he was delighted
when one admitted to him that patients seem to recover as well
without as with medical attention. "Princes of our time can't belch
or spit without a physician's prescription; but they don't live
longer or in better health for that," he said. He asked a celebrated
doctor why he didn't abstain from foods he forbade to patients.
He had the answer: "My dear friend, if a doctor did for himself
what he prescribes for others, or if he advised them to do what he
does, the doctor would lose either his health or his money." There-

fore, logically, Petrarch ordered that if he should fall seriously ill, no medical recommendations should be put in force; nature should take its course.

A Paduan physician, who was at the same time a close friend, took alarm at Petrarch's state. This was Giovanni Dondi dell' Orologio, Dondi O'Clock. His name derived from his father's achievement in constructing the town clock of Padua, and his own in building a *planetarium* or astronomical machine displaying the movement of the heavenly bodies, operated by a single weight turning more than two hundred wheels. Dondi wrote Petrarch in 1370, urging him to give up salted meat and fish, raw vegetables, fruit, water-drinking, and fasting. This salt-free diet might now be recommended to combat hardening of the arteries.

Petrarch replied with a long, friendly, and often amusing defense of his practices, though he agreed that it was time to give up salty meats and raw vegetables. But not fruits, surely, so lovely to sight, touch, taste, and smell! How could nature play such a trick on man, hiding poison in her loveliest creations? As for water, he had always drunk it in preference to wine, and he would continue to do so. "I drink water to follow my own nature, which understands what I am and tells me what's good for me. . . . Cato said the best guide is nature, and we should follow and obey her as God himself. So I have always submitted to nature, and always will, except in things forbidden not by Hippocrates but by God." Finally, in the matter of fasting, he would yield not a whit.

Nature decreed that the old body should be broken, bit by bit. In May 1371 he fell ill of a violent fever. The physicians assembled and opined that if he should fall asleep he would die by midnight. They ordered that, to be kept awake, he be bound uncomfortably with knotted cords. But Petrarch's own orders to his household were that the exact contrary of doctors' orders should be followed. He slept soundly, unbound. In the morning the doctors returned, expecting to see him dead; they found him triumphantly working at his writing-desk.

Such delightful victories could not be frequent. Fevers recurred; occasionally he would fall unconscious; and next day he would be all right again. Some have diagnosed his trouble as senile epilepsy, although there is no record of convulsions.

"May death find me reading and writing, or, better, praying and weeping," he wrote to Boccaccio in 1373. Perhaps he had his wish. He died in the night of the 18th to the 19th of July 1374, a day short of his seventieth birthday. According to an old story he was found, pen in hand, collapsed over his *Life of Caesar*. The story, of which the first extant record is dated fourteen years after his death, is now regarded as unreliable, being all too apt. It is at least possible, and fitting with all we know of his state of body and mind. I cannot willingly surrender the conviction that death found Petrarch reading and writing, praying and weeping. Nor the conviction that death gave him a kindly greeting, and that Petrarch responded with a welcome; for, as he said, what we commonly call death is in truth only the end of death.

He received a magnificent funeral, contrary to the wishes ex- pressed in his will. He was buried in the red amice of the canons of Padua. Soon afterward a marble tomb was erected in the open village square, in front of the church, and there it still stands. This became an object of veneration; a sick man offered a hundred gold pieces to have his bones inserted in it, beside the poet's. One of Petrarch's arms was stolen for a relic in 1630; when last heard from it was in the Royal Museum at Madrid. Even his pet cat, her career done, was embalmed and stuffed.

Boccaccio wrote a last letter to Petrarch in Paradise, with news that his new warm dressing gown was very welcome to him in his penury.

XXVIII: PETRARCH

Go to your goal, and your shadow will follow you.

—Secretum *III*

THERE IS A GOOD MODERN GAME, TO BUY AN ancient church or house in Europe, to number its stones, demolish it, and set it up again in New York, California, or Florida. But something is always missing in the rebuilding. The ghost of the house has been left behind; the church has lost its Holy Ghost. Similarly the biographer tries to demolish a man, number his qualities, and put them together again. He always fails, for half the qualities are always mislaid or wrongly numbered. And even if his structure crazily stands, the ghost comes not to inhabit it.

Many have tried to find in Petrarch a keystone quality, a dominant, a *faculté maîtresse*. For Wilkins, it is love; for Bartoli, *irrequietezza*, restlessness, inconsistency, insecurity; for Bosco. "lability," the sense of mortality, of slipping time; for Nolhac, the cult of fame. To Henry Cochin, his life was a long sublime mirage, a dolorous struggle, with perpetual recommencements and perpetual failures. If I must choose, I would say that the mark of his character is introspection, self-analysis, an absorbed contemplation of his own spirit and behavior. "Through him the inner world first receives recognition; he first notes, observes, analyzes, and sets forth its phenomena," said James Harvey Robinson. His gigantic self-portrait permits us to know him as well as we can know our closest friends—or better.

This very unmedieval prizing of his living person, not his soul, had its natural consequence in his longing for fame, or for the persistence of his little self in this base world after death. He dreamed of eternal life on earth rather than in heaven. His cult of fame impelled him to set down the least of his imaginations and observations, in the hope of capturing for a moment the attention of posterity. He even withheld his beloved *Africa* and his *Secretum* from his contemporaries, in order that a wiser posterity might judge them at their true worth.

But posterity is not likely to be any wiser than its parents. It is after all a vast *profanum vulgus,* which Petrarch affected to regard with contempt and loathing. The fact is that he loved the applause of the vulgar and his contemporary celebrity. Occasionally he was sincere with himself and his correspondents. "I am a member of the crowd, although I am a solemn contemner of the crowd," he wrote. And again: "I am not courting fastidious readers, or trying to please delicate ears. If I am read and approved by the humble I shall have the finest reward for my labors. I do not strive to be obscure, but to be clear. I want to be understood by intelligent men, and I hope they will read me with pleasure, though with application and attention."

He presented himself as completely as a man can do. He displayed confidently his signal merits, and also his evident faults, his vanity, touchiness, irresolution, volatility, self-distrust, pomposity. Out of the welter of qualities a few notable constants emerge.

Introspective though he was, he was a fascinated watcher and lover of nature and the external world. As such he was far ahead of his times. As traveler, mountain-climber, lyric celebrator of natural beauty, observer of human behavior, he opened windows in men's conventional understanding. He was the initiator of archaeological purpose. Though an enemy of Aristotelian science, he possessed at least the rudiments of scientific qualities, with his curiosity, clarity in observation, critical independence. He rejected supernatural explanations and dismissed alchemy, astrology, divination from dreams, on logical grounds. He had even an idea of scientific proof. Reporting that a diamond was said to distract a lodestone, he said: "As for me, I have wanted occasion and will to make the experiment or proof thereof; therefore I can affirm nothing." He said that all the Greeks in the world could not move him from a conclusion confirmed by long experience. I have told how he distrusted even Aristotle, in conflict with experience.

"I am anti-Aristotle whenever Aristotle is anti-common-sense." His intellectual curiosity was insatiable and far-reaching. He had opinions on everything, government, generalship, geography, education, medicine, music, gardening. His *De remediis* is essentially a collection of opinions on all of life's affairs. Such universal curiosity was later to be taken as the mark of the Renaissance man.

Chiefly he was concerned with literature, the problems of its creation and cultivation. He told Boccaccio: "Of all human pleasures the study of literature is noblest, most lasting, most comforting, constantly useful." The components of good writing, he said, are intelligence, culture, and memory, and for poetry warmth of emotion and liveliness of imagination. The author should possess good health, a mean of fortune between poverty and wealth, tranquillity in solitude, a mind well ordered and fed with noble thoughts. Since there was little pure literature in his own time he turned to the great storehouse of antiquity. "In order to forget my own times I have constantly striven to place myself in other ages." He recreated artistic Latin prose and poetry. Yet he was opposed to slavish imitation, a cowardly performance. Graft the new on the old, he told his disciples; the first inventors were men too. Meditate; keep thoughts long in mind; write, with long pauses to test your statements; have someone read your work aloud, and listen not as author but as judge. Don't believe the common statement that there's nothing new under the sun and that nothing new can be said. Solomon and Terence said that; but since their times how much is new! One of Petrarch's new things was an elementary system of literary, especially poetic, aesthetics, as in the theme of the *Triumphs,* that beauty conquers and outlasts death.

Intellectual curiosity merged with intellectual pride, a secure sense of superiority to the world. He recognized that such pride is sin; his St. Augustine, in the *Secretum,* makes the charge and his Franciscus protests only feebly.

He was not willing to be a poet and nothing more, as he had long since protested. Nor was he willing to be a scholar and nothing more. His superiorities imposed on him the duty to be a moralist, to correct others. This duty he fitted into the frame of conventional piety. He never had any doubts of Christian faith and practice; his devotions, prayers, and fastings were those of a professional ascetic. However, the moral code that he erected and proclaimed was based not so much on Church theology and philosophy as on classic, pagan authority. He tried to reconcile and blend the two traditions, to color classic memories with Christian values and to project pagan values into current teaching. He tried to make Cicero a Christian, himself a Cicero. Learning must be useful, he insisted. Thus he rejected the abstractions of scholastic philosophy and tried to turn philosophy into ethics. His concept of virtue was social, not metaphysical.

His classical learning was immense and profound. "I have read Virgil, Horace, Livy, Cicero not once but a thousand times, not hastily but dwelling on them. They are not only in my mind but in my marrow; they are a part of myself." Out of his knowledge he wrote much history, to preserve the past in the present. Says Panofsky: " . . . he revolutionized the interpretation of history no less than Copernicus was to revolutionize the interpretation of the physical universe." Billanovich adds that he sent the humanists back to history, permitted Machiavelli to write his studies of Livy, and Columbus to equip his caravels.

His scholarly purpose was to revive the past, as nearly entire as possible. As Giotto cast aside Byzantine formalism and rigidity to seek a new naturalism, he wanted to make his classic friends live as contemporaries. He insisted that scholarship should aim high, not lose itself in niggling details. "Neither grammar nor any of the seven liberal arts is worthy of the lifelong concern of a noble mind; they are means, not ends. . . . A smart boy is a pretty spectacle, but there's nothing worse than an old man doing a boy's lessons. . . . It is better to die in boyhood than grow old among puerilities."

The power of his learning was put to the service of an Italian patriotism, rare indeed in his time. Hence his constant clamor for the unification of Italy under the beneficent rule of Pope and Emperor in Rome. This larger patriotism, or Italianism, deriving in part from his lifelong exile from his proper home in Florence, takes shape in his great canzone, *Italia mia*. It was to work in Italian minds until the unification of Italy in the nineteenth century.

A final quality of his spirit may be clumsily defined as a penetrating goodness. His work is dotted with sudden shafts of wisdom, small revelations made to a man who loved men and animals and the great beautiful world. Here are a few, from a private anthology of Petrarch's wisdom. This, which is almost Pascal: "A man will

walk securely a narrow beam a little above ground, and will
tremble with fear on the solid top of a high tower. His weakness
is in Opinion, which destroys his natural courage." And this, which
is almost Montaigne: "All our afflictions are caused not by the
things themselves but by opinions; and these take their origin and
increase from custom." And this, which is almost La Rochefou-
cauld: "To offer immensities to one who asks a small favor is a
kind of refusal." And these, which are entirely himself: "Many
have not become what they might have because they believed they
were what people mistakenly said they were. . . . Why should one
give way to anger, when one can avenge oneself calmly, choosing
the noblest revenge—pardon? . . . To pardon offenses is a most
beautiful revenge, but to forget them is still more beautiful."

So far I have been reviewing the qualities of his mind and
character. If I should try to report the opinions emerging from his
qualities I should never have done. He had opinions on everything, especially on literature and style, on his writer's trade.
Many of his judgments sound flat and obvious today, but we have
had 600 years to digest them. The rapidity with which a discovery
becomes a commonplace is a measure of its truth.

"I am like a man standing between two worlds; I look both
forward and backward," he wrote. The context makes clear that
he pictured himself standing between an ancient world of light
and a present one of ominous darkness. But his statement contains another meaning. He stood between two worlds, the medieval
and the modern, the past and the present. He was the hinge of the
door, says Whitfield. He was necessarily medieval, a part of his
time, a product of his education. However, he was consciously a
rebel against his time. He looked for his sanction in the great
classic past of Rome; he tried to restore that past as a present
lesson to his world. The finest lesson to be learned from the mighty
dead is that, to be like them, we must be original creators.
Petrarch's numberless originalities, in literature, scholarship,
thought and life, are then the product of a noble kind of imitation.

This is humanism, the spirit of the coming Renaissance.
Petrarch is its father, by his demand for reformation, renewal, renaissance or rebirth. The disciples whom he directly stimulated
carried on his work to a later flowering. Even such men as Erasmus
were continuers of Petrarch's doctrines.

In the world of the poets Petrarch reigned for centuries. He set the model of what a lyric poem should be—a brief outburst of passion, developing a single thought, symbol, or fancy, within a frame of fixed and arduous form. Even today the formula holds. No other poet in all time has wielded such an influence, so long and so far.

And in the world of ordinary men, neither scholars nor poets, traces of Petrarch, immensely diluted, may still be discerned. He helped to define and form the modern sensibility, in its appreciation of the beauty in nature, in its sense of the mystery and marvel in everyday reality, in its idealization of romantic love, in its refinement of self-scrutiny. The posterity to which he looked so eagerly may have forgotten his name; it rewards him by feeling still some small quotum of his emotion.

Petrarch has frequently been called the First Modern Man. I would go farther. I would call him one of the Eternal Men.

ARQUA 1374

BIBLIOGRAPHY AND NOTES

THE ONLY nearly complete editions of Petrarch's works are the *Opera omnia* published in Basel in 1554 and 1581. Less nearly complete are the editions of Basel, 1496 and 1541, and of Venice, 1501 and 1503. An *Edizione nazionale* has long been in progress; the following volumes have appeared: I. *Africa*, ed. N. Festa (Florence, 1926); X–XIII. *Epistolae familiares* (first three edited by V. Rossi, the fourth by U. Bosco; Florence, 1926-42); XIV. *Rerum memorandarum libri*, ed. G. Billanovich (Florence, 1943). To these reference will be made whenever possible.

A valuable, and accessible, selection of Petrarch's Latin prose, with Italian translations, edited by G. Martellotti, P. G. Ricci, E. Carrara, and E. Bianchi, is entitled *Prosa* and published by Ricciardi (Milan and Naples, 1955). This includes, complete, the *Letter to Posterity*, the *Secretum*, *De vita solitaria*, *De sui ipsius et multorum ignorantia*, and *Invectiva contra eum qui maledixit Italiae*.

A scrupulous edition of the *Rime, Trionfi, e Poesie latine*, edited by F. Neri, G. Martellotti, E. Bianchi, and N. Sapegno (Milan and Naples, 1951) contains the *Rime* (often referred to as the *Canzoniere*) and *Trionfi* complete, but only selections from the *Rime disperse* and the Latin poems. This edition will serve as reference whenever possible.

A precious translation into Italian of the *Epistolae familiares* and *Epistolae variae*, with exhaustive notes, was made by G. Fracassetti (Florence, 1863-67). This will be often referred to. One must note that the numbering of the letters in Book I varies from that of Rossi. I follow Rossi.

The Latin text of the *Epistolae seniles* appears only in the early *Opera omnia*. They are translated into Italian by G. Fracassetti (Florence, 1869-70). His numbering of the books varies from that of the early editions. I have followed Fracassetti, as more generally available.

For other works of Petrarch I refer to the following editions:

Bucolicum carmen (Eclogues), ed. A. Avena (Padua, 1906).

Coronation Oration, in *Scritti inediti di Francesco Petrarca*, ed. A. Hortis (Trieste, 1874). Translation in English by Ernest H. Wilkins, in his *Studies in the Life and Works of Petrarch* (Cambridge, Mass., 1955).

De otio religioso, ed. G. Rotondi (Vatican City, 1958).

De remediis utriusque fortunae, in *Opera omnia*, 1558. Translated by Thomas Twyne as *Phisicke against Fortune* (London, 1579).

De viris illustribus, ed. with Italian translation by A. Razzolini (Bologna, 1874-79).

De vita solitaria, see *Prose,* above. English translation, *The Life of Solitude,* by J. Zeitlin (Urbana, Ill., 1924). The numbering of sections differs from that in *Prose.*

Epistolae metricae, in *Poemata minora,* ed. D. Rossetti (Milan, 1829-34). With Italian translation. I follow Rossetti's numbering, which differs somewhat from that of the early editions.

Epistolae sine nomine, in Paul Piur: *Petrarcas "Buch ohne Namen"* (Halle, 1925).

Invectivae contra medicum, ed. G. Ricci and D. Silvestri (Rome, 1950).

Poemata minora, ed. D. Rossetti (Milan, 1829-34).

Psalmi poenitentiales, ed. P. de Nolhac (Paris, 1929). With French translations.

Some minor poems, including the *Epitaph for Zabot,* first appeared in K. Burdach: *Aus Petrarcas ältestem Schüler-Kreise* (Berlin, 1929).

Critical and biographical studies of Petrarch are innumerable. Special indebtednesses will be recognized in the Notes. I must record my constant debt to the ten books and many articles by Ernest H. Wilkins, America's greatest Petrarchan. His *Life of Petrarch* (Chicago, 1961) has been a sure and unfailing guide. I am also under deep obligation to the uncompleted biography, *Francesco Petrarca* (2 vols.) by E. H. R. Tatham (London, 1925-26).

The following abbreviations are used in text and Notes:

De ignorantia: De sui ipsius et multorum ignorantia
De remediis: De remediis utriusque fortunae
Ep. metr.: Epistolae metricae
Fam.: Epistolae familiares
Rime: Rime, Trionfi e Poesie latine
Sen.: Epistolae seniles
Sine nomine: Epistolae sine nomine
Variae: Epistolae variae

CHAPTER I. BOYHOOD

PETRARCH's recollections of his ancestry, youth, and schooling are chiefly in the *Epistle to Posterity,* in *Fam.* I 1 and VI 3, and in *Sen.* X 2 and XVI 1. The opening quotation about his birth is from *Sen.* XIII 3; the description of his difficult birth from *Fam.* I 1. For Petrarch's father see N. Zingarelli, "Petrarca e suo padre," in his *Scritti di varia letteratura* (Milan, 1935), and C. Segrè, "I primi studi del Petrarca," in *Nuova Antologia* CCXCV (1921), pp. 115 ff., from which I take the quotation

about the importance of Petrarch's schooling. The letter to the Doge of
Genoa is *Fam.* XIV 5. The shipwreck story is in *Fam.* I 1. The memories
of Convenevole are in *Sen.* XVI 1. P. de Nolhac, in *Pétrarque et l'human-
isme* (Paris, 1907), I 260, doubts if the Cicero that Convenevole pawned
was actually the famous lost *De gloria.* The reference to F. Villani is in
A. Solerti, *Le vite di Dante, Petrarca, e Boccaccio* (Milan, 1904), p. 276.
Petrarch's recollection of his early devotion to Cicero is in *Sen.* XVI 1.
The quotation beginning "I was noting down the substance of the
thought" is from *Fam.* XXIV 1. "Latin culture was his life" comes from
C. Segrè, "I primi studi." The remembrance of his youthful piety is in
Secretum III (*Prose,* p. 150). The boyhood visit to Vaucluse is recounted
in *Sen.* X 2. The recollection of happy stays by the Sorgue is in *Sen.*
XIII 11.

CHAPTER 11. COLLEGE DAYS

THE QUOTATION from H. H. Milman is from his *Latin Christianity* (Lon-
don, 1872), VII 42. I lifted it from E. H. R. Tatham, *Francesco Petrarca*
(London, 1925-26), I 14. Petrarch's recollections of his university
career are mostly in the *Letter to Posterity,* in *Fam.* IV 16, IX 5, XVII 1,
XX 4, XXIV 1, and *Sen.* X 2. For the university career, see especially C.
Segrè in his *Studi petrarcheschi* (Florence, 1903), in "I primi studi del
Petrarca," *Nuova Antologia* CCXCV (1921), 115 ff., and in "Il Petrarca
a Montpellier," *Nuova Antologia* CCCXLIV (1929), 137 ff.; also A.
Foresti, *Anedotti della vita di Francesco Petrarca* (Brescia, 1928), and C.
Calcaterra, *"Bononiae triennium expendi,"* in *Studi petrarcheschi* II
(1949). The book-burning is related in *Sen.* XVI 1. Petrarch's threnody
on his mother's death is in the *Poemata minora,* ed. D. Rossetti. Petrarch
describes Bologna in *Sen.* X 2. The long quotation from Tatham is from
I 118-119. The reminiscence to Petrarch's brother is in *Fam.* XVII 1.
That to Guido Sette is *Sen.* X 2. The imbroglio about Niccolosa and
Selvaggia is well summarized by Tatham, I 183-195, although I do not
accept his conclusions. See also G. O. Corazzini, "La madre di Francesco
Petrarca," in *Archivio Storico Italiano,* Ser. V, vol. ix (1892); F. Lo Parco,
in *Rassegna Critica di Letteratura Italiana* XI 1-15 (1906); and Foresti,
Anedotti. Petrarch's statement about his loss of parental care is from the
Letter to Posterity. "In a single day Fate laid me low" is from *Secretum* II
(*Prose,* p. 118). "Though I experienced" is in *Fam.* IX 5. "This curse
followed us" is in *Fam.* X 3. The letter to Giovanni d'Andrea is *Fam.* IV
16. Petrarch's dislike of law is stated in *Fam.* XXIV 1 and XX 4. The
quotation about stilnovisti love is from Maurice Valency, *In Praise of
Love* (New York, 1958), p. 223.

CHAPTER III. AVIGNON, 1326

THE bit about thirteenth-century infidelity is from Matthew Paris, quoted in G. C. Coulton, *From St. Francis to Dante* (London, 1907), p. 188. "One who doubts his ability to live chaste" is borrowed from C. Dejob, *La foi religieuse en Italie au 14e siècle* (Paris, 1906), p. 150. The account of the great banquet is from Eugène Müntz, "L'argent et le luxe à la cour pontificale d'Avignon," *Revue des questions historiques* LXVI (1899), p. 403. The papal traveling order is from J. Girard, *Evocation du vieil Avignon* (Paris, 1958), p. 58. The background of everyday life in Avignon is drawn from many sources; see especially Iris Origo, *Merchant of Prato* (New York, 1957). The descriptions of Avignon quoted from Petrarch are from his *Ep. metr.* II 3 and *Secretum* II (*Prose*, p. 120). His characterization of the French is in *Sen.* IX 1. The outburst against men's fashions is in *De vita solitaria* I 8 (*Prose*, p. 388).

CHAPTER IV. YOUNG MAN ABOUT TOWN

THE opening quotation is from the *Letter to Posterity*. The one immediately following is from *Fam.* XXIV 1. The quotation from Boccaccio is from his *Life of Petrarch*, in A. Solerti, *Le vite di Dante, Petrarca, e Boccaccio* (Milan, 1904), p. 260. The selections from Petrarch's letter to his brother are in *Fam.* X 3. The reminiscence of his father's Cicero is in *Sen.* XVI 1. The passage from the *Trionfo d'amore* is I 52-57. The reference to a duel is in *Fam.* X 3. The letter to Boccaccio is in *Sen.* V 2. The description of Giovanni da Firenze is in *Sen.* XV 6.

CHAPTER V. LAURA

For Laura de Sade and the identification with Petrarch's Laura see especially P. A. de Sade, *Mémoires pour la vie de François Pétrarque* (Amsterdam, 1764-67); F. d'Ovidio, *Studi sul Petrarca e sul Tasso* (Rome, 1926); R. Carrara, *La leggenda di Laura* (Turin, 1935); and G. A. Cesareo, "Laura e le ragioni della signora de Sade," in *Annali della Cattedra Petrarchesca* III (1932). On the date of the enamorment, see N. Zingarelli, *Scritti di varia letteratura* (Milan, 1935), and C. Calcaterra, *La data fatale nel Canzoniere e nel Trionfi del Petrarca* (Turin, 1926). The Latin text of Petrarch's note on Laura in his Virgil has been often reproduced; e. g., in *Le rime di Francesco Petrarca*, ed. G. Carducci and S. Ferrari (Florence, 1899 etc.), p. 370. "I loathe seeing my lovely treasure" is from *Rime* CCLIX; the quotation from the *Secretum* is from Book III (*Prose*, p. 138). Petrarch's letter to Giacomo Colonna on the reality of Laura is *Fam.* II 9.

CHAPTER VI. LOVE—APPASSIONATO

FOR THE chronology of the *Canzoniere* see especially H. Cochin, *La chronologie du Canzoniere de Pétrarque* (Paris, 1898). The discussions of the book's composition are authoritatively summarized in E. H. Wilkins, *The Making of the "Canzoniere"* (Rome, 1951), pp. 154 ff.; from this is taken the quotation about "mingling of forms." The influence of Provençal poetry on Petrarch has been frequently studied; for a summary see G. G. Ferrero, *Petrarca e i trovatori* (Turin, 1959). See also G. Bertoni, in *Annali della Cattedra Petrarchesca* VI (1935-36), and Aldo Valloni, in *Studi Petrarcheschi* III (1950). The passage from Mario Casella is in *Annali della Cattedra Petrarchesca* VI (1935-36). That from Andreas Capellanus is from *De arte honesti amandi*, translated by J. J. Parry (New York, 1957), p. 17.

CHAPTER VII. SEEING THE WORLD

"WITH a hint in his calm face" is from *Variae* 25. The description of Giacomo Colonna is in *Sen.* XVI 1. See H. Cochin, "Pétrarque et Jacques Colonna," in *Annuaire-Bulletin de la Société de l'Histoire de France,* 1922. The obituary mention of Socrates is on the flyleaf of Petrarch's Virgil. The anecdote of St. Romualdus is in *De vita solitaria*, II 8 (*Prose,* p. 464). The tribute to Cardinal Colonna is in a letter to Luca Cristiani, printed in the notes to Fracassetti, *Familiari*, II, 314. The recollections of Cardinal Colonna's household are in *Fam.* V 2 and *Sen.* XVI 1. R. Weiss proves, in "Some New Correspondence of Petrarch," *Modern Language Review* XLIII (1948), that Petrarch's comedy was entitled *Philologia Philostrati*. The Latin epistle on Italy is *Ep. metr.* I 3. The "damnableness of the loss of manuscripts" appears in *Fam.* XVIII 12. G. Billanovich's discovery of Petrarch's Livy and his statements about the "literary codex" and Petrarch's scholarly standing come from his *I primi umanisti* (Fribourg, 1953), pp. 28-34. E. H. Wilkins describes the Livy text in his *Life of Petrarch* (Chicago, 1961), p. 16. Petrarch's report of his journey is *Fam.* I 4; his statements about the benefits of travel and the Parisianism of Parisians are in *Fam.* IX 13. His description of the wonders and delights of the world is taken from *De remediis* (*Phisicke against Fortune,* II 93). His recollection of seeing the point where the Rhine divides— which no critic seems to have noticed—is in *Fam.* XIX 13. His statement about being on the frontier of two worlds is in *Rerum memorandarum* I 2.

CHAPTER VIII. THE ASCENT OF MONT VENTOUX

THE references to Petrarch's sojourn by the Britannic sea are in *Fam.*
III 1 and 2 and in *Ep. metr.* I 7. In the Metrical Epistle he implies that
he had traveled by sea past Gibraltar to the north. Such a journey is to
be rejected for many reasons, well summarized by E. H. R. Tatham,
Francesco Petrarca (London, 1925-26) I 349-356. The poetic appeal
to Benedict XII is *Ep. metr.* I 2. For Dionigi da Borgo San Sepolcro see
U. Mariani, *Il Petrarca e gli Agostiniani* (Rome, 1946). Petrarch's testimony to the influence on him of Augustine is in *Sen.* VIII 6. The description of the ascent of Mont Ventoux is *Fam.* IV 1. G. Billanovich thinks,
on what seem to me insufficient grounds, that Petrarch wrote this letter in
1352 or 1353, as a sort of allegorical fairy tale, to provide after the event a
forecast of Gherardo's conversion (*Lo scrittoio del Petrarca*, Rome, 1947,
p. 194). The quotation from Wordsworth is *The Excursion* I 215; that
from Byron is somewhere in *Childe Harold's Pilgrimage.*

CHAPTER IX. ROME, 1337

THE passage casting doubt on the paternity of Giovanni is in *Fam.* XXII
7. The letter to Giacomo Colonna is *Fam.* II 9. The description of
Capranica is *Fam.* II 12. For the state of Rome see F. Gregorovius,
Geschichte der Stadt Rom (Stuttgart, 1875-81); E. Duprè Theseider,
Roma dal Comune di Popolo alla Signoria Pontifica (Bologna, 1952);
M. Andrieux, *Rome* (Paris, 1960); etc. The letter to Giovanni Colonna
di San Vito is *Fam.* VI 2; the anecdote of the vine-dresser comes from *Fam.*
XVIII 8. The old guide-book to Rome, *Mirabilia urbis Romae,* has been
often reedited. The characterization of Stefano Colonna is in the
Trionfo della fama II 262-263; his prowess is reported in *Sen.* XII 2; his
conversation with Petrarch is recorded in *Fam.* VIII 1.

CHAPTER X. VAUCLUSE, 1337-1341

THE opening quotation is from *Ep. metr.* I 6. "Harassed by so many obsessing cares" is in *Fam.* VII 18; "there are no riches or treasures" in
Fam. VIII 1. The comparison of Petrarch to Rousseau, etc., is made by
C. Segrè, in his *Studi petrarcheschi* (Florence, 1903), p. 95. "The consecration of a renewed human dignity" is from R. Ramat's introduction
to the *Rime* (Milan, 1957), p. 14. Petrarch's disgust with Avignon is
expressed in *De vita solitaria* I 6 (*Prose,* p. 354). The quotation from
E. H. R. Tatham is from his *Francesco Petrarca* (London, 1925-26), II
53. "Livers of busy lives do not live" is in *Fam.* XIII 4. Captain J. Y.

Cousteau tells of the dive in the Vaucluse fountain in his *The Silent World* (New York, 1953). The comparison of Sorgue's water with liquid grass is from A. Mézières, *Pétrarque* (Paris, 1868), p. 81. The recollections of Raymond Monet and his wife are in *Fam.* XIII 8, XVI 1, and *Sen.* IX 2. The passage on the joys of reading is from *Ep. metr.* I 6. The invitation to G. Colonna di San Vito is *Fam.* VI 3; that to Guido Sette is *Fam.* XVII 5. The quoted passage from *De remediis* is in Book I, Dialogue 57, in Twyne's translation, *Phisicke against Fortune*. The description of the *capinera* is in *Ep. metr.* I 8; that of the thunderstorm in *Ep. metr.* I 10. J. H. Whitfield, in his *Petrarch and the Renaissance* (Oxford, 1943), p. 90, speaks of "the cultured enjoyment of nature." The passage about the peasant's mattock is in *Fam.* XVII 5. The "mixed feeling of horror and delight" comes from the Introduction to J. Zeitlin's translation of *De vita solitaria*, *The Life of Solitude* (Urbana, Illinois, 1924), p. 70. The mountain-grass taste of good poems is in *De vita solitaria* I 7 (*Prose*, p. 366). Petrarch gives the Good Friday date of the conception of *Africa* in the *Letter to Posterity* and in a letter to Luca Cristiani printed in the notes to Fracassetti, *Fam.*, vol. II, p. 313. The remarks about food and drink are from *Sen.* XII 2. The invitation to Agapito Colonna is *Fam.* II 11. The reminiscent letters to Philippe de Cabassoles are *Sen.* XIII 12 and XVI 4. The locking up of Petrarch's books is recounted in *Fam.* XIII 7. The tribute to Philippe is in *De vita solitaria* II 14 (*Prose*, p. 576). The encounter with G. da Pastrengo's lady is in *Ep. metr.* III 3. The importunate lawyer is reported in *De vita solitaria* I 3 (*Prose*, p. 330). "No solitude so profound" is from *De vita solitaria* II 14 (*Prose*, p. 558). Zeitlin's remark about self-indulgence is from *The Life of Solitude*, p. 74. Petrarch's search for happiness, not salvation, in solitude is stated in *De vita solitaria* I 1 (*Prose*, p. 300). The quotation about the dangers of solitude is from *Fam.* XVI 14; that about "something unsatisfied in my heart" is in *Secretum* II (*Prose*, p. 94); that about the pursuing mind is from *De vita solitaria* I 5 (*Prose*, p. 344); that from *Childe Harold* is Canto I, lines 859-860; that about the carnality of philosophers and poets from *Fam.* VIII 3. The poem *Valle locus clausa* is in *Rime, Trionfi, e Poesie latine*, ed. Neri et al., p. 852.

CHAPTER XI. LOVE — MOLTO AGITATO

PETRARCH's letter of excuse to Guglielmo da Pastrengo is *Variae* 13. The bit about creating an inner solitude is in *De vita solitaria* I 4 (*Prose*, p. 338). The letter about the poet's continual burning in Vaucluse is *Fam.* VIII 3. The epistle to Laelius is *Ep. metr.* I 8. The reference to Umberto Bosco is to his *Petrarca* (Turin, 1946), p. 166. "Femina è cosa mobil" is from *Rime* CLXXXIII. "You opened your closed heart" is from *Trionfo della Morte* II 135. The quotation from Adolfo Bartoli comes from his *Petrarca*, Vol. VII of his *Storia della letteratura italiana* (Florence, 1884), p. 253. "Even sadness may have a delight" is from *Sen.* X 2. "There goes the man who wept forever" is from *Trionfo dell' Eternità*, 95-96. The quotations about pleasure in pain are from *Fam.* XI 3 and VIII 9.

CHAPTER XII. THE LAUREL CROWN

THE prevailing disesteem of poets is stated in *Fam.* X 5. The letter to King Robert is *Fam.* IV 3; that to Dionigi is *Fam.* IV 2; that to Cardinal Colonna is *Fam.* IV 4. The quotation from C. Calcaterra is from *Studi petrarcheschi* II (1949), p. 21. That from E. H. R. Tatham is from his *Francesco Petrarca* (London 1925-26) II 122. The recollection of King Robert's crossbowmanship is in *Rerum memorandarum* I 1. For references to Petrarch's presumed map of Italy see Jacob Burckhardt, *Civilization of the Renaissance in Italy* (New York, 1958), p. 295 note. The most ample description of the Coronation is in E. H. Wilkins, *The Making of the "Canzoniere"* (Rome, 1951), pp. 9-69. The Coronation Oration is to be found in Latin in A. Hortis, *Scritti inediti di Francesco Petrarca* (Trieste, 1874), and in English in E. H. Wilkins, *Studies in the Life and Works of Petrarch* (Cambridge, Mass., 1955), pp. 300-313. The quotation beginning "From the downfall of Rome" is from R. R. Bezzola, "Die Dichtung des Trecento," in *Das Trecento* (Zurich, 1960), p. 85. Boccaccio's remark is from his *Vita del Petrarca*, in A. Solerti, *Le vite di Dante, Petrarca, e Boccaccio* (Milan, 1904), p. 259. Petrarch's invectives. against a critic are in *Ep. metr.* II 11 and II 18. The quotation from Bergson is taken from *Selections from Bergson*, ed. by Harold A. Larrabee (New York, 1949), p. 114.

CHAPTER XIII. PARMA — AND AFRICA

FOR THE stay in Parma see especially A. Ronchini, *La dimora del Petrarca in Parma* (Parma, 1874), and F. Rizzi, *Francesco Petrarca e il decennio parmense* (Turin, 1934). Petrarch's description of Selvapiana is in *Ep. metr.* II 16. The lines from *Africa* beginning "Facili labuntur" are II 347-350. The quoted letter of 1349 is *Fam.* VIII 3. The admission of Petrarch's discouragement is in *Ep. metr.* II 11. The references to Vergerio and Beccadelli come from A. Solerti, *Le vite di Dante, Petrarca, e Boccaccio* (Milan, 1904), pp. 300 and 466; that to Leonardo Bruni from his *Dialogus de tribus vatibus florentinis* (ed. K. Wotke, Vienna, 1889), p. 21. The story of the blind poet is in *Sen.* XVI 7; that of the prophetic dream in *Fam.* V 7.

384 PETRARCH AND HIS WORLD

CHAPTER XIV. CRISIS

PETRARCH'S "shocking letter" is *Sine nomine* 1. His ecclesiastical career
is thoroughly examined in Wilkins' *Studies in the Life and Works of
Petrarch* (Cambridge, Mass., 1955). His depreciatory reference to Vaucluse is in *Fam.* VIII 3. The poetic epistle to himself is *Ep. metr.* I 14. The
letter to Guido Sette is *Fam.* V 18. On Gherardo, Henry Cochin's *Le
frère de Pétrarque* (Paris, 1903) is sympathetic and wise. Petrarch's love
of David is stated in *Fam.* XXII 10.

CHAPTER XV. THE SECRET BOOK

REFERENCES are to the edition in *Prose.* The only English translation is
Petrarch's Secret, by W. H. Draper (London, 1911). The tribute to
Augustine at the beginning of the chapter is from *De otio religioso* (ed.
G. Rotondi), p. 104.

CHAPTER XVI. NAPLES, 1343

AUGUSTINE'S "ecstatic appeal for Christ's love" is at the beginning of Book
IX of the *Confessions.* Petrarch's description of King Robert's death,
and his proposal to write Robert's biography, are in *Rerum memorandarum* III 96. The accounts of the Neapolitan journey are in *Fam.* V
1-6. The background of Neapolitan history has been amply treated; a
convenient résumé is E. G. Léonard, *Histoire de Jeanne Première*
(Monaco, 1932).

CHAPTER XVII. PARMA AND VERONA, 1343-1345

PETRARCH'S remarks on jealous men are in *Sen.* III 7. The epistle to G.
da Pastrengo is *Ep. metr.* II 19. The definition of poverty is in *Variae*
55. The reply to Socrates is *Ep. metr.* III 27. The letter to Moggio is
Fam. XIX 5. The escape from Parma is told in *Fam.* V 10. Petrarch's
continuing reputation in Reggio as a necromancer is reported in E.
Carrara, *Studi petrarcheschi* (Turin, 1959), p. 4. The letters to Cicero
are *Fam.* XXIV 3 and 4. The other letters to dead authors are *Fam.*
XXIV 5-12. The material from Hans Baron comes from the *Bulletin
of the John Rylands Library* XXII (April, 1938). The ideas are further
developed in Baron's *Crisis of the Early Italian Renaissance* (Prince-
ton, N. J., 1955). The definition of the scholar's duties is in *De vita
solitaria* I 6 *(Prose, p. 358).* The early history of humanism has been
much studied recently, particularly by Hans Baron, Paul O. Kristeller,

G. Toffanin, and Roberto Weiss. The date of *Italia mia* is much disputed; scholars have dated it all the way from 1328 to 1370. I would put it in 1344 or 1345.

CHAPTER XVIII. VAUCLUSE, 1345-1347

THE passage about the dog is in *Ep. metr.* III 5. The valley fishermen are described in *Fam.* III 19. The letter about the imprisoned villager is *Fam.* III 21. That to Cola di Rienzo about Vaucluse is *Variae* 42. The businessman's day is described in *De vita solitaria* I 2 (*Prose*, pp. 300-318); the life of the Brahmins, with the counsel of moderation, in II 11 (*Prose*, pp. 512-514). The criticism of superstition and the appeal to reason are in *Rerum memorandarum* IV 31-40, 101, 115-121. Petrarch's defense of quotation is in *Fam.* VI 4 and V 18. The praise of poetic difficulty is in *Invectivae contra medicum* III (ed. Ricci, p. 70). The letter on his bibliophily is *Fam.* III 18. It is commonly said that young Giovanni was sent to Verona in 1345 to be schooled; 1347 seems to me more likely.

CHAPTER XIX. LOVE—ADAGIO PATETICO

THE letter to Luca Christiani is *Fam.* VIII 3. For the poems to rivals of Laura, see especially G. A. Cesareo, "Gli amori del Petrarca," in *Giornale dantesco* VIII (1900), p. 13. The quotation from Edgar Quinet is from his *Les révolutions d'Italie* (Paris, 1878), I 188. That from A. Bartoli is in his *Petrarca*, Vol. VII of his *Storia della letteratura italiana* (Florence, 1884), p. 283.

CHAPTER XX. COLA DI RIENZO

THE story of Cola has been often told, most exhaustively by K. Burdach and P. Piur, *Briefwechsel des Cola di Rienzo* (6 vols., Berlin, 1912-29). Some will remember Wagner's early opera, some Bulwer-Lytton's romance. I have leaned heavily on E. Duprè Theseider, *Roma dal Comune di Popolo alla Signoria Pontifica* (Bologna, 1952). The quotation from E. H. R. Tatham is from his *Francesco Petrarca* (London, 1925-26) II 206. The meeting in St. Agricol is described in *Sine nomine* 7. "I think of you day and night" is in *Variae* 40. The paean to liberty is *Variae* 48. The "recently discovered letter" of Barbato is reported by R. Weiss in *Studi petrarcheschi* III (Bologna, 1950). The cynical view of the Avignon prelates is described in *Sine nomine* 3. The references to Theseider are to his *Roma*, pp. 602, 607. Stefano Colonna's stoic remark is in *Sen.* X 4. The reproachful letter from Genoa is *Fam.* VII 7. The letter about Cola's imprisonment is *Fam.* XIII 6. The appeal to the Roman people is *Sine nomine* 4.

CHAPTER XXI. THE BLACK DEATH

THE Verona earthquake is described in *Sen.* X 2. Petrarch's garden journal is quoted *in extenso* in an appendix to Pierre de Nolhac, *Pétrarque et l'humanisme* (Paris, 1907). The quoted letter to Luchino Visconti is *Fam.* VII 15. The material on the Black Death is drawn from many sources, especially Anna M. Campbell, *The Black Death and Men of Learning* (New York, 1913), Francis A. Gasquet, *The Great Pestilence* (London, 1893), Johannes Nohl, *The Black Death* (New York, 1926), and Egon Friedell, *Cultural History of Europe* (New York, 1930-32). "Sickness clung to their bones" is from Gasquet, p. 12; the phrase from Friedell from his I 86. Boccaccio's description is in the Introduction to the *Decameron*. Petrarch's own account is in *Fam.* VII 10 and VIII 7. Gherardo's heroism is described in *Fam.* XVI 2. Guy de Chauliac's account is in his *La grande chirurgie* (Lyon, 1552); it has frequently been quoted. Socrates' letter was first printed in J. J. De Smet, *Recueil des chroniques de Flandre* (Brussels, 1856) III 14-18.

CHAPTER XXII. ITALIAN JOURNEYS, 1349-1351

"IF Jacopo had lived longer" is in the *Letter to Posterity*. For the dream of a lay monastery see T. Kardos, in *Studi petrarcheschi* VII (1961), p. 211. The quoted regrets for Accursio are in *Fam.* VIII 7. For Petrarch's secondary loves see G. A. Cesareo, "Gli amori del Petrarca," in *Giornale dantesco* VIII (1900). For the letters, many studies by E. H. Wilkins, especially his invaluable manual, *Petrarch's Correspondence* (Padua, 1960); also G. Billanovich, *Lo scrittoio del Petrarca* (Rome, 1947). The characterization of his style as familiar is in *Fam.* I 1. "I can't stop writing letters" is in *Sen.* I 1. The complaint to Laelius is *Fam.* XV 1; the lost letter is reported in *Fam.* V 16 and 17. For the relations with Boccaccio, G. Billanovich, *Lo scrittoio* and *Suggestioni di cultura* (Naples, 1946). For Nelli and the Florentine Petrarchists see Henry Cochin, *Un ami de Pétrarque* (Paris, 1892). The quoted letters from Nelli are in Cochin, pp. 160, 172. The letter from Benintendi, with incipit "Nerius noster," is in the *Epistolae variae* of the sixteenth-century editions of Petrarch's *Opera*. For the Jubilee I found useful N. Zingarelli, in his *Scritti di varia letteratura* (Milan, 1935), pp. 372 ff. Clement's bull ordering the angels to take pilgrims to Paradise has been called spurious; see F. Gregorovius, *Geschichte der Stadt Rom* (Stuttgart, 1875-81) VI 309, note 2. There is a good description of the Jubilee in J. Jørgensen, *St. Bridget of Sweden* (London, 1954); also in Carlo Segrè, *Studi petrarcheschi* (Florence,

1903). The references to Petrarch's renunciation of lust are in *Fam.* XI 1, *Sen.* VIII 1, *Fam.* X 5 and XIX 16. The account of the horse's kick is in *Fam.* XI 1. Nelli's blast at the offending steed is in Cochin, p. 159. The visit to Arezzo is described in *Sen.* XIII 3. The letter to Charles IV is *Fam.* X 1; that to Urban V is *Sen.* VII 1; that to the Doge of Venice is *Fam.* XI 8. Petrarch's low opinion of teachers is stated in *Fam.* XII 3. The question whether he dreamed of a cardinalate is discussed in E. H. Wilkins, *Studies in the Life and Works of Petrarch* (Cambridge, Mass., 1955), pp. 63-80. Wilkins concludes that Petrarch desired but dreaded it. The poem *Linquimus Italiam* is in *Rime, Trionfi e Poesie latine*, ed. F. Neri and others (Milan, 1951).

CHAPTER XXIII. LOVE—DOLOROSO

THE quotation about life in Vaucluse is from *Fam.* XV 3; it is clearly of 1353. Matteo Longo's dog is described in *Fam.* XII 17. The epitaph on Zabot was first printed in K. Burdach, *Aus Petrarcas ältestem Schüler-kreise* (Berlin, 1929). For the chronology of the *Triumphs* see E. H. Wilkins, *Studies in the Life and Works of Petrarch* (Cambridge, Mass., 1955), pp. 254-273. For the physical structure of the *Canzoniere* see E. H. Wilkins, *The Making of the "Canzoniere"* (Rome, 1951). In my brief treatment of Petrarch's poetic theory I have been much helped by Alice Sperduti, "Petrarch on Poetry" (unpublished Ph. D. thesis, Cornell University, 1947). Petrarch's defense of poetry is in *Ep. metr.* II 11. "The law of poetry permits" is from *Fam.* IX 4. "If nature wouldn't give the word" is from *Fam.* XIII 7. The poet's duty is stated in *Sen.* XII 2. "Many things are required for good writing" is in *Variae* 54. The defense of imitation is particularly in *Fam.* XXIII 19. Petrarch's marginal comments are recorded in the notes to the edition of the *Rime* by G. Carducci and S. Ferrari (Florence, 1899, etc.). Ugo Foscolo's observation on cadences is in his *Essays on Petrarch* (London, 1821), p. 57. That from Villani I take from Theodor Mommsen, *Medieval and Renaissance Studies* (Ithaca, N. Y., 1959), p. 88. "The more difficult the search" is in *Invec-tivae contra medicum* (ed. Ricci) I, p. 37. "Style should be like a gown" and the following quotation are in *Fam.* XXII 2. Shakespeare's sonnet is CXXX. The quotation from Benedetto Croce is in his *Poesia popolare e poesia d'arte* (Bari, 1933), p. 72. That from Foscolo is from his *Essays on Petrarch*, p. 83.

CHAPTER XXIV. WAR WITH THE PAPAL COURT

THE standard modern authority on the Popes in Avignon is G. Mollat, *Les Papes d'Avignon* (Paris, 1912). Petrarch's reminiscence of the cardi-nal with an allergy to roses is in *Sen.* XII 2. His avoidance of the apostolic

388 PETRARCH AND HIS WORLD

secretaryship is told in *Fam.* XIII 5. For a summary of Petrarch's ecclesiastical career and his presumed ambition for a cardinalate see E. H. Wilkins, *Studies in the Life and Works of Petrarch* (Cambridge, Mass., 1955). The letter to the Genoese is *Fam.* XIV 5. His gross quotation from Seneca is in *Fam.* XIV 4. For the showering of unsolicited manuscripts on Petrarch and for the vogue of poetry in Avignon see *Fam.* XIII 6 and 7. The curious letter about the importunate woman is *Fam.* IX 3. The letter to Philippe about still-pursuing vices is *Fam.* XV 11. The letters about Giovanni are *Fam.* XIII 2 and 3. The important book on the *Epistolae sine nomine* is Paul Piur, *Petrarcas "Buch ohne Namen" und die päpstliche Kurie* (Halle, 1925), which includes the Latin text of the letters. Petrarch's letter to Philippe de Cabassoles suggesting that his denunciation be burned is *Fam.* XV 12. The "alarming advice" to Philippe is in *Fam.* XXII 5. His "vivid imagination" is characterized in Mollat, *Les Papes d'Avignon*, p. 487. The letter to Andrea Dandolo is *Fam.* XV 4; that to Boccaccio is *Fam.* XII 10; that to Lapo da Castiglionchio is *Fam.* XII 8. The meeting with the Roman ladies is described in *Fam.* XVI 8. *Ad Italiam* is *Ep. metr.* III 24; it is included in Neri et al., *Rime, Trionfi, e Poesie latine.*

CHAPTER XXV. MILAN, 1353-1361

THE description of Italy's sad state is in *De otio religioso*, p. 35. The reference to J. A. Symonds is from his *Age of the Despots* (New York, 1960), p. 92. The anecdote of the armed archbishop's Mass is from P. A. de Sade, *Mémoires pour la vie de François Pétrarque* (Amsterdam, 1764-67), III 172. For Boccaccio's letter see his *Opere latine minori*, ed. A. F. Messèra (Bari, 1928), pp. 136-140. Petrarch's excuses are *Fam.* XVI 11, 12 and 13 and XVII 10. "In appearance I lived with princes" is from *Sen.* XVII 2. The dealings with the astrologer are reported in *Sen.* III 1. The interview with the Emperor is described in *Fam.* XIX 2 and 3; the trip to Prague in *De otio religioso*, p. 36, and *Sen.* VII 1 and X 1; the visit to Paris in *Fam.* XXII 14 and *Sen.* X 2. Petrarch's itch for writing is stated in *Fam.* XIII 7. The project of an autobiography is in *Variae* 25. His characterizations of Fortune are in *Fam.* XXII 13 and *Sen.* VIII 3 and XVI 9. The quotation on *De remediis* is from J. H. Robinson and H. W. Rolfe, *Petrarch, the First Modern Man* (New York, 1898), p. 22. The contemptuous reference to art is in *De remediis (Phisicke against Fortune)*, I 41. The young theologian is described in *De remediis* I 12. The other quotations from *De remediis* are, in order, from I 14, II 93, and I 15. The quotation from Nelli is from Henry Cochin, *Un ami de Pétrarque* (Paris, 1892), p. 83. "Whoever ceases to learn" is in *Fam.* XVII 8. Boccaccio's praise of Petrarch's memory is from A. Solerti, *Le vite di Dante,*

Petrarca, e Boccaccio (Milan, 1904), p. 261. The letter to Guido Sette on Petrarch's daily routine is *Fam.* XIX 16; that to Nelli is *Fam.* XXI 12. The wounding by Cicero is recounted in *Fam.* XXI 10 and *Variae* 25. The warning against grafters is in *Fam.* XX 5. The letters on friendship are *Fam.* XVIII 8 and *Sen.* XVI 4. Petrarch's comments on Dante are in *Fam.* XXI 15; his scorn of the vernacular is quoted from *Sen.* II 1. His complaints of his son's behavior are in *Fam.* XVII 2 and XXII 7. Nelli's letter about Giovanni is in Cochin, *Un ami de Pétrarque*, p. 250. Petrarch's letter to Guido Sette about Giovanni is *Fam.* XXIII 12. The quotations from *De remediis* are taken from *Phisicke against Fortune*, I 70 and I 71. Nelli's letter on Giovanni's death is in Cochin, *Un ami de Pétrarque*, p. 289.

CHAPTER XXVI. PADUA, VENICE, AND

PAVIA, 1361-1369

"ONE builds the house" is from *Fam.* XXIII 13; "manners are corrupted" from *Sen.* X 2. The reprobation of male fashions is in *Sen.* VII 1. The trip to Avignon is proposed in *Sen.* I 2, 3, and 4. The letter to Nelli is *Sen.* I 2. The offer of his library to Venice and the Venetian acceptance are reported in E. H. Wilkins, *Petrarch's Later Years* (Cambridge, Mass., 1959), pp. 34-37. Fracassetti's horror of Venetian official Latin is in his edition of *Fam.*, vol. V, p. 376. Petrarch's praise of Venice appears especially in *Sen.* II 3, as does the vignette of the departing ships. The tourney is described in *Sen.* IV 3. His defense to Boccaccio of his liberty is in *Sen.* VI 2. The minatory letter to Pope Urban is *Sen.* VII 1. The Cardinal's jest is taken from Amy Bernardy, in *Annali della Cattedra Petrarchesca* VI (1935-1936), p. 44. Petrarch's regret that the Pope died before he could receive Petrarch's letter, and his accusation of papal mendacity, are in *Sen.* XIII 13. "Nothing is so proper to man as work" is from *Fam.* XXI 9. "I can't give up book-hunting" is from *Sen.* III 9. The praise of reading occurs often; see *De remediis* I 43, in which appears the complaint that cooks, not copyists, must take examinations, also *Fam.* XVIII 3, and *De vita solitaria* II 12 (*Prose*, p. 538), wherein he speaks of his identification with the author he reads. The quotation from G. Billanovich is from his *I primi umanisti* (Fribourg, 1953), p. 36. "Virgil uses too many conjunctions" is in *Sen.* V 2. The letter to Gherardo is *Fam.* XVIII 5. "There is no burden lighter than a pen" is from *Sen.* XVII 2. The remark about abundance of subject matter is in *Sen.* III 5. The scornful reference to philosophy is in *Fam.* XVII 1; the appeal from Aristotle to common sense in *Fam.* XX 14. "What am I? A scholar?" is from *Sen.* I 6. The descriptions of old age are in *Fam.* XXIII 1 and *Sen.* VIII 2. The confession of weari-

ness is in *Fam.* XXIII 9; the admission of inconsistency in *Fam.* XXIV 1.
Umberto Bosco's insistence on Petrarch's "lability" is in his *Petrarca*
(Turin, 1946). The remark about killing time is in the *De vita solitaria*
I 8 (*Prose,* p. 394). The passage about tapping the paper with a pen is
in *Fam.* XXIV 1. "Whatever is is hateful" is in *Sen.* III 9. The reference
to G. A. Levi is to his "Accidia e dubbio nel Petrarca," in *Rinascita* I
(1944), p. 48. "No one has got rich in my school" is in *Sen.* VIII 6. "Christ
our Apollo" is in *Fam.* XXII 2. The Averroistic cleric is in *Sen.* V 2. The
rational explanation of the stigmata is in *Sen.* VIII 3. Petrarch's delight
in music is often expressed, especially in *Sen.* XI 5. See, *inter alia,* W.
Osthoff, "Petrarca in der Musik des Abendlandes," in *Castrum Peregrini*
XX (1954). The regrets for Socrates are stated in *Sen.* I 3. "I feed on my
troubles" is in *Sen.* III 1. The lectures to Boccaccio are *Sen.* I 5 and V 2.
The descriptions of Pilatus are in *Sen.* III 6, V 3, and VI 1. The memories
of Giovanni are in *Sen.* I 2. Boccaccio's letter describing his second visit
to Venice is in his *Opere latine minori,* ed. A. F. Massèra (Bari, 1928),
and, in translation, in Fracassetti, *Familiari,* vol. III, pp. 16-19. The regrets for Petrarch's grandson are in *Sen.* X 4.

CHAPTER XXVII. ARQUA, 1369-1374

THE importunate visitors are characterized in *Variae* 15. The letter from
the scholarly guest is in *Romania* XIX (1890), p. 170. The descriptions
by other visitors are in A. Solerti, *Le vite di Dante, Petrarca, e Boccaccio*
(Milan, 1904), pp. 287, 280, 274, 269, 653. The letter on the conduct of
a good prince is *Sen.* XIV 1. The complaint that common people possess
and degrade his poems is in *Sen.* XIII 10. Petrarch's will has been excel-
lently edited and commented on by Theodor Mommsen, *Petrarch's
Testament* (Ithaca, N. Y., 1957). "Why should it shame me to be old?" is
from *Sen.* XVII 2. "I have lived long enough" is in *Sen.* XII 1. The quotations on doctors and health are from *Sen.* V 3. The letters to Dondi are
Sen. XII 1 and 2. "May death find me reading" is from *Sen.* XVII 2.

CHAPTER XXVIII. PETRARCH

THE quotation from James Harvey Robinson is from his *Petrarch: The
First Modern Man* (New York, 1898), p. 11. "I am a member of the
crowd" is in *Sen.* VI 3, and "I am not courting fastidious readers" in *Fam.*
XIII 5. The bit about the lodestone is in *De remediis,* Preface to Part
II. The rejection of the Greeks in favor of experience is in *Sen.* XII 1.
"I am anti-Aristotle" is in *Fam.* XX 14. The praise of literary study is in
Sen. XVII 2. The statement about good writing and good authorship is

from *Variae* 54. The advice to writers is in *Sen.* II 3. His impregnation with classical learning is stated in *Fam.* XXII 2. The quotation from Erwin Panofsky is from his *Renaissance and Renascences in Western Art* (Stockholm, 1960) I 10-11. The observation of G. Billanovich is in *Studi petrarcheschi* VII (1961), p. 31. "Neither grammar nor any of the liberal arts" is in *Fam.* XII 3. The random observations, or epigrams, are, in order, from *Sen.* VIII 3, *Fam.* II 2, *Fam.* VII 6, *De remediis* I 45, *Fam.* XII 2, *Sen.* XIV 1. "A man standing between two worlds" is in *Rerum memorandarum* I 2. "The hinge of the door" is from J. H. Whitfield, *Petrarch and the Renaissance* (London, 1943), p. 7.

INDEX

CPSIA information can be obtained at www.ICGtesting.com
Printed in the USA
242069LV00001B/2/P

9 780253 341228